HISTORY OF BROADCASTING: RADIO TO TELEVISION

HISTORY OF BROADCASTING: Radio to Television

History of Radio to 1926

GLEASON L. ARCHER

ARNO PRESS and THE NEW YORK TIMES

New York • 1971

Reprint Edition 1971 by Arno Press Inc.

Reprinted from a copy in The State Historical Society of Wisconsin Library

LC# 72-161132
ISBN 0-405-03557-8

HISTORY OF BROADCASTING: RADIO TO TELEVISION
ISBN for complete set: 0-405-03555-1
See last pages of this volume for titles.

Manufactured in the United States of America

Publisher's Note: The reader is directed to the *Addenda* at the end of the book for additions and corrections made by the author after the original edition was published.

HISTORY OF RADIO

TO 1926

GUGLIELMO MARCONI
When he gave to the world the art of wireless telegraphy.

HISTORY

of

RADIO

TO 1926

By GLEASON L. ARCHER, LL.D.

President of Suffolk University

The American Historical Society, Inc.

NEW YORK

PRINTED IN THE UNITED STATES OF AMERICA
AMERICAN BOOK—STRATFORD PRESS, INC., NEW YORK

ILLUSTRATIONS FROM THE AQUATONE PRESSES OF
EDWARD STERN & CO., INC.

PREFACE

THE PRESENT VOLUME is an outgrowth of the course on Radio Broadcasting in the College of Journalism of Suffolk University. Five years of personal experience as a radio lecturer on coast to coast networks beginning in 1929 had given the author an insight into the history of radio as well as an acquaintance with pioneers of the industry. In preparing a lecture course on the history of broadcasting, the author uncovered so much unpublished material of great historical value that he was constrained to undertake the task of preparing a detailed factual history of one of the greatest scientific developments of modern times.

Despite the fact that radio broadcasting began less than eighteen years ago, great confusion has arisen as to essential details of its beginning. Human memory is unreliable. Contemporary records, usually undated as to year or month, on paper that disintegrates in a decade, filed without regard to value, become perishable sources of information. Kaleidoscopic changes have occurred in the industry, the leaders of which have been too busy making history to give much thought to its preservation. There is need of settling controversial problems of historical nature while many of the pioneers of radio are still living. It has been the author's constant endeavor not only to gather the ordinary data available to a historian but after putting it into written form to submit it to veterans of the industry in order to test the same for accuracy of interpretation. In many cases radio pioneers who have generously given of their time have been able to furnish additional data and in some instances to supply original material susceptible of verification in newspapers, periodicals, in obscure correspondence files and radio station records. Thus much exceedingly valuable historical material has been rescued from oblivion.

The author was fortunate at the outset in his personal knowledge of the industry. He was fortunate also in the fact that the Executive Secretary of Suffolk University, Miss Carrolla A. Bryant, was for six years in the midst of radio history-making. At Station WEAF prior to the formation of the National Broadcasting Company and until 1932 in the Program Department of that great organization she acquired invaluable first hand knowledge of events. Her suggestions and aid deserve grateful recognition.

v

Miss Frances Sprague, the Librarian of the National Broadcasting Company in New York City, has been exceedingly helpful in making available books, periodicals, radio station records, miscellaneous files and other valuable material. Her co-operation during the months of research is beyond praise.

George H. Clark, Custodian of Historical Archives of the Radio Corporation of America, has been most generous in throwing open original files for the author's inspection.

Miss Esther Newsome, the Librarian of Suffolk University, deserves special praise for the assistance that she has rendered the author in checking historical data and in critical analysis of the manuscript from the literary angle.

The author would be remiss should he fail to acknowledge the courtesy and fairness of the great corporations concerned in this story of radio's beginnings. After the text had been roughly drafted the author applied to these corporations for the privilege of examining original records in an effort to verify every allegation of fact. Without exception they have accorded full and free access to records and in some cases high officials have spent days in repeated conferences with the author. The General Electric Company, The Radio Corporation of America, The Westinghouse Company, The American Telephone & Telegraph Company, The National Broadcasting Company, and The Columbia Broadcasting System have each been most co-operative. The publishers of *Fortune* have also furnished assistance.

A catalogue of individuals who have spent time in personal aid to the author would be voluminous. Deserving of special thanks, however, are Owen D. Young, David Sarnoff, William S. Paley, John Hays Hammond, Jr., Dr. Ernst F. W. Alexanderson, Elmer E. Bucher, Frank A. Arnold, Dr. Alfred H. Goldsmith, Captain S. C. Hooper, U.S.N., and Edward J. Nally.

For the illustrations used in the book special recognition is due to the following: The National Broadcasting Company, Radio Corporation of America, General Electric Company, The Westinghouse Company, Jones and Hare, George H. Clark and J. d'Agostino.

This volume carries the history of Radio through the pioneer period. In 1926 a new era began, the historical data of which has proved so engrossing and the material so rich in human interest as to deserve separate consideration. The author is already at work upon the twelve-year period since 1926, a period characterized by struggles for supremacy among great corporations and broadcasting networks in the grip of economic laws and government regulations.

G.L.A.

Suffolk University,
Boston, Massachusetts.
August 15, 1938.

CONTENTS BY CHAPTER

ILLUSTRATIONS

HISTORY OF RADIO

TO 1926

CHAPTER
ONE

Intercommunication of Signals in Early Times

Section 1. Introductory.

RADIO IS THE MIRACLE of the ages. Aladdin's Lamp, the Magic Carpet, the Seven League Boots of fable and every vision that mankind has ever entertained, since the world began, of laying hold upon the attributes of the Almighty, pale into insignificance beside the accomplished fact of radio. By its magic, the human voice may be projected around the earth in less time than it takes to pronounce the word "radio."

The story of wireless broadcasting has ramifications as ancient as civilization because since time began men have struggled with the very riddle to which this latest triumph of human ingenuity brings solution. Blind gropings of generations of experimenters have contributed to progress along the pathway to the pinnacle from which, in our own day, science suddenly glimpsed the secret of radio broadcasting. A brief summary of centuries of experimentation in communications is important as historical background of wireless telephony.

It will be set forth in these pages that radio broadcasting, as we know it today, began as a scientific novelty in East Pittsburgh, Pennsylvania, in the year 1920. Man's first recorded attempt to solve the problem of intercommunication of thought or intelligence dates back more than two thousand years. It is the purpose of this treatise to depict in chronological order those developments that may fairly be said to have contributed to this latest marvel of modern science.

Sec. 2. Fire Beacons in Ancient Times.

From the dawn of history, men have sought to solve the problem of intercommunication between persons separated by distance. The word telegraph, for instance, dates back to 300 B.C. It is a combination of two Greek words; tele, 'afar off' and graph, 'to write', or literally 'to write afar off'. The Greeks are credited by the *Encyclopedia Americana* with having invented the first telegraph system. Signals were given at night between military stations so located as to be visible from each other. Torches were used in combinations agreed upon, in units not exceeding five, as representing each letter of the Greek alphabet. Thus messages could be transmitted and conversations carried on. So the Greeks, 300 years before Christ, invented and put into successful operation a crude telegraph system.

Fire and smoke signals, even among primitive peoples, have also played their parts in the business of intercommunication.

The fire beacon is mentioned in Homer's *Iliad* as a recognized institution. According to legend it was such a beacon, previously agreed upon, that was a signal to the besieging army that the Greek heroes under command of Ulysses had come forth from concealment in the

Wooden Horse and were ready to open the gates of the city at the sacking of Troy. The Persians likewise employed the fire beacons in their military campaigns. Xerxes certainly relied upon this means of communication with his army in Greece after his flight to Asia. Xenophon, in the *Anabasis,* relates his experiences with the efficacy of the Persian system of fire beacons. He attempted on one occasion to capture the castle of a wealthy Persian noble near Pergamus. The besieged garrison, by fire signals, summoned aid that soon put Xenophon to flight. The Spartans were once worsted in a night attack on Salamis. Aid was summoned from Athens by fire beacons. Among the Romans fire-towers and signal lights played an important part in military campaigns.

In England the system was extensively employed up to the time of Queen Elizabeth. Macaulay's well-known poem depicting the arrival of the Spanish Armada contains the following significant lines:

"For swift to East and swift to West the ghastly war-flame spread, High on St. Michael's Mount it shone; it shone on Beachy Head— Far on the deep the Spaniard saw, along each southern shire, Cape beyond cape, in endless range, those twinkling points of fire."

Sec. 3. Heliographs and Semaphores.

Another form of signal that found widespread popularity for centuries was the heliograph, a device by which a flash of reflected sunlight could be thrown in any desired direction. This is said to have been the invention of a Dutch physicist named Gravesande. Johann Gauss, a German mathematician, later discovered by experiment that a mirror one inch square could flash a ray that could be seen seven miles distant. This system found favor in the United States in its coast survey and in 1861 it had been so far perfected that signal beams could be flashed ninety miles. By 1890 the United States Army had succeeded in flashing signals from mountain peaks to the distance of two hundred and fifteen miles.

A semaphore system [1] of military signaling was developed in France toward the end of the 18th century. Semaphore towers at distances ranging from six to ten miles were set up by various nations. Each tower was equipped with cross-arms similar to our modern railroad semaphores except that they were built on a larger scale. These cross-arms could be set so as to represent different letters of the alphabet and were read by means of telescopes. Operators could thus relay messages from station to station over long distances.

The invention of the semaphore system was the result of a juvenile

[1] *Encyclopedia Americana*—"Telegraphy," Vol 26, p. 328.

prank by which lads in two near-by schools managed to send signals to one another. Shortly before the French Revolution three pupils in two French boarding schools—brothers as it chanced—evolved this system of signaling. They were encouraged by the school authorities, the result being that the brothers later became ardent advocates of the system as a national institution. The first semaphore-telegram in history was sent August 15, 1794, announcing a victory of the French army then at war with the Austrians. During Napoleon's ascendancy in France the semaphore system was so extended that before the Emperor's downfall France had 1112 miles of semaphores served by 224 stations. Before the advent of electrical telegraphy the number of semaphore stations in France had increased to 533.

England was obliged to follow the French example and resort to semaphores for military signaling, but the system did not work out very well in England itself owing to the fogs that sometimes cut off communication with London, the heart of the nation.

Sweden, Austria and Prussia adopted the semaphore system shortly after France had demonstrated its success. Nicholas I of Russia, who reigned from 1825 to 1855, adopted the system on a grand scale. Handsome stone towers, five or six miles apart, spanned the nation from the German frontier to St. Petersburg. Two hundred and twenty stations, each manned by six operators, constituted Russia's semaphore-telegraph system.

Vast were the expenditures of nations in girdling their territories with semaphore lines, yet in the march of human events many a laboriously constructed system of one kind or another suddenly finds itself relegated to the scrap heap. Such was the fate of the system described, all because scientists working in another field of endeavor had discovered the art of electrical transmission of signals and even transmission of human speech. If we are to understand that development we must turn back the pages of time and survey the long story of development, discovery and invention that rendered possible electrical transmission of speech.

It is interesting to note that the visual-horizon limitation of the semaphore system which scientists no doubt regarded as forever banished by the development of electrical communication has returned as the chief obstacle to television. While short-wave broadcasting is unaffected by the curvature of the earth, yet when we get down into wave lengths that approach the light-spectrum we discover that the broadcast range corresponds to the visual horizon. Just as the semaphore was obliged to relay the message so also television requires some means of rebroadcasting at the visual horizon, which of course depends upon the height of the television antenna.

Sec. 4. Electricity the Riddle of the Ages.

The history of mankind has no more thrilling development than the manner in which human intelligence and human ingenuity have harnessed to man's use the mighty forces of electricity. From the dawn of civilization men had recognized an unseen force, latent in fishes, in a mineral termed a lodestone, or capable of being produced by friction in animal fur or in inanimate objects. This force has been known under the general terms electricity and magnetism.[2] The fact that the lodestone had attraction for metallic substances caused it to be the subject of experimentation by learned men of ancient times. Out of these experiments came the discovery that if a bit of lodestone were placed on a cork-float and left free in water the float would turn of its own volition until it came to rest with a particular projection of the stone invariably pointing to the North. Thus was discovered the essential principle of the magnetic compass that was so greatly to extend the horizon of knowledge not only of the continents and the seven seas but also of electricity itself.[3]

Men discovered that electrical phenomena could be produced by friction. Experimentation disclosed what objects were best adapted to the purpose. The use of amber, rubbed with silk or cloth, is even now one of the simplest of laboratory experiments in the production of static electricity, or electricity in a stationary state. In our own day, man-made electricity is generated in such tremendous currents that the most enduring metals melt in its fiery breath. It is difficult for us to realize that only a few generations ago the wisest of men could not manufacture electricity in greater quantity than any school child may now produce with an amber rod and a silken rag. Yet from this feeble beginning men have groped their way to the harnessing of a titanic force of nature which they can neither see nor fully understand.

---

[2] The term "electricity" comes from the Greek word electron (ἤλεχτρον), which means amber, the substance wherein the phenomenon of magnetism was most manifest. Magnetism comes from the name of the Greek city-state *Magnesia* in Asia Minor where great quantities of magnetic ores were found. Although magnetism had been known to the Greeks centuries earlier Socrates is known to have declared that the lodestone "not only attracts iron rings, but also imparts to them a similar power of attracting other rings; and sometimes you may see a number of pieces of iron and rings suspended from one another so as to form quite a long chain."

[3] The invention of the magnetic compass is claimed for the Chinese as early as 2637 B.C. but like other early inventions by the scholars of China it was apparently neglected by Oriental mariners. European nations were not familiar with the principles of the magnetic compass until the twelfth century of our era. This knowledge may have come to the Franks from the Arabs who may possibly have acquired it from the Chinese. While early compasses consisted of a magnetic needle on a splinter of wood floating in water, the first authentic account of a pivoted compass was written by one Peter Perigrinus de Maricourt in 1269 A.D. The mariner's compass shortly thereafter came into general use among European navigators.

DR. LEE DE FOREST
One of the great pioneers in wireless and radio; inventor of the audion.

Sec. 5. Mythical Powers of the Lodestone.

An Italian philosopher, della Porta, in his book *Magiae Naturalis,* published in 1569, advanced the fantastic theory that signals might be exchanged by utilizing a pair of magnetic compasses, each equipped with a circular alphabet and one supposedly controlled by the movements of the other.[4] The lodestone was credited by the superstitious people of that age with mystic qualities quite beyond its actual power. Della Porta's imaginative conception that two needles touched by the same lodestone would become so attuned that forever after one must obey the movements of the other had become, prior to 1600, an accepted notion even in scientific circles. Strada of Rome, in a book published in 1617, set down as a demonstrated scientific fact this alleged attribute of the lodestone. Singularly enough no painstaking philosopher had ventured to test the truth of the assertion and report the disappointing results.

As late as 1711 there appeared in Addison's *Spectator* an assertion that a certain lodestone (he does not credit all lodestones with such power) had "such virtue in it that if it touched two several needles, when one of the needles so touched began to move, the other, though at never so great a distance, moved at the same time and in the same manner." The article continues with the assertion that two friends, each equipped with one of these needles, set on a pivot in the midst of a dial ringed around by the letters of the alphabet, had been able to converse with each other at any distance by a simple turn of the needle to any desired letter on the dial. "By this means," Addison alleges, "they talked together across a whole continent, and conveyed their thoughts to one another in an instant over cities and mountains, seas or deserts." [5]

So delightful a fairytale as this had powerful appeal upon popular imagination. It is recorded that as late as 1744, Mark Akenside, an English poet, immortalized the legend in the following graceful lines:

> "Two faithful needles—from the informing touch,
> Of the same parent stone, together drew
> Its mystic virtue;—
> And though disjoined by kingdoms—though the main
> Rolled its broad surge betwixt—and different stars
> Beheld their wakeful motions—yet preserved
> Their former friendship and remembered still
> The alliance of their birth." [6]

Alas for dreamers of early days! The long-cherished fancy was later

---

[4] "The Radio Industry," Article by E. E. Bucher, p. 15.
[5] *The Spectator,* No. 241, Dec. 6, 1711.
[6] "Pleasures of Imagination," Akenside.

to be shattered by experimentation. Centuries were to intervene before the advent of radio in our own day rendered possible the dream of the poet. Men of early times, enthralled by the seeming magic of the magnetized compass needle and the fact that metallic objects could cause it to stir from its north-pointing position, did not realize that the magnetic currents of the earth controlled compass needles and that when separated from the other, the second compass would obey the earth current rather than the man-controlled movements of the first compass needle. The tuned-compass idea was futile at that stage of electrical development. It was essentially wireless control, impossible until centuries of progress should have provided the means of accomplishment.

Sec. 6. Attempts to Produce Electricity.

The feeble and elusive phenomenon of static electricity, created by the simple process of friction of silk upon amber or other substances, quite naturally failed to satisfy the scientists of early days. Electricity so produced bore but a faint semblance to the power which mankind longed to possess. A magnet capable of picking up light objects or of rotating a needle mounted upon a pivot was at best a child's toy. Yet scientists who were gifted with imagination glimpsed in electricity the riddle of the universe which they became determined to solve.

Their attempts were at first amateurish indeed. Then, too, the riddle was seemingly guarded by a sphinx more uncommunicative than that of Egyptian legend. The groping hands of investigators also were bitten by mysterious and resentful forces—as though the Almighty were forbidding impious hands to lay hold upon the Ark of the Covenant. That electric shocks of those days were not deadly was due wholly to the fact that men were unable to produce electricity of sufficient intensity to strike down the blundering novice in uncharted fields of danger.

The long story of experimentation, of patient groping for knowledge of electricity will perhaps never be written. Some investigators turned to mechanical devices for producing electricity. For instance, in 1672, a German physicist, Von Guericke,[7] constructed a globe of sulphur and mounted it on an axle that it might be revolved by turning a crank. He actually produced electricity by pressing his broad palm upon the sulphur-ball while it revolved—a primitive generator indeed! The charged globe of Von Guericke would attract light objects in the same manner as the rubbed amber rod, but it proved little more than a toy for the amusement of hopeful scientists. The singular fact remains that Von Guericke, in 1672, had hit upon the principle of the revolving generator, to be revived centuries later when men had

[7] *"The Radio Industry,"* 1928, p. 14.

at length learned how to capture and to store the electricity thus generated.

Other investigators tried still other forms of friction machines. In 1709 a revolving glass globe, constructed by Hauksbee, was experimented with and electricity was produced by pressing a cloth cushion against the globe while it revolved. This was the first machine capable of producing electric sparks. Many types of friction machines were tried by a succession of investigators. In the light of present-day knowledge we realize how closely some of these early philosophers pressed upon the key that centuries later was to unlock the flood gates to limitless electrical energy. Thus the groping fingers of men may toy with mysteries that later generations are destined to utilize in the reshaping of science or industry.

Sec. 7. Invention of the Leyden Jar.

There is some uncertainty as to the exact origin of the Leyden jar, the first known means of storing electricity, and the ancestor of the modern storage battery and power house. This uncertainty is due no doubt to the fact that a sort of freemasonry existed among scientists that led them to impart to one another the results of noteworthy experiments. Investigators in widely separated places might thus be pursuing similar lines of research and experimentation. The invention of the Leyden jar is said to have been made by Dean von Kleist of the Cathedral of Kamin in October, 1745, but it is generally credited to Professor Musschenbroek of Leyden. Musschenbroek was conducting an electrical experiment in January, 1746, attempting to introduce an electrical charge into water contained in a glass bottle. A friend was holding the bottle in one hand when he chanced to touch the charged conductor attached to a friction machine with the other hand. The man received a violent electric shock. Further experimentation confirmed the phenomenon. (The Leyden jar, so named years after its discovery, in its earliest stages consisted of a glass jar, partly filled with water.) The orifice was usually closed with a cork pierced by a wire or rod which dipped into the water. In charging the jar it was held in the hand by the operator and the free end of the wire was brought into contact with the prime conductor of an electrical machine. Upon separating the jar from its contact with the machine it was found to be electrically charged. When held in one hand, if the wire were grasped with the other a violent shock was experienced.

The Leyden jar was later developed so that water became unnecessary, the jar being lined with tinfoil for a part of its height. An outer covering of tinfoil was connected to a ground wire. Thus a crude condenser was created.

The important· fact had been discovered that an electric charge could not only be produced but by means of the Leyden jar could be stored for use at the will of the experimenter.

Sec. 8. Experimenting with the Leyden Jar.

These experiments with the Leyden jar were not unmixed with hazard. For the first time in history scientists had produced "a demon in a jar" that was capable of striking out with appalling swiftness and with paralyzing might. When news of the discovery swept over Europe and America, learned men began to try their hands at producing bottled electricity. The sting of the unseen current shooting through human bone and sinew fascinated not only scientists but the gaping multitude as well. Within a year following its invention, Daniel Gralath, an experimenter, had linked up a battery of three Leyden jars and had treated twenty individuals with linked hands to the dubious pleasure of sending the electric current through the human circuit thus established. In the same year, 1746, one Joseph Franz of Vienna had sent an electric current through fifteen hundred feet of iron wire. This may be said to have been a definite step in experimentation leading to the electric telegraph.

With no definite goal in mind, but following the usual cycle of blind experimentation, scientists of one country and another gradually accumulated experience that became of value to students of electricity, but purely from the standpoint of scientific research. A French priest, Abbé Nollet, for instance, demonstrated that a circuit a mile around, composed of alternate human conductors and iron wire held in the hands by the participants, could successfully be electrified by the discharge of several jars linked together. More than that, he demonstrated that every person in the unique circuit, when shocked by a charge of electricity, leaped into the air at the same instant.

Another scientist sent a shock through two miles of wire. In July, 1747, one Watson caused a wire to be carried across the Westminster Bridge over the Thames River. One end of the wire was connected with a Leyden jar and the other was held by an assistant, who carried in his other hand an iron rod. Whenever the iron rod was dipped into the river a shock was experienced, thus demonstrating that water completed the circuit in the same manner as if a second wire were used.

America's universal genius, Benjamin Franklin, was fascinated by the discovery of the Leyden jar. It was soon agreed among scientists that the electric spark that leaped the gap between two wires used as described in the foregoing demonstrated conclusively that electricity was a force capable of motion and of great latent power.

Sec. 9. Franklin's Electrical Discoveries.

Benjamin Franklin contributed two very important ideas to electrical science of his generation. The flash of the electric spark, leaping from one wire to another, suggested to his powerful intellect that the lightning flash from cloud to earth was similar in kind, hence that lightning was a manifestation on a mammoth scale of the same stored energy as that contained in the Leyden jar. How he demonstrated, in 1752, this theory to be correct, through the use of a kite directed into a thunder cloud, is a story known to all the world. It established his reputation as one of the greatest scientists of the age.

Franklin's second idea concerned the possible use of electricity as a means of communication. We think of Professor Morse as the inventor of the electric telegraph system, yet Benjamin Franklin is said to have been nearly a century ahead of him in the basic idea. The fact that electricity was demonstrated to flow in a current of inconceivable speed suggested to the practical mind of the American philosopher the idea of transmitting the electrical impulse over wires to distant points. In pursuance of this theory, Franklin actually caused to be strung four miles of wire.[8] The experiment failed because the Leyden jar was incapable of supplying a current sufficiently strong to produce the hoped for results at the other end of the four-mile circuit. Thus again a great invention destined to revolutionize modern life was obliged to accept defeat in one generation and to await fulfillment in another, when developments in science might render such fulfillment a possibility.

Sec. 10. The Electric Telegraph System Foreshadowed.

In Franklin's *Autobiography*, he comments on the jeers that greeted his first suggestion of the identity of lightning and electricity. Ridicule by European savants gave way, however, when experiments with a kite demonstrated the correctness of the American philosopher's deduction. It may be that his experiments with a telegraph line were at first greeted with derision but as early as 1753, a letter published in the *Scots Magazine*, in Edinburgh, from the pen of an anonymous writer, proposed a telegraph system in which would be strung a wire for each letter in the alphabet. "Electrical discharges," the writer declared, "should separately exhibit themselves by the diverging balls of an electroscope, or the striking of a bell by the attraction of a charged ball."[9]

However intriguing the idea of the electric telegraph may have been,

[8] "World Book," page 5736.
[9] Feb. 1, 1753, article entitled "An Expeditious Means of Conveying Intelligence."

yet it was a mere scientific abstraction. It was to be dreamed over for generations by scientists. Its fulfillment must await the further development of the science of electricity.

Prior to 1767, Joseph Bozolus, a Jesuit philosopher in the faculty of the College at Rome, suggested a telegraph line in which two underground wires would connect distant stations. The Leyden jar was to be utilized to produce sparks in the receiving station. An alphabet based upon sparks was suggested, but the learned priest did not go to the trouble of inventing such an alphabet.

In 1774, a scientist, Louis Le Sage, constructed, in Geneva, a telegraph system identical with that described in the *Scots Magazine* twenty-one years prior to that date. Twenty-four wires represented letters of the alphabet, each wire ending in a duly lettered electroscope to which was connected a pith ball that became agitated whenever the circuit was closed at the other end of the line. By watching the antics of the pith balls, an operator might be able to read the messages being sent over the Le Sage line.

During the next twenty years experimenters tried various combinations of wires, varying from one to thirty-six, but without genuine success. The great problem of insulation of wires was still to be solved. Men resorted to various methods, pitch, strips of cloth and even oil-painted covering being utilized in a process of trial and error. Exposure to the elements or the burial of wires under the ground resulted in speedy disintegration of whatever form of insulation was employed.

One of the most ingenious of the early devices for the electrical transmission of messages has thus been described: [10]

"In 1816, Francis Ronalds demonstrated a telegraph at his home in Hammersmith, England. He had suspended by silk strands eight miles of wire on his lawn. An electrical machine or a small Leyden jar supplied the power. The sending of the message depended upon two clocks at each end of the wire, synchronized to beat as nearly the time as possible. On each clock, on the axle which ordinarily turns the second hand, a dial with letters and figures around its circumference was fixed in place of the hand. Of course, it turned as fast as the hand would have done. In front of it and covering it was a stationary plate of similar size, with an aperture through which one of the letters or figures could be seen. At the instant when the desired letter passed the aperture, the inventor charged the wire and a pitch ball electrometer at the other end moved. The letter passing the aperture at that moment was written down by the receiver, and thus the word was spelled."

[10] Harlow, "Old Wires and New Waves," p. 41.

Sec. 11. Attempts to Utilize the Idea.

Chemistry was resorted to in an invention by Harrison Gray Dyar in 1828 to solve the problem of recording a telegraph message. By using rolls of blue litmus paper Dyar utilized the electric current to set up an acid reaction that produced red marks on the rolls of paper. In his experiments the inventor used several miles of wire strung around a race track on Long Island and so impressed those who witnessed his attempts that one hopeful investor agreed to go into partnership with him. They employed a promoter to raise additional capital in New York City and just as they were becoming confident of success their promoter, no doubt in an effort to extort a share in the project, brought suit against them for $20,000 for alleged services. The resulting litigation so discouraged the partners that the project was abandoned.

Even before this date scientists had become dissatisfied with the Leyden jar as a source of electrical energy. As early as 1774 Alessandro Volta of Como, Italy, discovered that electricity could be generated by means of cells in which two different metals were immersed in a weak solution of acid which would act with unequal intensity upon the two metals. The strength of the current produced bore definite relation to this inequality. The two metals thus formed the electrodes of the battery cell and the solution in which they were immersed formed the electrolyte. Zinc and copper in a sulphuric acid solution were soon discovered to be ideal for use in Voltaic batteries, the copper forming the positive pole and the zinc the negative pole.

Many years of experimentation elapsed before storage batteries were brought to a state where they could be said to have become genuine factors in industry. One of the most intriguing uses of the storage battery at this time was in connection with the age-long hunt for a means of electrical transmission of signals.

In 1819, Hans Christian Oersted, a Danish scientist, discovered that an electric current flowing along a wire would cause a pivoted compass needle to turn whenever the wire was held in a certain position over it. Reviving the idea of utilizing compass needles, vainly experimented with two centuries before when the lodestone was the only known source of electrical power, Oersted invented a so-called needle-telegraph system. The receiver was simply a magnetic compass with letters of the alphabet around its margin, the compass being placed within a coil of wire. Whenever the circuit was closed at the other end of the line the needle would oscillate and thus indicate letters of the alphabet. The system proved unsuccessful.

In 1823, Baron Schilling, a Russian nobleman, perfected a system of electrical signaling in which he employed five galvanometer needles, each needle equipped with a galvanic circuit of its own. The ingenious nobleman devised a code by which the motions of the needles might indicate letters of the alphabet. Experimentation led him to discard all but one needle and to so revise the code that this one needle might indicate all of the letters of the alphabet. In 1835 the inventor exhibited his device to a group of German physicists gathered in convention at Bonn. Schilling was later permitted to stage a public demonstration of his telegraph system in Vienna. Wires were suspended from housetops in that city. Two years later he made plans to lay an insulated cable across the Gulf of Finland in a project to connect St. Petersburg and the Russian fortress of Kronstadt. Death of the inventor, however, cut short his career and the cable-laying experiment was abandoned.

Sec. 12. Improvements in Electro-Magnets.

Electro-magnets were relatively feeble in the early days of experimentation. They were incapable of retaining magnetic properties beyond certain limits. In 1824, William Sturgeon, an English experimenter, discovered a novel method of constructing electro-magnets. By using soft iron in horseshoe form, coating it with a non-conducting varnish and winding loose coils of copper wire around the legs of the horseshoe, he discovered that a single galvanic battery connected to the wire transformed the horseshoe into a magnet capable of sustaining heavy weights. This power vanished, however, whenever the current was turned off. The invention of the magnetic armature was destined to play an important part in solving the baffling problem of electrical transmission of signals.

It remained for an American inventor, Joseph Henry, to develop the electro-magnet to the point of genuine utility.

"In 1828, at the age of thirty-one, he first exhibited at the Albany Academy his electro-magnet wound with copper wire, which had been insulated by covering it with silk thread. To him belongs the credit for inventing the magnetic 'spool' or 'bobbin', that form of coil since universally employed for every application of electro-magnetism." [11] In 1830, he bent a piece of iron 20 inches long into a horseshoe magnet and lifted 750 pounds with it. Then he bent a bar 30 inches long, and it lifted 2,300 pounds—eight times more than any magnet hitherto known in Europe could cope with. "Professor Henry," remarked Sturgeon, a contemporary scientist, "has been enabled to produce a magnetic force which totally eclipses every other in the whole annals of magnetism; and no parallel is to be found since the miraculous suspension of the celebrated oriental impostor in his iron coffin."

[11] William B. Taylor in 'An Historical Sketch of Joseph Henry's Contribution to the Electro-Magnetic Telegraph.'

"Henry," says Taylor, "was the absolute creator of the intensity magnet."

"In 1831, he suspended around the walls of a large class-room in the Academy a mile of copper wire, interposed in a circuit between a battery and an 'intensity' magnet. At each excitation of the magnet, a rod which had been in contact with a limb of the soft iron core was repelled from it, and its other end struck a bell. Henry explained to his classes that signaling might be done in this way, but that was as far as he went with it. He did not formulate a code of language, nor attempt to develop an actual telegraph instrument; yet his simple circuit and bell had elements which no previous telegraph had had, and which were destined to be essential to the telegraph of the future. It is therefore claimed by those who think that Henry's contribution to the science has been underrated that it was he and not Morse who 'invented' the telegraph." [12]

It is probable that Joseph Henry, although fully aware of the scientific success of his experiment, nevertheless regarded it as a mere experiment and never looked beyond it to the possible utility of the invention. Professor Henry was later chosen to be the first Secretary of the newly-formed Smithsonian Institution in Washington. He no doubt considered this elevation as a definite dedication to public service of his scientific talents. At any rate he rendered generous aid to other investigators of electrical phenomena and to his improvement of the electro-magnet is undoubtedly due some of the success of Morse and others in the field of telegraphy.

[12] Harlow—"Old Wires and New Waves," pp. 46-47.

CHAPTER
TWO

Invention of the Electric Telegraph

Section 13. Inventors Approach the Goal.

SCIENTIFIC PROGRESS has ever been slow and groping in its advance. Men in widely separated places have often struggled with similar scientific problems. It has frequently happened that identical discoveries have been made without collaboration of any sort. The invention of the electric telegraph is an instance in point. Several men claimed the invention as their own and protracted litigation resulted. It is certainly true that no one man ever originated all the vitally necessary elements of a successful telegraph system. Many of these ideas had been utilized in laboratory experimentation for years before the invention was perfected. In a sense they were the common property of scientists. It was only after an enterprising and persistent American artist had invaded the field and had combined ideas into a commercially successful system that rival claimants went into court to attack the originality of the Morse patents. Let us make a brief survey of the state of telegraph experimentation at the time when Samuel F. B. Morse entered the field.

At the University of Göttingen were two scientists, Karl Friedrich Gauss and Wilhelm Eduard Weber, who had spent much time with the idea. In the year following Samuel Morse's first attempt to invent a telegraph system, 1833 to be exact, they set up a telegraph line a mile and a half long, using two wires and carrying the same over the housetops of the city, employing glass insulators to protect the current from loss by leakage. Their receiving instrument was the familiar magnetic needle, deflected to the right or the left by the influence of an electric current. The strangest feature of their device was a reflecting mirror and a telescope which were placed about twelve feet distant from the needle. An observer sighting through the telescope toward the mirror was to read the messages by interpreting different combinations of movement that had been agreed upon to indicate the various letters of the alphabet. It is needless to point out that the system was highly technical and far from satisfactory.

Gauss later turned the device over to Professor C. A. Steinheil of Munich to continue investigations as to how its defects might be remedied. Steinheil later set up a galvanometer telegraph line between Munich and Borgenhausen, a distance of two miles. He was able to employ greater electric currents than had before been possible. In the place of needles the inventor substituted two magnetic bars which, being alternately attracted and repelled by manipulation of the electric current, were made to strike bells of different tones, thus indicating letters of the alphabet. Steinheil also experimented by attaching fountain pens to the ends of the bars and arranging a roll of paper turned

by clock-work. Thus he was able to produce dots capable of being inter-
preted as letters of the alphabet.

The ingenious German scientist soon made the important discovery that only one telegraph wire would be necessary if the line were
grounded, since the earth could be relied upon to complete the electrical circuit necessary for the sending of messages.

While these experiments were being tried in Germany, Professor
John Frederick Daniell, in England, had made great improvements in
the galvanic battery. With the Daniell battery it became possible to
enjoy a steady and continuous action of the electric current, a circumstance that proved decidedly helpful to inventors.

As early as 1830, Charles Wheatstone, a young Englishman, began to
experiment with electricity. In 1834 he devised a revolving mirror capable of measuring the velocity of electricity passing through a half-a-
mile-long copper wire. Two years later he invented a telegraph system
in which he used five needles. Each needle was capable of six variations,
giving Wheatstone thirty possible characters. At about this time William F. Cooke produced a working model of a telegraph line with
three needles instead of five. Finding that he and Wheatstone were
working along similar lines, Cooke effected a sort of partnership with
the latter, their express object being to perfect a telegraph system.

It so happened that Professor Joseph Henry, the American scientist,
then recently appointed Secretary of the Smithsonian Institution, paid a
visit to England in April, 1837. While there he visited the Wheatstone
laboratory and gave valuable advice and assistance to the inventors.
Wheatstone took out an English patent on his telegraph system in July,
1837. This date is important because at that time the Morse telegraph
system had not been patented. Bitter controversy was later to arise between the English and the American inventors. Englishmen in general
still regard Wheatstone as the real inventor of the telegraph.

Edward Davy, of Devonshire, England, was another inventor of a
telegraph system. His idea involved the use of six wires with balls at
each end. An electric spark, under his system, applied to one ball would
electrify the ball at the other end of the line. By combinations of signals he contrived an alphabet. In March, 1837, learning that Wheatstone was about to try for a patent on an electric telegraph, Davy filed
a caveat (legal notice that he was at work on the device) and deposited
a sealed description of his own invention. There was one very important idea of Davy's that was destined to have great bearing upon the
development of the electric telegraph. He devised an "electrical re-
newer" or a local battery to relay a feeble electric current. The Solicitor-General was so impressed by the novelty of Davy's invention that
he permitted a patent to be issued to him also.

Various other inventors in Germany, France and Scotland brought forward inventions of telegraph systems. The whole scientific world, it seemed, was on the trail of the elusive electric telegraph. It is small wonder that Samuel F. B. Morse caught the contagion, so to speak.

Sec. 14. Morse Invents a Telegraph System.

Samuel F. B. Morse was born April 27, 1791, in Charlestown, Massachusetts, the son of a Congregational minister. After his graduation from Yale College in 1810, he took up the study of painting. His success in art was outstanding but the rewards were disappointing. After spending many years in America, he went to Europe where he continued to study art and to practice his profession. Morse finally embarked for America aboard the packet *Sully.* The ship sailed from Havre, October 6, 1832, having aboard a small but distinguished group of passengers. Among them was a Dr. Charles Jackson of Boston. Up to this time it does not appear that Morse had ever given much thought to the electrical science. One day at dinner, during the early part of the voyage, Dr. Jackson discoursed upon electro-magnetism, which was somewhat of a hobby with him. His conversation became absorbingly interesting to Morse, especially his comments upon the fact that scientists had discovered that the presence of an electric current in any part of a circuit could be detected by breaking the circuit.

Scientists, as we have seen, had for decades accepted this fact as no longer a cause for wonderment, but to novices such as the company on the *Sully* the idea was new and striking. Morse was profoundly impressed. No doubt without knowledge of the telegraph systems devised by others, he set to work to invent one of his own. Possibly if he had been trained in electrical science he might have approached the subject in the same manner as had all previous investigators in this special field. The artist, with nothing but his inventive instinct to guide him, attempted to solve the riddle of the ages. There is some dispute as to how much help Dr. Jackson actually gave to the would-be inventor while the idea of an electric telegraph system was germinating in the latter's mind.[1] Morse made sketches at the time in his note-book that reveal familiarity with magnets wound about with wire, but it may be that this was the result of tutelage by Dr. Jackson. At any rate during the six weeks' voyage to America Samuel F. B. Morse worked out on paper the proposed machinery of his telegraph system with which to open and close circuits in order to print messages at the receiving end of the line.

Thus it will be seen that the amateur inventor had blundered upon a solution that scientists had overlooked. Morse did not at that time

[1] For an interesting account of the controversy see Harlow—"Old Wires and New Waves," pp. 58-62.

fully comprehend the importance of his discovery. None of the passengers regarded the invention as more than an academic abstraction that had helped to while away leaden hours of a long sea voyage. Later, however, Dr. Jackson was to cause a great deal of trouble for Professor Morse.

Sec. 15. Disheartening Years for the Inventor.

Morse, the artist, was without funds. However enthusiastic he may have been over his new telegraphic device, he could not find means to make a working model or to try out his theories. He was, moreover, a widower with several motherless children to support. While his brothers generously financed him for a time, he was soon forced to resume his palette and brush in an effort to earn a livelihood. During three bitter years of struggle with poverty he was unable to do anything with his invention. There was a time when he entertained hopes of winning a government job to paint murals in several of the then unfilled panels in the Rotunda of the Capitol in Washington. It is interesting to note that in his application for appointment as one of the artists he recited that he had devoted twenty years to the study of art, seven of those years in Europe. Notwithstanding the undoubted talent of the artist his application was rejected.

Fortunately, in 1835, Samuel Morse was appointed Professor of Literature of the Arts of Design in the University of the City of New York. The University was then in the process of formation and its salary budget was limited, but by virtue of his official position Professor Morse was able to rent spacious quarters in one of the University buildings. Here he maintained a studio for his artistic activities and also a laboratory and workshop where he might devote odd moments to his electric telegraph scheme.

The first model of the invention was constructed by Morse himself. The recording apparatus involved the use of a ribbon of paper passing over rollers and so arranged that a pencil point attached to the lower end of a wooden pendulum made contact with the paper in response to the opening and closing of the circuit by the sending apparatus. In order to regulate the length of time and the manner of opening and closing of the circuit Morse invented saw-tooth type that he cast by hand. This type could be set up as in a composing stick and fixed upon an endless belt of carpet-binding revolving over two rollers. When a message was to be transmitted the rollers would be turned by a crank thus drawing the type forward. As the type progressed the free end of the circuit-lever would rise over the points and then fall into the notches, thus opening and closing the electrical circuit. At the receiving end of the line the pencil point recorded a straight line along the paper-ribbon so long as the pendulum was at rest, but whenever the circuit was closed by the passing of a tooth under the circuit-lever the armature of the magnet affixed to the pendulum would pull it aside temporarily, thus producing a zig-zag line, short or long according to the character that was being recorded. This was the forerunner of the dot and dash system later devised.

In 1836 Morse procured forty feet of wire and set up his instruments. To his dismay, however, the system would not work. He was then so very ignorant of the science of electricity as to be unable to figure out why his theories had failed. In his distress he turned to a professor of chemistry of the University, Dr. Leonard D. Gale, and was advised that a single battery was insufficient and also that the coil formed around the poles of his electro-magnet should consist of hundreds of turns instead of the few that Morse had given it.

The inventor was now introduced to a magazine article on the subject from the pen of Professor Joseph Henry, published in 1831. Employing the Henry method, the two men substituted a number of small batteries and built up a battery of intensity. When the new coils had been installed Morse was delighted to find that he could send a message through two hundred feet of wire. Then he added wire until he had a thousand feet in the circuit. The system worked as before. Imagine the elation of Samuel F. B. Morse when, having strung ten miles of wire on reels around the lecture room, it was found that messages could be flashed through the entire circuit!

Sec. 16. Morse Applies for a Patent.

The Morse Telegraph System was still no more than a laboratory wonder, as every preceding system had been. The inventor realized that his apparatus was crude and amateurish in appearance. He lacked the means to hire skilled artisans to build a proper model. Capitalists were not interested in the contraption. Only a few scientists could glimpse the practical utility of the invention. News of it became noised abroad and on September 2, 1837, several English and American scientists came to the University to witness a demonstration of the Morse Telegraph. Fortunately for the poverty-stricken inventor a young man in the group became very enthusiastic over the demonstration. He proved to be Alfred N. Vail, son of the proprietor of the Speedwell Iron Works at Morristown, New Jersey.

Young Vail presently agreed to become a partner with Morse in the invention, undertaking to conduct experiments and to manufacture parts of the apparatus at his father's iron works. Not only that but Alfred N. Vail also persuaded his father and brother to advance money to assist the project. Thus aided, the inventor who for five years had dreamed over the venture was now able to file a caveat in the United States Patent Office on October 3, 1837. The caveat contained the following significant statement:

"The machinery for a full and practical display of his new invention is not yet completed, and he therefore prays protection of his right till he shall have matured the machinery." He described his invention as "a new method of transmitting and recording intelligence by electromagnetism."

It appears that the Secretary of the Treasury in March of 1836 had issued a circular-letter seeking advice as to the possibility of establishing a government telegraph system. Morse had received one of these letters and had written to the Secretary at that time concerning his invention. He had kept this important official informed as to his progress, hoping, of course, that the United States Government would adopt the system as soon as it could be perfected.

Judge Vail, the father of Morse's partner, had invested some money in the invention more because of his son's enthusiasm than because of his own faith in the idea. Neighbors and friends jeered at him so much that the father at length grew irritated at the slowness of progress on the invention. Finally, when the elder Vail was ready to withdraw all support from the partners, he was invited to witness a demonstration of the system. This was held on January 6, 1838.

An important improvement had been made in the recording instrument. The pendulum, instead of swinging to and fro as had the first model, now moved up and down in response to the opening and closing of the electric circuit. No longer did the pencil-point describe a zigzag line but instead it made actual dots and dashes. The skeptical manufacturer came to the shop with several friends. He wrote on a slip of paper, taking care that Morse should not see it, the following sentence: "A patient winner is no loser." This bromidic sentiment he handed to his son for transmission. The inventor was still using sawtooth type in the sending of messages. Young Vail set up the words, inserted the type in the machine and turned the crank. Morse at the receiver took down the message and presently brought it over to the waiting group. It was exactly as the elder Vail had written it, a fact that so astonished the manufacturer that he instantly became an enthusiast in support of the invention.

Morse very wisely insisted upon a long period of experimentation before permitting the invention to become public. Saw-tooth type was soon discarded in favor of the familiar key by which the operator sent messages by simple action of the fingers and wrist. The system of using numbers in a sort of code for letters of the alphabet shortly gave way to the more sensible plan of sending letters instead—letters for which

THE ALEXANDERSON ALTERNATOR
(with inventor watching its operation)

THE FESSENDEN ALTERNATOR
Built by Ernst F. W. Alexanderson at the General Electric plant in
Schenectady, N. Y., in 1906.

dots and dashes were the symbols. The receiving instrument continued to make a written record of the message, for at that time no one supposed that messages could be read by ear.

Sec. 17. Rivalries and Bickerings.

It was perhaps inevitable that among persons closely associated in originating an epoch-marking invention such as the electric telegraph there should have developed heartburnings and jealousy. Morse was apparently too much inclined to claim for himself credit for the ideas of others. Vail resented injudicious references to himself as "my assistant," since he considered that he was a co-worker, contributing not only money but ideas as important as any advanced by the original inventor. It is certain that after Vail joined forces with Morse many impractical ideas were discarded and exceedingly important improvements were made. Since the two men were working side by side in their workshop it may have been difficult to determine who was chiefly responsible for ideas evolved in the progress of their work. In after years there was much speculation on this point. Despite their occasional clashes, however, the two men continued to labor at their common task and still remained friends.

In the meantime an unexpected controversy arose with Dr. Jackson, previously mentioned as a passenger on the *Sully* in the memorable voyage of October, 1832. After a lapse of five years Morse paid a visit to Boston in August, 1837—this being prior to his meeting with the Vails as previously recorded. While in Boston he had attempted to renew acquaintance with Dr. Jackson. The Doctor was not at his office when Morse called, so the inventor wrote him a letter telling of the progress of his invention. Jackson promptly replied, expressing his pleasure at the success of the effort and adding: "I have seen several notices of it in the newspapers, but observe that my name was not connected with the discovery." He went on to say that it was no doubt an accidental inadvertence of the editors, who were unaware of "our mutual discovery."

The inventor was considerably upset by this development. After five years of silence from Dr. Jackson it was dumfounding to have the latter calmly assume that the Morse Telegraph was the joint invention of Morse and Jackson. It was of course true that on shipboard the two had been full of enthusiasm over the idea. Dr. Jackson had even promised to investigate and report on some substance easily decomposed by electricity with the idea of utilizing chemistry for the printing of telegraphic messages, but had never collaborated in the manner agreed. This failure to act enabled Morse to reply with truth: "Your neglect retarded my invention and compelled me after five years' delay to consider the result of that experiment (they had made a trial of glauber salt on a colored paper) a failure and consequently to devise another mode of applying my apparatus—a mode entirely original with me."

That this letter would clear up misunderstanding was too much to hope. Far from pacifying Dr. Jackson it rather intensified his desire to claim for himself a share in the credit for discovering the electric telegraph. If Morse had been better acquainted with the history of the long quest by physicists for a satisfactory telegraph system he would have known that as early as 1816 a chemical telegraph had been suggested and in 1828 an inventor named Dyar had conducted successful experiments along this line. Dr. Jackson's idea was therefore not original nor did it prove of any value to Samuel F. B. Morse. Dr. Jackson was evidently a contentious man, for as events were to demonstrate he became a thorn in the flesh to Dr. Morse, especially after the telegraph system assumed commercial importance.

The advent of Alfred Vail followed closely on the exchange of letters between Jackson and Morse. The situation grew more complicated as Vail and others entered into co-operation. The state of ownership in its early days is indicated by a letter written to Francis O. J. Smith, chairman of the Committee on Commerce of the United States House of Representatives, February 15, 1838. In this letter Morse declares: "It is proper that I should here state that the patent right (It was an error to refer to it as 'patent right' since the patent had not then been allowed. Ed.) is now jointly owned in unequal shares by myself, Professor Gale, of New York City University, and Messrs. Alfred and George Vail."

Out of the welter of conflicting claims it is difficult to reconcile the views of partisans of this or that person as having played the leading role in the invention of the telegraph. Alfred Vail, whose claim to chief honors has been stoutly maintained, certainly weakened his own claim to pre-eminence when, in March, 1838, at the very time when he was supposed to have been the chief inventor, he wrote to Morse in the following strain:

"I feel, Professor Morse, that if I am ever worth anything, it will be wholly attributable to your kindness. I now should have no earthly prospect of happiness and domestic bliss had it not been for what you have done. For which I shall ever remember with the liveliest emotions of gratitude, whether it is eventually successful or not."

Sec. 18. Efforts to Secure Foreign Patents.

Now that the Morse telegraph system had passed the laboratory test it was resolved to lay the matter before the National Congress in the hope that a modest appropriation might be voted for the erection of a line between Washington and some near-by city, such as Baltimore. Apparently the inventors did not at that time glimpse the commercial possibilities of their invention. Their hope was to sell it to the government to be used as an adjunct of the mails or in government service.

A successful demonstration of the device was made in February, 1838 before a group of Congressmen and government officials. The matter of appropriation for an experimental line was referred to the Committee on Commerce. The hope of the inventors ran high when the Committee recommended an appropriation of $30,000 for the purpose, the same to be expended under the direction of the Secretary of the Treasury. A bill was duly prepared and presented to the Congress. Opposition at once developed. The idea was regarded by many as fantastic and impractical. They were opposed to spending so much money on a mere experiment, especially when the country was still debilitated by the financial panic of 1837. The bill failed to pass.

Smith, the chairman of the Committee on Commerce, disregarding the proprieties that should have dictated a policy of "hands off," now approached Morse for a share in the invention. He pointed out the need of securing foreign patents and offered to accompany Morse to Europe, paying his own expenses, in an effort to arrange for patenting the device in the chief countries of Europe. The inventor fell into the scheme but in arranging for Smith's quarter-interest he insisted that it should be carved out of the shares already owned by his three partners, Professor Gale, Alfred and George Vail, refusing to part with any of his own half-interest.

When Smith and Morse reached England in the Summer of 1838 they aroused a veritable hornets' nest. Wheatstone and Cooke had already patented their own telegraph system and they now opposed the granting of a patent to the American inventor. The Solicitor-General found some excuse for denying the application for a patent.

In France their reception was little better than in England. A patent so loaded down with "jokers" that it was of little value was finally allowed. Smith had returned to America for the session of Congress but Morse pushed on to Russia. Here he met with hostility from Czar Nicholas, who conceived such an antipathy for the device that he forbade all Russian publications to describe the workings of the Morse telegraph.

After these disheartening experiences, Morse returned to the United States to find that Dr. Jackson was suing him in an effort to establish his alleged claim as co-inventor. Congress had taken no action on the bill to appropriate funds for the experimental line. To make matters worse, the financial depression had smitten Morse's partners so sorely that they now turned deaf ears to his pleas for help.

Morse wrote a letter to Smith at this time that reveals in dramatic fashion his state of mind. "I had hoped to find on my return some funds ready for prosecuting the enterprise. . . . I return with not a farthing in my pocket, and have to borrow even for my meals."

Further to complicate matters the University had fallen into financial distress. Professor Gale had gone to a Southern college to teach. Morse's own services were no longer required. By sheer necessity he was driven to open a small studio and to seek art pupils. This was a mere temporary "pot-boiling" expedient that proved very distasteful to the inventor. The few pupils who came to him paid barely enough tuition to keep him from want. It is recorded that on one occasion he was completely destitute and unable to procure food notwithstanding the fact that one of his pupils was $50 in arrears on his tuition. Driven by desperation Morse dunned the student and succeeded in collecting $10, which he gratefully declared saved him from starvation.

The only bright feature of the depressing months was that Professor Joseph Henry, then at Princeton, generously gave the harassed Morse valuable advice and assistance in electrical problems. Without this encouragement it is problematical whether the inventor could have carried on. His associates had withdrawn financial support. Wheatstone, the English inventor, had applied for an American patent. A promoter of a semaphore telegraph was now bombarding Congress with appeals to appropriate money for his system.

Then came the day when Wheatstone was awarded a patent, with Morse's application still pending. The old adage that it is always darkest just before dawn certainly applied in this case, for ten days after the Wheatstone patent was issued Samuel F. B. Morse was granted similar privileges, this event occurring in June, 1840.

Sec. 19. The National Congress Takes Action.

During the years of delay Morse had worked out an improvement in electric batteries, producing one more powerful than had hitherto been available. He continued to haunt the halls of Congress in a vain endeavor to persuade the vision-lacking law makers to grant a subsidy for an experimental telegraph line. If he had fancied that the winning of his patent would turn the tide in his favor he was doomed to disillusionment. Congress remained unimpressed and decidedly unfriendly. Thus two more years passed. Toward the end of the year 1842 Morse contrived to string a wire between two committee rooms at Washington. The demonstration was highly successful but produced no immediate results.

Morse had by this time come to be regarded by certain members of Congress as half-demented and an object of mirth. As late as February 21, 1843, an alleged humorist, for the purpose of making sport of the perennial telegraph appropriation bill, offered an amendment to the effect that one-half of the sum appropriated should be devoted to trying experiments in mesmerism under the direction of the Secretary of the Treasury. The debate on this absurd amendment was no doubt amusing to all save the long-suffering inventor then sitting in the House balcony. Fortunately the effort to laugh the measure out of Congress failed in its purpose and a few days later the appropriation bill passed the House by a vote of 89 to 83.

Scarcely more than a week of that session of Congress remained. The bill must be gotten through the Senate or fail for the year. In a last desperate effort the half-starved inventor haunted the Senate lobbies in an effort to win votes for his cause, conscious that hostile forces were at work to defeat the appropriation. On the last day of the session, March 3, 1843, President Tyler came to the Capitol to sign bills as fast as they might come through the final stages of enactment. So many bills were ahead of the telegraph appropriation that Morse lost all hope and, thoroughly exhausted, went to his room and to bed only to learn next morning that the bill had actually passed and had been signed by President Tyler. Miss Annie Ellsworth, a daughter of the Commissioner of Patents, was the messenger who brought the glad tidings. The overjoyed inventor then and there promised the girl that the first message to be sent over the line should be hers. This promise was later fulfilled but more than a year was to elapse before that glad day.

Sec. 20. The First Telegraph Line.

The money appropriated for the construction of an experimental telegraph line was to be spent under the direction of the Secretary of the Treasury. Morse, Vail, Gale and Fisher were put on the payroll at modest salaries. Since forty-four miles of telegraph lines were to be constructed, expenditures must be kept down. The associates were divided on the question of whether the line should be strung on poles or carried underground. The danger of damage from storms, exposure to the elements and possible human vandalism led the group to decide upon the underground laying of wires. In order to protect the wires from dampness and resultant erosion they encased them in lead pipes, soldered at the joints. Four copper wires wound with cotton yarn of different colors, black, red, green and yellow, and coated with shellac, were placed in the lead cable. Ezra Cornell, the future founder of Cornell University, then a plow salesman, became foreman of the trench gang and thus associated himself with the enterprise that was to bring him wealth and fame. When several miles of the line had been laid and much money wasted in the process, Morse discovered to his sorrow that something had gone wrong with the underground pipe and that the wires had short-circuited. Thus nine months had been lost.

It was finally decided to string the wires on poles. Tests were made as the work progressed. News reporters and Congressmen kept close watch upon the progress of things. When five miles had been constructed the line gave satisfactory performance, yet there were many skeptics who refused to be convinced. When the line had progressed halfway from Washington to Baltimore in May, 1844, the Whig National Convention was in session in Baltimore. With a shrewd sense of news values Morse prepared to relay the names of the nominees to the Capital City. When the train from Baltimore reached Annapolis bringing advance news of the convention Vail was at a telegraph instrument ready to flash the result of the balloting to Morse, stationed at the railroad depot in Washington where a throng had gathered. Within two minutes the feat had been accomplished and an hour before the train puffed into Washington it was known in that city that Henry Clay and Theodore Frelinghuysen had been made the Whig nominees. To be sure, many persons were skeptical as to the truth of the report concerning the name of the Vice-Presidential candidate, but when the train arrived with confirmation of the first news-flash in telegraphic history, Morse was thereupon acclaimed as something of a wizard instead of a madman as formerly supposed.

The last half of the line from Washington to Baltimore was completed in double-quick time. May 24, 1844, was the day appointed for the transmission of the first message between the two cities. True to his promise of fourteen months before, Professor Morse gave Miss Annie Ellsworth the honor of choosing the language of this historic message. She and her mother, being intensely religious, turned to the Bible for inspiration. The twenty-third verse of the twenty-third chapter of Numbers was their choice. Thus originated the historic inaugural message of the Morse Telegraph System, "What hath God wrought." The actual ceremony of the opening of the line was deeply impressive. The Supreme Court room in the National Capitol had been utilized for the purpose. Justices of that high tribunal, government officials and a few of the members of the National Congress who had been active in behalf of the measure were there in readiness for the great event. The inventor Morse was the man of the hour. Before seating himself at the telegraph instrument he made a brief and impressive speech calling attention to the fact that his fellow worker Vail was at this moment in the Mount Claire station of the Baltimore and Ohio Railroad in the city of Baltimore. He impressed upon his listeners the fact that Vail had no advance information as to the message to be transmitted. Morse seated himself and clicked off the words that Annie Ellsworth had selected. He had no sooner finished than there came a signal that

Vail had received the message correctly. Then came the thrilling moment when Morse's receiver began to click off the words, indenting the symbols on a strip of paper that progressed through the machine. The message came back in identical language. The overjoyed inventor was thereupon obliged to signal Vail to stand by while he was being congratulated in Washington. The historic strip of paper was claimed by Congressman Seymour of Connecticut and now reposes in a museum in Hartford, Connecticut.

CHAPTER THREE

Development of Telegraphy—The Atlantic Cable

Section 21. Public Indifference to the New Invention.

IN THE LIGHT of present-day knowledge of the importance of the telegraph in modern life we might naturally suppose that the people of the United States would have hailed the successful demonstration of the Morse system as a great national event. On the contrary, not a ripple was created by the invention. Men went their way as before, sending messages between Washington and Baltimore by slow moving mail instead of by the time-annihilating electric telegraph. To be sure, on the day following the inauguration of the system, the Baltimore *Patriot* indulged in the novelty of having a reporter send three brief news dispatches from Washington. This was featured as a great journalistic exploit, yet strangely enough months elapsed before the editor resorted to the telegraph for further news from Washington.

Had it not been for the fact that the Democratic National Convention assembled in Baltimore within a few days, Morse and his co-workers might have had no telegraphic business at all. Then occurred an event that should have overwhelmed them with business. The Convention, after a spirited contest in which former President Martin Van Buren was the leading candidate, nominated for the Presidency a "dark horse," James K. Polk. The news of this event when flashed to Washington created consternation and disbelief. Then came a dispatch to the effect that U. S. Senator Silas Wright of New York had just been nominated for the Vice Presidency. This news was rushed to the Senator, who immediately declared his refusal to run. Within ten minutes following the nomination of Wright a telegram from Morse in Washington was handed to the chairman of the Convention in Baltimore informing him of Senator Wright's decision. The convention was thrown into uproar over the announcement. The delegates, by majority vote, refused to credit the telegram as representing the wishes of Senator Wright. The convention was suspended until a committee could be sent to Washington by rail. When the group returned with the dismal tidings that the telegram had been authentic the convention voted to plead with the Senator. This was done through the medium of the telegraph system. A committee from the convention sat with Vail in Baltimore and Senator Wright himself sat beside Morse in Washington while pleas and excuses were being exchanged. Wright remained firm in his refusal. A crowd gathered in Washington and surrounded the Morse office, eager for news of the convention. When he was at length able to report that George M. Dallas had been nominated in Wright's place the crowd broke into wild cheers, not for Dallas but for Professor Morse, the modern wizard.

A small amount of the Congressional appropriation remained unexpended. Morse and his partners had at first no thought of private exploitation of what they believed to be a great public utility. They finally agreed among themselves that if the Federal Government would be willing to pay them $100,000 for their joint interests they would surrender the system to the nation. For nearly a year the telegraph was maintained as a free institution, open to all and sundry. Singularly enough very few people made use of it, with the result that the operators found their task monotonous and uninteresting.

Sec. 22. Private Exploitation of the Telegraph.

Had the development of the telegraph industry been left to the Federal Government it is probable that it would have been laid aside as a mere theory of science that under government largess had been tried and proved correct. Had it awaited public demand, the inventors would certainly have gone to their graves with nothing more to their credit than the successful demonstration of a means of communication that nobody cared to use. That apathetic giant, The General Public, needed a great deal of downright prodding to awaken him to the importance of what the gods had dropped into his lap. How that awakening was brought about is as long and involved a story as can be found in the annals of inventions that have revolutionized society.

It is observable in all ages that the Power that shapes the destinies of men frequently utilizes the cupidity of man to advance causes in which the hopes of humanity are later demonstrated to have been inseparably linked. So it proved with the development of the Morse Telegraph.

While the inventor and his associates were patiently and hopefully awaiting government action, Smith, the avaricious politician who had virtually extorted a quarter interest in the invention some years back, decided to organize a corporation to exploit the invention in New England. His plan was to build a telegraph line between New York City and Boston. The associates decided to stage a sort of sideshow in Boston as a means of arousing interest in the projected company. A line was set up from City Hall to Sudbury Street and a small admission charge was made to all who desired to see messages sent. Cornell and Morse assisted in staging the show but hard-headed Bostonians were unwilling to invest in stock of the proposed company. The disgusted promoter Smith then changed his plans. His line should run from New York City to Philadelphia. The side-show was moved to the Metropolis. Cornell and Wood were the operators at the two experimental stations in New York City. They slept on hard chairs in their offices, but so few people paid admission to witness the marvel of science that both men nearly starved for lack of money to buy food. Smith was a skillful promoter, however, and by the Autumn of 1845 he had sold enough stock to start building his Magnetic Telegraph Company line between New York and Philadelphia.

In the meantime the Postmaster General had decided that the government should operate the Washington-Baltimore experimental line as an adjunct to the Post Office Department. He fixed the very modest charge of a quarter of a cent a word for messages transmitted over the line. The receipts for the first four days of operation were one cent. During the first six months the total receipts were $413 as against an operating expense of $3,925. Two years later the government gladly relinquished its losing venture and stepped out of government ownership of a telegraph line.

By January, 1846, Smith's Philadelphia-New York line had reached Newark, New Jersey. The Hudson River proved to be too great an obstacle for wires to be strung and so an attempt was made by the enterprising Cornell to lay across the river a cable encased in lead pipe. The cable was not a success. Messages were therefore ferried across in row-boats by youthful "racketeers" who managed to collect double for their services.

Sec. 23. Tribulations on Pioneer Lines.

The line had no sooner begun operation than difficulties developed. Faulty poles broke down under impact of storms. Marksmen amused themselves by using the glass insulators as targets. People who lived near the line and who may have needed wire for any purpose simply climbed a pole and cut down a telegraph wire, helping themselves to as much as they desired. Repair men were constantly on the alert but during the first five months of operation the line was out of commission a total of thirty-six days. Patronage under such conditions of uncertainty was naturally quite as uncertain in its nature.

The indefatigable Smith, in his pursuit of elusive profits, promoted a line between Boston and Lowell and presently succeeded in connecting New York and Boston. This was merely the beginning of telegraph expansion. In July, 1846, the line between New York and Philadelphia reported a net profit for the preceding three months of $516. By this time promoters had discovered that to sell stock brought them a profit and to extort a share of the rewards of the contractor who constructed the line was another avenue of gain. A wild scramble to build lines resulted—a mushroom enterprise in which gullible individuals invested.

Nature itself struck with paralyzing might at frequent intervals. During one storm in the Winter of 1847 the line between Philadelphia and Wilmington, a distance of twenty-seven miles, was broken down in seventeen places. The line from New York City to Boston sustained in one night one hundred and seventy **breaks** in a short span of thirty miles. It was indeed a costly and more or less ghastly process of trial and error by which linemen and technicians gradually learned to master the major difficulties of the maintenance of lines.

The most unlovely phase in the development of the electric telegraph was not the smearing of wires with tar to protect the metal from corrosion but the smearing of reputations by rival promoters and claimants. An enterprising genius named Henry O'Reilly matched wits with Smith in a contest for supremacy in the field of line expansion and for many years was a dominant figure in telegraph history. During his career O'Reilly built eight thousand miles of telegraph lines.

Sec. 24. Fame and Fortune for Morse and His Associates.

The inevitable result of the building of telegraph lines as well as the acrimonious controversies that developed between rival promoters and inventors was to focus public attention upon the system itself. As the industry developed and the transmission of messages became more and more a certainty rather than a disappointment because of the sudden breakdown of facilities, the general public began to patronize the lines.

The Associated Press became one of the important agencies for popularizing the telegraph. To be sure there was conflict at first between the proprietors of the telegraph and the officials of the Associated Press, all because of rates to be charged for the sending of messages. The railroads and westward expansion likewise had important bearing upon the growth of patronage of the new means of communication. The broader the national boundaries became the more necessary grew this agency. Without the telegraph it is hard to say what might have happened to the nation when its caravans of westward journeying pioneers pushed into the wilderness. As it proved, the invention of Samuel F. B. Morse was providential, since it annihilated distance and bound together the great American public in bonds more enduring than the slender wires that spanned the hills and dales from Maine to the new territories of the West.

Fluctuations of fortune attended the growth of the telegraph industry but eventually every original investor or pioneer who had had faith to cling to the stock originally issued to him became wealthy—some of them very rich indeed. Ezra Cornell perpetuated his name by endowing Cornell University. Sibley and Kendall also became generous in their public benefactions. Morse himself became rich not only in material wealth but in that intangible wealth of public acclaim and academic honors. He lived to see the industry that he had created wax mighty in the land. The Western Union Telegraph Company and the American Telegraph Company each became giant corporations during his lifetime.

Sec. 25. Attempts to Invent Submarine Cables.

It has previously been noted that in the attempt to carry the first telegraph line from Philadelphia to New York the builders attempted unsuccessfully to lay a cable on the bed of the Hudson River. Water was the bugaboo of amateur electricians, since dampness penetrating the insulation of wires caused the electric current to desert the metal conductor and play baffling pranks. In the costly school of trial and error electricians gradually mastered the major problems of insulation. The glass insulator was their first great triumph, for by it they managed to keep the precious current from deserting the wires on wet days and flashing down wet poles to the earth, thus tying up the telegraph line.

In their attempts to devise waterproof covering for wire, scientists had resorted to various water-resisting substances. Cable wound about with layers of cloth and coated with resin and beeswax was found to be ineffective. The substitution of melted rubber proved little better. Then came the all-important discovery that gutta-percha, a resinous exudation of a tropical tree, was ideal for the purpose. This discovery became known in the United States about 1847. Two years later the substance was first used in a submarine cable across the Connecticut River at Middletown, Connecticut. The experiment proved so successful that telegraph builders generally adopted gutta-percha as the standard insulation for under-water cables.

Wheatstone in England had already conceived a plan for a submarine line across the English Channel between Dover and Calais. John and Ronald Brett, in 1845, put on record an ambitious plan for a submarine cable between England and America. Both plans were merely on paper. In 1850, however, John Brett laid the first cable across the English Channel. Messages were actually exchanged between the two countries, but after one day of service the cable ceased to function. Although gutta-percha had been used yet the insulation proved so thin that the combined action of tide and the gravel bottom abraded the cable and exposed the wires. The cable was relaid, using a thicker coating of gutta-percha enclosed in lead pipe. This effort proved successful. Within the next few years three cables were laid between England and the Continent and two between England and Ireland. Brett seems to have been the leading spirit in this movement.

The success of Brett's ventures naturally led to serious thoughts of a submarine cable across the Atlantic. One of the first outspoken advocates of the idea that eventually ripened into the Atlantic Cable is said to have been a Roman Catholic Bishop of St. John's, Newfoundland, who wrote a letter to a local newspaper in 1850 urging the construction of such a cable from the United States to Newfoundland. His idea was that vessels passing Cape Race bound for European ports could be given the latest news from the States and ships headed for the United States could disclose the latest happenings in Europe at least two days prior to their arrival in New York. The idea found favor with the telegraph companies. Money was raised for the project and in 1852–53 the first cable was begun from Newfoundland to New Brunswick. The company promptly went into bankruptcy upon the failure of the cable to work. Faulty insulation and the corrosive action of sea water accounted for the catastrophe.

F. N. Gisbourne, the manager of the ill-fated project, attempted in 1854 to revive the company. Among the New York capitalists whom he consulted was a retired paper manufacturer, Cyrus W. Field. Field was only thirty-five years of age and had already become dissatisfied with a life of inactivity.

Out of Field's talks with Gisbourne came the dawning of a new interest in life. It is said that one day the two men chanced to be standing beside a globe that gave an inaccurate scale of the width of the Atlantic between Newfoundland and Ireland. The distance appeared so inconsiderable that Field said to himself: "If a cable to Newfoundland, why not a cable all the way." Thus was born in the mind of the eventual builder of it the Atlantic Cable.

Sec. 26. Field's Efforts to Promote an Atlantic Cable.

Fortunately for Cyrus W. Field the United States Navy had just published the results of a survey of the ocean bottom between Newfoundland and Ireland. Soundings had established the existence of a virtual plateau between the two with no ocean depths greater than two thousand fathoms, thus rendering the task of cable-laying less hazardous than if great depths were to be encountered.

In the history of humanity few instances have been recorded of such enduring zeal for a cause, however worthy, as of Cyrus W. Field's for the Atlantic Cable. It is probably true that Mr. Field was first attracted to the project by the very human desire for personal glory. To be the creator of one of the greatest boons to humanity that had ever been achieved by man—the annihilating of distance, as it were, between the continents of the earth—was an alluring thought. It is true that Field was ignorant of the magnitude of his task, else he would never have undertaken it so confidently. Peter Cooper, one of New York's public-spirited citizens, was a friend of Field and probably the first to agree to share in the venture. Moses Taylor, Chandler White and Marshall

O. Roberts were the other New York capitalists who joined in the project. A corporation was formed May 6, 1854 to be known as the "Newfoundland and London Telegraph Co." with an authorized capital stock of $1,500,000. The government of Newfoundland had already promised generous co-operation. It promptly granted a subsidy of £50,000 to aid in the work. It also gave to the corporation fifty square miles of public land with a promise of an additional fifty square miles upon completion of the cable. To complete its generosity the Newfoundland government gave the cable corporation a fifty-year monopoly of cable-laying within its borders. Prince Edward Island, which was to be utilized in the cable-laying project, also granted a liberal charter.

Field immediately went to England to arrange for manufacture of the cable, English manufacturers having had experience in such work. It was not until the Summer of 1855 that the cable arrived in American waters. It was fabricated of three copper wires, each insulated by gutta-percha and rope yarn. A gutta-percha covering over all was strengthened by iron wire heavily smeared with tar. Thus it was hoped the problem of laying a deep-sea cable of great length had been successfully solved.

Field and his associates staged a grand ceremony for the laying of the first section of the cable across the Strait of Cape Breton, a distance of 55 miles. Four clergymen, sundry poets and authors and even the great Samuel F. B. Morse graced the occasion, or would have, had not the sea proved so rough that grace was not the word for this christening party. Indeed there was something prophetic about the whole affair. When two miles of the cable had been laid it had to be cut in order to save the vessel from being cast onto the rocks by a sudden tempest. Later the cable was spliced and a fresh start made. Yet the splicing shortly gave way under the strain as the long cable descended into the ocean depths. Again the cable was spliced. An obstinate sea-captain who paid little heed to the charted course of the cable route gave the promoters no end of trouble. A violent storm in mid-channel finally obliged them to cut the cable and to give up the attempt with forty miles of wire on the sea bottom.

Not to be thwarted by this disaster, the original backers contributed more money and in July, 1856, had the satisfaction of completing the cable across the treacherous Strait of Cape Breton. To their dismay, however, the expense of the venture had already exceeded a million dollars, and had exhausted the resources of the promoters of the enterprise. Although Morse had at first been enthusiastic over the project he lost interest when it was discovered that even in a fifty-five mile submarine cable his system would not work. A more sensitive type of signaling was needed and Field was driven to adopt the earlier type

of needle-telegraph supplemented by a delicate reflecting galvanometer. Professor William Thomson, who later became the world-
famous Lord Kelvin, was the scientist who perfected this device.

The Thomson invention was almost magical in its sensitivity. A
needle weighing but an ounce and a half was so mounted that friction was minimized. A tiny mirror reflecting a ray of light indicated
with exceeding accuracy the slightest stirrings of the super-sensitive
needle. Not only that but the operator of the receiving station observed the oscillations of the needle as recorded by the mirror and
indicated the same to another operator by means of a telegraph instrument that printed the symbols agreed upon. This second operator
translated the symbols into words. The symbols were somewhat similar to the Morse code, being based upon the number of oscillations of
the needle and the duration of each. It was a complicated system, but
it worked.

It was hoped that this system would function even in a cable long
enough to span the broad Atlantic. To be sure, there were those who
pooh-poohed the idea that a cable could successfully be laid between
Europe and America. Robert Stephenson, the famous engineer and
bridge builder, told Field with finality that it would be impossible to
lay a cable in deep water.

Sec. 27. The First Atlantic Cable.

Since the resources of the original backers had already been exhausted in the venture, Field went to England for help. In December,
1856, he succeeded in organizing the Atlantic Telegraph Company of
Great Britain with a capitalization of £350,000. Best of all, the issue
of stock was over-subscribed. The British government, moreover,
pledged financial support by guaranteeing cable business up to a certain figure. The United States Congress took similar action on March
3, 1857.

Thus encouraged, Field made ready to lay the cable. On August 5,
1857, in the midst of imposing ceremonies, the shore end of the cable
was installed at the proposed terminal on the coast of Ireland. In
four days the cable-laying ship paid out three hundred and sixty miles
of wire. Then for no observable reason the cable parted. The ship
returned with flags at half staff to Ireland. Thus a half-million dollars had been wasted. The promoters nevertheless decided to carry on.
Field had a new plan. If two ships, each carrying half the cable, were
to start at mid-Atlantic, splice the cable and proceed one toward
Newfoundland and the other direct to Ireland the feat might be
accomplished. On June 25, 1858, the cable-laying ships and their con-
voys began their task in accordance with this unique plan.

They had scarcely separated, being but three miles apart, when the machinery of one of the ships fouled the cable and broke it. Again the ships met and spliced the cable. As a precautionary measure operators on each ship were signaling to each other through the cable as it was being paid out. Thus they were enabled to discover, when forty miles of wire separated them, that the cable had ceased to function. It was thereupon decided to repeat for a third time the splicing process. One of the ships, however, now had so inadequate a supply of coal that fears were entertained of being obliged to return to Ireland should any more accidents befall the cable.

Fate again proved unkind. When two hundred miles of cable had been laid the line again broke and the two ships steamed sadly back to the Irish shore. The directors of the cable company were in despair. Field, despite his repeated failures, still had faith in the project. The chairman of the directors resigned and one other prominent member failed to attend. Field's eloquence, however, won an affirmative vote of the remainder of the directors. So swiftly were new preparations made that on July 17th the ships again set forth from Valentia, Ireland. This time there were no speeches and no enthusiasm. Even Field, who was aboard one of the ships, must have realized that this was his last chance.

On July 29, 1858, the cable was spliced and the ships parted in mid-Atlantic. Was it prudence on Field's part that the ship he was on steamed for America? He must have realized that should this attempt fail he would be far from popular in England. It may be that cable-laying, like every other feat of skill, requires experience for successful completion. If so, the mechanics aboard the two ships had profited by their former mishaps, for there was no breaking of cables on this trip. The black line rolled evenly out of its coil in the hold of each ship. Signals were exchanged at regular intervals throughout six anxious days. On the seventh day Field's ship, the *Niagara,* entered Trinity Bay, Newfoundland, and the joyous operators flashed the good news to the *Agamemnon* to learn that the latter was within sight of the Irish coast.

Sec. 28. Failure of the Cable.

The exultant Cyrus W. Field with a single companion landed that very evening and walked fifteen miles to the nearest telegraph station to send the glad tidings of the successful laying of the cable. By August 12th the stations in Ireland and Newfoundland were in communication but the signals proved distressingly feeble. Plans went forward, however, for the formal inauguration of the line by an exchange of messages between Queen Victoria and President Buchanan. It was not until August 16th that the attempt was made to send the Queen's message.

After two hours of effort, repetitions being necessary, only twenty-four words had been received in America. A pause for repairs then became necessary and not until the following day did the balance of the Queen's message cross the Atlantic. On August 18th President Buchanan's reply was labored through. The public on both sides of the Atlantic rejoiced mightily at this triumph of modern science and human perseverance. Rejoicing soon gave way to misgivings when it became generally known that great difficulty was being experienced in transmitting messages.

Plans went forward, however, for a grand celebration in Field's honor to be given by the City of New York. Six hundred guests sat down at the banquet. Eloquent speeches were made to which Field was obliged to respond, even though he was at the moment consumed with secret anxiety lest his great project had utterly failed. The cable, for some unknown reason, was slowly but surely dying. Feeble responses and unintelligible signals continued to be exchanged until October 20, 1858, when the cable ceased to function.

Field was thereupon bitterly assailed on both sides of the Atlantic for having perpetrated a fraud upon the investing public. Some enemies went so far as to allege that no messages had ever been exchanged—the purported cablegrams having been faked for the evil purpose of selling worthless stock. Field was not without his champions, however, for even investors who had lost heavily came to his defense. It was finally decided that a fault of manufacture had caused the cable to become exposed in places to the action of sea-water, thus accounting for the gradual destruction of the cable service.

Sec. 29. Other Unsuccessful Attempts.

Field became so unnerved by his failure that it required months for him to recover, but recover he did and as early as May, 1859, we find him crossing the Atlantic to confer with the British authorities about the laying of a new cable. The government was not in an agreeable mood, since it had just met disaster in a cable venture at the Red Sea. Then, too, the stock in Field's company had become so ill esteemed that one speculator was said to have purchased a $10,000 certificate for $10. Months passed with little progress being made.

The outbreak of the Civil War, while it demonstrated the need of an Atlantic cable and proved the tremendous value of a telegraph system on land, nevertheless so dislocated financial structures in both English-speaking nations that Field's efforts were completely frustrated. Month after month and year after year he struggled with the hopeless task of raising money. He soon came to be regarded as so great a nuisance that men avoided meeting him by crossing the street whenever he was seen approaching. During the anxious years of pro-motion Field crossed the ocean more than a score of times, never re-questing a dollar of remuneration for the time and effort thus wasted.

Toward the close of the Civil War the prospects of the cable com-pany began to revive. The Reuter news agency, for example, came forward with a guaranty of a considerable volume of business. One of the most encouraging circumstances of all was the fact that the owners of the *Great Eastern,* a mammoth steamship that had become a sort of white elephant, offered to charter the ship for a year as a cable-layer on the most generous of terms. If the cable-laying should prove suc-cessful the ship owners would be entitled to £50,000 in stock of the company, but if the venture turned out unsuccessfully the steamship company would not be entitled to any compensation.

Thus encouraged, Field and his associates made successful efforts to raise money for the gigantic enterprise. In July, 1865, the cable was attached at the Irish terminus. It would seem that sad experience should have cured Field of the ceremony habit but such was not the case. His irrepressible enthusiasm found vent in banqueting and speechmaking to mark the historic setting forth of the *Great Eastern* on its unique voyage—a passenger ship now heavily laden with 2300 miles of cable—tanks and cable weighing 9000 tons.

The ponderous craft with its mighty burden headed for Newfound-land. An operator on shipboard kept up continuous communication with the shore station in an effort to avoid the costly errors of earlier attempts when defective cable had cut off communication and need-less miles of wire had been wasted. There was need enough for this precaution. Whenever the signals faded out, the *Great Eastern* turned back, reeling in the cable from the ocean depths until the defect was discovered. Strangely enough, the first defect was caused by a short piece of wire that in some manner had been thrust through the heavy insulation. More strangely still, the second and third defects in the cable were found to be of the same nature. Experts explained these defects as due to carelessness in reeling the cable rather than deliberate sabotage of the cable venture. A more grievous accident was in store for them. When the *Great Eastern* was less than seven hundred miles from the Newfoundland shore the end of the cable slipped from the clutch of the paying-out device and vanished into the deeps of the ocean.

For ten days the great ship cruised about in an endeavor to grapple the lost cable. Then when the cable had been found and was in process of being raised to the surface the hawser broke and the cable plunged to the bottom once more. There was no help for it—they were beaten again.

Sec. 30. The Atlantic Cable at Last.

The undaunted Cyrus W. Field returned to England and after months of effort organized a new corporation, the Anglo-American Company, which made a contract with its predecessor, the Atlantic Telegraph Company, to manufacture and lay the cable. Again the *Great Eastern* was loaded with more than 2300 miles of cable. Again the cable was made fast at the Irish terminus in Valentia Bay and once more the great ship turned its prow toward America.

"Day after day, night after night, her great pistons glided in their channels, and the cable poured over the stern without a hitch. At last they had learned how it was done!" [1]

Indeed they had, for on July 27th the *Great Eastern* steamed into Trinity Bay, Newfoundland, not a single break or delay having occurred in the trans-Atlantic passage. The most glorious moment of life for Cyrus W. Field must have occurred on that day, for when the cable was landed at 5 o'clock it was found to work perfectly. The great task of connecting the continents with means of instantaneous communication had at last been accomplished. The intrepid pioneer was now the unquestioned man of the hour—yea, of the century. In the words of Justin McCarthy: "The history of human invention has no more inspiriting example of patience living down discouragements and perseverance triumphing over defeat." [2]

To cap the climax of achievement and to dumfound his critics, Field now turned the *Great Eastern* back to the spot where it had lost the cable of the previous year. Equipped with adequate grappling devices, after much searching of the ocean depths, it picked up the lost cable and brought it triumphantly aboard, September 1, 1866. In the meantime the excited electricians were busy testing the cable and creating vast astonishment in the Irish cable office. "Night and day for a whole year," declared the London *Times* on September 5th, 1866, "an electrician had been on duty, watching the tiny ray of light through which signals are given and twice every day the whole length of wire—1240 miles—has been tested for conductivity and insulation. . . . Suddenly last Sunday morning at a quarter to six, while the light was being watched by Mr. May, he observed a peculiar indication about it which showed at once to his experienced eye that a message was near at hand. In a few minutes afterwards the unsteady flickering was changed to coherency, if we may use such a term, and at once the cable began to speak: 'Canning to Glass—I have much pleasure in speaking to you through the 1865 cable. Just going to make a splice.'"

[1] Harlow—"Old Wires and New Waves," p. 294.
[2] McCarthy in *History of Our Times.*

The recovered cable was duly spliced and the *Great Eastern* turned back toward Newfoundland. On September 8th the second cable was carried triumphantly ashore while the whole world rejoiced. The recapture of the lost cable and its flawless operation after a year at the bottom of the sea appealed more strongly to popular imagination than had Field's success in landing the cable of 1866. He was now acclaimed as one of the great heroes of the world. After eleven years of unremitting endeavor he had triumphed gloriously.

One of the significant triumphs of the day was now added by Professor Thomson. This great scientist had been dissatisfied with the workings of the mirror galvanometer and had set to work to invent a siphon recorder. A curved metal tube about the size of an old-fashioned knitting needle was made to siphon ink from a reservoir and automatically to record in Morse characters the cable message on an endless ribbon of paper.

It is pleasing to note that the Atlantic Cable, unlike Morse's Telegraph, was a financial success from the very beginning. Within two years Field had paid in full, with interest, all creditors with whom he had been obliged to compromise at his bankruptcy in 1860. The success of the Feld cables led to a virtual epidemic of cable-laying not only in the Atlantic but in other oceans as well.

CHAPTER
FOUR

Invention of the Telephone

Section 31. Reis Makes a Beginning.

The invention of the telephone, according to popular fancy, dates from that historic day in Boston in the year 1875 when Alexander Graham Bell and his mechanical assistant, Thomas A. Watson, working on a telegraphic device for reproducing sound, accidentally stumbled upon the secret of the electrical transmission of the human voice. So pleasing a fiction, however, will not stand the test of historical research. For at least eighteen years prior to that March evening scientists on both sides of the Atlantic had been experimenting with the idea of a telephone.

Even before the invention of the telegraph men had discovered that mechanical vibration set up in tightly stretched parchment or other sensitive medium could be transmitted over a taut string or wire to another device similar to the sending apparatus and that the voice would be reproduced. The limitations of such a telephone, however, rendered it little better than a toy. The invention of the telegraph at once stimulated interest in the new field of transmission. Men began to dream of talking to one another in human tones over electrically charged wires.

Philip Reis, a German professor, apparently invented the first electrical device that might truly be called a telephone. It is noteworthy that great inventions usually originate from the crudest of beginnings. The first automobiles, for instance, were much like an ordinary riding wagon of the period. It required decades of experience to evolve the luxurious motor cars of the present.

The Reis telephone was a crude affair. Since the human ear was the accepted symbol of hearing, Reis decided to pattern his telephone as closely as possible on nature itself. He carved out of wood an imitation of the human ear. A tightly stretched drum of pig's bladder formed the tympanum. A dot of wax on the inside of the membrane held a curved platinum wire in such a manner that it moved with every vibration of the tympanum and as it moved the wire made contact with a spring which was attached to a charged wire. The receiver was even more crude. The instrument itself was a knitting needle set in a coil of wire and resting on a violin as a sounding board.

It reproduced musical notes. There were those who claimed that they could distinguish over it words and phrases. The inventor manufactured a dozen or so of his telephones and learned professors lectured upon them as marvels of science. Although the Reis telephone created a mild sensation at the time, no one in Germany could see any practical value in the invention. Not until Bell produced his famous telephone did they awaken to the world-opportunity that they had thus blindly thrown away.

Sec. 32. American Efforts to Invent the Harmonic Telegraph.

By a singular coincidence two American inventors, one in Chicago and the other in Boston, each pursuing the elusive harmonic telegraph will-o'-the-wisp, invented a telephone similar in many respects to that of the other. So close proved the race for patent rights that the two men filed papers in the Patent Office on the same day and within two hours of each other.

The first man was Elisha Gray, an orphan who had worked his way through college and had later built up an extensive electrical manufacturing enterprise which eventually became the Western Electric Company. Prior to 1873, Gray had invented an automatic self-adjusting telegraph relay, a telegraph switch, a telegraph repeater and various other practical devices. He had been intrigued, as had other men possessing knowledge of the science of electricity, with the fact that by means of different musical tones more than one message might be sent at the same instant over the same wire. No really efficient system had as yet been invented, so Elisha Gray undertook the task.

In 1874 Gray had made some progress toward accomplishing his object. The Western Union, eager to be first in the field, after much publicity exhibited the Gray instrument in New York City. They called it a telephone because it could reproduce sound by the medium of an electric circuit. In fact they used 2400 miles of wire in their demonstration and reproduced musical notes at the receiving end. Gray had stumbled upon the fact that if magnets were adjusted or attuned to each other and connected by wire, a sound operating upon one magnet, by the variations in the electric current, would reproduce the same tone in the other. By multiplying magnets attached to the same wire it was hoped that any number of messages could be sent over the same circuit. Although the experiment proved disappointing in so far as the sending of multiple messages was concerned yet it led one of the Western Union officials to declare that in time "operators will talk with one another instead of telegraphing."

Alexander Graham Bell, the second inventor, had come to the United States from Scotland in 1870 at the age of twenty-three because of ill health. His father and his grandfather before him had been celebrated teachers of speech and sound in Scotland. Young Alexander had been trained in the family profession. Finding that a year in Canada had done much to restore his weak lungs, Alexander Bell came to Boston in 1871 and lectured on diction at Boston University for one year. Then he established in Boston a school of his own for the correction of defects of speech, such as stammering and vocal difficulties of persons who were deaf.

Sec. 33. Bell's Experimentation.

It was no doubt Bell's efforts in behalf of the very deaf that led him into serious investigation of the phenomenon of vibration of the human voice and the possibility of transmitting it over an electrical circuit. While only a youth in Scotland he had met the inventor Wheatstone, a rival of Morse for telegraphic honors. At that time Wheatstone had been experimenting with electro-magnets and tuning forks. This being closely allied to Bell's present inquiry, he took up Wheatstone's old-time quest and established a workshop in which he could tinker to his heart's content. The electrical world was then quite agitated over the possibility of sending more than one message at a time over a telegraph wire. Bell soon conceived the idea of inventing a telegraph system involving the use of eight magnets, each equipped with a reed tuned to one of the notes of a musical scale, thus to send eight messages simultaneously. It was an alluring thought but difficult of accomplishment.

Fortunately for Bell, the father of one of his pupils was Gardiner G. Hubbard, a Boston lawyer who had specialized more or less in telegraphic litigation. Mabel Hubbard, the lawyer's daughter, became romantically interested in her teacher and he in her, but what is more to the point, Hubbard himself and the father of another pupil became jointly interested in Bell's idea of perfecting his harmonic telegraph scheme. They encouraged him to devote his time to the invention and agreed to finance the expenses of his investigation. This was indeed fortunate, since it enabled Bell to employ skilled mechanics to construct electrical apparatus which he himself would have been powerless to make.

Fate moves in mysterious ways. It so happened that in the Charles Williams' machine shop in Boston was working a brilliant young mechanic, Thomas A. Watson, who was destined to become Bell's co-worker in the invention of the telephone. Watson was only twenty years old in 1874 when he first met Alexander Graham Bell, having already constructed according to the inventor's plans parts of the receiver and transmitter of the harmonic telegraph. In his efforts to assist the inventor to realize his dream Watson in turn became deeply interested in the project. Sanders and Hubbard, the financial backers of Bell, realizing the importance of having a clever mechanic working at all times with the inventor, persuaded Watson to cast his lot with him and agreed to pay him $9.00 a week for his services. Neither of the sponsors of the effort had any idea of inventing a speaking telephone, the harmonic telegraph being the agreed object of experimentation.

On June 2, 1875, Bell and Watson were busy at their harmonic telegraph when an astonishing thing happened. They were trying to adjust two instruments so that the steel reeds of the receiving instruments would vibrate in tune with the sending device. Bell was in one room with the receiver while Watson, sixty feet away in another room, was plucking the reeds with his fingers in order to keep them in vibration. One of the reeds stuck so that a continuous flow of electricity had passed through the circuit while Watson was endeavoring to free the thin strip of steel. To the trained ears of Bell came an astounding signal—a genuine sound instead of a mechanical vibration. Instantly Bell dashed to the room where his assistant was at work crying out, "What did you do then? Don't change anything! Let me see!"

It was the author's great privilege to have known Thomas A. Watson quite intimately during the last thirty years of his life. The invention of the telephone was a frequent topic of discussion between them. In a social visit to the Watson study in Boston just prior to the inventor's death, Mr. Watson made the following significant remark to the author:

"I verily believe that Fate had a hand in the invention of the telephone. No ear in all the world save the trained and sensitive ear of Alexander Graham Bell could probably have recognized that hum as a sound wave. By Fate he was in that room listening at the very instant when I was having trouble with that reed."

Sec. 34. Rival Claimants for Patent Rights.

In the history of other great inventions we have observed that many years—sometimes centuries—have elapsed between the first glimmering recognition of a phenomenon and its eventual mastery by man. Yet in this case two men of unusual mental endowment at once set to work to conquer the mystery which Providence had thus unexpectedly placed before them. Bell's knowledge of the mechanics of speech, the sound waves that the delicate vocal chords were capable of setting in motion, gave him a clue as to how this new type of electrical sound-wave might be transmitted and reproduced.

Thomas A. Watson was given immediate instructions to build a device in which the maximum vocal vibrations might be harnessed to the purpose in hand. A small drum-like disk of tightly stretched gold-beater's skin was mounted over a receiver. The center of the drumhead was joined to the free end of a receiver spring in the hope that the human voice directed to the drum through a funnel or mouthpiece would cause the electrical circuit to convey to another similar device the impulses which, being reproduced, would cause the receiving instrument to talk.

Months passed, however, in futile attempts to make the telephone talk. Bell journeyed to Washington and discussed his perplexities with the venerable Professor Joseph Henry. The latter gave him the very frank admonition to learn more of the science of electricity, yet to persevere in his undertaking. By this time Bell had learned that Elisha Gray was also hot on the trail of the elusive telephone. This knowledge caused anxiety lest Gray should reach the goal ahead of him. Bell's backers now took alarm and insisted upon rushing the invention to the Patent Office.

It was fortunate indeed for Bell that action was taken promptly, since Gray had apparently learned of the activities in Boston and had himself taken alarm. On a stormy day, February 14, 1876, Gray arrived in Washington to file in the Patent Office a caveat, or notice to the world, that he was at work on an invention of a telephone. On the same afternoon, two hours before Gray reached the desk of the filing clerk, however, the patent attorney who represented Bell had filed a formal application for a patent. Years of litigation were to follow before Alexander Graham Bell was to be officially declared the winner in this contest. There were charges that one important feature in Gray's caveat was immediately thereafter used by Bell and Watson, giving rise to the suspicion that there had been collusion at the Patent Office and that Bell had unlawfully been permitted to see a document whose contents should have remained secret until a formal application for a patent could have been made.

Bell claimed that this feature had already been invented but by inadvertence had been omitted from the hastily drawn application of February 14th. Whatever the facts of this dispute may have been it is unquestioned that on February 29th, 1876, Bell amended his application for a patent by describing the missing feature, which was a variable resistance device consisting of a short wire extending from the diaphragm or drumhead of the instrument and dipping into a cup of acid, the depth varying with the nature of the vibration.

Sec. 35. Bell's First Talking Telephone.

It is an extraordinary fact that Bell's telephone was actually patented three days before the inventor succeeded in making the instrument talk. The usual fate of inventors is that hard-headed and unimaginative patent officials delay approval of their inventions for months and sometimes years after actual demonstration of successful operation. Yet here was a case where a merely theoretical device was patented before it was ever demonstrated that it could accomplish what was claimed for it.

The first successful operation of Bell's telephone occurred on the evening of March 10, 1876, when Bell and Watson had a never-to-be-forgotten experience. They were working as usual upon their telephone device, the two men now in lodgings at 5 Exeter Place, Boston. Watson had constructed a new transmitter in which was included a cup to be filled with dilute sulphuric acid. The two attic rooms used by the pair had been connected by wire and a telephone receiver had been installed in Bell's bedroom. All being in readiness for the test, Watson poured acid and water into the cup. He then hurried to Bell's room, closed the door and applied his ear to the receiver. To his astonishment he heard Bell's voice crying out in agitation: "Mr. Watson, come here! I want you." The professor had accidentally spilled some of the acid on his clothing and needed help to remove it before it could harm the fabric. Watson's shout of triumph when he came dashing into the room must have been enough to make even the impecunious Bell forget the damage to his pants. "Professor Bell," he cried excitedly, "I heard every word you said." The inventor, in his turn, rushed into the next room and listened while Watson talked into the transmitter. This was but the beginning of a glad, mad evening in which the two joyful experimenters took turns at declaiming and listening. Having made this beginning, it was easy to construct a return circuit in order that two-way conversation might be carried on between the attic rooms. The next logical development was to run a wire from Bell's lodgings to the Williams' shop, half a mile distant, where they worked daily at their alluring task. Sure enough the telephone worked, although faintly, thus confirming their belief that they had unlocked the secret of electrical transmission of speech.

The story of Morse's struggles to secure the adoption of the telegraph had its counterpart in a milder degree in the case of the Bell Telephone. The success of the telegraph had no doubt somewhat prepared the public mind for marvels of science, and the announcement that an instrument had been invented whereby any person might converse with another over miles of distance could not fail to attract attention. The Centennial Exposition in Philadelphia gave Bell his first great opportunity of publicity. Dom Pedro, the Emperor of Brazil, one of the visitors to the Bell exhibit at the exposition, greatly assisted in the process of publicizing the invention.

Public recognition of an invention, however, does not solve the financial problems of an inventor and his financial backers. Until the invention can be sold or exploited there are bound to be lean days for all concerned. Bell had spent every dollar he could earn or borrow and Sanders had $110,000 tied up in the enterprise before he was able to get any of it back. Hubbard and Watson were deeply involved and various others had investments that stood to win or lose according to the success or failure of the invention.

Hubbard, with an eye to the needs of his son-in-law Bell, began to arrange public lectures in various New England cities at which admission fees were charged. The procedure was for Bell to lecture on the wonders of the device while Thomas A. Watson at some distant point would talk to him over the telephone, a not very satisfactory loud speaker being on the stage. Watson usually had a cornetist, organist or other musician to furnish entertainment. Shortly before his death Mr. Watson told the author quite gleefully of a time when he sang to a distinguished audience in Symphony Hall, Boston, although the Watson vocal ability was nothing to boast about. The reason for his being called upon was simply that when some famous singer was scheduled to do the vocal part of the lecture from Salem or some other distant point so many people along the telephone line tried to listen in that the great man's voice could not be heard by the Boston audience. When Watson took over the song, however, the line was quickly cleared, with the result that the audience heard the voice of a skilled mechanic rather than that of the famous singer.

The financial returns from these lectures were meager indeed. It was not until lines had been built and contracts for telephone service began to come in that the backers of the enterprise felt that the telephone had a future as a business investment. The first payment of $20 for a year's lease of two telephones was received at the Boston office in May, 1877. The Bell Telephone Company was organized July 9, 1877, 5,000 shares of stock being issued. Bell, Hubbard, Sanders and Watson were the stockholders, the last named being allotted 499 shares while the other three divided the remainder nearly equally among them or their dependents.

The financial rewards that later were showered upon the fortunate possessors of this stock are now a matter of history. Seldom has inventive enterprise met with such universal recognition and reward as in the case of the Bell Telephone.

The effect of the telephone in enlarging the scope of life of individuals cannot be overestimated. It is probable that no invention in the history of humanity has meant more to the average man than the telephone. For him it has conquered distance, enabling him to converse as if face to face with friends, relations or business acquaintances who may be hundreds or even thousands of miles away. Without the telephone the speed and bustle of modern life would be an impossibility.

CHAPTER
FIVE

Wireless Telegraphy

Section 36. Early Attempts at Wireless Communication.

Although Guglielmo Marconi is justly acclaimed as the father of wireless telegraphy he was by no means the discoverer of the electrical phenomena upon which his invention is based. Scientists had known for generations that leakage of electrical current in telegraph wires in some mysterious manner could magnetize metallic objects at a considerable distance. As early as 1843 Professor Joseph Henry of the United States, whose name has frequently been mentioned in connection with the telegraph, succeeded in magnetizing needles over a distance of 220 feet from the electrically charged wires. Faraday in England performed similar experiments.

In 1865 James Clerk Maxwell, an English physicist, wrote an essay on electro-magnetic phenomena that aroused widespread interest among scientists. He advanced the theory, and presented evidence in its support, that electrical impulses travel through space in the form of waves that speed with the velocity of light. The relation between waves of light and waves of electricity in terms of vibration was soon perceived to be so close that they differed chiefly in number of vibrations per second. Light waves were demonstrated to be so very short that in order to be visible to the human eye there must be from thirty thousand to sixty thousand of them in an inch of space, whereas electrical waves may have vibrations anywhere from a few inches to miles in length. Thus a new avenue of scientific speculation was added to the field of electrical phenomena.

With the development of telegraph and telephone systems, having vast networks of wires, came the annoying phenomenon of interference, or of sounds picked up by induction by telephone wires from near-by telegraph lines or from other telephone wires. Thomas A. Edison at one time turned his attention to this problem, not with the idea of finding a remedy but hoping to utilize the phenomenon in an attempt to devise a means of telegraphing to moving trains.

Edison took out a patent in 1885 on a system of induction telegraphy. By affixing a tin-foil-covered plate to the top of the locomotive or coach the inventor found it possible to attract from telegraph lines bordering the roadbed what amounted to wireless messages. However rapidly a train might be moving at the time, the Edison device continued to function. One fact that militated against it as an answer to the problem of how to maintain telegraphic communication with a moving train was that the device was too democratic in its operation. Any near-by telegraph wire over which a message might be passing found equal favor with the Edison collector of signals. One wire might be carrying a message to the train but any number of near-by wires might alike contribute to a jumbled collection of signals. The manifold difficulties of the problem and the fact that Edison was working on more universally important inventions led him to suspend activities in this field of endeavor.

While the Edison attempt narrowly missed the goal, there was an English inventor, Sir W. H. Preece, who approached even nearer to the secret of wireless telegraphy. In 1885 he set up two squares of insulated wire eighty rods across and eighty rods distant from each other. By the use of powerful currents he managed to cause messages to leap by induction from one square to the other, which was wireless telegraphy in crude form but not of a type to offer any advantages over the ordinary telephone. By a process of trial and error, however, scientists were gradually acquiring knowledge of the true characteristics of electrical discharges into the air.[1]

Sec. 37. Discovery of Hertzian Waves.

A brilliant young German scientist, Heinrich Hertz, experimenting in electrical phenomena, in the year 1887 finally unlocked the secret of the elusive wireless waves. He proved that electric waves could be sent out at will around an oscillating circuit. Hertz set up two hoops of wire some distance apart. In one hoop he left a break across which a spark of electricity would leap whenever the current was thrown on. The spark thus produced was found to excite corresponding currents in the opposite hoop. By placing the hoops farther and farther apart he discovered that he could operate over a distance of several hundred feet and by successive experiments he demonstrated that the waves traveled from one hoop to the other with the speed of light. He discovered, moreover, that the waves could be reflected by polished metal mirrors and also that they could be focused by using lens-shaped cylinders of pitch. From these facts he deduced the arresting conclusion that there must be a special medium other than air in which these waves traveled, in fact which transmitted even waves of light. Thus originated the theory of the existence of an all-permeating medium which by common consent scientists called ether.

According to this theory, ether occupies all space throughout the universe, existing even in solid substances, within the structure of the same, so that waves of electrical energy are capable of penetrating even stone and metals, flowing freely with the speed of light.

[1] Lt. W. L. Howard, U.S.N., writing in "Wireless Telegraphy," November 1, 1899, makes the following statement:

"In 1884 it was noticed that telegraphic messages sent through the usual lines buried in iron pipes under the streets of London were received on telephone circuits on poles carried above the housetops. W. H. Preece in 1885 found that ordinary telegraphic circuits produced disturbance 2,000 feet away.

"In 1892, messages were sent by induction from Penarth to Flatholm, 33 miles, but the most practical test was in 1895, when the cable between Oban and the Isle of Mill broke down and communication was established by electro-magnetic induction."

FESSENDEN AND A GROUP OF EARLY CO-WORKERS

The ether theory, like other scientific abstractions, is perhaps not the true solution. Scientists have recently questioned the existence of ether as an all-permeating medium, yet no one can dispute the fact that waves of electrical energy flow freely with incredible speed. To Heinrich Hertz belongs the credit for having discovered this all-important fact.

Hertzian waves, as they were called, became the subject of laboratory experiments in all lands. It was not until 1892 that Sir William Crookes, in a magazine article,[2] pointed out the possibility of utilizing these waves in "telegraphy across space" by specially tuned instruments employing definite wave lengths. "What remains to be discovered," he wrote, "is—firstly, a simpler and more certain means of generating electrical waves of any desired wave-length, from the shortest, say a few feet in length, which will easily pass through buildings and fogs, to those long waves whose lengths are measured by tens, hundreds and thousands of miles; secondly, more delicate receivers which will respond to wave-lengths between certain defined limits and be silent to all others; thirdly, means of darting the sheaf of rays in any desired direction, whether by lenses or reflectors, by the help of which the sensitiveness of the receiver . . . would not need to be so delicate as when the rays to be picked up are simply radiating into space in all directions and fading away. . . . Any two friends living within the radius of sensitivity of their receiving instruments, having first decided on their special wave-length and attuned their respective receiving instruments to mutual receptivity, could thus communicate as long and as often as they wished by timing the impulses to produce long and short intervals on the ordinary Morse Code."

This amazing forecast of future events, so reminiscent of the old fantasy of the mystic powers of the lodestone as discussed in Chapter I, had given the idea of wireless telegraphy a tangible form. In 1892, the same year in which the Crookes prophecy appeared, Edouard Branly, aided no doubt by discoveries of Sir Oliver Lodge, devised an appliance for detecting electro-magnetic waves, known as the Branly "Coherer." This was to play a very important part in the history of wireless telegraphy. It remained for a gifted and persistent Italian youth to undertake the task of conquering the obstacles that lay in the path of a great scientific achievement. That youth was Guglielmo Marconi, born of Irish-Italian parentage in Bologna, Italy, in 1874.

Sec. 38. Marconi Enters the Field.

Guglielmo Marconi was privately educated in Italy and England, manifesting at an early age a great interest in the science of electricity.

[2] "Some Possibilities of Electricity" in the *Fortnightly Review.*

One of his friends [3] proved to be an enthusiastic experimenter, especially in the mystery of Hertzian waves. Thus the youth was introduced to the field of science in which he was to make his name immortal. It appears from Marconi's own testimony that in his teens he conceived the idea of the practicability of wireless telegraphy. Even then he set it definitely as his life ambition to perfect and establish wireless communication throughout the world. After reading the essay by Sir William Crookes, however, he feared that the idea would be worked out by scientists before he could be ready to compete with them in so highly technical a field.

The eager young man set up an experimental station on his father's farm, the father encouraging the son by supplying him with means to pursue his investigation.

Young Marconi made his first experiments in the Marconi vegetable garden. Across the lowly domain of beans and cabbages the young man was to conduct experiments that were destined to influence the fate of empires. His sending and receiving apparatus were of home origin. Up to a certain point he followed the well-known experiments with the Hertz broken coil, with which very short distances could be attained. He then used a more open form of Hertz radiator, two rods in line, the adjoining ends provided with spark gaps, the outer ends of the rods fitted with metal wings to form a capacity area. Greater distances were obtained with this apparatus. The touch of genius was to introduce a Morse telegraph instrument into the circuit. Thus he was able to regulate the spark that leaped the gap at his lightest touch. Now for the first time in history the Morse code was introduced to wireless waves—dots and dashes flung into space from the Hertz spark-gap with which scientists had long dallied. It had remained for the Italian youth to lead the world to the solution of the great secret of wireless telegraphy.

Marconi had studied the Branly coherer and was well informed as to methods employed in constructing the receiving apparatus in which a mass of metal granules were employed. Under the influence of an electric current these granules combined to form a network or webbed-chain through which the current filtered in passing. Professor Branly had overcome the tendency of the metal filings to adhere to each other after the current had passed through them by attaching a tiny hammer that automatically tapped the tube to shake the filings apart after each flash. This was the type of detector used by Marconi in his early experiments.

Sec. 39. Wireless Telegraph Patented.

The Branly "Coherer," as it was called, did not accomplish all that

[3] Professor Righi of University of Bologna.

Marconi hoped for it, so the young inventor set out to improve the device. After testing various types of metal filings he hit upon nickel with a small percentage of silver as best suited to his purpose. By using a silver plug in each end of the tube and attaching platinum wires to either end of the device he produced a much more serviceable coherer. The automatic decoherer was made to tap the tube and shake the filings apart after every dot or dash.

Marconi's originality led him to depart from accepted patterns of thought. In one of these excursions into new realms of experimentation, in the year 1895, he discovered the principles of the modern aerial. He had been using, in orthodox fashion, the Hertz dipole oscillator and needless to say attaining only orthodox results. One day he conceived the idea of connecting half of the oscillator with the earth. The other half he elevated and prolonged into the air, at once gaining much greater distance in the transmission of signals. Since wires thus extended bore a natural resemblance to the feelers or antennae of some monster insect the name was soon applied to the Marconi device. So effective was the new system that the young inventor was soon able to flash messages across a distance of more than a mile. Wireless telegraphy was now a reality—capable of achieving dependable transmission of signals.

In 1896 the young inventor went to England and took out the first patent ever granted anywhere in the world for wireless telegraphy. Thus at an age when the average youth is just completing his college education the ambitious Marconi, who had feared that older scientists might beat him in the race, attained the coveted honor of becoming the original patentee of a globe-girdling means of communication. To be sure wireless telegraphy was not then globe-girdling, nor even capable of bridging the English channel, but it had made a beginning that astounded the scientists of the world. Marconi had not yet done more than bring to greater perfection the ideas of others. He had combined these ideas into a workable system. He realized all too well that wireless telegraphy on a commercial scale would be possible only when problems of distance-coverage should have been solved.

Under the auspices of the engineer-in-chief of the British Post Office, Sir William Preece, Marconi was now enabled to try out his theories on an extensive scale. Experiments were made on land and sea and to the young man's satisfaction it appeared that the device worked far better over the ocean than over the land. Telephone and telegraph lines were common conveniences on land but at that time ships on the ocean had no means of communication.

English capitalists became interested in the new device. On July 20, 1897, the Wireless Telegraph and Signal Company, Ltd., was incorporated, with a capital of £100,000 to acquire the Marconi patents in all countries except Italy and its dependencies. Marconi himself was engaged as chief engineer of the new company, whose name was presently changed to Marconi's Wireless Telegraph Company, Ltd. This first wireless company in the world has since been popularly known as the British Marconi Company.

Upon his return to Italy in 1897 Marconi enlisted the co-operation of the Italian Navy. In one of his experiments he succeeded in attaining a message-radius of twelve miles. Later in the same year Lloyd's Corporation of London invited Marconi to establish wireless communication between two lighthouses on the North Irish coast, an especially rugged and difficult shore with a high cliff intervening. The distance between the lighthouses was seven and one-half miles. Not only did Marconi's trained workmen set up a wireless system that worked perfectly but they had no difficulty in teaching the lighthouse keepers to operate the instruments.

From this time forward Marconi was in great demand. In July, 1898, he reported by wireless the Kingstown Regatta. In the following month he set up a station at Queen Victoria's summer residence on the Isle of Wight in order that the aged Queen might be in daily contact with the Prince of Wales, whose yacht was equipped with the new device.

Sec. 40. Increasing the Range of Wireless Transmission.

Sir Oliver Lodge, the brilliant English scientist, rendered great aid to Marconi in the years 1897 and 1898 by experimenting in principles of tuning of wireless instruments. Thus was originated the technique of sending out electric waves of definite length from instruments resembling huge tuning forks, so tuned that they would always give forth impulses of the same wave length. These experiments included also the devising of receiving sets that could be tuned to receive impulses of definite wave length. Without in the least realizing it, Lodge and Marconi were paving the way for the advent of radio broadcasting.

Now that British ships were being equipped with wireless apparatus it was inevitable that some marine disaster should sooner or later focus public attention on the vital importance of the invention. Such an occasion arose in the Spring of 1899 when the lightship on Goodwin Sands near Dover, England, was accidentally rammed by a freighter. These shoals are very dangerous to shipping. By means of wireless the lightship summoned aid. Within a few months following this first call for help wireless messages from this one lightship saved lives and property sufficient to create a demand for the Marconi invention in naval circles throughout the world.

Had Marconi been less of a scientist he might have contented himself with exploiting short range wireless systems, but he soon began to dream of spanning oceans. He had at first believed that the curvature of the earth would prevent him from flashing messages very far. Had these electrical impulses followed the same laws as waves of light he would indeed have been powerless to conquer the vast reaches of ocean. His experiments, however, indicated that the invisible waves in some mysterious manner followed atmospheric strata or at least traveled in an arc paralleling the earth's surface rather than in straight lines.

It is evident that the ambitious young man was not overlooking any possibilities of developing a market for his invention. In the Autumn of 1899 we find him in the United States. He had crossed the Atlantic to report the international yacht races. Officials of the Navy Department were keenly interested in the experiment. As a consequence Marconi was permitted to try out his wireless telegraph under naval auspices. The tests occurred on November 2, 1899.

In testing the Marconi system the *New York* and the *Massachusetts* were equipped with wireless apparatus. They exchanged messages across thirty-six miles of ocean. A news item of that date was as follows: "Rear Admiral Phelps received the first official message by the wireless. Rear Admiral Farquhar, on his flagship, the *New York,* twenty miles out at sea, presented his compliments to the Commandant and reported that he would be at the Navy Yard on Friday morning. The message was ticked off from the transmitting spar lashed to the topmast of the *New York,* caught by the receiver at the Navesink station, 20 miles away; then it was sent over the wires to the Navy Yard. Admiral Phelps immediately acknowledged the receipt of the message and reported that the coal dock would be made ready for the *New York.*" [4]

Mr. Marconi was on the *New York* in personal charge of the apparatus when the above message was sent (Nov. 2, 1899).

The youthful inventor was evidently ably chaperoned by business associates from the British Marconi Company. Young Marconi had no sooner attracted the attention of naval authorities in this country than a new corporation blossomed under the Stars and Stripes. The Marconi Wireless Telegraph Company of America was organized. Hereafter in this narrative the corporation will be referred to as the American Marconi Company. A large and probably a controlling interest in the new corporation was held by the British Marconi Company. No doubt the astute Britons had already conceived a plan to dominate wireless communications of the world. On no other reasonable hypothesis may we account for the speed with which they acted in forming an American branch of the Marconi Company.

[4] New York *Herald,* November 4, 1899.

The American liner *St. Paul* on November 15, 1899, succeeded in communicating with a wireless station on the Isle of Wight over a distance of sixty-six miles. Up to that date no commercial message had been detected at so great a distance, although Marconi himself in his experiments had sent messages across seventy miles of ocean. In the following year, having discovered how to send waves in powerful succession, he succeeded in covering two hundred miles. This feat gave encouragement to capitalists and in 1900 the Marconi International Marine Communications Company was organized with the definite plan of establishing strategically located wireless stations. Such stations were promptly set up on the shores of England and Ireland as well as on the continent. Newfoundland and Canada were friendly to the idea.

So rapidly and efficiently did Marconi and his engineers work that by December, 1901, they were ready to try the experiment of flashing a message across the Atlantic. At Poldhu on the coast of Cornwall they built a powerful experimental station. Two lofty masts set far apart and connected by a powerful cable supported the antenna through which this epoch-marking attempt was to be made.

Sec. 41. The First Trans-Atlantic Signal.

Marconi himself crossed the ocean in order to superintend the experiment on the Newfoundland shore. He crossed, moreover, without public announcement of his purpose. His landing in Newfoundland was made quietly, for unlike Cyrus W. Field he was averse to publicity, preferring to accomplish results before beating the drums of victory. Believing that signals might be received as readily through wires carried aloft by powerful kites and balloons as by an expensive receiving station, Marconi made preparations for the test. Two assistants, G. S. Kemp and P. W. Paget, had accompanied him from England. The place selected was on the seashore near the harbor-mouth of the city of St. John's, Newfoundland. On December 12, 1901, Marconi, having cabled to his English assistant, Fleming, at Poldhu that he was ready to listen, settled down to wait.

Arnold has thus described Marconi's experience:

"Before he left England Marconi had given detailed instructions to his assistant at the signal station that the test was to be conducted by the transmission of the Morse telegraphic letter 'S' represented by three dots. The signal was to be transmitted at a fixed hour each day as soon as word had been received by them that the receiving station at St. John's was ready. At noontime on Thursday, December 12, 1901, Marconi sat in his little room in the old barracks waiting for the appointed time to arrive when England would begin transmitting his signal. There were only two persons in this receiving room, Mr. Marconi and his assistant, Mr. Kemp. . . . For half an hour not a sound was heard, then suddenly the assistant, Mr. Kemp, heard the sharp metallic click of the tapper as it struck against the coherer.

"In a moment, faintly yet distinctly, there came the three little clicks or dots spelling out in Morse code the letter 'S,' which had been sent out a fraction of a second before from the sending station in England. Again and again the signal came through until both Senatore Marconi and Mr. Kemp were positive that there could be no mistake. It was thus that history was made, for on that day the principle of wireless communication over great distances was established, constituting one of the greatest wonders of modern science." [5]

Marconi has given us his own story of the event, published in the *Evening Herald*, St. John's, Newfoundland, in its issue of December 16, 1901, under the heading "The Inventor's Story." It reads:

"On arriving in Newfoundland and installing my station on Signal Hill, at the entrance to St. John's, I sent up kites every day this week with the vertical aerial wire appended by which our signals are received. I had previously cabled to my station at Cornwall to begin sending the prearranged signal. On Wednesday my kite blew away, and nothing resulted. Thursday, however, I had better luck. My arrangement was for Cornwall to send at specific intervals between 3 and 6 o'clock P.M. the Morse letter 'S', which consists of three dots, thus (. . .). The hours were equivalent to from noon to 3 P.M. at St. John's, and Thursday during these hours myself and my assistant, Mr. Kemp, received these signals under such conditions as assured us they were genuine. We received them through a specially sensitive telephone attached to our instrument, which enables us to detect signals which the instrument would not record."

Marconi was listening in at the time the first signals were detected. Making sure that he was not mistaken, after a few moments he handed the telephone to his assistant, saying "Kemp, do you hear anything?". Kemp listened, heard the unmistakable low pitched whine of the Poldhu signals, and assured his chief that the "three dots" had been heard by him. Then, and only then, did Marconi admit that he, too, had heard them. And not until the following day, when for a short time, during another lull in the roaring atmospherics, the signals came through audibly, did Marconi report officially his success. On Thursday, December 12, a momentous date in wireless history, and again on December 13, the Atlantic was conquered by the wireless waves.

Unlike other inventors who have ventured all in pursuit of a theory only to discover that the practical application of the theory is a vir-

[5] Arnold—"Broadcast Advertising," p. 3.

tual will-o'-the-wisp, Marconi thus had the amazing good fortune at the first trial to realize one of the sublimest visions that was ever entertained up to that hour by mortal man. Eighteen hundred miles of ocean space without wires or current-boosting devices had been spanned by the genius of a twenty-seven-year-old scientist.

Sec. 42. Awakening of a Giant Industry.

News of Marconi's triumph had no sooner spread abroad than the Anglo-American Cable Company took alarm. This new means of trans-Atlantic communication might prove a dangerous rival to the established cable companies. Taking advantage of the fact that the cable company had a grant of exclusive rights from the Newfoundland government for telegraphic communication with all points outside the colony, representatives of the company warned Marconi out of Newfoundland. The youthful inventor thereupon made arrangements to set up an experimental station at Glace Bay, Cape Breton Island, the Nova Scotia government having offered him the site.

Despite the fact that signals could be flashed across the Atlantic from the outset, months were to elapse before the Marconi Company had progressed enough in overcoming the difficulties of atmosphere and distance to be able to transmit genuine messages. The Company had sold stock and in fact it experienced little difficulty in thus financing expansion of facilities. Ships were being equipped with wireless apparatus and this meant that shore stations must be established as rapidly as possible. Thus two fields of service were thrown open simultaneously—the purely commercial telegraphic service and marine telegraphy from ship to shore. This latter phase was difficult indeed because the Marconi Company was not equipped to supply the overwhelming demand for marine radio apparatus that came pouring in as soon as the new agency had demonstrated its ability to enable ships on the high seas to maintain continuous contact with stations on land. Marine disasters in which wireless operators on shipboard flashed news to other ships or life-saving stations, thus avoiding losses in goods and in human lives, were soon common occurrences.

Popular imagination had been fired as never before in the history of inventions. Mechanically minded individuals began to construct amateur wireless sets. Nor were the nations content to sit idly by and permit a world-wide monopoly in space-telegraphy to be built up by one company, even though it was headed by the acknowledged inventor of the system. This does not mean that there were not rival inventors in the field. Marconi, as already pointed out, entered a more or less crowded array of investigators of wireless phenomena. The Germans, for instance, were working on the problem. Scientists in England and America were likewise veterans in wireless research. The scene was thus set for a race to pre-empt the business in various parts of the world, with or without the consent of the Marconi Company.

The American branch of the great Marconi system was not destined to fare very well in the United States. Our citizens have never been enthusiastic concerning British enterprises. This was so obviously of British origin that it remained an alien despite all efforts of its promoters to convince the American people that it was owned and controlled on this side of the Atlantic. It was true that the majority of its stockholders and directors were American citizens, yet the control of the corporation was decidedly in the parent company in England.

In a conference with David Sarnoff, former Commercial Manager of the Marconi Company (May 11, 1938), the author propounded the question of British control. Mr. Sarnoff replied emphatically that the corporation was dominated by the parent company. "It was organized," he declared, "by Marconi's Wireless Telegraph Company Ltd., of England, which was the largest individual shareholder and the controlling influence in the American Marconi Company. In 1912 the late Mr. Godfrey Isaacs, who was a brother of the late Lord Reading of England, was the head of the British Marconi Company. . . . In that year Mr. Isaacs came to the United States and reorganized the capital structure of the American Marconi Company. That reorganization provided the capital with which was undertaken the program of erecting a series of trans-oceanic high-power Marconi Wireless Telegraph Stations for communication between the United States and England, between the United States and Norway and between the United States and Hawaii and Japan."

Going back to the beginning of the American Marconi's relations with the United States Navy Department we find the following facts:

In 1900 the Secretary of the Navy in his annual report declared that the Marconi tests had proved so satisfactory that the Board of Investigation had reported favorably upon the invention for ship to ship and ship to shore communications. He asserted that if interference could be eliminated the Navy would adopt the Marconi device. It appears from the records that in 1901 the Department was considering discontinuing the use of homing pigeons in favor of wireless telegraphy. The choice then seemed to be between Marconi and deForest. The latter claimed to be able to overcome interference by using mechanically tuned sending and receiving instruments. In 1902 the Navy Department had crossed the Marconi system off its list of possibilities because it had refused to sell its apparatus to the Navy, insisting upon a rental basis for a period of years and imposing other terms that stamped the Marconi organization as a foreign controlled corporation. It is small wonder that the German Slaby-Arco system was adopted in 1903 by the United States Navy.

*Sec. 43. Confusion on the Air and First International Wireless
Conference.*

Great confusion resulted from early attempts to utilize the new
agency. Men are not unlike boys when introduced to a new plaything and this was a tremendously fascinating plaything. To be able
to capture from thin air messages from unexpected sources, perchance
from sailor friends on other ships, gave new zest to life. To be able
to send out messages, to carry on conversations by wireless, made the
new device a joyous boon to the sailor-man. Operators, whether on
Naval or merchant ships, attained importance out of all proportion
to their actual daily duties. They were in a class by themselves. Soon
they began to run wild. Their newly found liberty became license to
follow their own devices except when sending or receiving official
messages. There were no laws, national or international, to govern
their conduct. Human nature in its most arrogant form soon be-
deviled the new medium of communication. Gossip between friends
could and did crowd out messages of life and death on the high seas.
It is said that the terrible *Titanic* tragedy might have been averted
had not a gossiping pair refused to yield precedence to an operator
who tried vainly for half an hour to warn the doomed ship of the
presence of icebergs.

The only way in which urgent messages could be gotten on the air
when two gossiping cronies held the ether was to lay a book or other
weight upon the transmitting key and thus blanket them with such
a roar of interference that they were obliged to desist. This process,
however, was time-consuming and provocative of feuds. What was true
on the sea was also of common occurrence on land. The blessing of
wireless, under the blight of human frailty, became a virtual curse.
In all parts of the world the same phenomenon was observable. Self-
ishness and arrogance flourished in all lands and on seas the world
over.

So intolerable became this condition that in 1903 the first International Wireless Conference was held in Berlin for the express
purpose of formulating regulations for wireless telegraphy. The most
important result of the conference, which was naturally exploratory
in nature, was the question of adopting a distress signal that might
be recognized by the operators of all nations. While every delegate
agreed that a distress signal should have precedence over all other
forms of wireless communication, they were unable to agree upon an
international signal. The British CQ, long used as a distress call on
English railroads, was naturally favored by the delegates of that country, yet as a concession to the new industry the letter D was added.
CQD continued to be used for many years as an international distress

signal. The Germans, however, used SOE and with characteristic firmness held out for its adoption. A second Wireless Conference in 1906 fixed upon SOS as the most appropriate distress signal. This signal was eventually adopted by all nations, but in the sinking of the *Republic* in 1909 and the *Titanic* in 1912 both SOS and CQD were used.

CHAPTER
SIX

Wireless Developments in the United States

Section 44. Fessenden Attempts to Improve Wireless Telegraphy.

NEARLY TWO CENTURIES of experimentation in electrical transmission of signals had preceded wireless telegraphy. Marconi had raised the electric telegraph from its earthbound fetters of pole and wire to unfettered freedom of the skies. The Morse Code no longer followed a slender wire from sender to receiver. It now clattered off into space in all directions and could be picked up by any receiver tuned to the same wave length. Marconi perhaps did not realize how near he had come to the great secret of how to broadcast the human voice in the very tones of the speaker.

It was inevitable that this new field of scientific endeavor should attract the attention of multitudes of ambitious amateurs. Thousands of youths in all lands were already tinkering with home-made wireless apparatus. It was inevitable also that out of the multitude of mere imitators of others should emerge a few men capable of blazing new trails—of carrying the science to new heights of achievement. Two such men now appeared in the United States, Professor Reginald A. Fessenden of the University of Pittsburgh, a former engineer in the Westinghouse Electrical plant in Pittsburgh, and a brilliant young Yale graduate, Lee de Forest.

Fessenden had been tinkering with wireless for several years prior to 1900, at which date he was hired by the U.S. Weather Bureau to conduct experiments in wireless telegraphy as an aid in weather forecasting and in storm warnings. He had already reached the conclusion that the coherer type of receiver then universally used was unsatisfactory. The coherer, as previously noted, was a glass tube filled with metal filings that had to be shaken down by an automatic tapper after reception of a signal. Fessenden was striving for some efficient substitute for the coherer which would produce results with less expenditure of electrical energy and with low resistance. He desired also to devise means by which vocal and musical tones might be reproduced. The human voice or musical notes were utterly drowned out by the rock-crusher din of the wireless transmitters then in use.

As early as 1892 [1] Professor Elihu Thomson, the famous American scientist, had discovered that a direct current arc could be used to convey through a circuit definite electrical oscillations. Taking advantage of this fact, about 1901 Fessenden began experimenting with this, attempting to make use of it for wireless telephone purposes. But he had no suitable detector which would follow the undulations of the human voice. The coherer, then the standard detector, would reproduce only dots and dashes. So he began work on a detector which was virtually a miniature electric light bulb having an exceedingly fine fila-

1 Schubert—*The Electric Word*, p. 46.

ment. This, while not differing greatly in sensitiveness from the coherer, did have the advantage of reproducing voice undulations. This detector never came into commercial use, however, due to its lack of sensitiveness. Strangely enough it led quite by accident to the invention of a detector which for many years was the world's standard.

In his efforts to produce the "hot wire barretter," as Fessenden named his lamp with a fine filament made of Wollaston wire, one of Fessenden's assistants one day noted a very greatly increased efficiency of operation of the device, and later it was found that he had discovered a new and more effective type of detector, which Fessenden at once called the "liquid barretter," but which was universally known to the wireless fraternity as the "electrolytic detector." Fortunately in the records of the Federal Courts in a suit between the National Electric Signalling Company v. DeForest Wireless Company (140 Fed. 449) we find important dates. The patent for the hot-wire barretter was granted August 12, 1902 and for the liquid barretter, May 26, 1903. In an address before the Twentieth Anniversary Convention in Pittsburgh, April 7, 1932, Samuel M. Kintner of the Westinghouse Electric and Manufacturing Company gave an excellent description of this important discovery:

"The hot-wire barretter needed to have the silver coating removed for a very short length by a nitric acid treatment. It was during such treatment that Fessenden observed that one of several of such barretters, in this silver-dissolving part of the process, was giving indications, on a meter attached to the circuit, of signals received from an automatic test sender making D's. An examination revealed that this one had a broken filament while the others were complete. A brief investigation disclosed the fact that this Wollaston wire dipping into the twenty per cent nitric acid solution was far more sensitive and reliable than any other known type. This was the standard of sensitivity for years, in fact until it was displaced by the vacuum tube about 1913." [2]

The importance of this discovery on the history of the future great industry of radio cannot be overestimated. While Fessenden had previously been able with his hot-wire barretter to distinguish tones of the human voice he now found a detector so sensitive and reliable that when hooked up in circuit with a telephone receiver he could hear the sound given off by each wireless station to which he tuned his instrument. The coherer was capable only of reproducing dots and dashes. Early in his experiments in modulating the current through an aerial the inventor was able to hear faint but recognizable tones of

[2] *Proceedings of the Institute of Radio Engineers*, Vol. 20, No. 12, December 1932.

the voice of his assistant at the sending station. Thus the wireless telephone was foreshadowed in Pittsburgh, Pennsylvania, in 1901.

Sec. 45. Fessenden Advocates High Frequency Apparatus.

Fessenden's first trials of wireless telephony were made with a spark transmitter, which emitted a continuous din which completely drowned the voice-signals that Fessenden was also impressing on the antenna. He then tried increasing the spark frequency, trying to get it above the range of audibility of the human ear, and managed to accomplish fair results. The highest frequency then possible, however, was 10,000 cycles per second, which was still audible to the listener and spoiled the reception of the voice to a considerable extent.

This led Fessenden to the idea of trying extremely high frequencies, so high that the machines would generate in themselves the radio waves needed to carry the telephone signals to a distant receiving point. This involved terrific speed.

Ordinary alternators, or generators used to generate electric light current, change the direction of their current flow 120 times a second. Hertz waves, on the other hand, change their current from twenty thousand to sixty million times per second. To attain this result by means of a rotating machine one would have to increase greatly the number of poles in the alternator, and still more greatly increase the speed. It was thus apparent that an alternator would have to be speeded a thousand times faster than such a machine had ever been made to run, if its oscillations were to create radio waves. Fessenden had faith that such an alternator could be built. He believed that with a sustained wave transmission and a high frequency alternator of this type he might accomplish genuine wireless telephony.

"Take a high frequency alternator of 100,000 cycles per second," declared Fessenden at the time,[3] "connect one terminal to the antenna and the other one to the ground, then tune to resonance." When asked how he could get sufficient voltage he replied, "Several hundred volts will be ample, as by resonance I can raise the voltage in the antenna one hundred times, which will be all I require."

Practical wireless men, however, declared that no such high frequency machine could be built. Professor Fleming, one of England's foremost scientists in wireless research, declared that if built "no appreciable radiation would result."

Professor Fessenden not only had faith in the idea but, realizing that the wireless telephone would be an impossibility without such high powered alternator, he set deliberately to work to invent such a ma-

[3] See Kintner address—*Institute of Radio Engineers,* Vol. 20, No. 12, December 1932.

chine. Years were to elapse, however, before the dream would be
realized. In the meantime there were many practical problems of wireless telegraphy which the ingenious inventor was to be called upon to
solve. Wireless telegraphy was in fact a field in which competition was
keen. A more or less feverish contest was in progress. Then too, some
inventors were not overscrupulous in making use of another's discoveries, so that infringement of patents was to furnish a fruitful field of
litigation.

Sec. 46. Lee de Forest Enters the Field.

Lee de Forest won his Ph.D. at Yale in 1899. He had read Sir William Crookes' prophetic magazine article, the same that had inspired
Marconi, as previously related. It had a similar effect upon Lee de
Forest. Nikola Tesla's book on "Electrical Phenomena" was likewise
an inspiration. More than that de Forest visited Tesla in his New
York laboratory. Having a decided bent for scientific research and a
natural talent as an inventor, young Dr. deForest worked for some
time for various electrical concerns in the vicinity of Chicago, but his
heart was in wireless telegraphy. His first invention was his "electrolytic anti-coherer," a new type of wireless detector. He first tried
this out on Chicago housetops, utilizing a series of iron barrel hoops
connected by wires for an antenna.

When later tried on Lake Michigan, deForest attained with this
crude device a range of four or five miles. These experiments occurred
in the summer of 1901, and the youthful inventor was so encouraged
by them that he decided to try reporting the International Yacht
Races to be held near New York that fall. He had difficulty in raising
money for his fare to New York, where disappointment awaited him.
The Associated Press had already made a contract with the Marconi
Company to have the races reported by wireless. DeForest now
turned to the Publishers Press Association, and was able to arrange
for a reporting contract. The Association was to supply a tugboat.
DeForest lacked equipment but he finally persuaded a friend to advance a thousand dollars to purchase parts and equipment.

In order to raise this money deForest had promised to reimburse
his friend by means of stock in the American Wireless Telegraph
Company which had not then been organized. The Press Association
provided the tug as agreed and the hopeful inventor embarked to
witness and to report the yacht races. Rival stations had been set up
on shore by the Marconi people and by deForest with operators eager
to start reporting the progress of the great international contest. The
races had no sooner begun than the operators on shore experienced
the baffling and maddening phenomenon, soon to be so well known in
their fraternity, of interference between the electrical waves sent out

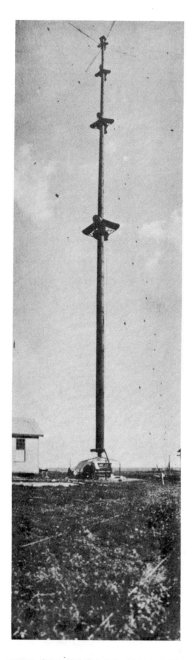

DE FOREST AUDION

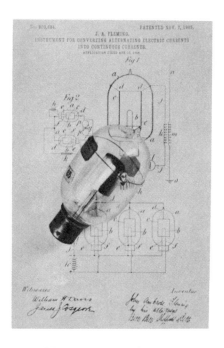

THE BRANT ROCK ANTENNA
Carrying Fessenden's pioneer work
in wireless telephony.

FLEMING VALVE IN 1905

by the rival tugs. They blanketed each other so completely that not an intelligible word could be received on shore. Although the principles of tuning were then known, neither party had believed that it would be necessary in this case. The rivals learned of the trouble but continued through the race. The New York newspaper clients, unwilling to admit defeat, published their news as "Received by wireless telegraphy from tug following the yachts."

Following this misadventure Dr. deForest nevertheless rented an old machine shop in Jersey City as headquarters for his company with its ambitious title "American Wireless Telegraph Company." Here he experimented for months, using for the first time in this country alternating current. The youthful inventor was having difficulty to keep from starving when a promoter, Abraham White, persuaded him to reorganize his venture as the "American deForest Wireless." Nothing immediate came of White's promotional activities, but deForest himself had the good fortune to win the approval of the United States Navy Department that in 1902 tried out the three systems of Marconi, deForest and Fessenden.

A short time after the tests were made deForest was called to Washington and asked to manufacture several of his wireless sets for the government. Two stations were to be set up, one in Washington at the Navy Yard and the other at Annapolis. By Christmas week in 1902 the stations were in operation. Government officials were so well satisfied with the deForest products that during the winter of 1902–03 the little factory in Jersey City worked overtime to fill orders. Prosperity enabled deForest to open an experimental laboratory in New York City. There was need enough for such an adjunct to his work because in the rapidly developing science of wireless telegraphy there was intense rivalry. Danger existed that new discoveries might give his competitors overwhelming advantage.

Sec. 47. Fessenden Organizes a Wireless Company.

The activities of the deForest Company had no doubt inspired Pittsburgh friends of Reginald A. Fessenden to believe that the scientist in their midst should be encouraged to put his ideas into practical use. While other physicists, even the great Marconi, were still absorbed in the problems of the mere mechanical sending of the Morse Code, Professor Fessenden had not only conceived the brilliant idea of transmitting the human voice through the ether but had actually invented an instrument capable of doing it. True it was a mere laboratory triumph as yet—a glimpse as it were of the Promised Land of Radio— yet to far-seeing men who were privileged to be in Fessenden's circle of friends it was inspiration indeed.

In his first experiments with his liquid barretter Fessenden had

used the spark transmitter. The crash and clamor of the spark virtually drowned out the voice of the sender, for Fessenden was valiantly
endeavoring to project his voice even on the shoulders of the thunder
clap. In this he succeeded but it was still a far cry to wireless telephony. He must invent apparatus capable of sending as well as receiving vocal tones by wireless. Fortunately for Fessenden and for the
world there were in Pittsburgh two wealthy men, Thomas H. Given
and Hay Walker, Jr., who saw in the Fessenden idea the opportunity
of the ages. It was not an opportunity to make money but rather to
lose money in furthering a great ideal. Lesser men would have formed
a corporation and have sold stock to the public, but these men in the
language of one of their intimate friends "dug down into their own
pockets for the necessary funds to carry on. Mr. Given remarked to
me several times, 'If this radio business turns out as I expect it will,
I'll be satisfied with my returns on what I've put into it; if it does not,
I, at least, will not have on my conscience the thought that I've wasted
the savings of poor scrub-women, widows with dependent children, or
others who fall such easy prey to the high-powered stock salesmen.'

"The courage of these two men who put more than $2,000,000 of
their own money into this radio company is one of the most striking
recollections I hold of genuine confidence in the future of radio. Unfortunately, neither reaped the benefits of their sacrifices, as Mr. Given,
who bought Mr. Walker's interest during the war, died about one year
before broadcasting raised radio to its full stature, and it has always
been a great regret to me that he could not have lived to see his dreams
come true." [4]

In that regret the people of the world who now enjoy the inesti-
mable benefits of radio may earnestly join, for it was with the financial backing thus generously given that Professor Fessenden embarked
in the great adventure of inventing means and methods of translating
his vision of wireless telephony into terms of everyday life.

The three men, Given, Walker and Fessenden, organized the National Electric Signalling Company capitalized at $100,000 as a means
of developing the Fessenden inventions and of affording the inventor
unlimited opportunity for research. Realizing that the seashore was a
more favorable location for experimentation than Pittsburgh itself,
Fessenden went to Chesapeake Bay and presently set to work at the
construction of three experimental stations, at Old Point Comfort,
Cape Charles and Ocean View. The task he had set for himself, however, was one that required infinite patience along the tortuous trail
of trial and error. Fessenden was confronted with the problem of how
to produce the proper type of wireless waves on which to project the

[4] From address of S. M. Kintner, "Pittsburgh's Contribution to Radio." *Proceedings,* Institute of Radio Engineers, Apr. 7, 1932.

human voice. He felt sure that in his liquid barretter he had a detector capable of picking up vocal tones from any distance, could he but get away from the spark system of sending messages.

Sec. 48. Naval and Maritime Wireless Problems.

The United States Navy was by this time keenly alive to the necessity of keeping abreast of wireless developments. Under the dynamic leadership of President Theodore Roosevelt the nation was not content merely to imitate others. The experiments being tried by Lee de Forest under naval auspices have already been noted. In the meantime several naval officers had been in Europe studying the wireless systems then being used by the various nations. In 1902 these officers reported four different types, German and French, for trial in the naval laboratories in Washington and Annapolis.

"In the spring of 1903," writes Schubert, "the Slaby-Arco apparatus —with which the German Navy was equipped—was finally decided upon as the best of the four systems being tested, and a dozen sets were ordered from Germany. Late that summer these arrived and were installed in the battleships of the North Atlantic Fleet, which was growing to be a respectable force. Signalmen and electricians were trained in their use by the men who had carried out the tests, and when, in the autumn maneuvers, the Fleet divided and fought a sham battle in Long Island Sound, the 'Blues' beat the 'Reds' through the aid of a radio message that rallied the forces in the dark." [5]

This emphatic demonstration of the value of wireless in naval operations convinced forward-looking naval officers that wireless apparatus should be installed on all fighting craft of the United States Navy. Not all of Uncle Sam's high command were of this opinion. There were captains and even admirals who were so reactionary in their views and so jealous of their prerogatives while on the high seas that they resented the idea of receiving orders by wireless. They opposed with might and main the new agency of communications.

During the year 1903 six experimental stations were established by the United States Navy. In these stations elaborate tests were conducted not only of the wireless apparatus from abroad but also those of deForest and Fessenden. A special training school for wireless operators was now started in the New York Navy Yard.

During the year 1903 a virtual chaos existed in wireless systems in the United States. The Marconi system was now largely commercial in its phases. The United States Navy had been using the Slaby-Arco apparatus. The Army had been struggling with the Braun system. The Weather Bureau was using the Fessenden system while deForest had his own circle of influence among naval officers.

[5] Schubert—*The Electric Word*, p. 54.

Sec. 49. DeForest and Sir Thomas Lipton.

As noted in a previous section, deForest had already been called upon to equip two experimental stations for the Navy. The success of the equipment there installed was to have influence upon the fortunes of deForest. Sir Thomas Lipton made a new attempt to capture the international trophy in the fall of 1903. Three rival wireless systems were put into operation to report the progress of the great sporting event. The Marconi Company had a tug equipped with its standard apparatus and both deForest and Fessenden had tugs in the wake of the yachts as well as signal stations on shore. The rivals had taken the precaution to agree upon separate wave lengths of their respective signaling and to their joy the plan worked very well. To be sure, there was some interference, but then the effort to use wireless signals in the recently held war games of the British Navy had been a dismal failure because the signals used by the opposing fleets had blanketed each other.

Sir Thomas Lipton had been persuaded to permit a deForest instrument to be installed on his private yacht from which he viewed the efforts of his *Shamrock III* to lift America's cup. As usual the Lipton craft was beaten but the gallant commander was so impressed by Lee deForest's invention that he invited the inventor to England and endeavored to persuade officials of the English government that there was merit in the American device. The Marconi interests, however, were so thoroughly entrenched in high circles that deForest found himself checkmated at every turn. Out of his English trip came one important development. The London *Times* engaged deForest to supply information by wireless as to developments in the Russo-Japanese War that was then impending and regarded by international experts as inevitable. With his usual alertness deForest turned this event to double advantage by persuading the New York *Times* to join in employing the deForest service in the war zone.

Sec. 50. Wireless in Russo-Japanese War.

The Russo-Japanese War began February 6, 1904. DeForest did not go to the Far East himself but sent two of his most expert operators. They reached Shantung, China, shortly before the outbreak of hostilities and by dint of great industry and by utilizing all available bamboo in the locality they erected a wireless station. This station was located just east of Wei-Hai-Wei on a cliff that towered 150 feet above the water, the mast of the wireless station rising another 150 feet. A small steamer was engaged to cruise the war zone on the lookout for news which it was to send by wireless to the station at Wei-Hai-Wei.

The Russo-Japanese War had powerful appeal to the newspapers of the world as well as to all nations having interests in the Orient. Had it not been for discoveries in the art of tuning of wave lengths the air would have been filled with an indescribable babel of wireless signals, since there were at least seven different wireless systems in operation in the war zone. The London *Times* was employing the deForest system, whereas the British Navy had a score of its fighting craft equipped with Marconi service in which the Branly Coherer was in use. The Italian Navy on the other hand, while using the Marconi system, had a different type of coherer. The Germans and French had the Braun system and the Russians used a variation of the same. The Japanese employed a system that was believed to be based upon the Marconi system but which they stoutly declared was of Japanese origin.

Wireless certainly demonstrated its utility in this war. A typical instance occurred when the observation steamer connected with the deForest outfit was halted by a Russian warship. A shot was fired across the bow of the news-gathering craft and notice was given that the staff were to be questioned. The wireless operator at once notified the deForest station on shore and asked that the nearby British fleet be informed of the outrage. Promptly word came back that British fighting craft were hoisting anchors. This evidently gave alarm to officers in charge of the Russian warship, thus demonstrating that its wireless operator had listened to the exchange of messages. Hastily abandoning the announced intention of holding the steamer, the Russian war craft swung about and rushed away under full steam.

Sec. 51. Wireless Stations in the United States.

The Marconi Wireless Telegraph Company of America was chartered in 1899 by the State of New Jersey.[6] One of its first radio stations on the coast of the United States was built at Wellfleet, Massachusetts, using a 1500 meter wave length. In January, 1903, this station succeeded in sending messages across the Atlantic. President Theodore Roosevelt and King Edward VII exchanged felicitations. The station did not prove to be a commercial success, since it lacked power. Wireless was then in its infancy and much was to be learned before it could come into its own as a means of trans-Atlantic communication. The Marconi. Company built various stations on the Atlantic and Pacific coasts of the United States.

The Navy itself was active in developing wireless stations. By the end of the year 1904 twenty shore stations were in actual operation; ten more were being constructed and the naval authorities were making plans for fifty additional wireless outposts in order that our extensive coast line might be protected. Twenty-four war craft now

---

[6] Jome—"Economics of the Radio Industry," p. 22n.

carried wireless equipment. Apparatus had been ordered for ten more. Plans had been made to equip sixty-eight additional fighting ships with wireless outfits.

The British Navy with upwards of fifty wireless stations had found it necessary to create some governing body for this new branch of national defense. In August, 1904, the British Parliament passed the Wireless Telegraph Act of Great Britain, which placed all wireless activities under the control of the Post Office. No wireless station might thereafter be erected except under license from the postal authorities. Stations must operate under definitely assigned wave lengths.

In the United States there was a rapidly growing need for regulation. Wireless stations had sprung up under the auspices of various branches of government service. Commercial stations were also multiplying. President Theodore Roosevelt promptly appointed a committee to study the question. The committee submitted its report in August, 1904, recommending that the War Department should have charge of military stations in the interior; whereas the Navy was to control all coastal stations. Commercial stations were to be under the supervision of the Department of Commerce and Labor.

The report of the Roosevelt Board was destined to have profound influence upon the future of radio in the United States. Although it never became a law its recommendations were in effect adopted, especially by the Navy Department. It launched the Navy on a wireless system of its own, a system upon which the United States Government was to spend millions of dollars. In few fields of national endeavor have public funds been expended more wisely than in developing the wireless arm of the Navy. It will be pointed out hereafter that to the United States Navy wireless telegraphy and its offspring radio broadcasting owe an everlasting debt. Not only did Navy technicians contribute to the development of the art but private inventors and private manufacturers with their research departments found in Navy patronage the encouragement and inspiration that led them to persevere in their endeavors.

CHAPTER
SEVEN

Beginnings of Wireless Telephony

Section 52. International Rivalries of Wireless-Telegraphy.

COMMERCIAL RIVALRIES BETWEEN NATIONS frequently lead to war. Rivalries of similar nature between industrial organizations that may be competing for pre-eminence in world markets are notoriously bitter. The Marconi companies of Great Britain and of the United States were at first very hostile to other wireless systems or companies, regarding them no doubt as presumptuous upstarts in a field that belonged to Marconi by right of discovery. Rival systems, moreover, were regarded, and perhaps rightly, as being unlawful borrowings of Marconi's ideas. So great was this resentment that for several years the Marconi people would not exchange messages with competing systems. This was bitterly resented by Germany and other nations whose ships might be in desperate need of communicating with land, and the only station within range an unfriendly Marconi station.

A Radiotelegraphic Conference was held in Berlin in August, 1903, while the Russo-Japanese War was still a mere cloud on the horizon. It was by this time realized the world over that wireless telegraphy had ceased to be a novelty and plaything and had assumed the importance of a maritime necessity. Then too the example of telegraph and cable lines nationally controlled was seen to be entirely inappropriate as guidance in the newly born type of communication. Hertzian waves by their very nature radiated in all directions and were essentially international in character. Any satisfactory approach to the subject must recognize this fundamental fact.

All the great powers as well as smaller nations were represented at the Berlin Conference. The matter of division of wireless tolls between ship stations, shore stations and telegraph lines over which messages might be relayed to their destinations, heretofore an unsettled and vexing problem, was the first item on the agenda of the Conference. Fortunately the delegates were able to arrive at a satisfactory solution of the matter of tolls.

The storm broke, however, when the question of free interchange of wireless messages was propounded by Germany. Both England and Italy, in which the Marconi interests were strongly entrenched, opposed the German plan of exchange of messages, with the unfortunate result that the Conference turned into a bitter wrangle. Charges and countercharges were hurled. German delegates bitterly declared that there was more behind the Marconi policy than appeared on the surface— that Great Britain, already having a strangle hold on the cables of the world, was attempting to establish a monopoly of wireless communication. It was pointed out that unless Germany and other nations were to establish shore stations of their own, ships flying their flags might as well not carry wireless equipment when near English or Italian territory. The British delegates retorted that the Marconi Company was under no duty to aid its competitors—that unless ships were equipped with Marconi apparatus they had no right to expect Marconi stations to serve them. The analogy was cited of one who might wrongfully tap a telephone line and then complain that the telephone company had refused to accept messages. However mistaken was this comparison and however narrow the view of the Marconi Company, there is no question of sincerity of the parties to the controversy. The Conference thus became deadlocked, and adjourned leaving the main question unsolved.[1]

One result flowed from the controversy that was highly pleasing to the Marconi interests. Since Marconi stations were now numerous and being erected in strategic locations all over the world the failure of rivals to secure the right to interchange of wireless messages gave the Marconi system a great advantage over its competitors. No ship owner could thereafter afford to equip his craft with anything but Marconi apparatus. Thus a virtual monopoly of wireless business accrued to the pioneer company.

Sec. 53. Infringement of Patents in Wireless Inventions.

During the period of the Russo-Japanese War which continued from February, 1904, to the surrender of Port Arthur on January 2, 1905, there was a great deal of wireless development in the United States. The American Marconi Company was especially active. Fessenden was busily engaged at Chesapeake Bay, making such progress that he was already dreaming of spanning the Atlantic. A site for a station on the Massachusetts coast was under discussion and also a trans-Atlantic experiment station in the British Isles. Fessenden's revolutionary plan of utilizing an electric light bulb as a detector was to turn the thoughts of other investigators into the same avenue of research. DeForest had long been working with a gas-flame as a hoped-for solution of the problem.

Heretofore it had been customary for scientists to use one another's inventions and discoveries with complete freedom. They were regarded as mere scientific abstractions. Now that an age of commercial development had dawned in this field rival inventors soon became involved in legal complications over the use of inventions not their own. It has previously been noted that in 1901 Professor Fessenden had invented a liquid barretter which involved the use of acid in a sealed detector tube. DeForest and his assistant, Clifford D. Babcock, now attempted to make use of the idea in devising a wireless detector of their own. Since this was the first of several infringement controversies that deForest got into it is worthy of special attention.

[1] Jome—"Economics of the Radio Industry," p. 24.

DeForest's biographer, Carneal, has thus described the device: "A fine platinum wire was flattened out and sealed in a small tube. Then the end of the tube was broken off and ground down so that only a small edge of wire was exposed to the acid in the tube. The glass tube was mounted on a brass shank, which could be screwed into a holder which in turn was suspended over the lead cup holding the acid. . . . This little device, mounted on a rubber base to minimize vibration, acted as a second electrode to the detector. Actually it was based on the original discovery by Professor Pupin. It proved to be a very reliable type of electrolytic rectifier. The Navy found these little 'spade electrode' detectors exactly suited for their purpose and ordered hundreds of them."

While the discovery of the idea involved in the invention may well have been made by Professor Pupin as alleged, yet the fact remains that Reginald A. Fessenden had put it to practical use and had taken out a basic patent on the invention. This explains the following quotation from the deForest biography:

"With practical success achieved at last, patent complications arose. It must be remembered that the wireless stations installed thus far and for some time thereafter were all using deForest's alternating current transmitter and the electrolytic detector. Now a long patent suit covering the electrolytic idea was started by Professor Reginald Fessenden, well known inventor, which was not finally adjusted until 1906 when the deForest-Babcock electrolytic detector was declared by the Federal Courts to be an infringement upon Fessenden's patent." [2]

This patent litigation extending over a period of years was only one of many such suits. Actions and cross-actions in which deForest, Fessenden, the Marconi Company and others were parties, plaintiff or defendant, were to be features of an unlovely scramble for legal rights. To the casual observer it might well have seemed that the great inventive geniuses of this period were of pirate blood and that they boldly seized one another's ideas without regard to consequences.

Sec. 54. Invention of the Fleming Valve.

The ancestry of inventions is sometimes an interesting study purely from the historical angle. In the case of the far-famed audion tube of radio we find three distinguished inventors intimately involved. Thomas A. Edison produced the ancestor of the audion tube at a time when there was apparently no human use for such a device. In a process of trial and error while the great inventor was striving to produce a satisfactory electric light he noticed that one side of the carbon

[2] Carneal—"Life of deForest," pp. 150-51. See National Electric Signalling Co. v. DeForest Wireless Co., 140 Fed. 449. (decided November 8, 1905).

filament behaved differently from the other. It caused a blackening of the glass bulb. Edison tried the experiment of inserting a small electrode, whereby he demonstrated that a battery connected to this electrode would operate only when the positive side of the battery was connected to the electrode—hence it formed a one way valve. These experiments disclosed a curious electrical phenomenon that must have made a very profound impression upon another experimenter in the electrical field, since twenty years later he is said to have remembered and resurrected the device as a means of solving the great problem of an electric detector of wireless waves.

Dr. J. Ambrose Fleming was that man. He was now one of Marconi's technical advisers. In studying the problem of how to provide means of detecting and decoding, as it were, the rapid vibrations of wireless waves thrown off by the sending apparatus of a Marconi station, the thought occurred to him that an electric valve permitting the current to flow in one direction only would answer the purpose. The discarded two-electrode light that Thomas A. Edison had invented twenty years previously had possibilities. This light consisted of a little plate of metal connected with the base of the bulb and on a separate wire from the light-filament as one electrode, whereas the filament constituted the second electrode within the glass chamber. It was known by scientists that, whenever the Edison device was so connected that the plate was in contact with the positive terminal of a battery and the filament with the negative pole, the current flowed through it, but whenever the position was reversed no current would flow.

"It occurred to Fleming," writes Harlow, "that if the plate of the Edison effect bulb were connected with the antenna, and the filament to the ground, and a telephone placed in the circuit, the frequencies would be so reduced that the receiver might register audibly the effect of the waves. He made improvements, however, by substituting a metal cylinder for the flat plate, and improved the sensitivity of the device by increasing the electronic emissions. This 'Fleming valve' so-called, was one of the great ideas of wireless communication. It was one of the earliest of the vacuum tubes which had come to be the life and soul of radio." [3]

The third scientist to figure in the development of the three-electrode vacuum tube was Lee deForest. His contribution will be discussed hereafter in the chronological development of this historical narrative.

Sec. 55. Fessenden's Experiments at Brant Rock.

Reginald A. Fessenden had original ideas on the subject of high frequency vibrations. He believed in the possibility of developing a

[3] Harlow—"Old Wires and New Waves," p. 462.

smooth and continuous flow of high frequency vibrations, which was of course impossible with the intermittent spark-gap system then in vogue. He had glimpsed the dazzling idea of superimposing the human voice on this continuous flow in much the same manner as Bell had caused ordinary electric currents to carry the human voice in the telephone circuit. How to produce this high frequency vibrations flow was the great problem. Fessenden believed that a generator might be built with a sufficiently high frequency to produce a carrier for the human voice.

He was familiar with the high frequency dynamo built by Elihu Thomson of the General Electric Company in 1889, and also with generators later constructed by Tesla, but none of these machines was capable of more than 5,000 cycles. Fessenden himself had applied for a patent, May 20, 1901, on a high frequency dynamo.

In 1903 Charles P. Steinmetz, the famous electrical engineer, had built a 10,000 cycle alternator on Fessenden's order at the General Electric plant in Schenectady. This machine gave 1 k.w.* In the autumn of 1904 Fessenden applied to the General Electric Company for an alternator capable of 100,000 cycles. The inventor perhaps fancied that the matter would be turned over to Dr. Steinmetz and for that reason did not include a design or instructions of any sort.

It so happened that the Fessenden order was assigned to the brilliant young engineer, Ernst F. W. Alexanderson,[6] a newcomer to the Schenectady plant. Apparently free to build whatever he felt would accomplish satisfactory results Alexanderson prepared a design for an alternator with a stationary laminated iron armature between two rotating disks. When the design was submitted to Prof. Fessenden, however, he objected to the iron armature, not believing that iron could be used for such high frequency operation. The General Elec-

* Information in letter Fessenden to Alexanderson June 3, 1909.

[6] Ernst F. W. Alexanderson was born January 25, 1878 in Upsala, Sweden, the son of Prof. A. M. Alexanderson then on the faculty of Upsala University but later at the University of Lund in southern Sweden. Young Ernst developed an interest in electrical engineering at an early age. After one year of academic work at the University of Lund he entered the Royal Technical University in Stockholm from which he was later graduated as an electrical mechanical engineer. Thereafter he took a year of postgraduate work in Berlin, studying under Professor Slaby, the wireless inventor. A book by Charles P. Steinmetz so intrigued the young man that he decided to go to America and endeavor to make contact with Steinmetz. After five months in America young Alexanderson succeeded in securing a position with the General Electric Company in February 1902. Then he met for the first time Charles P. Steinmetz, whom he had pictured almost as a god—only to find him a misshapen hunchback, clad in a black bathing suit, crouched over a table and barking monosyllabic answers. The first meeting was a shock but acquaintance with the little wizard restored all of the youth's feelings of hero-worship toward him. Alexanderson's Alternator was an epoch-marking invention that won him world-wide acclaim.

tric Company had already taken steps to safeguard patent rights in the Alexanderson device. As a consequence of Fessenden's objection, Alexanderson being at the time unable to convince him of his error, the task began of constructing an alternator using a wooden armature. This would require months of experimentation.

In 1905 the National Electric Signalling Company decided to abandon the experimental stations on the Chesapeake Bay. The Company had acquired a building site at Brant Rock on the Massachusetts coast for the erection of a powerful wireless station which it at once proceeded to build. In this construction work Fessenden again displayed originality. The sending tower was simply a great metal tube, three feet in diameter, resting upon a steel sphere as a base and towering four hundred and twenty feet high. The tube was built in eight-foot sections bolted together and held erect by guy wires from four points along its length. The tower and guy wires were carefully insulated from the earth. A similar wireless station was in the meantime being constructed at Machrihanish, Scotland.

On the night of December 11, 1905 the Brant Rock station put into operation its newly installed apparatus with such astonishing results that the Bureau of Equipment of the United States Navy began to investigate the Brant Rock phenomenon. In a letter written to Fessenden under date of December 19th the Department declared: "The operator in charge at San Juan (Porto Rico) reports as follows, 'on December 11th at 9:15 P.M. heard a new spark. Had never heard it before. Was making signals "BOZ" and kept repeating "BOZ" in continental code.' " In a later letter the operator at San Juan reported that the Fessenden signals came through clearly even in June 1906 when the Marconi stations were cut off by static.

It is thus apparent that the Brant Rock station contented itself at first with ordinary wireless activities, not yet having apparatus capable of voice transmission. On January 1, 1906 the station made its first exchange of wireless messages with the newly completed station in Scotland. Reception proved to be excellent. Fessenden and his associates were overjoyed at their apparent success. Message after message was exchanged for three days and then for some unaccountable reason communication suddenly ceased. Using the same instruments and the same power as before Fessenden could not get his messages across the Atlantic. For three weeks this baffling condition continued and then messages came through again. Triumph was short, however, for again a pall of silence shut off the long-distance circuit although the Brant Rock signals continued to be sensational on this side of the Atlantic.

In an effort to achieve greater sending and receiving power Fessenden added an umbrella-like structure to the top of his antenna tube, which made possible a considerable spread of wire. Disaster lurked at the Scottish station. In a heavy gale the antenna blew down and so great was the damage to station and tube that no attempt was made to rebuild the station. The date of this calamity is a matter of uncertainty. Schubert sets it at December, 1906,[7] but Professor Kintner declares that the tower blew down in July, 1907.[8]

Even though Fessenden had been obliged to rely upon a "spark" transmitter in his first year at Brant Rock he was nevertheless looking forward to a new machine capable of sending out continuous waves. This machine, however, was still in the experimental stage in the G. E. shops at Schenectady. Let us follow the history of the machine, going back to its inception. "On February 2" (1905), reports Alexanderson, "I submitted a design of an alternator without iron but reiterated my opinion that iron is preferable. During the rest of the year 1905 I directed experiments with a number of models in accordance with Fessenden's own design. These designs differed radically from my original ones and I did the work contrary to my own opinion, hoping to ultimately persuade Fessenden to go back to my early designs. On October 16, 1905, I reported to Fessenden on the test of one of his models and pointed out the great difficulties and suggested the abandonment of this line of designs and the adoption of one which is a compromise between his design and my early one."

It later developed that Fessenden had already placed an order for an alternator with the Rivett Lathe Mfg. Company in Boston but it became necessary to call upon Dr. Alexanderson for engineering advice as the work progressed. Unfortunately for Fessenden the tests were unsatisfactory. On December 18, 1905, Alexanderson reported that the machine was defective from mechanical as well as electrical standpoints. "I do not consider it worth while to spend any more time on the machine," was his verdict. On March 27, 1906, Alexanderson was obliged to give Prof. Fessenden a disquieting report on the experimental machine then being tested at Schenectady. At a speed of 50,000 cycles "the belts commence to slip and get hot," but it was hoped to discover means to cure the defect. In May, 1906, a De Laval turbine gear was ordered, to be used in an effort to develop the necessary mechanical speed.

By arrangement with Fessenden the turbine gear was to be tested in the Schenectady plant. It arrived in July, 1906, but proved disappointing. Because of the great speed the gears generated such heat that the bearings of the machine burned out and the experiment ended in failure.

[7] Schubert—"The Electric Word," p. 76.
[8] Kintner—"Institute Radio Engineers"—Vol 20, No. 12.

Sec. 56. The Wireless Telephone at Last.

Despite the failure of the De Laval machine Fessenden believed that an alternator properly constructed would be able to function as he desired. Expense meant nothing to the eager scientist, although Given and Walker, who were financing the National Electric Signalling Company and paying Fessenden a salary of $300 a month, as well as giving him a large block of stock in the company, must have winced at every expensive failure.

In the meantime the alternator under construction at Schenectady was nearing completion. Alexanderson states that "a machine was completed in the summer of 1906 which was successfully used for one kilowatt at 50,000 cycles. . . . However, this machine was made without iron (i.e., without an iron armature) in accordance with Fessenden's ideas and the compromise in the shape of the disc limited the usefulness of the machine on account of mechanical distortions at speeds higher than 50,000 cycles." This machine was delivered to Fessenden at Brant Rock in September, 1906. At the first trial the device did not work, but when it was taken apart mechanics discovered that either in transit or by some mishap in assembling the machine a wire had been broken.

Hope reviving, the wire was mended and the machine reassembled. Its first demonstration deserves to go down in history as one of the greatest events in scientific annals.[9] Then for the first time the human voice was projected hundreds of miles by wireless telephony. This occurred on Christmas Eve, 1906.

"Early that evening," writes Harlow, "wireless operators on ships within a radius of several hundred miles sprang to attention as they caught the call 'CQ, CQ' in the Morse Code. Was it a ship in distress? They listened eagerly, and to their amazement, heard a human voice coming from their instruments—someone speaking! Then a woman's voice rose in song. It was uncanny! Many of them called to officers to come and listen; soon the wireless rooms were crowded. Next someone was heard reading a poem. Then there was a violin solo; then a man made a speech, and they could catch most of the words. Finally, everyone who had heard the program was asked to write to R. A. Fessenden at Brant Rock, Massachusetts—and many of the operators did. Thus was the first radio broadcast in history put on." [10]

[9] George H. Clark, Custodian of Historical Records of RCA, writing of the Christmas Eve broadcast: "I asked J. V. L. Hogan, H. E. Hallborg and Arthur VanDyck what machine was used to generate power for this, apparently the first American test of wireless telephony." (Hogan and Hallborg were positive that it was the alternator. VanDyck said it might have been.) "Thus it is well assured that it was the alternator; also that it was a water-cooled microphone that was used."

[10] See speech by Dr. S. M. Kintner, Vice-Pres. Westinghouse Electric & Mfg. Co. before Institute of Radio Engineers reported in Radio World, May 28, 1932.

DR. ERNST F. W. ALEXANDERSON
Whose originality of mind and persistence in effort gave the world the Alexanderson Alternator and other extremely important inventions in wireless and radio fields.

It seems almost incredible that so great an event as this could have received so little recognition at the time or that fourteen years could have elapsed between this first historic broadcast and the rise of radio broadcasting in 1920. Such was the fact and there is ample proof in existence.

"It is well known," writes John V. L. Hogan, one of the pioneers of radio, "that in 1906 Fessenden gave numerous practical demonstrations of radio-telephony between his experimental stations at Brant Rock and Plymouth, Massachusetts, and that in 1907 he increased his range from this distance of about twelve miles to such an extent that Brant Rock was able to communicate with New York, nearly two hundred miles away, and Washington, about five hundred miles." [11]

The author has availed himself of the fact that Brant Rock is but a few miles distant from his summer home. He has visited the neighborhood in the hope of finding old residents who lived in the vicinity while Fessenden was conducting his experiments and who may have personal knowledge of the pioneer broadcasts.

Fortunately there is still living in Duxbury in honorable retirement a man who from 1884 to 1926 was Superintendent of the cable office in Duxbury—William Facey. In January, 1937, Mr. Facey stated that he had very definite recollections of the first occasion, although he could not recall the month or year, on which he encountered the amazing phenomenon of a human voice coming from a wireless set in the den of his cottage in Duxbury. It appears that his own son and a lad of the neighborhood were wireless enthusiasts and Mr. Facey had assisted them in assembling a machine. Since they could not read the Morse Code readily the veteran cable operator was much in demand. One afternoon [12] the trio were dumfounded to hear Fessenden and an assistant talking back and forth as though in telephone conversation. For experimental purposes Fessenden then had a shack on the Plymouth shore and it was between this point and the Brant Rock station that the conversation was going on. Facey stated that the voice came in vibrations from the regular telephone head-set in the same manner as the sound of the Morse code. Thus we have corroboration by responsible witnesses now living that the astonishing performance of the telegraph instruments on shipboard on Christmas Eve, 1906, is Gospel truth. [13]

[11] Hogan—The Outline of Radio (1928) p. 20.
[12] Tests of this nature were made by Fessenden, Dec. 11, 1906. Blake—"History of Radio Telegraphy," p. 210.
[13] A well known lawyer of New York City is the son of a lawyer who handled patent applications for the National Electric Signalling Company. When a mere boy this lawyer visited Brant Rock and on one memorable occasion in the fall of 1906 was privileged to speak into the crude transmitter used by Fessenden at the time. He describes the "microphone" as a casing formed of asbestos with a small aperture for the voice, and remembers well that he scorched his lips by getting too close to the transmitting arc within.

In years to come, the words "wireless," "radio" and "broadcasting" were to acquire new significance. In early days, the term "wireless" was used to indicate wireless telegraphy, both in England and in America. About 1912, however, the United States Navy felt that the term was inadequate, because it meant telegraphy by Hertz waves, yet actually included all other forms of communication without wires, such as by induction and conduction. Orders were given to the Service that thenceforth the term "radiotelegraphy" would be used, to supplant the earlier term. The American public accepted the term almost instantly. The British clung to the older term, however, and still do. Radiotelegraphy, and radiotelephony, therefore, are entirely synonymous with wireless telegraphy or wireless telephony, but are more modern American terms.

Since wireless waves spread out in all directions, such transmission is, in the last analysis, "broadcasting." But the term was not used in the art, as such, in cases where a radiotelegram was sent to a specific receiving station, as was the status in almost all cases. However, when —as during the World War—it became necessary to send messages to a number of vessels of the Fleet without calling them individually, these messages were said to have been "broadcast" or "sent broadcast."

From the advent of wireless telephony, however, the idea of sending the voice signals "broadcast" became much more common. Fessenden in 1906 addressed his entertainment to a number of vessels of the United Fruit Company and the United States Navy. De Forest, later, had amateur listeners by the hundreds. However, the noun "broadcasting" today has a very clear meaning to listeners; it means the dissemination of speech or music, purposely for entertainment or education, to a listening audience of non-technical people, on a regular program, which program is known to them in advance. Therefore, the word "broadcasting," as a noun, can be applied to the first program of KDKA, and all that follow. Radiotelephone tests, and radiotelegraph messages addressed to a group, should be more properly expressed by the verb, namely, by stating that they were "broadcast." Radiotelephone and radiotelegraph messages addressed to a specific station are not "broadcast," they are sent by "point-to-point communication." Admittedly, the terms have been used very loosely in the past. It is hoped that clearly drawn definition today will be of value.

Sec. 57. The Heterodyne Receiving System—Marconi Company and David Sarnoff.

Even though Fessenden was toiling at the task of harnessing the thunderbolt to provide means for broadcasting the human voice across oceans and continents, he did not neglect the necessary task of providing for the means of receiving and decoding, as it were, these high frequency impulses. In 1905 Fessenden invented the so-called heterodyne receiving system.

In the language of Kintner: "This was another bold stroke of Fessenden, in which he departed radically from methods practiced by others. Like his other great inventions, it was made before he had suitable equipment with which to practice it. He required a source of local oscillations of adjustable frequency, and a high frequency alternator or oscillating arc was all that was available. These could be made to work, but with considerable inconvenience and a high degree of unreliability. The discovery of the oscillating tube provided the principal need of this great system to make it what it has proved to be, the best method of reception thus far devised. Upon it Major Armstrong, six or seven years later, built his superheterodyne system." [14]

The term heterodyne has a technical meaning which may in general be explained as follows: When currents of two different frequencies or beats flow in the same circuit they will produce a new frequency and are said to heterodyne (from the Greek words, *heteros* —other or different, and *dynamis*—power) and the new frequency is called a heterodyne frequency. Further to simplify the matter: If frequencies are being received that are of such rapidity as to be beyond the range of the human ear, such as 300,000 cycles per second, in order to "heterodyne" one would generate in the receiving apparatus a frequency say of 301,000 cycles per second. The result of combining the two would be that the "beat" note would equal the difference between the two or 1000 cycles per second which could easily be transformed into tones suitable for the ear of the listener. Mysterious and magical no doubt, but a scientific fact nevertheless.

Professor Fessenden, who had devised the system, applied for letters patent in 1905. His triumph was more theoretical than real for he was years ahead of the industry. His own continuous-wave apparatus was the only system then capable of utilizing the heterodyne system. Not until 1912 when the triode or audion tube of deForest became available for the general public did the heterodyne invention assume its true importance in the art.

In the meantime the American branch of the Marconi Company was carrying on a modest enterprise in New Jersey. It had a factory at Roselle Park where it manufactured wireless apparatus for installation on merchant ships. A staff of wireless operators and technicians was maintained to serve its shore stations—four in number—and the merchant ships that were equipped with wireless apparatus of Marconi origin. It is not usual to make mention in any serious work of

[14] Kintner—Institute of Radio Engineers, Vol. 20, No. 12.

the mere hiring of an office boy, yet on September 30, 1906, the Marconi Wireless Telegraph Company of America hired an office boy who deserves mention in any volume dealing with the wireless industry or with radio broadcasting.

That boy was fifteen-year old David Sarnoff. Russian born, he had been in the United States but six years. The death of his father had forced young David, the eldest of five children, to become a wage-earner at ten years of age. He had been a newsboy. He had worked as a messenger in a telegraph office. Out of his meager earnings the lad had contrived to purchase a telegraph instrument. In six months of self-tutelage young Sarnoff had qualified as a telegraph operator—or at least he thought that he had. In September, 1906, he applied to the chief engineer at the Marconi Wireless headquarters for a job as a telegraph operator. The chief smiled at the boy's request but hired him—as an office boy at $5.50 a week.

Young Sarnoff promptly bought technical books on wireless telegraphy and set himself to the task of mastering their contents. He even spent his week-ends in the experimental shop of the Marconi Company —mastering with hand and brain the technical details of a great new science. Promotion came in 1908 when David Sarnoff was sent to the Marconi station on Nantucket Island, off the southern coast of Massachusetts. Here he remained for two fruitful years of study and practice of wireless telegraphy. A story has come down to us of those Nantucket days that throws a flood of light upon the character of one of the most forceful and dynamic men in the radio industry. In 1924 Jack Irwin, chief operator at the island station, wrote an article entitled "Historic Days at a Famous Wireless Station" [15] in which the following paragraph occurs:

"Young David Sarnoff, now Vice-President and General Manager of the Radio Corporation of America, received his early training at this station. After commencing his career as office boy at the head office of the Marconi Company he was sent to Siasconset as an operator. I particularly welcomed Sarnoff. He was so enthusiastic about radio that he stood a great part of my watch, voluntarily, and thereby allowed me to play tennis and otherwise enjoy the summer advantages of Nantucket."

Sec. 58. The Crystal Receiver.

It has been noted in the development of wireless telegraphy that the coherer was for years the chief reliance of Marconi as a receiving device. Metal filings were used in the coherer tube. Somewhat suggestive of the then discarded coherer was the so-called crystal receiver invented by General Henry H. C. Dunwoody, of the United States

---

[15] Radio Broadcast, September 1924, p. 419.

Army, in 1906. He discovered that carborundum, an electric-furnace product, might be used as a detector of electric currents. At about the same time G. W. Pickard discovered that silicon and other substances might be utilized in the same manner. Lead ore (galena) and iron pyrites were also popular.

The Pickard crystal detectors were to have profound effect upon the popularization of wireless telegraphy and later upon the development of radio broadcasting. The crystal detector was inexpensive. Any amateur, however modest his means, need not hesitate in providing himself with crystal detectors, whereas the vacuum tube detector was an expensive device. This was one of the reasons why this type of detector became standard equipment for home-made sets. When used in the receiver the crystal detector acted like a valve in suppressing half of the wave frequencies coming from the antenna.

Thus at the very period when it was important that the general public be educated to the possibilities of radio the efficient crystal detector came along to boost the industry. It is true that at this period there was no radio industry in the modern sense. A few manufacturers like deForest were kept busy in supplying the growing demand by amateurs all over the country for wireless equipment. The Morse code had great appeal to boys and young men, but when music and spoken words might occasionally be picked up out of the ether there arose a veritable army of enthusiasts for the new science. Boys love to tinker, to experiment with chemistry or mechanics, and here was the opportunity of the ages. Then, too, the more or less dormant instinct of humanity to eavesdrop on a neighbor or upon anybody, that had already proved so objectionable on country telephone lines, now found joyous and legitimate expression in the new science of wireless. Messages by this magic system were given to the world and anyone with sufficient skill and ingenuity to assemble a wireless or radio outfit was privileged to listen in on any or all messages that might be flashing through the skies. Marine disasters, calls for help, progress of rescue ships and all the soul-thrilling experiences in which wireless telegraphy soon played such dramatic part, were now open to ambitious amateurs. Is it any wonder that eager youths began to delay bedtime into the morning hours while they fiddled with unreliable and exasperating radio sets in the hope of fishing new thrills out of the trackless ether? The humble crystal receiving set was thus a godsend to such amateurs.

"The best of these so-called crystal receivers," writes Hogan, "were nearly equivalent in sensitiveness to the earlier liquid type, and because of their ease of manipulation they almost entirely superseded the older devices." [16]

[16] Hogan—Outline of Radio (1928).

Sec. 59. DeForest and His Audion.

Lee deForest had no sooner gotten through with his disastrous litigation with Fessenden over the electrolytic or liquid receiver than he turned his attention to perfecting the work of another inventor and thereafter of utilizing the invention, thus eventually involving himself in one of the most famous of all radio infringement controversies. Reference has already been made to the Fleming electric valve or tube patterned upon the Edison experiment, discarded by the great inventor twenty years before—the two-electrode tube.

It appears that Fleming lectured before the Royal Society of England in February, 1905, describing the operation of his detector of wireless signals. Fleming had taken the precaution to patent the device in England, November 16, 1904. He later assigned his rights to the Marconi Company that took out American patents in November 1905.[17] In litigation over patent rights it was alleged that deForest had read the report of the meeting and had immediately thereafter adopted the device in his own experiments in America.[18] Now comes a very significant development. DeForest was not satisfied with the Fleming-Edison device. He tried the experiment of inserting between the Fleming plate and the filament a tiny grid-iron with bars of fine wire—the famous grid that was later to transform radio reception.

"This may not mean much to the uninitiated," writes Harlow, "but that miniature gadget was the truest 'little giant' in all history, perhaps the nearest approximation to an all-powerful genie that the brain of man ever created. It set unbelievably powerful currents in motion, magnifications of those which flicked up and down the antenna wire, and thus produced voice amplification which made radio telephony a finished product. By adding another tube and another, the amplification was enormously increased—millions, billions of times." [19]

The importance of the third element in the deForest audion cannot be overestimated. While in its original form it proved weak in operation owing to the presence of gas in the imperfect vacuum, yet the principle of operation was superb. When connected to a radio antenna it became alternately positive and negative in response to the incoming Hertz waves. When positive it increased the flow of current between filament and plate; when negative it retarded the flow, thus acting as a true valve.

The third element was added to the vacuum tube December 31, 1906, in a laboratory test. The fact that he could now receive telegraph

17 Jome—Economics of the Radio Industry, pp. 207-208.
18 Marconi Wireless Telegraph Co. of America v. deForest Radio Telephone & Telegraph Co., 236 Fed. 942; affirmed 243 Fed. 560.
19 Harlow—Old Wires and New Waves, pp. 462, 463.

signals with clarity and power led deForest to file an application for a patent on January 29, 1907, two weeks after the issuance to him of a patent on a three-electrode tube that did not call for a grid. This new device was promptly labeled the deForest Audion. The inventor shortly thereafter organized the "deForest Radio Telephone Company," to manufacture and market his new product and to develop radio telephony.

Alas for his hopes! The public had not yet been educated to the point where any radio invention, however valuable, could become commercially profitable. Then, too, inventions were elbowing each other out of the way so rapidly in this field that there was no certainty that any device would retain pre-eminence for any length of time. Fessenden's heterodyne claims, Dunwoody's crystal detector and deForest's audion tube were all three brought forward within a few months of each other. The public was naturally hesitant.

During the summer of 1907 deForest carried on extensive experiments in telephone broadcasting between two buildings, three blocks apart, in New York City. Several scientists who were amateur wireless enthusiasts soon began to tune in on these telephone conversations. Peter Cooper Hewitt, the inventor of a mercury-vapor light, then had a laboratory in the tower of the old Madison Square Garden. He became interested in deForest's experiments and assisted in various tests. This led to the installation of the deForest system of wireless telephony on a luxurious private yacht that during the summer of 1907 was cruising in Lake Erie. The greater convenience of the telephone as a means of communication in contrast to the ordinary Morse Code in ship-to-ship conversations was conclusively demonstrated by the Lake Erie tests. The Navy Department decided to install the deForest apparatus on two battleships. The range of signals was found to be limited to a few miles. Admiral Robley D. Evans nevertheless became a militant advocate of the wireless telephone, believing that when perfected it would become a necessary equipment of every war craft in the fleet. The Navy Department became the chief customer of the deForest Radio Telephone Company. When the United States Fleet made its memorable cruise around the world, in the late fall of 1907, over twenty vessels were equipped with the de Forest radio-telephone. Through its patronage the struggling inventor was able to keep out of the financial disaster that threatened him at all times.

In discussing the phenomenon of public indifference to the marvelous invention of radio, which from 1906 to 1920 was virtually unknown in America, Owen D. Young, in a conversation with the author on February 5, 1937 expressed opinion that this was the fate of nearly every great invention.

"Fifteen years is about the average period of probation," he declared, "and during that time the inventor, the promoter and the investor who see a great future for the invention generally lose their shirts. Public demand even for a great invention is always slow in developing. That is why the wise capitalist keeps out of exploiting new inventions and comes in only when the public is ready for mass demand."

CHAPTER
EIGHT

Travails of the Wireless Industry

Sec. 60. DeForest Broadcasts from Eiffel Tower.

REGINALD A. FESSENDEN must have experienced some heartburnings at seeing deForest step thus suddenly and dramatically into the field of wireless telephony. The pioneer was still toiling at his experiments in the station at Brant Rock, and incidentally developing friction with his backers, Given and Walker. These unfortunate gentlemen had already advanced huge sums to the company since the formation of the National Electric Signalling Company in November, 1902. For six years the company had been paying three hundred dollars a month to Fessenden for his services as director of the work of experimentation. That work had been exceedingly expensive, being essentially of a research character. Professor Fessenden was apparently one to whom expense meant little when hot on the trail of an idea. That he had a proper regard for the value of his own services is evidenced by the fact that directly after his successful Brant Rock experiments with voice broadcasting he demanded of his backers an increase in salary. So clamorous did he become that in September, 1908, his salary was advanced to eight hundred dollars a month—an unusual experience for an inventor who had not yet brought his inventions to a point where they could earn money for his backers.

In contrast to the heavy losses incident to Fessenden's endeavors, the enterprising and spectacular deForest was reaping financial returns from wireless telegraphy. Although Fessenden had emerged victorious from a patent infringement suit, his resourceful rival had invented a gadget that was now being acclaimed as the greatest invention in wireless history, one that might easily supplant the Fessenden liquid barretter in its own field. It is probably true that the Brant Rock scientist believed that deForest with his audion tube was again treading on dangerous ground since the Fleming patent, now held by the Marconi Company, covered two of the three elements in the audion—consequently deForest had apparently taken out a patent that might successfully be questioned in the courts.

DeForest was a bold and energetic man who had apparently never hesitated to advance his claims to originality even when the same might be contested by others. The fact that his new invention, the audion tube, had already been adopted by the Navy Department was of great value to him, yet he longed for new worlds to conquer.

His next move was one of the most original and audacious of his entire career. It was nothing less than to go to Europe and to stage a wireless telephone broadcast from the Eiffel Tower. This demonstration would involve a great deal of expense, but the publicity value of the exploit might be expected to prove of tremendous value to the newly formed corporation—the deForest Radio Telephone Com-

pany. In the summer of 1908, with several assistants in his party, the
inventor sailed for France. The details of his experience on that momentous mission have thus been set forth by Carneal:

"The first day in Paris saw negotiations completed for use of the
Eiffel Tower for his experiments, and the second saw that notable
structure changing its aspect as the first radio phone was installed on
French soil. From the sides of the Tower antennae were hung and in
its base the American's generator was installed. No sooner had this
work been completed than tests with the French military stations near
Paris were begun. At slightly more than twenty-eight miles beyond the
Eiffel Tower the signals began to fade out. Within a few days a range
of twenty-five miles had been established as dependable under all
conditions.

"When the night for the big test arrived, having learned that he
would be allowed to use the main antenna which ran almost to the
top of the Tower for experiments, deForest and his assistants, chief
among whom was his wife, stayed at the transmitter all evening, feeding records to the Pathé talking machine which was modulating the
carrier current. All night long they stayed at the Tower, returning to
their hotel in the early morning to await results. The stations had all
received the program. But deForest's success went deeper. A letter
postmarked Marseilles written by an engineer who had listened in exactly five hundred miles away, told of the complete reception of the
program." [1]

Sec. 61. Caruso Sings into the Microphone.

DeForest's triumphant experience in Paris had been attained entirely by mechanical means—by the use of phonograph records. As a
lover of music, deForest well knew that a mere phonograph record
lacked the tonal qualities of great operatic performances. There were
difficult problems to be solved, however, before an operatic performance could be picked up by the wireless telephone. A record might be
played a few inches distant from the microphone, yet an opera required different technique. The inventor was eager to undertake the
task. Within a year following his return from Europe he began experiments with speakers and musicians. To be sure, the audience who
might be expected to listen to the tests was very small, yet all concerned realized that they were engaged in blazing new trails.

Early in January arrangements were concluded with the Metropolitan Opera Company in New York City for a broadcast of one of its
performances, and since the world-famous Caruso was to sing the leading role the few friends of the inventor who might be privileged to
listen at the factory and such amateurs in the district as then owned

[1] Carneal—Life of deForest, pp. 221-22.

crude radio sets were agog to participate as a listener audience. De-Forest had given the expected broadcast all possible publicity. The operatic stars were sympathetic and perhaps a bit amused at the eagerness of the inventor.

"The first program," writes Carneal, "was one of the Metropolitan's double bills, 'Cavalleria Rusticana' and 'Pagliacci,' with Caruso appearing as Turridou in the former. A little half-kilowatt telephone transmitter through which the chief arias were to pass was installed in a vacant room at the top of the Opera House. . . . Listeners-in were stationed at the Park Avenue laboratory, at the Metropolitan Life Building and at the Newark plant, supplemented by many curious engineers and amateurs and a specially invited audience at one of the hotels in the Times Square district. In spite of the crude arrangement, crude indeed by contrast to the present-day elaborate broadcast studios, Caruso's voice went out over the ether on that date memorable in the history of radio, January 20, 1910, (actual date January 13, 1910. G. L. A.) and was heard by perhaps fifty listeners. Wireless operators on ships in New York Harbor and nearby waters, and at the Brooklyn Navy Yard, and a group of newspaper men who had gathered with great interest in the factory in Newark, all were lavish in their praise of the reception. DeForest's idea had materialized into a public event. The inventor felt convinced from that minute that broadcasting was destined to go forward, perhaps even as far as his own wild dream of uniting the scattered corners of the globe." [2]

Sec. 62. Radio Enthusiasts Multiply.

Despite the fact that scarcely more than fifty persons heard the Caruso broadcast and the public press paid little heed to the affair, it nevertheless formed a very important forward surge of radio as a

---

[2] Carneal—Life of deForest, pp. 231, 232. Evidently Author Carneal was over-enthusiastic in this statement. An examination of newspaper reports dated next morning indicates that reporters were not entirely satisfied with the opera broadcast. The New York *Times* reporter among other statements declared: "At the receiving station in Mr. Turner's office the homeless song waves were kept from finding themselves by constant interruptions, said to come from the Manhattan Beach Station, which, it was explained, despite all entreaties attuned to the same 850 meter length of waves as the Turner instrument. Signor Caruso and Mme. Destinn, it was learned later, sang finely at the Opera House. Mr. Turner said that sometimes he could catch the ecstasy . . . but the reporters could hear only a ticking."

A part of the New York *Sun* report was as follows: "Some of the guests took turns fitting the receivers over their ears and one or two of them thought they heard a tenor; they were not positive. They all did hear a constant tick-ta-ta-tick. . . . There was an operator somewhere who was carrying on a ribald conversation with some other operator, greatly to the detriment of science and an evening's entertainment."

The New York *Herald* reporter had a similar experience but he stated that in offices of the Metropolitan Opera House the reception was not marred by the wireless pest and came in clearly.

science. It was in the nature of a laboratory test carried out of doors and demonstrated to fulfill claims concerning it. For several years schoolboys in increasing numbers had been experimenting with wireless telegraphy. This involved learning the Morse code and the mastery of technicalities that many lads lacked patience or ability to accomplish. Now, however, came a new and thrilling development—the possibility of picking up music and even the human voice. Small wonder, therefore, that deForest's activities gave great impetus to a movement that had flattened out more or less because of its lack of human appeal. People began to speak of the new type of electrical transmission as "radio", although ten years were to elapse before the public in general was to adopt the name.

"At just about this time (1910)", writes Carneal, "the word 'radio', heretofore a mysterious 'force' that only the scientists understood, sprang into being. It was ushered in by a motley group of people, mostly boys and young men, working all alone on crude homemade apparatus in the isolation of their own homes. These young people, scattered over the country, were engaged in the strange pastime of 'fishing' things out of the invisible space about them, at first dots and dashes and later words and music that came from nowhere. . . . Parents, at first indulgent of the strange and not inexpensive devices their youngsters brought into the home, began to gape in wonder as they donned the head sets and actually listened to music coming to them out of the air. They did not in the least understand how it happened. It seemed mysterious beyond words. Their amusement died out as they found themselves listening to an explanation of the vast intricacies of 'radio'. These young amateurs, working in isolation upon the crudest kind of apparatus, had become an important element in the plans of Lee deForest. . . . Even at that time, from the constantly increasing number of scribbled notes, telegrams, and once in a while a brave young visitor in person, deForest had begun to realize the importance of these young 'fans' who by their enthusiasm and persistence might well sponsor a great industry."

The enterprising Elmer E. Bucher, of the American Marconi Company, now turned author, writing technical books on wireless telegraphy in so clear and lucid a style that even amateurs could follow directions. These books became best sellers, Mr. Bucher's royalties rising into six figures before the craze for home-made wireless sets subsided.

Sec. 63. Litigation over Patent Infringements.

One of the most amazing features of the history of radio concerns the pirating of inventions by those who had no legal rights to them or who having made some improvements on basic patents boldly seized the ideas of others in order to manufacture and to sell radio equipment.

The Marconi Company had many infringement cases on its hands in the United States at an early date, the most important of which involved the United Wireless Company that for a time was the most extensive American company in the business. It is apparent that the United Wireless Company was an unethical concern, for when infringement cases came to trial its officers pleaded guilty to infringement of the Marconi patents. The court issued sweeping injunctions against further infringement and lo! it appeared that the company could not continue to operate its stations either on the Atlantic or Pacific seaboard nor on ships equipped by the company. Another calamity had befallen the organization. On June 30, 1911, the president and several officers of the company were convicted of selling stock under false pretenses. Receivers were appointed for the company in four states.[3]

Thus the United Wireless Company became utterly helpless and at the mercy of the Marconi interests. The British Marconi Company on June 29, 1912, purchased the assets of the United Company and later resold them to the American Marconi Company. "The absorption of the assets of this company," writes Jome, "gave the American Marconi Company a practical monopoly of the supply of apparatus and operators for radio communication in the United States. This relief from a powerful source of competition added to the business prestige of the American Marconi Company and indirectly to the earning capacity of the parent British Company. Partly in order to finance this consolidation and partly to take care of normal growth the authorized and issued capital of the American Company was increased in 1912. A traffic agreement was also made with the Western Union." [4]

David Sarnoff has informed the author that prior to 1912 the American Marconi Company was a relatively unimportant concern, engaged in ship-to-shore communications and in manufacturing wireless equipment.

As a result of this purchase of the assets of the United Wireless Company the American Marconi Company, with five wireless stations, increased to approximately fifty coastal stations from Maine to Texas on the east coast and from Oregon to California on the west coast, with some fourteen wireless stations on the Great Lakes. In coastal shipping equipped with wireless the gain was even more impressive, increasing from four or five to approximately four hundred. These ships were engaged in coastwise or South American trade.

[3] "Moody's Manual" for 1911.
[4] Jome—Economics of Radio Industry, p. 30.

Sec. 64. Fessenden Meets Disaster.

Reginald A. Fessenden was essentially a scientist—an engineer with a strong flair for research in new and untried fields. For many years at great expense to his backers he had conducted experiments at Brant Rock and elsewhere in an effort to develop satisfactory apparatus for the sending and receiving of wireless telephonic messages. So far in advance of others was he that neither his radio telephone nor his alternator device had commercial value, simply because nobody was yet equipped to use them. The spark-gap device was then in universal favor, which meant that Morse code was all that could be sent by wireless instruments.

Fessenden finally sensed the hopelessness of financial returns from the wireless telephone. In 1909 he produced a new type of spark-gap apparatus that promised to revolutionize wireless telegraphy. It was a 500-cycle alternator that generated "damped" waves and gave forth a clear note that penetrated static with amazing success.

Although Fessenden had experienced little demand for other inventions, the spark-gap device now met with instant success. The United States Navy, also the United Fruit Company, purchased several of the new transmitters. A transmitter of one hundred kilowatt capacity was sold to the Navy for the proposed radio station at Arlington. Given and Walker, the financial backers of the National Electric Signalling Company, began to entertain hopes that their investment might at last have some chance of being safeguarded. They were not content, however, with mere manufacturing of equipment. They aspired to greater things, desiring to build up a system of communications that might challenge even the Marconi Companies. Trans-Atlantic communications by them had failed several years before, yet in 1910 the company applied again to the British Post Office for licenses for wireless stations.

The British Post Office officials demanded proof that the company could send messages across so great a distance and declared that if the Brant Rock station could communicate with the United Fruit Company station at New Orleans, 1800 miles distant, this would be considered a satisfactory test, and a nine-year license would be granted. Fessenden had conducted the negotiations in person and when news of the terms of the license was communicated to Given and Walker, they urged the inventor to press for a longer period. He did so and in December succeeded in getting a promise of a fifteen-year license provided the tests should prove satisfactory. Fessenden now returned to the United States and presently succeeded in exchanging messages between Brant Rock and New Orleans.

Now came a distressing development that has been well explained in Schubert's *The Electric Word.* "The whole project crashed into the

HISTORY IN THE MAKING

Secretary Daniels in his office in Washington telephones by wireless to President Wilson when the latter was 900 miles at sea. The inventor, Ernst F. W. Alexanderson (with mustache), is seen back of Secretary Daniels.

rocks of internal dissension when the engineer and his backers split wide apart. The point at issue was a proposed Canadian subsidiary, which was to operate the Canada-England circuit. Professor Fessenden, born in Canada, had felt that for reasons of propriety—this circuit being an all-British affair—the Canadian Company should be controlled by himself and his British and Canadian associates to the exclusion of Messrs. Given and Walker, who were, however, to advance part of its cost as a non-voting investment, and had secured an agreement from those gentlemen to that effect before he started for England to conduct the negotiations. This may have been patriotic, and a splendid idea from the British standpoint, but as time went on it seemed that between the Professor and his British associates, the whole venture was becoming one in which the Pittsburgh bankers, who had sunk nearly two million dollars in financing the Fessenden experiments and who controlled the National Electric Signalling Company, were in danger of emerging on the short end of things. Bad feeling and suspicion between them and their engineer became so great that it was impossible for them to continue together. Fessenden maintained that they were trying to freeze him out; he made a British-American issue out of it, quit the company in high dudgeon, and brought suit for damages. In July, 1912, a jury rendered a verdict in his favor and allowed him four hundred and six thousand dollars—a straw that broke the camel's back." [5]

Straw is scarcely the word to use in this connection when we consider that to the unfortunate backers there had been nothing but expenses for eight years. This staggering verdict must have fallen upon them not like the proverbial straw but like the collapse of the temple when Samson executed vengeance upon the Philistines. At any rate, the company was ruined in one stroke. It went into bankruptcy and receivers were appointed.

Thus the American Marconi Company found itself the beneficiary of the Fessenden collapse. It was now without a competitor.

Sec. 65. DeForest Is Arrested and Charged with Fraud.

It was inevitable that out of the mad scramble for wealth in the field of wireless and radio communications, where hope and disaster crowded each other, there should have occurred ugly scandals. The United Wireless Company, as previously indicated, had met with disaster because of fraudulent practices—the pirating of Marconi inventions and stock swindles by its officers. It is usually difficult to determine in what cases genuine fraudulent intent might be present even when convictions occur, since the law operates against persons who are guilty of constructive fraud—which may mean extreme optimism not justified by any basis of

[5] Schubert—The Electric Word, pp. 79-80.

fact. At any rate, with so many investors ruined by the collapse of wireless stock it was inevitable that scandals and criminal prosecutions should arise.

The greatest wireless scandal of the age was that which shook the British Empire in 1912. A phenomenal rise in Marconi stock between December, 1911, and April, 1912, was followed by a tremendous crash in prices. Then it was discovered that high public officials of Great Britain had bought Marconi stock at a low figure and had sold the stock at peak prices. While in some instances this may have been a mere coincidence, when it was demonstrated that rise in stock quotations was influenced by the action of the British Government in contracting with the Marconi Company for naval equipment it was believed quite generally that government officials had acted corruptly. A parliamentary committee was appointed to investigate these ugly charges with a view to setting aside the agreement between the government and the Marconi Company should the facts warrant such drastic action. While the investigation caused some embarrassment to certain government officials, yet the committee reported in favor of the continuance of the Marconi agreement.

The Marconi scandal in England caused definite repercussions in the United States. Disappointed investors in the deForest Radio Telephone Company were not slow to raise hue and cry against the inventor and his associates. Whether there were sinister influences at work or the whole deplorable affair was due to the zeal of reactionary prosecuting officers who could see nothing but visionary buncombe in radio we shall perhaps never know, but in March, 1912, Lee deForest and other officers of his company were arrested on charges of having used the United States mails in a scheme to defraud investors in radio stock.

DeForest had no difficulty in securing release on bail, yet the shame and harmful publicity virtually destroyed the fortunes of his company. To be sure, he was out on bail, yet sooner or later he must face criminal prosecution in the courts of New York. Thus the unhappy inventor to whose genius the world stands indebted was for the time being under a heavy cloud of public disfavor—branded as a swindler and cheat.

Sec. 66. Chaos in Wireless Telegraphic Transmission.

Amateur operators, especially in the United States, multiplied amazingly. It was natural, however, that having mastered the art of capturing the elusive waves and decoding them into intelligent speech that these "hams", as they were called, should have aspired to the greater feat of sending out messages on their own account. Thus a great number of amateurs set up transmitters of varying degrees of efficiency, each of them capable of cluttering up the ether with man-made static.

As early as 1906, when President Theodore Roosevelt visited the naval fleet off Cape Cod, the nearby Newport Naval Station was unable to communicate messages to him by wireless because of amateur interference. Destroyers were obliged to carry messages back and forth.

Radio magazines multiplied. Popular science periodicals also were full of articles on the new marvel of wireless telegraphy. Diagrams and instructions galore fed to young America guidance in the assembling of radio sending and receiving sets, while manufacturers of radio parts vied with one another in supplying the means whereby amateurs might satisfy their desire for wireless tinkerings. Radio towers of grotesque home-made variety began to disfigure the landscape here and there throughout the countryside.

To make matters even more serious a few irresponsible and mischievous amateurs began to send out false messages that caused no end of distress and confusion. Harlow thus describes the situation: "Amateurs would send out fake orders to naval vessels, purporting to come from admirals; they broadcast false distress calls and had Coast Guard and other vessels running wildly about, trying to find the ship in distress. This 'joke' was even perpetrated on the other side of the world. In May, 1914, a message was received in Japan, allegedly from the American liner *Siberia*, saying that it was aground and sinking off the coast of Formosa. Vessels at once rushed to her aid, but meanwhile the *Siberia* arrived at Manila next day, having been nowhere near Formosa and knowing nothing of the distress call. There being no law to cover most of the amateurs' tricks, few or no police searches were made for them, and the names and locations of the worst offenders were unknown. When remonstrated with by air, these were apt to respond with curses and obscenity." [6]

Sec. 67. The Federal Government Takes a Hand.

It was inevitable that the Federal Government should sooner or later bestir itself in the matter. A bill was introduced into the Congress in 1912 seeking to place all wireless transmission under government regulation. News of the proposed measure caused violent protests by amateurs and others. The congressional committee was virtually swamped with conflicting evidence, but the fact that other nations had already adopted government regulation and that a third International Radio Telegraphic Conference was shortly to be held in London were important considerations that led the committee to take a strong stand.

A significant development that should not be overlooked in this connection was that the Congress already had before it a bill to require passenger-carrying vessels to have at least two skilled radio oper-

6 Harlow—Old Wires and New Waves, p. 469.

ators in charge of radio apparatus of sufficient power to be capable of summoning aid in time of need. This act no doubt reflected the public reaction to the terrible *Titanic* disaster of April 15th, 1912. The *Titanic*, it should be noted, had been considered the "last word" in ocean liners. It was on its maiden voyage and traveling at great speed when it collided with an iceberg and shortly sank. Owing to the fact that the great ship was equipped with wireless apparatus the heroic operators were able to summon aid and seven hundred of the passengers were saved. Fifteen hundred others were lost—many of them famous men and women. The incident had made the whole world wireless-minded. The fact that ships nearer than those that dashed to the rescue of the stricken liner might have saved many lives had their radios been in operation when the distress signals went out roused the nation to the need of some such regulation.

In 1910 an act had been passed amending the Interstate Commerce laws by extending their operation to interstate transmission of intelligence by wire and wireless. The proposal now was to further extend the scope of the law to include regulations of radio-telegraphic communication. The bill became a law August 13, 1912, and regulation was lodged in the Department of Commerce. Since the Federal Government could have no jurisdiction over radio communications occurring entirely within any individual state, being limited by the Federal Constitution to matters of interstate commerce, the act was obviously entirely inadequate to cope with the situation. On the other hand, not even amateurs could guarantee that electrical impulses set up by them might not cross state borders, hence the new law proved more effective than it might otherwise have been.

The law provided for the licensing of operators (Chap. 287 Paragraph 1) on forms furnished by the Secretary of Commerce (Paragraph 2) but limited to United States citizens; punishment was specified for employment of unlicensed operators (Paragraph 3); and penalties were named for violation (Paragraph 4). Regulation of wave lengths and the beginnings of their restrictions were included in the bill. Willful and malicious interference with radio communication was prohibited and penalized (Paragraph 5). Uttering or transmitting false or fraudulent signals called for a penalty of twenty-five hundred dollars fine or imprisonment for not more than five years or both (Paragraph 7).[7]

Sec. 68. DeForest and American Tel. & Tel. Company.

Shortly after deForest's release on bail, with ruin staring him in the face, the unfortunate inventor looked about him for some means of escape from his financial woes. Since the American Telephone and

[7] See Vol. 4, United States Compiled Statutes of 1913.

Telegraph Company was known to be interested in trans-continental transmission, deForest on October 30, 1912, went to the officials of the company in an effort to sell or lease patent rights in his far-famed audion amplifier. To be sure, he was involved in litigation over wireless rights to the invention, but as a technical matter the Fleming patent, being confined to wireless, could not operate to bar use of the audion in long distance telephone transmission. Hopefully deForest demonstrated his device. The matter was taken under advisement. After some weeks of delay deForest, now quite desperate, made inquiries but was coolly rebuffed.

To the disappointed inventor this treatment was later regarded as evidence of a deliberate attempt to overreach him by pretending lack of interest in an exceedingly valuable device. To the engineers of the American Telephone Company, however, there appear to have been genuine difficulties in adapting the instrument to their needs. Then, too, there was obvious danger of future litigation with the Marconi interests over the use of the principle involved in the Fleming valve. Greater still was a defect in the audion itself.

It is true that the audion was a great improvement over other forms of detectors of radio signals, but its amplifying characteristics were decidedly limited, especially when applied to wire telephony. The Telephone Company needed a relay or booster of current, yet the audion could operate only on a very low current—one one-hundredth of a watt. If forced higher than this it caused voice distortion and then broke into a blue glow and ceased to function as an amplifier. The fact that telephone engineers were able to pass one watt of electrical energy through an ordinary telephone transmitter, even though the results were not very satisfactory, caused them to be impatient with the deForest audion. No one at that time realized that the presence of gas in the imperfect vacuum of the audion was largely responsible for the erratic behavior of the device.

The above facts represent the other side of the picture and to a considerable extent refute the ugly charges made by the friends of deForest that he was deliberately robbed by a heartless corporation. There is no doubt, as events were to demonstrate, that an unfortunate bargain was eventually made by the inventor.

Sec. 69. DeForest Sells the Audion Amplifier.

The goal of the American Telephone and Telegraph Company engineers was to produce a system of land-wire telephony that would enable telephone conversation between New York and San Francisco. In the latter city was shortly to be held a World's Fair and the telephone industry needed some spectacular achievement as its contribution to the event. The electric current used in telephone wires was incapable of traveling across the continent, since it dissipated or faded out on the way. Amplifiers were needed at intervals along the route to give the fading current new strength to continue its journey. DeForest's audion, despite its defects already noted, gave promise of becoming the answer to the problem. A Dr. H. P. Arnold, in the research department, was now at work upon the problem of producing a better vacuum tube than deForest had accomplished, hoping thus to get more power out of it and thus also to eliminate disastrous ionization of the gas in the imperfect vacuum.

Dr. Arnold's theory that a better vacuum would improve the audion was accordingly tried out in laboratory tests. At the same time and without the knowledge of Dr. Arnold another research was being conducted in the possibilities of the audion by Dr. Irving Langmuir, a physicist and chemist in the research department of the General Electric Company. For several years Langmuir had been investigating what went on inside vacuum tubes when powerful electric currents flowed through enclosed filaments. He had thus developed what was known as the "pure electron discharge tube" in his laboratory, which, with a drawn tungsten filament invented by a Dr. W. D. Coolidge, also of the General Electric Company, was producing remarkable results. Dr. Langmuir was thus equipped to apply his discoveries to the deForest audion.[8]

He at once demonstrated that the device could be of great value as a radio accessory. Since the General Electric was not in a position to commercialize its wire telephonic possibilities, Dr. Langmuir turned his attention to its radio-telephonic potentialities. His report coincided with that of Dr. Arnold of the Telephone Company—the audion had distinct promise. The Telephone Company at this time ordered its agents to purchase the rights to use the device for long distance telephony.

The manner in which the lawyer representing the American Telephone and Telegraph Company set about his task of purchasing rights to the audion from Lee deForest may have been his own idea of proper procedure. The company perhaps had no knowledge of the facts. To deForest, however, the affair later appeared to have been one in which he was overreached. According to his version the transaction was as follows:

[8] John Hays Hammond, Jr., still in the early twenties, began his scientific career at this time, his special interest being wireless telephony. In May, 1911, he engaged the services of Fritz Lowenstein as consulting engineer. Young Hammond had invented an automatic wireless selective system which gave promise of becoming commercially valuable. Lowenstein was a physicist of standing and well qualified to collaborate with the younger man. It is apparent from correspondence of the period that the New York laboratory was testing the three electrode tube for possible use as an amplifying device as early as November, 1911.

One day in the summer of 1913, the penniless and harassed inventor was alone in his laboratory in the old Biograph Building on 14th Street in New York City when a young man came to see him. The visitor proved to be a lawyer who announced that he had a client who was mildly interested in purchasing the patent rights to the audion. DeForest had optimistically believed that these rights should bring half a million dollars but the stranger declared that his client would not pay more than fifty thousand dollars for a license to use the device. DeForest endeavored to discover the name of the client, but the stranger refused to reveal the latter's identity except to deny "on the word of a gentleman" that it was the American Telephone and Telegraph Company.

The unhappy deForest, reluctant to sell at so modest a figure but in grave financial difficulties, consulted the board of directors of his company. The stockholders voted to sell to the stranger, assigning the exclusive right to the deForest patents for wire telephone and telegraphic purposes. The money would save the company from bankruptcy and also supply needed capital for manufacturing. The transaction was accordingly concluded and deForest at once plunged into his work again. The sequel of the story may be told in the words of deForest's biographer:

"In the midst of the excitement of new activities, a strange story reached deForest's ears. It concerned a record purported to have been seen in the United States Patent Office, dated just six weeks after the execution of the deal with a party bearing the same name as the attorney who had purchased the patents, that showed a transfer of these licensed rights to the audion amplifier to the American Telephone and Telegraph Company. DeForest recalled the suave, good-looking, young man, with his honest manner and his outstretched hand and his 'word of a gentleman.'" [9]

DeForest believed that he had been swindled. He accepted as fact a rumor that the board of directors of the company had actually voted a maximum of five hundred thousand dollars to purchase the patent rights if it should become necessary to pay that much. The needy inventor facing prosecution for overzealous promotion of an industry that later justified his faith, was no doubt imposed upon by a shrewd lawyer.

Sec. 70. DeForest on Trial for Alleged Fraud.

Although deForest and his associates had received a temporary reprieve from disaster by the sale of the patent rights, they knew all too well that a grievous ordeal awaited them. The criminal action in

[9] Carneal—Life of deForest, p. 257.

which deForest and other officers of his company were out on bail was
soon to come up for action in the Federal courts. DeForest and several
of the directors of the Radio Telephone Company went on trial in
New York City, November 12, 1913, charged with using the mails to
defraud the public by selling stock in a company whose only assets
were the deForest patents "chiefly directed by a strange device like
an incandescent lamp, which he called an Audion, and which device
had proven to be worthless." The language of this indictment reveals
how completely the prosecuting authorities failed to grasp the significance of deForest's radio inventions. In the light of subsequent events
there is irony indeed in the fact that the Federal District Attorney in
his all-seeing wisdom heaped upon the badgered inventor the following epithets of scorn:

"DeForest has said in many newspapers and over his signature that
it would be possible to transmit the human voice across the Atlantic
before many years. Based on these absurd and deliberately mislead-
ing statements of deForest, the misguided public, Your Honor, has
been persuaded to purchase stock in his company, paying as high as
ten and twenty dollars a share for the stock." The impassioned District
Attorney pleaded that deForest be sent to the Federal penitentiary at
Atlanta. After a trial lasting more than six weeks a jury of twelve men
found two of the directors guilty but acquitted deForest and one of
his associates of criminal intent. The Federal judge, in a speech that
must later have caused him a measure of chagrin at his own lack of
understanding, lectured Lee deForest severely, reprimanding him as
though he were a cheat who had narrowly escaped well-deserved punishment, admonishing him to give up all pretense of being an inventor. The fatuous jurist wound up his homily by advising deForest to
get "a common garden variety of job and stick to it." Thus one of the
foremost inventors of the age escaped criminal conviction because the
twelve men in the jury box had greater ability to perceive the truth
than the jurist who presided over one of the most important districts
in the Federal judiciary.

*Sec. 70a. David Sarnoff Makes Wireless History—Forecasts Radio
      Broadcasting.*

The John Wanamaker stores at an early date recognized the utility
and advertising value of wireless telegraphy and later of the wireless
telephone. In 1910 this enterprising organization made arrangements
with the American Marconi Company for experimental point-to-point
wireless stations to be installed in their New York City and Philadelphia stores. Young David Sarnoff, manager of the Marconi station
at Sea Gate, N. Y., had read every treatise on wireless telegraphy that

he could lay hands on. He was now consumed with ambition to take a special electrical engineering course at the Pratt Institute in Brooklyn. When Wanamaker announced that the New York and Philadelphia stores were to be equipped with the latest and best in Marconi apparatus David Sarnoff applied for the assignment and was promptly transferred to the Wanamaker store in New York City, thus enabling the ambitious youth to enjoy free evenings and regular hours for attending the Pratt Institute.

On one notable occasion, however, David Sarnoff failed to appear in his classes at the Institute. For seventy-two hours of unceasing vigil the young operator sat at his instrument board in the Wanamaker store and picked up the heart-rending details of the *Titanic* disaster. By order of the President of the United States every wireless station except those engaged in rescue work was ordered closed on April 16, 1912, in order that there be no interference with the reception of wireless messages concerning the disaster.

"The *S.S. Titanic* ran into iceberg. Sinking fast," was the first message that was plucked from the ether. For three agonizing days young Sarnoff stuck to his task while rescue ships combed the seas for survivors of the tragedy. Seven hundred and six souls, largely women and children in lifeboats or clinging to driftwood were taken out alive but fifteen hundred and seventeen who had been aboard the sunken craft perished in mid-ocean. That any were saved at all was no doubt due to wireless telegraphy.

"The drama of this struggle against the sea," wrote one of the biographers of David Sarnoff, "caused millions throughout the world to grasp at every word that came through the Wanamaker station. Not until he had given to the world the name of the last survivor, three days and three nights after that first message came, did Sarnoff call his job done. The loss of the *Titanic* and the great service of radio aroused public consciousness to the importance of this new service. Congress passed a new law making much stricter the requirements regarding equipment and operators on seagoing vessels."

The Wanamaker stores were shortly to lose their star operator. The Marconi Company transferred him in 1912. David Sarnoff became a Radio Inspector and an Instructor in the Marconi Institute, where wireless operators were being trained. In 1913 he was promoted to the position of Chief Radio Inspector and Assistant Chief Engineer. In 1914 he became contract manager of the Marconi Company. While fulfilling the duties of this dual position young Sarnoff—but twenty-three years of age—was sent to New Orleans to attend a Convention of Railway Telegraph Superintendents scheduled for May 19th to 22nd, 1914. He left New York on the *S.S. Antilles* with a group of delegates. When about sixty miles at sea he entertained the group by picking up

the wireless program from his old station at Wanamaker's. Keenly
alive to the possibilities of wireless telephony, the youthful Assistant
Chief Engineer was already carrying on experiments in transmitting
music from the Wanamaker Store, tests being made on a regular schedule. Sarnoff had a surprise for his companions when he connected a
number of headphones to the ship's wireless receiver. To their amazement not the Morse code but music, clear and strong, came to them
on shipboard. This experience and the enthusiasm of his companions
no doubt further stimulated the active brain of David Sarnoff.

In 1916 Mr. Sarnoff embodied in a written recommendation to
Edward J. Nally, the General Manager of the Marconi Company, the
details of his proposed "Radio Music Box" scheme. Mr. Nally's reply,
dated November 9, 1916, is in existence and has been examined by
the author. Elmer E. Bucher, at that time an engineer of the Marconi
Company, has informed the author that he was with Mr. Sarnoff in
1916 when the latter dictated the following statement:

"I have in mind a plan of development which would make radio a
'household utility' in the same sense as the piano or phonograph. The
idea is to bring music into the house by wireless.

"While this has been tried in the past by wires, it has been a failure
because wires do not lend themselves to this scheme. With radio, however, it would seem to be entirely feasible. For example—a radio telephone transmitter having a range of say 25 to 50 miles can be installed
at a fixed point where instrumental or vocal music or both are produced. The problem of transmitting music has already been solved in
principle and therefore all the receivers attuned to the transmitting
wave length should be capable of receiving such music. The receiver
can be designed in the form of a simple 'Radio Music Box' and arranged for several different wave lengths, which should be changeable
with the throwing of a single switch or pressing of a single button.

"The 'Radio Music Box' can be supplied with amplifying tubes and
a loudspeaking telephone, all of which can be neatly mounted in one
box. The box can be placed on a table in the parlor or living room,
the switch set accordingly and the transmitted music received. There
should be no difficulty in receiving music perfectly when transmitted
within a radius of 25 to 50 miles. Within such a radius there reside
hundreds of thousands of families; and as all can simultaneously receive from a single transmitter, there would be no question of obtaining sufficiently loud signals to make the performance enjoyable. The
power of the transmitter can be made 5 k.w., if necessary, to cover even
a short radius of 25 to 50 miles; thereby giving extra loud signals in
the home if desired. The use of head telephones would be obviated
by this method. The development of a small loop antenna to go with
each 'Radio Music Box' would likewise solve the antennae problem.

"The same principle can be extended to numerous other fields as, for example, receiving lectures at home which can be made perfectly audible; also events of national importance can be simultaneously announced and received. Baseball scores can be transmitted in the air by the use of one set installed at the Polo Grounds. The same would be true of other cities. This proposition would be especially interesting to farmers and others living in outlying districts removed from cities. By the purchase of a 'Radio Music Box' they could enjoy concerts, lectures, music, recitals, etc., which may be going on in the nearest city within their radius. While I have indicated a few of the most probable fields of usefulness for such a device, yet there are numerous other fields to which the principle can be extended. . . .

*   *   *

"The manufacture of the 'Radio Music Box' including antenna, in large quantities, would make possible their sale at a moderate figure of perhaps $75.00 per outfit. The main revenue to be derived will be from the sale of 'Radio Music Boxes' which if manufactured in quantities of one hundred thousand or so could yield a handsome profit when sold at the price mentioned above. Secondary sources of revenue would be from the sale of transmitters and from increased advertising and circulation of the *Wireless Age*. The Company would have to undertake the arrangements, I am sure, for music recitals, lectures, etc., which arrangements can be satisfactorily worked out. It is not possible to estimate the total amount of business obtainable with this plan until it has been developed and actually tried out but there are about 15,000,000 families in the United States alone and if only one million or 7% of the total families thought well of the idea it would, at the figure mentioned, mean a gross business of about $75,000,000 which should yield considerable revenue.

"Aside from the profit to be derived from this proposition the possibilities for advertising for the Company are tremendous; for its name would ultimately be brought into the household and wireless would receive national and universal attention."

*   *   *

Sec. 71. Armstrong-deForest Litigation.

Edwin H. Armstrong was destined to make important contributions to the science of wireless telephony. An ardent amateur at fifteen years of age, he began his career as an experimenter in radio phenomena. He read with eagerness all the literature on the subject that he could lay his hands on. By the time he was ready to enter college he had put himself well abreast of the art of radio amplification. While a student at Columbia University he continued to experiment with the audion. His active mind and his natural originality led him to make deductions that had escaped veteran investigators. He was in fact on the trail of the "feed-back" principle whose discovery was to revolutionize the industry. Penniless college student that he was he could not apply for a patent without financial aid, and he was prudent enough to realize that he could not safely proceed with his experiments unless protection of this nature could be obtained. The youth's father was unimpressed by his son's enthusiasm and refused to assist him financially. Armstrong's uncle likewise declined to aid the hopeful inventor. He did, however, offer the valuable suggestion that the youth make a drawing of his invention and have it witnessed by a notary. Armstrong took this advice and the drawing later became his chief reliance in a long-drawn contest with deForest.

Although the boy had failed to enlist the support of his own family he did succeed in convincing Professor Michael I. Pupin of Columbia University that he had discovered a valuable principle. Prof. Pupin took him into the university laboratories and enabled him to continue his investigations.[10] Although deForest had already evolved what he called a "Cascade amplifier" by which three audions in succession were made to amplify the results of a single audion twenty-sevenfold, yet the amateur Armstrong brought forward a new feed-back principle in receiving circuits that produced astonishing results. It was not unlike feeding back a part of the current as a means of attaining stronger effects just as live steam is fed back and used over again. Armstrong was awarded a patent October 6, 1914.

To be sure, deForest claimed that he had already evolved the plan before Armstrong originated the idea. Long-continued litigation was to result. For more than twenty years the contest was destined to continue in the courts with alternate victories for the rival inventors, but in 1934 the Supreme Court of the United States was to decide that deForest had a right to priority in the matter.

Sec. 72. Contest Over deForest's Audion Amplifier.

The deForest Audion proved to be one of the most prolific sources of litigation in the history of inventions. It has previously been noted that the device had a three-phase development. The first phase was the two-electrode tube made by Thomas A. Edison in his attempts to devise an effective incandescent electric light. This had proved useless as an incandescent light and had been discarded by Edison. In his experiments, however, the inventor had discovered that the two-electrode tube possessed the peculiar property when connected to an alternating electric circuit of permitting the current to flow in one direction only. This was known by scientists as the "Edison Effect"—one of the peculiar manifestations of electricity.

[10] Radio Broadcast, May 1922.

Twenty years later, in 1904 to be exact, we reach the second phase when Dr. J. A. Fleming resurrected the discarded Edison device, improved it and renamed it the Fleming valve. The use to which it was now put was distinctly novel and entitled Fleming to patent rights. But even though it was a move in the right direction, the Fleming valve proved of little value until deForest added a third element known as a "grid". It has previously been noted that deForest applied for letters patent on the entire device and that in 1907 the U. S. Patent Office issued a patent on the deForest Audion. For several years thereafter deForest manufactured the audion and gradually built up a considerable demand for the invention.

Now came an important development: On October 24, 1914, the Marconi Wireless Telegraph Company of America brought an action against the deForest Radio Telephone Company in the Federal District Court of New York to restrain the latter from manufacturing and selling the audion tube. Thus was launched a momentous struggle that was destined to tie up in litigation one of the most valuable devices known to radio. It was a moot question in legal circles whether victory for either could operate in any way except as a defeat for both. It was admitted that the two-electrode device was valueless without the grid element but if the Marconi interests owned the one and the deForest Company the other then neither could manufacture the complete device without the consent of the other. Consent between these warring factions seemed indeed remote.

Sec. 73. Evolution of the Alexanderson Alternator.

The history of any great invention almost invariably discloses that the device is not the product of one human brain but rather the culmination of the gropings of a multitude of searchers for truth in the general field. Sometimes the invention itself may await the coming of a clear-visioned thinker who, surveying the field, recognizes in the seeming maze of apparently unrelated discoveries by other men the needful components of the great invention. The inventor's function in such case is to combine in a workable system the ideas and mechanical gadgets that others have fumbled with yet have never brought to perfection. The Alexanderson Alternator is an instance in point. Elihu Thomson, as we have previously noted, built a high frequency generator as early as 1889. Tesla did the like somewhat later and produced a more powerful generator.

Utilizing the same principle Reginald A. Fessenden invented a high frequency alternator (so-called because it was an alternating current generator) in 1901. Following history a bit further we find Charles P. Steinmetz building a 10,000 cycle alternator for Fessenden at the General Electric plant in 1903. In the following year, however, an order from Fessenden for a 100,000 cycle alternator fell into the lap of the brilliant young electrical engineer, Ernst F. W. Alexanderson, at the General Electric plant. He it was who possessed the clarity of vision to recognize in all that had gone before such elements as might be combined in producing a high frequency generator. Alexanderson realized that the Steinmetz device could not operate at more than 10,000 cycles. To produce a machine capable of ten times that frequency required a distinctly new mechanical approach.

The first design submitted by Alexanderson, as previously indicated, involved the use of a laminated iron armature. Because the Steinmetz machine had employed the same material Fessenden at once manifested a prejudice against it, believing that 10,000 cycles was the maximum for an iron armature. He accordingly rejected the Alexanderson design in this respect and insisted upon using wood.

It was, therefore, fortunate that the younger man had crystallized his own ideas on the subject before he had learned of Fessenden's disbelief in an iron armature, otherwise he might have been turned aside from the quest that was to result so gloriously.

Attention has already been called to the alternator with a wooden armature that Alexanderson built for Fessenden in 1906. Despite its limitations this was the device by which the human voice was broadcast on Christmas Eve, 1906. It is a singular fact that Professor Fessenden continued to insist upon the wooden armature despite all that Alexanderson could do to dissuade him. Finally the young inventor found an opportunity to try out his own theory! The American Tel. & Tel. Company was then struggling with the problem of producing an alternator or relay capable of stepping-up the current in long-distance telephone lines. An appeal to the General Electric Company for aid [11] caused Alexanderson's employers to turn the matter over to him. His pet project could now be tried out in earnest! On April 2, 1907, the factory began work on the Alexanderson high frequency machine. The two inventors, Fessenden and Alexanderson, were corresponding freely at the time and on June 13, 1907 Alexanderson wrote to Fessenden explaining the design of the new machine. On June 18th Fessenden replied, urging Alexanderson to abandon the iron armature. The latter was not to be turned aside from his purpose. In the latter part of September, 1907, the telephone relay was ready for testing. The results were so remarkable that Fessenden himself came to Schenectady to witness a demonstration. Then and not until then did Fessenden abandon his wooden armature idea. The new machine gave such a good account of itself that the Brant Rock pioneer decided to adopt the Alexanderson plan.

[11] The letter from the A. T. & T. Company to the General Electric Company concerning this desired telephone relay was dated March 11, 1907.

The situation was a bit complicated at the time since Fessenden had already placed an order with the General Electric Company for a 10 k.w. machine similar to the one that had been built for him by Alexanderson and on which he had made his famous Christmas Eve experiment of the year before. Writing in 1915 for the Patent Department of General Electric, Alexanderson explained the incident thus:

"Fessenden placed an order for a 10 k.w. machine of this type and this requisition by a mistake in the routine went to Mr. Conway Robinson, who was one of the designing engineers in the A.C. department, and he started work on the machine without my knowledge. . . . Fessenden on a visit to Schenectady saw the test of the telephone relay and decided that this type of alternator was so much more promising that he wished to cancel the requisition for the 10 k.w. alternator on which work was being done and authorized an expenditure of $5,000 in developing the new type. Report of this was made by Mr. Edwards to Mr. Pratt on February 24, 1908 and after further conferences Prof. Fessenden agreed to pay $1,225 for the cancellation of the requisition."

A further development should be noted: Fessenden had already placed an order with the De Laval Company for an alternator with a wooden armature but he now substituted iron for wood. It will be remembered that at about this time Prof. Fessenden invented a rotary spark-gap device for wireless telegraphy. This invention scored so great a success that the National Electric Signalling Company embarked on a campaign of commercial expansion that led to disastrous conflict within the company as previously recorded. From this unhappy controversy came the elimination of Prof. Fessenden as a factor in the further development of the alternator. The General Electric Company had by this time expended thousands of dollars in experimentation. Patents had already been applied for covering the Alexanderson ideas. It was logical therefore that the quest should be continued and that Ernst F. W. Alexanderson should have been given *carte blanche* to carry on. In a letter to Albert G. Davis of the Patent Department of General Electric under date of June 29, 1915, Alexanderson speaks thus of progress attained after Fessenden faded out of the picture:

"The important mechanical features in alternators of our present design are covered by patents 1,110,029 and 1,110,030, which refer to mechanical details that were developed after I ceased to co-operate with Fessenden on account of his separation from the National Electric Signalling Company. These improvements were embodied in some of the later machines furnished to the National Electric Signalling Company on a contract for six machines at a definite price but they were added on our own responsibility and not by any request of the National Electric Signalling Company."

Every important improvement in the alternator called for the filing of a fresh application for a patent. It is interesting to note that on April 26, 1909, Alexanderson applied for a patent on his alternator and also in the same year read a paper before the American Institute of Electrical Engineers describing the successful operation of a two kilowatt, 100,000-cycle alternator. This, by the way, was the machine used by Major Squier of the U. S. Signal Corps in experimenting with high-frequency telephony over wire lines. One of the most significant of the patent applications made by Alexanderson in the alternator series was dated December 7, 1912. It did not ripen into a patent until November 28, 1916 (U. S. Patent No. 1,206,643).

Sec. 74. Alexanderson's Magnetic Amplifier.

Having developed a powerful instrument for the production of smooth continuous waves, a new problem presented itself to Alexanderson—how to control these powerful currents by the minute energy contained in the human voice. Fessenden had already made use of the known fact that a carbon microphone acts as an amplifier. Microphones such as were then in use in telephony fell far short of being able to cope with the energy generated by the new alternator. In his tests with a 1/2 k.w. alternator Fessenden had tried the expedient of a water-cooled microphone. It was apparent that this type of microphone could not be utilized with alternators of high power. Alexanderson set to work upon the problem of producing an amplifier, or as it was then called, a telephone relay—it being intended to relay power into fading telephone circuits.

It will be observed that the telephone proper and the wireless telephone were thus facing similar problems of amplification. It was fortunate for young Alexanderson that a demand existed for the immediate development of such a relay. With the active support of Caryl D. Haskins, one of the executives of General Electric, the inventor pushed on in his quest. His first approach was to equip the alternator with a laminated field structure in order to introduce the telephone current into the field and thus to realize the amplification within the alternator itself. Successful results were attained, yet Alexanderson became convinced that greater success might be realized by separating the functions of generating the alternating current and controlling the same.

The great problem was how to harness the weak power circuit of the microphone to the high power circuit of the antenna without having the antenna power burn out the microphone. This was accom-

OWEN D. YOUNG
Whose genius as an organizer brought the Radio Corporation of America
into being.

plished by utilizing the well-known magnetic saturation effect in iron. Thus by using an iron core as the harnessing link Alexanderson accomplished the feat of producing what may popularly be termed a one-way valve. When thus harnessed the weak current from the microphone operated like the throttle-control of the modern automobile —a tremendously effective device. This was a new and distinct contribution to the science of electrical transmission. The Alexanderson Magnetic Amplifier was perfected prior to 1912.

It proved highly successful in telegraphy and telephony, yet the tireless inventor later discovered a new means of amplification that soon superseded the magnetic amplifier in the field of wireless telephony. The story of that discovery will be set forth in the following pages. The magnetic amplifier, however, was destined to play a mighty role in wireless history.

A characteristic anecdote of this period of development is found in young Alexanderson's modest announcement to E. W. Rice, Jr., Vice-President of General Electric Company, that he had at last perfected his magnetic amplifier. He hoped that Mr. Rice would come with him to see it work, the inventor expressing belief that it would be possible to use the device in trans-Atlantic wireless telephony. Mr. Rice was immediately interrupted by the arrival of another official of the company who desired a conference on company matters. Rice explained that Alexanderson had produced a device that might be the answer to trans-Atlantic telephony, whereupon the other exclaimed: "Why do you waste time on such foolish dreams?"

Mr. Rice replied: "If Alexanderson thinks he has discovered the means of telephoning across the ocean I feel it my duty to look into it." Needless to say the "foolish dream," in the fullness of time, did come true!

Sec. 75. Alexanderson's Electronic Amplifier.

The manner in which Ernst F. W. Alexanderson discovered the new "harnessing link between microphone and antenna," later known as the Electronic Amplifier, has a distinct human touch. Even though the inventor had scored a great success in the magnetic amplifier he still maintained the open mind of the scientist, hoping that some even more effective means might be discovered in this field. He had already invented a mercury vapor tube with an ignitor control and had taken out a patent on it as a telephone amplifier. At that time no means existed for manufacturing the ignitor.

It seems that John Hays Hammond, Jr., an eager young scientist who has since made a brilliant record in various fields, such as radio control of torpedoes, airplanes and the like, was installing two of Alexanderson's 100,000-cycle alternators in his experimental plant at

Gloucester, Mass. In September, 1912, Alexanderson visited Hammond in connection with tests being conducted by the young inventor. During the progress of the tests the two men discussed, among other topics, the problem of telephonic modulation of high frequency energy.

"During these discussions," Alexanderson testified in the patent interference case, No. 42,158, "Mr. Hammond told me about the characteristics of the deForest audion,[12] and I gained from him the impression that while the audion had proved to be an efficient amplifier of telephone currents, it could not be used as a relay for radio frequency currents because of an inherent sluggishness in its action." Alexanderson at once concluded that this sluggishness was due to ionized [13] vapor within the deForest tube and reasoned that with a more perfect vacuum the tube would have more amplifying power. He was familiar with the experiments of Dr. Langmuir and Dr. Coolidge in connection with X-ray tubes. To continue with his testimony: "I therefore conceived the idea that the three-electrode valve of the deForest type might be improved by the methods of evacuation used by Dr. Langmuir and Dr. Coolidge and that the tubes so improved might be substituted in the system for radio telephonic transmission described in my Patent 1,042,069."

Alexanderson promptly conferred with Dr. Coolidge and others, later experimenting with the valve and adding to it very important technical improvements, thus eventually perfecting what he called an electronic amplifier, popularly known as a vacuum tube, a simple device for controlling radiated energy. It was capable of stepping up the power in terms of kilowatts (thousands of watts) instead of watts. Best of all this power could be directly controlled by an ordinary microphone. This electronic amplifier was to prove of extreme importance in the development of radio telephony. It is the basic principle of the present-day radio broadcasting transmitter. Tubes of this type are now built up to 100 k.w. rating.

[12] Hammond apparently mentioned to Alexanderson in the Hammond New York laboratory that Lowenstein was conducting experiments with an ionic detector invented by Hammond. On October 21, 1912, Alexanderson wrote a letter to the Gloucester inventor in which he offered suggestions for overcoming certain difficulties that had been encountered. "If the disturbing impulses are greater than the capacity of one detector," he wrote, "it would be feasible to connect a number of them in series until sufficient capacity is reached. . . . Each element of inductance and capacity would be tuned for the same frequency as the whole circuit, and with the detector belonging to the same would form a separate receiving unit."

[13] An atom seems to be composed of one electron which represents the negative charge of the atom whereas the ion is the positive charge, in mass far in excess of the other. According to estimates by some scientists the ion is 1840 times the mass of the electron. Naturally the pure electron discharge produced by methods devised by Dr. Langmuir overcame the sluggishness inherent in tubes containing ionized vapor.

Sec. 76. Alexanderson's Multiple Tuned Antenna.

One of the great problems to which Alexanderson devoted his talents at this time was the development of a practical and commercial system of trans-oceanic communication. This required not only an efficient transmitter but also a type of antenna very much more effective than any then existing. The custom then was of having but one connection between the antenna and the transmitter. Alexanderson had a theory that a series of down-wires each equipped with a tuning coil and each leading to ground connections along the antenna would greatly increase the efficiency of transmission. Wireless experts in general scoffed at the idea, yet Alexanderson, nothing daunted, tried out his theories at the experimental wireless station in Schenectady. The antenna of this station was 900 feet long. The inventor added a tuned down-wire to the far end of the antenna. To his satisfaction he discovered that the efficiency of the antenna had been more than doubled. This historic experiment was made on February 5, 1916.

Guglielmo Marconi was one of the first responsible officials in the wireless field to recognize the possibilities of multiple tuning of the antenna. Shortly before the United States entered the World War he invited Mr. Alexanderson to try out the plan at the New Brunswick wireless station. The antenna at this place was a mile long. Alexanderson installed six tuned down-wires at regular intervals along the antenna and lo! the power of the same had increased tenfold. The far-flung Marconi Company at once conceived the ambitious project of equipping their stations with the Alexanderson system and thus of girdling the globe. The Alexanderson system had assumed international importance. The genius of one man was to alter the current of history. How profound was to be the influence of the Alexanderson system upon Anglo-American relations—in fact upon world politics— will presently appear.

CHAPTER NINE

Wireless Telegraphy in the World War

Sec. 77. The United States Navy and Wireless Experimentation.

THE UNITED STATES NAVY is entitled to great credit for its part in the development of radio transmission. What private individuals or private electrical manufacturers may have dreamed about, the Navy technicians, with the resources of the nation behind them, were able to bring to pass. The direct contributions of Navy technicians, however, were slight in comparison to the indirect contributions of the Navy as a potential customer of private electrical manufacturers and inventors. So alert were naval officials to every development in the wireless industry that any inventor, however impecunious, might be sure not only of a hearing but of a thorough testing of his device. We have already observed how the United States Navy conducted elaborate tests of the Marconi, the Fessenden, the deForest and the German Slaby-Arco systems even when the wireless industry was in its swaddling clothes. The same open-minded scientific attitude continued. Whenever a new device could be demonstrated to be of practical value the Navy became a generous purchaser of equipment.

One of the greatest experiment stations in early radio history was the mammoth naval wireless station near the Nation's Capital—across the Potomac in Arlington, Virginia. This station was begun about 1910 and was three years in building. Three self-supporting steel masts, one six hundred feet high and the other two four hundred and fifty feet each, were the supporting members for the giant antenna of this remarkable station. One night in 1912, when but one wire had been stretched from the tallest mast to the ground, a naval engineer who chanced to be listening-in heard signals in the Morse code in a foreign language. These dots and dashes were later demonstrated to have originated in the Radio Station of the Eiffel Tower in Paris. The incident served to quicken the naval technicians in their quest for an effective means of broadcasting wireless signals. They were already trying out Fessenden's spark transmitter but soon discovered that the "arc" type of sending apparatus was more effective.[1] No device yet available, however, was capable of accomplishing all that they desired.

The arc transmitter was an invention of Valdemar Poulsen, a Danish scientist who had migrated to the United States. It was a generator of continuous waves and differed from the usual arc in that it burned in an atmosphere containing hydrogen and in a strong transverse magnetic field. The device was manufactured by the Federal Telegraph Company, which specialized in Poulsen products. Lee deForest was for a time in the employ of this company in an engineering capacity.[2]

[1] Schubert—The Electric Word, p. 100; History of Engineering During World War, p. 95.
[2] Schubert—The Electric Word, p. 95.

The Federal Telegraph Company became one of the first important rivals of the American Marconi Company, since it erected a number of radio stations in strategic points in the United States.

The Poulsen arc transmitter was installed by the Federal Telegraph Company in the Arlington Radio Station shortly after it went into commission in February, 1913. The Fessenden spark apparatus was already in operation in the same station. Thus two rival systems were tested out on the greatest proving ground imaginable. The arc transmitter demonstrated greater distance coverage and more freedom from static.

Arc transmitters of various sizes up to five hundred kilowatts were tested by the United States Navy. Battleships and other fighting craft were equipped with arc transmitters. Experience demonstrated, however, that the Poulsen invention emitted a broad wave and had the further disadvantage of developing such an enormous amount of heat that the device required a water-cooling system.

After the outbreak of the World War and months before there was any likelihood of the United States becoming embroiled, the attention of the national government was quite naturally focused upon wireless communication and the necessity of perfecting existing facilities. A special board was appointed to reorganize the Naval Radio Service. The board was officially authorized on December 5, 1914. A report was filed by the board two months later and in May, 1915, this report was officially adopted. Thus originated the Naval Communications Service, whose first director was Captain (afterward Admiral) William H. G. Bullard. Captain Bullard had already attained distinction in the electrical and radio field.

The survey of available wireless facilities revealed not only the considerable network of government-owned stations—manned by naval and army experts—but also an impressive list of privately-owned stations. The chief wireless stations operated by the Navy were at Arlington, Virginia; at San Diego, California; at Darien in the Canal Zone; at Pearl Harbor, Hawaii; at Guam and an important outpost in the Philippines. Among privately-owned stations the Federal Telegraph Company was pre-eminent on the West Coast while the American Marconi Company maintained a large group of stations in strategic locations in the United States. German interests had also developed a powerful station at Sayville, Long Island, and were beginning a high power station at Tuckerton, N. J.

The Naval Communications Board, with an eye to future possibilities, was keeping watchful oversight of developments in the research laboratories of the various rival manufacturers of radio and wireless equipment. The Alexanderson Alternator was naturally the center of interest at this time because it was seeking to accomplish one of the dreams of wireless enthusiasts—the conquest of distance.

The historian of the future may be able to write the full story of the achievements of the United States Navy in developing wireless telegraphy and wireless telephony during the war period, but we are still too near the events for the government to release all data concerning the Navy experimentation. They were state secrets at the time and due to the continuous nature of experimentation still possess something of the same attributes.

Sec. 78. The World War and Wireless Developments.

The outbreak of the World War in 1914 had focused the attention of all belligerent nations upon the importance of wireless communication. Germany, as befitted a nation of scientists, was probably better prepared to compete with the Marconi-served Great Britain than any other nation. Her Navy was fully equipped for the needs of the hour and two high power stations at Nauen and Eilvese were in operation with far-reaching wireless coverage.

France was somewhat backward in this respect but since the French Navy was insignificant in comparison with either that of Britain or Germany the need was not as great. The grim business of land warfare also required short range wireless equipment. Wireless, however, had one grave disadvantage—it could be heard by enemies as well as by friends. Wireless waves could also be blanketed by hostile broadcasts, hence no certain reliance could be reposed in it in the war zone. Obviously there were great problems to be solved before wireless could hope to equal the humble telephone as an avenue of military signaling. For this reason the signal corps of every army unit in the war zone was obliged to face deadly barrages and sniping while valiantly endeavoring to string telephone and telegraph wire from headquarters to exposed trenches and outposts. The telephone thus became all-important in Flanders.

On the sea, however, wireless reigned, especially for Germany and her allies after the early days of the war. Britain, mistress of the seas and of the chief cable lines of the globe, promptly cut every cable that could be of value to her enemies. Germany was obliged to exert all efforts to build up lines of wireless communication with her U-boat and war craft fleets. Strangely enough the supposedly astute Teutons allowed themselves to be hoodwinked by the British.

Schubert declares: "Germany promptly fell back upon radio.[3] The ether of the Channel was full of the smooth efficient wireless talk of her fleet as her ships and their bases exchanged messages in intricate

[3] Meaning wireless telegraphy.

cipher, hurrying as if to get them through before 'interference' came.

"It never came; she was granted the utmost freedom to use her radio all she wished—and she took the bait. For the British vessels were pursuing a policy that it was more blessed to receive than to give. While they themselves maintained 'wireless silence' except in emergencies, they listened, ears glued to receivers, 'eavesdropping' for all they were worth. Every recorded message was telegraphed by land-wire to the British Intelligence Headquarters at the Admiralty and there, day by day, the whole was co-ordinated, pieced together—a continuous record of the Teutons' radio communications." [4]

The British were not at first able to make anything out of these elaborately coded messages but they bided their time until a German cruiser was sunk in a sea fight with the Russians. Divers then went hopefully into the depths to locate the vessel's safe. Sure enough, when the heavy receptacle was recovered and cracked open a set of the latest German codes was found. Somewhat later a German submarine, all its occupants dead, came rolling in on the beach at Yarmouth, England, with another set of codes. Thus the British Intelligence Office was able to decode German messages and to keep fully informed of German plans and plots. As the war progressed so many of these codes were found that even the frequent changing of codes offered little hindrance to British experts. Not only that but experts in British and American intelligence service soon learned to decipher German codes without the aid of the code books.

Another development of wireless proved of great value in the World War. A wireless "director-finder" was developed by John Stone Stone in 1905. He arranged two vertical single wire antennae, each on a separate mast of a ship, and each leading to a separate primary system acting on a common secondary. If the ship were directly at right angles to the line between it and the sending station, currents of equal amplitude and phase would be set up in each antenna, and if—as was usually the case—the two primaries were wound "opposing", the signals would cancel each other and nothing would be heard in the telephones. On the other hand, if the ship were in line with the pathway of the signals, the currents in the two antennae would be somewhat out of phase, and a resultant current would be transmitted to the secondary. This system was tried out by the U. S. Navy Dept. and worked fairly well. The requirement of moving the ship was a very serious detriment to success, however.

Shortly after, the Bellini-Tosi direction finder came into play. Here two triangular loop aerials were used, their apices coincident, and

4 Schubert—The Electric Word, p. 138.

their planes at right angles to each other. In each was a primary coil, and these coils acted on a single, rotatable coil. Signals set up in the two loops created a resultant field, and the rotating coil gave greatest signals when it embraced this field to its maximum. Therefore the movement of coil, and not of the ship, indicated the direction of the distant sending station.

This system worked out well on passenger ships, but with the metal masts and other adjacent masses of iron on U. S. battleships it gave very poor results. Moreover, its pick-up, due to the relatively small loops used, was very inferior. The American Marconi Company improved it to some extent by making each loop consist of four turns, a forerunner of improvements later to come, but even this did not remedy the difficulty.

Frederick A. Kolster, a radio engineer in the employ of the Bureau of Standards at Washington, was the first to remedy both of the faults of older systems at one and the same time. He used as his pick-up a multiple loop antenna, or coil antenna, and he arranged to have this move about a vertical axis. Therefore, by moving the loop for maximum (or minimum) signal one could determine by pointer the direction from which the signal came. This multiple loop gave a much greater pick-up than any of the preceding systems. At the same time, Kolster improved the sensitivity of the apparatus by adding to it the vacuum tube amplifier, then just coming into general use. This was just before America's entrance into the World War.

Lieutenant-Commander Hooper, then in charge of the Navy's radio work, saw Kolster's device, and at once had it tested under service conditions, finding that here he had the first radio compass that would give good results on a battleship. He therefore arranged to obtain exclusive rights to this apparatus for two years, and extensive work was begun in the Navy to design various types of Kolster direction finders for the different forms of ships to use them. The results were uniformly satisfactory, and completely justified the far-sightedness of Lieutenant-Commander Hooper in making the deal.

After the War, commercial adaptation of the rotating coil form of direction finder lagged for a time, due to a conflict of opinion. The Navy felt that the best way to obtain bearings was to have the ship itself send signals, and have the bearings obtained by two or more Navy shore stations fitted with direction finders, and connected by wire lines. Thus cross bearings could be taken, the position of the ship determined by chart, and the exact position sent by radio to the vessel.

Each of the coastal radio stations in European waters, during the war, was equipped with a radio compass of Italian origin. Thus

British war craft were enabled to locate and sink a surprisingly large number of German submarines, whereupon divers would be sent down to recover German secret documents.

It is said that the Battle of Jutland brought out in full the strength and weakness of wireless telegraphy. Wireless was of tremendous value to the commander of an embattled squadron while messages could be gotten to ships of the fleet, but interference inevitably blanketed radio transmission and turned everything into chaos.

Propaganda found a mighty vehicle in wireless broadcasts. Thus Germany was able to reach out beyond the ring of steel that encircled her and pour into the ears of the world her version of the causes of the war and the aims of the Central Powers. Not only that but Germany carried on—always in code which British agents could readily decipher—world-wide intrigues that did much to align neutral nations against her. It was, for example, a decoded wireless message to the government of Mexico seeking to inflame her against the United States and thus to induce her to enter the war on the side of Germany that did much to swerve public opinion in the United States in favor of war with Germany.

Sec. 79. The Allies Turn to American Radio Experts for Aid.

Early in the war European nations began to make overtures to American electrical research experts for solution of problems that had baffled their own scientists. Shortly after the outbreak of hostilities the British Government sent agents to the Westinghouse Electric and Manufacturing Company in Pittsburgh, Pennsylvania, with a request that it set its research engineers to work upon certain special problems of wireless telegraph and telephone transmission. This naturally involved "laboratory" work that might approximate actual conditions and involved the establishment of transmitting and receiving stations sufficiently separated by space to permit accurate testing of results. One station was set up near the Westinghouse plant in East Pittsburgh while the other was located at the home of Dr. Frank Conrad, one of the chief technicians of the company, in the Pittsburgh residential district, a distance of four or five miles. From this effort on the part of the Westinghouse Company was eventually to develop the first great triumph of radio broadcasting.

The General Electric Company, in Schenectady, New York, had already accomplished notable results, especially in its development of the Alexanderson Alternator. So intriguing were the reports of the tests being conducted with this marvel of science that, as indicated in the previous chapter Marconi, the father of wireless telegraphy, became personally interested. In April, 1915, the great scientist came to America in connection with litigation over a patent infringement case. While here he made a pilgrimage to Schenectady and investigated the Alexanderson Alternator.

At that time a comparatively unknown lawyer had been advanced to the position of chief counsel for the General Electric Company— Owen D. Young. His knowledge of wireless was nil and he had never taken any special interest in it. Yet when a letter came to him from the great Marconi inviting him to a conference at the latter's hotel, Mr. Young would have been more than human if he had not experienced a thrill at the prospect of meeting in a business conference one of the greatest inventors of the age—at the latter's express invitation.

Since Mr. Young was to prove the organizing genius of the radio industry, his history prior to the momentous conference with Marconi should be summarized at this point. Owen D. Young, the future founder of the Radio Corporation of America and the author of the Young Plan for the Settlement of World War Reparations, had practiced law in Boston from 1896 to 1912. Public utility companies had found him unusually capable in handling difficult problems of high finance and public relations. On April 28, 1912, the head of the legal department of the General Electric Company was killed in an automobile accident. Owen D. Young was invited to accept the vacant post. In January, 1913, he began his notable career with the Company.

The beginning of the World War in 1914 brought many pressing legal problems to Mr. Young's attention but until the Spring of 1915 the subject of wireless telegraphy had never caused him any serious concern. The day came, however, when Owen D. Young suddenly awoke to the great international aspect of wireless. Ida Tarbell in her *Life of Young* states that his first "wireless" message came to him when he received by mail the letter signed by the famous inventor Marconi inviting him to the conference. This must have occurred on May 19th or 20th, 1915, since Marconi, having arrived in New York aboard the *Lusitania* on April 24th,[5] to testify in the case of Marconi Wireless Telegraph Company *v.* Atlantic Communications Company, was called home suddenly by the Italian War Office. The trial adjourned May 21st.[6]

Fortunately we are able to fix the date of the Schenectady visit, since Dr. Alexanderson has kindly permitted the author to inspect his personal files of 1915. We know that the conference with Mr. Young must have occurred after the Schenectady visit and before May 21st.

In a letter to Dr. Alexanderson, signed by Marconi personally, under date of April 28, 1915, the Italian inventor stated that his New York office was making arrangements for him to visit Schenectady to

[5] Wireless Age, May 1915.
[6] *Ibid.*, June 1915.

witness a demonstration of the Alexanderson Alternator. It was not until May 18th, however, that a telegram to Alexanderson brought the long-expected news:

Coming by train leaving Grand Central at ten thirty today (signed) Marconi.

Dr. Alexanderson has stated to the author that the Marconi party spent the afternoon of that day in studying the alternator and in a tour of the General Electric establishment.

Sec. 80. Marconi and Owen D. Young Confer.

In testimony before a Senate Committee investigating the cable situation January 11, 1921, Mr. Young stated that Marconi's purpose in calling the conference was to arrange if possible a business agreement whereby the Marconi interests might acquire "the rights and if possible, the exclusive rights in this machine" (the Alexanderson Alternator). In a private conference with the author February 5, 1937, Mr. Young elaborated upon this statement in the following manner:

"At this conference between Mr. E. W. Rice, Jr., President of General Electric, Mr. Marconi, Mr. Steadman and myself, a tentative trade was agreed upon under which the General Electric Company would give to the Marconi Companies exclusive right of use in the alternator in consideration of their purchasing a substantial number of alternators at prices which were then discussed, General Electric to retain exclusive rights to manufacture".

It should be explained that Mr. Steadman was the general counsel for the British Marconi Company, thus occupying a position similar to that of Mr. Young in the employ of the General Electric. It appeared also that prior to this meeting with Young, Marconi himself had visited Schenectady to witness a demonstration of the Alexanderson invention. He was, therefore, fully aware of the value of the Alternator in the future development of radio transmission. The negotiations were destined to be tentative only, since the recall of Marconi to military service of Italy frustrated consummation of the deal.

Later in the same year Mr. Steadman returned to America and informed Mr. Young that owing to the war and the resulting disorganization of the radio industry it would be difficult to go ahead with the contemplated program. Thus negotiations languished until the United States entered the war, whereupon the British Marconi Company was notified of the cancellation of all understandings on the subject. The letter from E. W. Rice, Jr., to the Marconi Company bore the date of May 10, 1917.

The year 1915 witnessed notable developments in wireless telephony. The American Telephone and Telegraph Company had long been interested in some means of overcoming the limitations of wire installations. The success of wireless telegraphy had indicated that with the march of science space might yet be conquered for telephonic communications. Fessenden's spectacular feats at Brant Rock had raised hopes for a time but the failure of his company had cancelled the promise of wireless telephony from his endeavors.

The acquisition of a right to use the deForest audion in 1913 had enabled telephone engineers to develop a vacuum tube that produced astounding results in long distance transmission of speech over land wires. Dr. Langmuir, previously mentioned, and Dr. Arnold, each of whom had worked on the deForest audion, were soon in a legal wrangle over patent applications for an improved vacuum tube.

The improved tube, however, was now in operation. By its superior qualities the Telephone Company in 1915 succeeded in its great ambition—telephone conversation between New York City and San Francisco. Nor was this the height of its achievements during the year. In this same year the Telephone Company built a large experimental transmitter and with the permission of the Navy installed it in the wireless station in Arlington, Virginia. This was not a single tube but a huge bank of tubes—five hundred small tubes so arranged as to generate continuous waves and thus render possible projection of the human voice across vast distances.

Now for the first time the voice of man, riding the ether waves, crossed the Atlantic. A speaker in Arlington was heard in Paris. Not only that but the voice flashed across the continent and girdled the Pacific as far west as Honolulu. The result was unbelievable!

The *Electrical World* for February 5, 1916, thus commented upon the Arlington experiment: "Radio-telephony has in the past year begun to come into its own. . . . Within the past few months, experimental demonstrations of radio transmission of speech from Arlington to San Francisco, Paris, Panama and even Honolulu have been announced."

In the meantime at Schenectady, the General Electric Company had at last perfected the Alexanderson Alternator. This instrument was no mere bank of small tubes but a powerful instrument capable of accomplishing with greater certainty the desired result. It was a spinning giant generating powerful waves but so delicately adjusted as to be responsive to the slightest manipulation by its operator. This was the instrument that Marconi had made a pilgrimage to see and for which he negotiated in his conference with Owen D. Young. It is small wonder that Mr. Young himself soon became deeply impressed with the miracle of science that had been achieved in the laboratories of the company whose legal interests he was in duty bound to protect.

The year 1915 may thus be entitled to another distinction—since it was the year in which Owen D. Young, whose genius as an organizer eventually put together the "jigsaw puzzle" of conflicting patent claimants and rival manufacturers, first became acquainted with radio.

In 1915–1916 the experimental station of the American Radio and Research Company at Tufts College in Massachusetts was brought to completion. A tower over 300 feet high, the third largest in the United States, supported by four porcelain insulators set in 15 tons of reinforced concrete, was to be used in experiments in wireless telephony. (See *Electrical World,* Feb. 5, 1916.)

Sec. 81. Lee deForest Resumes Radio Broadcasting.

Although the great secret of wireless transmission of the human voice had now been known to scientists for several years, few had glimpsed its significance. The World War, even though it still seemed that the United States would be able to avoid active participation therein, had absorbed the energies of the leading electrical engineers of the country—Lee deForest among them. But not even war work could wean the great inventor from his passion for probing the mysteries of radio broadcasting. He, it will be remembered, had broadcast the golden voice of Caruso in 1910. Since that date the great inventor had tasted the cup of defeat and had endured nation-wide humiliation. Even now his greatest invention, the audion, was tied up in litigation.

By 1916, however, deForest was able to indulge once more his penchant for radio broadcasting. To be sure, voice transmission was still regarded by the world at large as a mere scientific abstraction that could never become a force in the affairs of men. Much pioneer work must be done before the great awakening. In the light of subsequent events it is little short of amazing that so much was done by Fessenden and deForest in this field without public recognition of the significance of the new science. The true explanation no doubt lies in the fact that the wireless-minded multitude was listening for signals in the Morse code and had no means of capturing voices singing in the wilderness of the skies.

Among the artists who co-operated with deForest at this time was a young lady whose name is familiar to radio listeners, Miss Vaughn de Leath. She is said to have been the first woman to sing into the deForest microphone—a circumstance that led to her being known as the "Original Radio Girl". In describing Miss de Leath's first experience with radio the National Broadcasting News Service, 1938, declares that she was obliged to climb three flights of creaky stairs to reach the deForest workshop. When the inventor introduced her to the crude microphone he waxed poetic and declared:

"You are about to become the first woman ever to sing for people and continents invisible".

DeForest was operating his experimental radio broadcasting station at Highbridge in the Bronx prior to the hotly contested national election of November 7, 1916. With a shrewd eye to its publicity value deForest arranged to flash election bulletins at regular intervals during the evening. The New York *Times* for Wednesday, November 8, 1916, contained the following news item:

"The Bronx produced an election-night innovation when, shortly after dark last evening, the deForest radio laboratories in Highbridge began flashing returns by wireless. Amateur operators within a radius of 200 miles had been forewarned of the new information service, and it was estimated that several thousand of them received the news, many of them through using the newly manufactured wireless telephones."

These wireless telephones, the purchase of which was thus stimulated by their manufacturer, were crude affairs indeed in comparison to radio receiving sets of later years. DeForest was never highly regarded as a manufacturer—his wares being more or less unreliable for continuous service. Since he was pioneering in an uncharted field it was understandable that his wireless telephones should have been afflicted with temperament, static and interference from wireless signals in the Morse code.

DeForest's biographer has thus described the activities of the inventor during the months preceding America's entrance into the World War: "In the summer and fall of 1916, while still engaged in war work for the Allies, deForest started what was considered by the layman to be the first regular broadcasting. The first of the programs were placed on the air from the Columbia Phonograph Laboratories in New York City, consisting chiefly of the company's new records, and picked up by a notable group on the roof of the Hotel Astor where a number of celebrities were celebrating the occasion. At the dinner table were placed many pairs of regular telephone receivers with headbands which were connected to a standard receiver and amplifier. The programs came in strong and clear. Next morning the press heralded the event with big headlines. DeForest saw that radio might at last become an actual public service which could be enjoyed by everyone. Artists who had been engaged to make records now appeared before the microphone. New interests were added to the program. Before long, letters began to pour in praising the station's service and asking for more.

"The first use of the radio broadcast for dissemination of news was in the presidential election of 1916 when the New York *American* ran a special wire to the deForest plant in Highbridge (he had moved his station from New York City to Highbridge) and broadcast news bulletins from hour to hour. At the closing Lee deForest, radio's first announcer, informed his public that 'Charles Evans Hughes has been elected President,' only to be contradicted in the next morning's newspapers.

"DeForest was probably the original broadcast announcer. He personally made many of the announcements in the early years, though his engineers took regular turns at the microphone night after night. This early broadcasting aroused a tremendous amount of interest throughout the East. It was heard in Toronto, Canada, and ships far out at sea, resulting in an increasing demand among amateurs for the deForest products. The company's business was growing rapidly up to the beginning of 1917, when the gathering war clouds compelled the government to shut down on all amateur radio activities, a ban that was not removed until the spring of 1919." [7]

Sec. 82. United States Court Decides against deForest.

On September 20, 1916 the long controversy between the Marconi Company and the deForest Radio Company was at last decided by the District Court of the United States—the decision being adverse to deForest. With a thoroughness characteristic of the court and well merited by the case itself the court went into the history of the controversy and established for all time the facts. From the standpoint of the historian engaged in research concerning a very controversial situation, where claims and counterclaims as to essential facts have been made by partisans, it is refreshing indeed to find court decisions that establish truth so far as human tribunals can hope to establish it.

The language of this decision, in discussing the origin of the audion tube, is very illuminating. For this reason it is reproduced in the court's own words:

"Stripped of technical phraseology, what Fleming did was to take the well-known Edison hot and cold electrode incandescent electric lamp and use it as a detector of radio signals. No one had disclosed or even intimated, the possibility of this use of a device then long known in another art. Cohering filings, magnets, electrolytes, and sensitive crystals, *at that time,* failed to give any hint of the utility in this art of the Edison lamp. What led Fleming to his result was his adherence to the theory of the 'rectified' alternating currents."

[7] An amateur station 2ZK, New Rochelle, N. Y., run by Geo. C. Connor and Charles V. Logwood, broadcast music between 9 and 10 P.M. week days, November, 1916.

The court went on to decide that this new use of the Edison device was patentable by Fleming. After discussing the contentions of the defense that deForest had produced an essentially new device the court said:

"DeForest had long been proceeding on a theory different from that of Fleming. Having read Fleming's article he began to experiment with the incandescent lamp. He probably doubted its efficiency at first but within a very short space of time—perhaps a week, perhaps a month—he changed his mind, and, discovering that Fleming was right, wrote his solicitor, after he had filed his application for No. 824,637, that the new receiver is the best yet. Thereafter he used the language of the incandescent lamp. . . . DeForest in his three-electrode audion has undoubtedly made a contribution of great value to the art . . . but on the other hand Fleming's invention was likewise a contribution of value, and is to be treated liberally and not defeated either by unconfirmed theory or by association in apparatus, where later developments have taught how other useful adjuncts can be employed."

The conclusion was that the deForest invention had infringed that of Fleming, hence that he could not manufacture the three-electrode audion without the consent of the Marconi Company, the owners of the Fleming patent. [8]

Sec. 83. Telephone Company Buys Full Rights to Audion.

Despite the fact that the United States Court had decided that deForest had no right to manufacture the audion for radio purposes since it included two elements of the Fleming patent, yet this decision did not affect the right to use it for telephonic purposes. It was for such wire-line rights that it had paid deForest $50,000 in 1913. Now they wished to obtain the radio rights as well, and in 1914 they purchased these from deForest, for the sum of $90,000, deForest retaining, however, the right to use the invention for certain limited purposes, such as to manufacture and sell it to radio amateurs.

In 1917, a rumor spread that deForest was about to sell his remaining patent rights, over and above the audion proper, to the Atlantic Communications Company. The American Telephone and Telegraph Company sensed that it might lose an invaluable weapon in the field of radio-telephony, toward which its thoughts were rapidly turning. So they made a bid to deForest, and after the usual jockeying for terms, purchased from him for $250,000 all the still outstanding rights under his patents, and under all his applications issued and to be applied for during the next seven years. Among these latter were the then pending feedback or regenerative audion patents.

[8] Marconi Company v. DeForest Radio Telegraph and Telephone Company 236 Fed. 942.

This decision must have given great satisfaction to Lee deForest. Whatever regrets may have been his over the previous transaction he now had an opportunity to retrieve his error. A quarter million dollars was his price—and the Telephone Company paid it.

Upon the outbreak of war, however, all amateur wireless stations had been ordered dismantled, so the right to manufacture for the amateur trade remained valueless throughout the duration of the war. To be sure, rebellious individuals still continued to maintain amateur stations here and there throughout the country, yet they did so at their own peril. Wartime zeal of military and police forces left little opportunity for successful evasion. Even the discontinued Brant Rock station over which Fessenden had conducted his epoch-marking experiments in radio-telephony went down before this command.[9]

An article in *Wireless Age* of October, 1917, put the case thus bluntly to amateur wireless operators:

"It is within the range of possibility that the uninformed amateur experimenter may unintentionally violate the President's executive order in regard to dismantling his wireless apparatus. The following communication from the United States Navy Department calls for attention on the part of the members of the National Amateur Wireless Association:

" 'It has come to the notice of the Navy Department that the President's Executive Order which called for the dismantling of private radio stations has been misinterpreted by many experimenters, publishers and amateurs. By dismantling is meant the *complete disconnection of all pieces of apparatus and antennae, and the sealing and storing of same.* Apparatus which is not dismantled as outlined above is subject to confiscation.'

"The precautions taken by the Navy Department to prevent hostile radio communications are entirely in order and it behooves all experimenters to co-operate with the Government and comply with the President's order to the smallest detail. It is clearly evident that amateurs who attempt to rebuild or improve their apparatus take the risk of meeting with punishment and having their equipment confiscated."

It may well be that the abrupt cutting off of the amateur trade in radio parts had important bearing upon deForest's subsequent career.

[9] Wireless Age, January 1918, p. 268
"A firm of contractors has bought the 420-foot wireless tower at Brant Rock, Mass., a familiar sight to summer visitors, and converted it into junk. The only signal tower like it in the world is on the north coast of Scotland. The station cost the International Signal Company $1,000,000 to build, it being the first erected on the Atlantic Coast, at which early experiments on the 500-cycle transmission apparatus were made, in the United States. The tower was cylindrical in shape and supported by wire cable stays. The plant made 60 tons of scrap iron and steel, including the cylindrical standard and the wire cables."

While he continued in war work until the conclusion of hostilities, yet his inventive genius had by this time turned into other fields. The rising film industry offered scope for men of scientific bent. In this field deForest has accomplished notable results. His audion, however, was probably his greatest contribution to science.

The Federal Telegraph Company, the chief rival of the Marconi Company, had built up a considerable business in wireless transmission, especially on the west coast. It owned patents of considerable value. Early in the summer of 1917 there were rumors that the Federal Telegraph Company was in negotiation with the Marconi Company in regard to a consolidation whereby the latter would take over the patents and physical assets of the Federal Company. Whether these rumors were fed to the Navy Department as a means of stimulating a hoped-for sale to the Government is by no means clear. The probabilities are that there was a basis of fact for the report. Subsequent disclosures, however, indicate that the sale to the United States Government was engineered under suspicious circumstances. A scandal of major importance was averted by the suicide of one of the chief actors in the transaction and the resignation of suspected officials. [10]

Sec. 84. The Government Takes Over All Wireless Stations.

By proclamation on the day following the declaration of war in April, 1917,[11] President Wilson directed the Navy to take over all wireless stations in the United States and its possessions that were not already under the control of the Army. With patriotic zeal wireless officials complied wholeheartedly with the proclamation and turned over to the Government not only their physical equipment but all available talent, technicians and research workers.

The grim business of war now gave great impetus to the development of the art of radio transmission. The Government could do what

[10] History of the Bureau of Engineering—Navy Dept.—During World War (1922 —a Government Bulletin)

"About 10 months after our entry into the war negotiations were begun by the Navy Department with the Federal Telegraph Co. for the purchase of its patents and shore stations. These negotiations were concluded satisfactorily and on May 15, 1918, the Government acquired the patents of this company and its shore stations —three high-power and five coastal—for the sum of $1,600,000. . . . The Marconi Company would consent to sell their ship installations only on the condition that the Government buy also their coastal radio stations. This was agreed to, and the purchase of 330 ship installations and 45 coastal stations was effected, as of November 30, 1918, for the sum of $1,450,000."

[11] Wireless Age, May 1917, p. 549

Acting under instructions from the Navy Department at Washington on April 8th, the military and police authorities throughout the country began dismantling all sets of wireless apparatus, with the exception of those used by the Government or under the direct supervision of United States officials.

private firms could not—combine the scientific resources of all electrical manufacturers in one common endeavor. Because of national necessity all claimants must bow their heads to the inevitable and so long as that necessity should continue there was no redress for infringement of patents except to file claims for damages with the Court of Claims.[12] Patent infringement barriers were thus broken down and electrical engineers in the employ of the Government were able to utilize anything and everything that might aid them to accomplish their objective.

It so happened that at the time of the taking over of wireless stations there was being installed in the New Brunswick, N.J., station of the Marconi Wireless Telegraph Company an instrument that was to revolutionize wireless transmission—the famous Alexanderson Alternator previously described in these pages. The General Electric Company had spent large sums in developing this powerful transmitter. As we have seen, the great Marconi himself made a pilgrimage to Schenectady in May, 1915, to witness a laboratory test of the device. The Italian inventor had become so convinced of its value that he had thereupon endeavored to purchase exclusive rights for the British Marconi Company in the Alexanderson Alternator. Negotiations had been broken off. Now, however, the General Electric Company had made arrangements with the Marconi Company of America to install a 50 k.w. alternator for the purpose of testing the device on trans-oceanic communications.

There is some controversy over whether the 50 k.w. alternator was purchased by the Marconi Company, or loaned by the General Electric Company. Owen D. Young and Dr. Alexanderson are of the opinion that it was loaned. Mr. Nally and David Sarnoff declare that it was purchased by the Marconi Company. In an effort to clarify the matter the author wrote to Captain S. C. Hooper, the naval official who had charge of the purchase of wireless equipment during that period. Captain Hooper's reply, under date June 21, 1938, gives the following illuminating information:

[12] For evidence of this action of the Government see letter of Franklin D. Roosevelt, Acting Secretary of the Navy, April 3, 1918, to Marconi Wireless Telegraph Company:

"The Department, having in view the Government's interests and the exceptional public necessity that the apparatus called for in your contracts be procured as soon as possible, hereby directs and requires you to proceed uninterruptedly and expeditiously with the fulfillment of the said contracts, using and embodying in such apparatus, any patented invention necessarily required for that purpose. In order that you may be protected against hindrance by litigation for any purpose, by reason of infringement of patents, the Department hereby guarantees to hold and save you harmless against claims of any and all kinds for or on account of the use of patented inventions in the manufacture and production of said apparatus, and your contracts are each and severally hereby modified accordingly."

"When the trans-Atlantic German cables were cut, it was necessary to improve radio communication between the United States and Germany. This matter was so urgent, and existing equipment so inadequate (it was what one might call experimental), that in an effort to improve matters the Navy initiated an arrangement with the General Electric Company and the Marconi Company that the 50 k.w. Alexanderson machine be installed at New Brunswick, one of the American Marconi Company's stations. . . . Actually, in a nutshell, the Navy initiated and pushed through the whole matter; the Marconi Company assisted in every way; and finally the Marconi Company paid for the equipment after the War because it was in their station, they wanted it and the Navy had no further use for it."

It should be pointed out that the final paragraph in the above refers not only to the 50 k.w. alternator but also to a 200 k.w. alternator that was later installed. The reason for the confusion as to the facts is thus apparent: The Navy Department did not pay for the alternators in cash but made suitable allowances for use of them when the station was restored to the Marconi Company. The latter, at the time of the return of the New Brunswick station, was transferring its physical assets to RCA, which in turn was dealing with the General Electric Company. In the adjustment of equities between the three corporations the cost of the alternators would naturally have been taken into consideration. It is small wonder that confusion developed as to the facts of sale or loan.

Turning to the records of the General Electric Company we find that on February 9, 1917 the Marconi Company wrote to the General Electric Company about shipping the machine from Schenectady to New Brunswick, N.J. On February 14th a second letter was written by the Marconi Company with reference to arrangements for trucking the alternator. It is certain that not until July, 1917, was the apparatus fully installed. On July 12, 1917, Marconi himself visited the station to witness trans-Atlantic tests both for telegraphy and telephony.

During the summer of 1917 the 50 k.w. Alexanderson Alternator demonstrated great superiority over other types of equipment. The Navy Department was well aware that the General Electric Company was then building a 200 k.w. alternator. Believing that this machine would prove of great value to navy communications, Lieutenant-Commander S. C. Hooper, U.S.N., on October 1, 1917, wrote to the General Electric Company concerning it. The following extracts from his letter and from the response are of great historical significance:

"Further information is requested," wrote Hooper, "as to whether you will have at an early date any of the Alexanderson high frequency machines ready for delivery. Circumstances have arisen that make it necessary to have from one to several high power frequency machines at a comparatively early date."

In response to this inquiry E. P. Edwards, Assistant Manager of the Lighting Department of the General Electric Company, wrote in part as follows: "We are now building a 200 k.w. Alexanderson Alternator which we expect to bring to test together with other elements of the Alexanderson system of which the Alternator forms a part, during January of 1918. If our expectations are realized these tests will be of short duration; their purpose being to determine the mechanical balance of the adjustment of the air gap, etc. We do not believe it will be necessary to conduct any electrical tests. This equipment, therefore, should be ready for shipment some time in January. . . . While the 200 k.w. outfit will be approximately four times the capacity of the set now installed at New Brunswick, we are recommending the installation of two 200 k.w. outfits in each station; each being capable of radiating at least 400 amperes from a suitably designed and constructed antenna, similar to the New Brunswick antenna of the Marconi Company but modified to provide for multiple tuning. The two 200 k.w. alternators can be operated as a unit when necessary, to meet the most unfavorable conditions. . . . One unit could, of course, be used by itself under ordinary conditions of sending."

The installation of the 200 k.w. alternator was completed during the winter of 1918. The United States Government was thus enabled to communicate by wireless telegraphy with the embattled Allies and with our own Expeditionary Forces in France. It has been pointed out in a previous chapter that Alexanderson had already invented his system of multiple tuning of antennae and also his tuned amplifier radio frequency. These improvements were being tested at the New Brunswick wireless station. So successful did they prove that this station became at once the most powerful wireless station in the world. Thus the United States had added a new and powerful instrumentality to the service of mankind in general and to the Allies in particular. The great Republic of the West was no longer separated from Europe by a vast ocean because the genius of its scientists had evolved a dependable means of wireless communication.

The call letters of the New Brunswick, N. J. station were NFF. It is said that battleships in all parts of the world were able to pick up the wireless signals of this station. So clear and powerful was its operation that even portable field sets in France could tune in on NFF. Field newspapers distributed among the American soldiers in France depended quite largely upon NFF for the latest news from home. It thus operated as a daily news service of international character that kept the American troops in touch with home events and with public opinion in the United States.

Sec. 85. President Wilson Speaks to the World.

The Naval Communications Board that had been functioning since 1914 had an unrivaled opportunity to demonstrate its effectiveness in the World War. The new 200 kilowatt Alexanderson Alternator was accomplishing undreamed-of results. With powerful stations in the Pacific it was possible for the United States to girdle the globe with its wireless messages.

President Woodrow Wilson had a keen appreciation of the power of the spoken or written word to mold the opinions of men. Germany had already set the example of utilizing wireless messages to circulate propaganda in enemy territory. The American President, therefore, resolved to demonstrate the power of the pen in a world of unsheathed swords. Carefully he prepared his first great wireless message to the world. The story of how this event was engineered has thus been set forth in the January, 1918, issue of *Wireless Age:*

"The record of two extraordinary circumstances will go down to posterity with President Wilson's masterly message giving the aims and basis for World peace. The first circumstance is the manner in which it was distributed throughout the reading world; second the remarkably short time—one hour and forty-five minutes—it took to spread it broadcast. A full half hour before the President's message was flashed to all the ends of the earth—to every point in Europe, Asia, Africa, Australia, South and North America, every island in the Atlantic, Pacific and Indian Oceans, possessing a telegraph or wireless instrument, newspaper or courier service—word had gone out to 'clear the way for an important address by President Wilson.'

"The mighty naval radio stations at San Diego and Darien [14] were primed to play their part. Shortly after Darien, which is on the Isthmus of Panama, flashed the word to the Pacific, Atlantic and Indian Ocean islands that something big was coming and to lend an ear, the operator at Helgoland, it is believed by naval officers, became immediately attentive. There was extraordinary power and punch in the Darien operator's key, and it is fair to assume the Prussian operators at the Hamburg, Kiel, Berlin, Karlsruhe, Frankfort, Prague, Vienna, Constantinople, and Philippopolis radio stations were brought to a sharp state of wakefulness.

"Promptly at 12:30 o'clock, New York time, the director of the Division of the Foreign Press Service of the Committee of Public Information signalled the cable companies and the Naval radio station

[14] The 200 k.w. Alexanderson Alternator not yet being installed at New Brunswick, N. J.

at Brooklyn to begin sending the President's message. Until the message was fully transmitted seven men in the room were kept under lock and key. Advance word on the message would have been of tremendous importance in Wall Street. The message from Washington came over the Government's private wire. After it was received it was read back to Washington by telephone to make sure that every word was correct. . . . When the message was verified by Washington it was split into 'cable takes' of about 100 words each, and the operators started their work. The message contained about 2700 words."

The President, in this famous speech to a joint session of the Congress, January 8, 1918, struck out with the vigor of a Jeremiah. "We entered this war," he declared, "because violations of right had occurred which touched us to the quick and made the life of our own people impossible unless they were corrected and the world secured once for all against their recurrence. What we demand in this war, therefore, is nothing peculiar to ourselves. It is that the world be made fit and safe to live in; and particularly that it be made safe for every peace-loving nation which, like our own, wishes to live its own life, determine its own institutions, be assured of justice and fair dealings by the other peoples of the world as against force and selfish aggression. All the peoples of the world are in effect partners in this interest, and for our own part we see very clearly that unless justice be done to others it will not be done to us."

The President then went on to enunciate his famous "Fourteen Points" as essential to a just peace.

"For such arrangements and covenants we are willing to fight and to continue to fight until they are achieved," he declared, "but only because we wish the right to prevail and desire a just and stable peace, such as can be secured only by removing the chief provocations to war, which this program does remove. . . . The moral climax of this, the culminating and final war for human liberty, has come and they (i.e., the people of the United States) are ready to put their own strength, their own highest purpose, their own integrity and devotion to the test."

What a pity that our great moral spokesman could have been so deceived by his own exalted optimism!

Sec. 86. Radio Highlights of America's War Time.

Although the Government had closed down all except Federally operated radio stations for the duration of the war, this did not mean that radio opportunities were to be denied the ambitious amateur. Quite the reverse was true. Spurred by wartime necessity, the Government established in each district radio schools for preliminary training in radio telegraphy in order to supply the demand for trained operators. One or more advanced schools of radio were needed. In the summer of 1917 Harvard University offered dormitory and other facilities to the Government for such a school. From a small beginning was speedily recruited a mammoth radio school. The courses being intensive and the need great, a group of operatives would finish the four months' training and graduate into active service—a new group of fifty to one hundred operators each week. Classes were recruited wholesale through the Navy recruiting office and moved from preliminary training schools to the Harvard Radio School.

A similar school was established by the Government on the Pacific Coast at Mare Island, Calif. with equally amazing results. By December, 1917, nearly five thousand radio students were attending Harvard and the Mare Island Training School.[15] Radio amateurs thus discovered that the disappointment involved in the closing of their homemade wireless plants was more than compensated for by the unexpected opportunity to receive technical training at Government expense.

It was soon discovered by these Government schools that students who were formerly amateur experimenters outshone all others from every standpoint, possessing a certain keenness in manipulating wireless equipment which land line telegraphers required several months of close application to acquire.[16]

The Naval Communications Service also made notable progress during the first six months of America's participation in the War. Radio communication was established between the United States and its island possessions in the Pacific and between the United States and Europe. For the first time Italy and the United States were thus united. Three important high-powered wireless stations were completed—one at San Diego, Calif., another at Pearl Harbor, Hawaii, and a third at Cavite in the Philippines. By December, 1917, all three of these stations were in operation.

The United States signal corps in France performed notable service, especially in the science of wireless reception and transmission. A problem that had baffled Allied engineers for a long time was that of German high frequency wireless messages that were being sent out by military units beyond No-Man's land. Each unit had its wireless equipment. Prior to every German attack it was observable that the massing of troops brought wireless concentration. No satisfactory means had been discovered to capture and decode German high-frequency messages. If this could be accomplished the Allied forces might determine the location of the units and the military strength that was being assembled for an offensive. Edwin H. Armstrong, previously mentioned in connection with the invention of the "feed back" or regenerative

15 Wireless Age, October 1918, p. 42.
16 *Ibid.*, January 1918, p. 707.

principle of wireless, then an officer in the United States signal corps in France, is entitled to the honor of having solved the problem. He had long been familiar with Fessenden's heterodyne system. The German signals, however, could not be heterodyned to audio-frequency. Armstrong invented a highly technical system in the spring of 1918 which he called "Super-Heterodyne". Radio engineers at once adopted the super-heterodyne as one of the great technical advances in the field of wireless.

Much of the progress accomplished by technicians working under Government supervision during the war was necessarily shrouded in mystery. Not even technical journals were informed of what was going forward, as witness the following item in *Wireless Age* for June, 1918, p. 781:

"It is again necessary to state that we have no definite information concerning the vacuum valve situation. Just when amateurs will be able to purchase evacuated tubes after the war we cannot say; but it is highly probable that such tubes will be available for amateurs' use. It is equally possible that the vacuum tube will come in for considerable use on the part of amateurs for purposes of transmission. At least the tube will permit communication over short ranges and it will provide a transmitter of greater simplicity than the amateur ordinarily is accustomed to use."

It should also be noted that at the request of the Navy Department all litigation then pending over patent infringements was suspended for the duration of the war,[17] all persons aggrieved having a right to apply for redress to the court of claims. This involved the various important actions instituted by the Marconi Company as well as those in which domestic companies were parties plaintiff.

Sec. 87. President Wilson Speaks to German People.

By this time the General Electric Company had put into the hands of the Navy Department a weapon more powerful and far-reaching than anything previously devised by man—a 200 k.w. Alexanderson Alternator in the New Brunswick, N.J., station. Thus in June, 1918, when the World War was at its most critical stage the 200 k.w. marvel of science was put into operation—made available for President Woodrow Wilson's efforts to end Christendom's orgy of bloodshed.

The part played by President Wilson in the events leading to the Armistice cannot be overestimated. His "Fourteen Points" had ten months earlier captured the imagination of a war-weary world. He was the one man in Christendom whose views could command uni-

[17] Wireless Age, July 1918, p. 796.

versal respect. Fortunately wireless telegraphy had provided a medium through which his logic could appeal directly to the common people of all nations and even strike real blows at the tottering throne of the Kaiser. Numerous notes had been exchanged relative to a peace conference, especially with Austria-Hungary, whose war organization was visibly crumbling. On October 6th the German Government began overtures for a peace conference on the basis of the "Fourteen Points" speech and other similar addresses. After several exchanges President Wilson decided upon the bold stroke of a subtle appeal to the German people to repudiate their war-guilty rulers. The part played by wireless is thus described by the New York *Evening Post* (quoted in the *Wireless Age*):

"It was 12 o'clock noon—one day about October 20 last—when every Government wireless operator on duty in the Allied Countries was startled out of his wits by a signal call from the radio station at New Brunswick, N. J. The operators of the wireless stations of the Central Powers could not have been more surprised.

"'POZ-POZ-POZ-deNFF' buzzed the wireless. The Allied operators saw immediately visions of brazen treachery or equally brazen German spy operations in the United States. They saw visions of American war scandal, such as the world had never known, court martials and firing squads and possible revolution in America.

"For POZ is the radio call for the German Government station at Nauen, a suburb of Berlin and NFF is the radio address of the United States naval sending station at New Brunswick, and the two had not been on speaking terms for a long time.

"There must have been a real Prussian at the Nauen switchboard, for within two or three minutes he responded patronizingly: 'Your signals are fine, old man.'

"Whereupon the 'old man' in New Brunswick proceeded to dispatch through the ether a message which was not so fine as it was clear. No code was used. The message was in plain English. It was the first of President Wilson's statements to the German people carrying the suggestion that the Allies would conduct no negotiations for an armistice and peace with the German Government as then constituted." [18]

When we consult President Wilson's state papers we discover that he indeed addressed plain language to the German people, as witness the following extract:

"The nations associated against Germany cannot be expected to agree to a cessation of arms while acts of inhumanity, spoliation and desolation are being continued which they justly look upon with horror and with burning hearts.

[18] Wireless Age, July 1919, p. 8.

"It is necessary also, in order that there may be no possibility of misunderstanding, that the President should very solemnly call the attention of the Government of Germany to the language and plain intent of one of the terms of peace which the German Government has now accepted. It is contained in the address of the President delivered at Mt. Vernon on the Fourth of July last. It is as follows: 'The destruction of every arbitrary power anywhere that can separately, secretly and of its single choice disturb the peace of the world, or, if it cannot be presently destroyed, at least its reduction to virtual impotency. The power which has hitherto controlled the German nation is the sort here described. *It is within the choice of the German nation to alter it.*' The President's words just quoted naturally constitute a condition precedent to peace, if peace is to come by the action of the German people themselves. The President feels bound to say that the whole process of peace will, in his judgment, depend upon the definiteness *and satisfactory character of the guarantees which can be given in this fundamental matter.*"

Sec. 88. The Alexanderson-Beverage Static Eliminator.

During the war period serious doubt arose that wireless telegraphy could ever be more than an intermittent service, particularly during the summer months when static became severe. At such times wireless communication was either completely interrupted or materially slowed down. Radio experts at that period, therefore, devoted much thought to the problem of static elimination. Many theories were advanced as to how this might be accomplished. One of those efforts was to attempt to devise some new type of receiver by which static might be eliminated by a process of filtration. These efforts naturally led to hopes and illusions of success that were invariably doomed to disappointment. Another line of thought was that new antenna systems might be devised which would pick up the signal and reject the static. The difficulty in all these efforts was that the true nature of static was not yet understood. Experimental work on false premises was naturally unproductive of satisfactory results.

Roy A. Weagant, for example, believed that static came from above. He was so capable an experimenter, however, that notwithstanding this misconception he accomplished genuine advance in antenna construction. The discovery of the actual nature of static came about as discoveries often do, by an accident. That discovery is a story in itself and brings us again to that capable personage—Ernst F. W. Alexanderson. Alexanderson and his assistant, Harold H. Beverage (now Chief Research Engineer of RCA but then a young man less than three years out of college) were working on the problem of outwitting man-made static, or the German radio barrage that was then in operation.

At an Inter-Allied Conference in February, 1918, bitter complaints had been voiced that German wireless was being used to blanket the wireless messages of the Allies. Appeals for a solution were made and Alexanderson was one of the engineers to whom the problem was presented. With characteristic ingenuity he set to work and produced what was labeled Alexanderson's "Barrage Receiver." This ingenious device could be used to neutralize signals or to destroy interference. When set up within three miles of the powerful New Brunswick, N. J., trans-Atlantic station it successfully cut off the powerful signals from that station but permitted the signals originating in Europe to be heard.

The accident involved in that case was that the barrage receiver actually cut off not only the New Brunswick station but the baffling enemy, static, as well. The new system was exceedingly simple. A wire two miles long extended from the point of junction in a northeasterly direction—this being the general direction of Europe. The wire rested upon the ground. A second wire of similar length extended in the opposite direction. The wires were joined in a set of balancing coils through which one type of signal could be subtracted from the other. When it was observed that the demon static that had so plagued them no longer whistled and howled Alexanderson and Beverage immediately understood that they had discovered the nature of static and had hit upon a means for its elimination. They had discovered that static in the eastern United States is an electro-magnetic wave motion similar to a wireless signal and originating in the region of the Gulf of Mexico except in case of thunder storms occurring on the northerly side of the station. By great good fortune their line, extending in the southwesterly direction, pointed at the Gulf of Mexico.

This discovery was reported to the Navy Department. Quick to seize upon the idea the Naval officials at once sent Beverage to Bar Harbor to install a barrage or anti-static receiver at that point. When this task had been completed Alexanderson sent Beverage to the northern end of Long Island to conduct experiments in length of receiver. Beverage's daily reports soon established that the longer the line the greater its efficiency in static elimination. When the line had reached ten miles it was discovered that static had been almost entirely eliminated without the necessity of using the balancing coils.

Further analyzing the results Beverage found that the ground connections in the northeast end, due to the sandy soil of Long Island, were exactly right for maximum results. This gave him the clue that led to a scientific study of the phenomenon. He was assisted in this important work by Chester W. Rice. He later presented the result of these studies to the Institute of Radio Engineers. The device was patented as the Beverage Antenna.

An interesting story is told by Dr. Alexanderson of an experience that befell the two inventors when they were installing the experimental antenna near the New Brunswick station. He and Beverage made their headquarters at an old barn, it being necessary to work with secrecy. This being in the days when German spies were greatly feared, the simple country folk decided that the mysterious strangers must be German spies. One night a posse gathered and rushed the barn, but neither Beverage nor Alexanderson was there at the time. A hapless tramp was captured but not even a suspicious mob could picture the disheveled derelict as a German spy.

Sec. 89. Wilson Goes to France for Peace Parleys.

Having thus departed from diplomatic usages, thereby earning the applause of the world, President Wilson continued to address the German people, although ostensibly replying to their Premier. The disastrous effect upon the fortunes of the German Kaiser is too well known to need extended mention in this connection. By wireless the energetic American President, with his extraordinary ability as a writer of rapier-like English, broadcast messages to the disheartened hosts of the Central Powers. The might of American arms and the resurgence of hope in the Allied ranks because of America's entrance into the war lent force to every word that Woodrow Wilson uttered touching the subject of peace during those trying weeks terminating in the Armistice of November 11, 1918.

The New Brunswick station had already demonstrated that it was more powerful than any other wireless station in the world.[19] This no doubt had influence upon the President's decision to attend the coming Peace Conference in Paris. Arrangements were accordingly made to equip the *S.S. George Washington,* on which the President was to travel across the Atlantic, with wireless equipment that would enable the Chief Executive to keep in constant touch with Washington during the voyage. The naval flagship, the battleship *Pennsylvania,* which accompanied the *George Washington,* was likewise equipped with up-to-date receiving apparatus as well as having the most powerful transmitter afloat.

Of great significance to radio is the fact that both ships were equipped with radio telephones by which the President might talk with the commander of the *Pennsylvania.* The arrangement for shore station co-operation was as follows:

"At three special naval radio receiving stations, one in Maine, one in New Jersey, and one in the Navy Building, Washington, expert operators listened continuously for the *Pennsylvania's* messages. The messages when received were forwarded with utmost despatch to the

[19] Wireless Age, January 1919, p. 7.

trans-Atlantic radio division of the office of the Director of Naval Communications in the Navy Department, and the three copies compared to insure accuracy. All outgoing messages passed through the same office in Washington.

"As the Presidential party approached Europe, by arrangement with the Navy Department, special receiving stations in both England and France listened for messages from the *Pennsylvania* and one of the French high power stations forwarded messages direct to the ship. The President was thus kept in touch with Washington and Paris or London simultaneously."

The record of that memorable voyage shows the following facts: The S.S. *George Washington* sailed from New York harbor December 4, 1918 and arrived in France December 13th. The Peace Conference itself did not convene until January 12th, 1919. The intervening period was occupied by preparations for the conference, not the least of which was the triumphal progress of President Wilson through the Allied countries, where he was hailed by the common people as their deliverer and by the rulers with the deference due to his high station. The wily diplomats with whom he was to match wits no doubt regarded him as a publicity-loving idealist who must be flattered and cajoled, but whose impractical idealism must be checkmated at all costs.[20]

Four weeks of adulation in Allied countries, the center of interest in mighty throngs of cheering humanity, could not fail to have convinced Woodrow Wilson that he had acted wisely in coming to Europe to oversee the Peace Conference. His words carried to the four corners of the earth by the magic of wireless telegraphy had accomplished the undoing of the Central Powers. Germany had agreed to the Armistice in reliance upon the terms that had been outlined by the American President, especially the terms popularly known as the "Fourteen Points" contained in his first world-wide wireless message of January 8, 1918.

President Wilson would have been more than human if he had not thrilled at the discovery that even in humble villages in Europe, school

[20] Intimate Papers of Col. House, Vol. IV, p. 250.
"The coming of President Wilson to Europe stimulated lively interest in political circles. The statesmen recognized the influence which he exercised over the popular mind and were somewhat disturbed by their ignorance of his intentions. How was he minded to apply the principles with which his name had become synonymous, and what sort of revolution in international affairs would his application imply? Of all the European leaders, only Mr. Balfour and M. Tardieu had met and talked with the President. They set themselves to learn everything possible about him, his background, his tastes, his prejudices. Mr. Lloyd George, inviting Sir William Wiseman to luncheon, cross-examined the latter for upwards of an hour regarding the President. Possibly they were less sorry for the inevitable delay in calling the Peace Conference, since it gave them a chance to study the attitude they would take toward the President."

children were studying his "Fourteen Points" as reverently as though they were articles of religious faith. He must have realized that he now occupied the most exalted place in the hearts of the common people of every nation that was ever enjoyed by mortal man. In his eloquent words they had found their own yearnings for peace and justice powerfully and adequately expressed. The universal adulation encountered in Europe must have convinced our own war-weary President that he was indeed the prophet who should have the glory hereafter of having ushered in the millennium when nations should learn to war no more.

What a disillusionment must have been his at the Peace Conference when the hardened sinners of diplomacy gathered in conclave! Altruism and lofty purpose were on his tongue and in his heart but on their tongues were honeyed phrases intended to beguile the unsuspicious American President while they secretly labored to accomplish age-old chicanery and selfish spoils-gathering so characteristic of Old-World diplomacy.

President Wilson's first shock of disillusionment must have come to him on the opening day of the Conference. One of his "Fourteen Points" had been "open Covenants of Peace openly arrived at," yet to his dismay the delegates of the Allied nations at once refused to permit representatives of the press to attend the sessions. Not only that but they banned publicity. Wilson was thus placed in a most awkward position. Journalists from all over the world had gathered in Paris to report the much-heralded new diplomacy—the diplomacy of righteousness and high ideals, for Wilson had promised that "diplomacy shall proceed always frankly and in the public view,"—yet the event proved that the sinister diplomacy of secret sessions still held sway.

Tooth and nail the American President fought his crafty associates, battling for his "Fourteen Points" and especially for his pet project—the League of Nations. To a man of Wilson's temperament, a pedagogue from his youth up, and the imperious ruler of a great people, this flouting of his advice must have been very hard to bear. The Allied leaders had encouraged him to violate a national tradition by crossing the sea in order that they might have his personal counsel in the interpretation and application of his "Fourteen Points." They now treated him as though he were a noisy demagogue in an arena of fighting men.

Wilson saw with clear vision that he had walked into a sordid mêlée in which every nation was seeking advantage for itself. What could he do in such a contest to safeguard the interests of the United States? There was obviously one great international advantage possessed by his own countrymen—their great inventions in the field of wireless communications that had enabled him to speak to a world audience.

ALBERT G. DAVIS
Vice-President of General Electric.

GEN. JAMES G. HARBORD
Second President of RCA.

EDWARD J. NALLY
First President of RCA.

*Sec. 90. Did Wilson Take Action to Safeguard American Pre-eminence
in Radio?*

Since there has been considerable controversy [21] over what if anything President Wilson did while abroad to safeguard American interests in wireless communication, it may be well to present the following pertinent circumstantial evidence: Walter S. Rogers was the communications expert of the American Commission to Negotiate Peace.
On February 12, 1919, while President Wilson was locked in battle
with the Old World diplomats, Rogers presented to him a masterly
brief on world communications in which the following stinging reference to Great Britain's monopoly of the cables occurs:

"When communication facilities are controlled by one nation which
gives its commerce and its press preferential service or rates, misunder-
standings are sure to arise. The attached memorandum contains constructive suggestions aimed to prevent animosities growing out of unfair use of communication facilities, or arising from a lack of facilities,
and to provide for a generous flow of intelligence in all directions." [22]

This thought to a statesman of Wilson's keen intellect might have
been sufficient to stir him to action, but Rogers was so deeply moved
by the subject that in the portion of the brief in which he discusses
wireless and radio he makes direct appeal to the President.

". . . There is also a call to the newer world statesmanship not only
to further the breaking down of barriers, but actively to assist in the
development of wire and radio communications. Science stands ready
to do its part.

". . . High-power radio, with its unlimited possibilities for broadcasting messages to the ends of the earth, presents a startling opportunity
for disseminating intelligence." [23]

With such a document in his hands is it likely that President Wilson
could have failed to give thought to the interests of his own country?
Let us proceed to other evidence: It is well known that the President
won a partial victory in securing the assent of the Peace Conference to
his League of Nations plan, after which he made a hasty trip to the
United States to lay the League Covenant before the Congress and to
attend to his Constitutional duties in connection with the expiring
session of Congress. He left France on the *S.S. George Washington* February 15th and returned to French soil on March 14th. During the
eighteen days on shipboard he had kept in touch with the world by

[21] See Hearings December 9, 17, 1929 before Committee on Interstate Commerce,
United States Senate.
[22] Ray Stannard Baker—"Woodrow Wilson and World Settlement," Vol. III, p. 428.
[23] *Ibid.*

wireless telegraphy, all because the genius of American engineers had made possible so great a marvel of science.

On February 22, 1919, while President Wilson was still 900 miles from Washington, the wireless telephone on the *George Washington* received a call from the national capital that must have thrilled the American President. The office of the Secretary of the Navy was calling by wireless telephone, desiring to talk with President Wilson. The Chief Executive picked up the receiver and from far-off Washington came a familiar voice. We have no report of the exact conversation on that historic occasion but we do know that the event was an everlasting testimonial to the genius of Ernst F. W. Alexanderson. Previous to this time large antennae tuned for long-wave telegraphy had not been capable of the modulation needful for wireless telephony. Alexanderson had recently perfected his new system of multiple tuning. In response to a request from the Navy Department he had arrived at the New Brunswick, N. J., station on February 18th to endeavor to arrange for the telephone conversation. The antenna was so busy with telegraphic communication that only two hours out of twenty-four could be allowed for telephonic testing. In the last testing period, when the station was at length equipped for telephonic communication, it was necessary to have conversation going on constantly. Sailors were called upon to keep the lines busy by talking with their girl friends. It is probable that no call to volunteer for God and country was ever answered with such alacrity as on this occasion. The station was tuned and made ready for the great moment. This round-trip voyage should have given President Wilson opportunity to decide what to do about American wireless without the following frank reminder from Washington.

Postmaster General Burleson sent him a cablegram that was placed in the President's hands on March 15th, 1919. In the cablegram was the following paragraph:

"Our ships and merchant marine now have to depend upon the courtesy of foreign-controlled means of communication to get home connections. The world system of international electric communications has been built up in order to connect the Old World commercial centers with that World business. The United States is connected on one side only." [24]

Sec. 91. Admiral Grayson's Testimony.

It will appear in the following chapter that Owen D. Young declares that Admiral William H. G. Bullard came to him while the President was in Paris, saying that Wilson had sent him on a special mission to

[24] Baker—"Woodrow Wilson and World Settlement," Vol. III, p. 425.

see to it that British interests should not gain possession of the Alexanderson Alternator, and other inventions held by American manufacturers. No direct evidence has yet been discovered of the authenticity of Bullard's mission, yet we have another bit of circumstantial evidence:

At the hearing before the Senate Committee in 1929 when Mr. Young was challenged by anti-monopoly Senators—Admiral Bullard and President Wilson both being dead—Admiral Cary T. Grayson came forward voluntarily with important testimony:

Senator Pittman: And were you with President Wilson in Paris in 1919?

Admiral Grayson: Yes, sir.

Senator Pittman: In what capacity were you with him at that time?

Admiral Grayson: As physician and Naval aide.

Senator Pittman: You have heard my statement here with regard to the misunderstanding concerning some testimony. I will ask if you know anything with regard to the President's action in connection with Admiral Bullard's carrying a message to Mr. Owen D. Young relative to radio?

Admiral Grayson: One morning the President, when the question was being discussed about radio, and I was out with him in the morning, soon after breakfast, driving, said to me, "I wish you would remind me today to get in touch and communication with the Navy Department officially or with Admiral Bullard. I have an important message that I want to send to Mr. Owen D. Young relative to the protection of American rights and possibilities in radio communications."

Senator Pittman: Did you carry out these instructions?

Admiral Grayson: I did, sir.

The Chairman: Do you recall what date that was?

Admiral Grayson: No, sir. I do not recall exactly. That was in 1919.

The Chairman: What part of 1919?

Admiral Grayson: Well, I would think it was—I do not remember exactly. I do not know the month.

Senator Dill: Was Admiral Bullard in Paris then?

Admiral Grayson: I think he was. He was there off and on. I saw him a number of times. I do not know whether he was there that day or not.

Senator Wheeler: How do you come to remember this conversation so distinctly?

Admiral Grayson: Well, when the question was brought up, and I heard some question about it three or four years ago, I happened to be with Senator Pittman, and I told him the story, and he came by this morning and asked me would I come down and repeat the story that I told him once.

Senator Wheeler: Did you have any other conversation with President Wilson at that time that you recall?

Admiral Grayson: Well, I had a good many, but this was—

Senator Wheeler: Do you recall where it was, or when it was?

Admiral Grayson: Well, it was in Paris, and on this morning it was soon after breakfast. It was in the Bois, to be exact. We were on a motor ride together to get a little fresh air right after breakfast, before the meeting of the Big Four at 10 o'clock.

Senator Dill: Do you know what the message was that he sent to Admiral Bullard?

Admiral Grayson: I do not know any more than what I just said, that he wanted to be reminded to get into communication with him for that purpose.

Senator Pittman: Well, Admiral, I do not care about your going into the whole story, because it is a long story, as I remember it, but was there considerable discussion in Paris at that time with regard to radio regulation and control?

Admiral Grayson: Yes, sir. Mr. Marconi was there, Senator.

Senator Dill: Of course, nothing happened then that has anything to do with the present practices that have developed with radio, as the result of that message? President Wilson had only in mind having the Alexanderson Alternator from going to the British Marconi? I take it that is what he had in mind? That is what Admiral Bullard tried to prevent being sold to the British Marconi?

Admiral Grayson: I think so.

Senator Hawes: Admiral, was not this the situation, that the President, fearing that there might be a sale of this property, sent for Admiral Bullard to communicate with Mr. Young and others that he thought it was the duty of patriotic Americans to retain this property in their possession and not part with it, either financially or in a power way?

Admiral Grayson: Yes, sir.

Senator Hawes: That was your idea of the appeal that was being made by the President to Mr. Young, through Admiral Bullard?

Admiral Grayson: Yes, sir.

The Chairman: Is that all?

Senator Pittman: That is all I wanted to ask, Mr. Chairman. I did not want him to go into the conversation with President Wilson or anybody else. This story was told to me four or five years ago, and I found that Admiral Grayson was in town, and phoned to him this morning, and on my way down I called and picked him up and brought him down here. The one thing that I wanted was that President Wilson did have some connection with it. That is all I wanted.

Sec. 92. U. S. Government Intervenes to Prevent British Domination of Radio.

This testimony of Admiral Grayson is in harmony with the known facts that President Wilson had previously received two urgent requests from responsible associates to take action to safeguard American interests. These urgings, coupled with his own dependence upon wireless communication for dissemination of his own views of world affairs; coupled also with his natural resentment against the monopolistic tactics of Great Britain, would render it extremely probable that he would have taken precisely the action reported by Admiral Bullard.

Admiral Bullard, moreover, had been the first director of the Naval Communications Bureau. That he was then reassigned by President Wilson while in Paris to take charge of this department is a certainty. There is evidence that he returned to America from Paris in March, 1919, to reorganize the Naval Communications service. The Admiral arrived in Washington to assume his duties at the Navy Department on March 31, 1919. According to the story by Commander Stanford C. Hooper, U.S.N., who wrote in the June, 1922, issue of *Radio Broadcast,* Hooper and Commander Sweet called upon Admiral Bullard April 3 who "but three days before had arrived in Washington." They called moreover to discuss ways and means of blocking sale of the Alexanderson Alternators to the British Marconi Company, agents of whom were then in negotiation with the General Electric Company for purchase of the same.

If President Wilson had discussed the necessity of safeguarding American control of the Alexanderson Alternator with Admiral Bullard the latter said nothing to his visitors about it. His first mention of it, as we shall see, came in his later conference with Owen D. Young. Whether the doughty mariner at that conference for the purpose of impressing the General Electric Company elevated a mere conversation with his chief to a positive command to proceed post haste from Paris to see them, we shall probably never know. Such evidence as we now possess indicates that the Admiral may have exaggerated a bit at the time. That evidence will be discussed in the following chapter.

The probabilities are that Captain Hooper's alarm at a letter that had been received by the Navy Department from Owen D. Young was what stirred the Admiral to action. Once stirred, however, the Admiral took dramatic lead in a great international drama that quite overshadowed the really vital part played by Captain Hooper in the affair. Irrespective of what President Wilson may or may not have said in Paris, it was what Hooper said in Washington on April 3, 1919, that caused Admiral Bullard to rush to New York to save the Alexanderson Alternator from being sold to the Marconi Company.

CHAPTER
TEN

Contest for American Control of Wireless

Section 93. Contest Over Bill for Government Monopoly of Wireless.

THE SUDDEN CLOSING of the World War left wireless communications still under the control of the National Government. Private commercial stations could not hope to receive their property back automatically, since it could not be returned without official action of the government. As for amateurs, there was no property to receive back except their sealed-up equipment that was now eighteen months in disuse. To make the prospect for amateurs all the more dubious, two bills were shortly introduced into the Congress tending to perpetuate government monopoly of all wireless communications.

The Alexander Bill (H.R. 13159), introduced November 21, 1918, and its duplicate in the Senate (S. 5036) provided for experimental and technical training school stations, with no mention whatever of amateur stations. Despite the fact that President Wilson and Secretary Daniels of the Navy Department were each reported to be in favor of the legislation, furious opposition at once developed.

The National Wireless Association came out with a scathing denunciation of government monopoly of radio and wireless. The fact that government control must be limited by the Interstate Commerce clause of the U. S. Constitution was no consolation to the N.W.A.

"Perhaps some genius," they bitterly protested, "might design an amateur station that would not transmit signals outside his state boundaries or receive outside signals—and be permitted to operate. But this is a ridiculous and valueless assumption. Yet that is the only opportunity the present bill offers. It frankly and unreservedly gives the Government permanent possession of radio and its unrestricted operation. . . . The Alexander bill is a high-handed and unjustified attempt to trespass on the rights of American citizens and a legislative boomerang that will do incalculable damage to its undoubted exponent, the Navy itself. . . . It is sought, rather, that all future activity center about the radio establishment of the Government—that the development of a communication method still in a transitory state from an art to a science be committed to the hands of a few workers on the Government payroll, or in technical schools or professional laboratories. The individual worker, in a phrase, is to be suppressed. No opportunity is to be given for independent investigation and possible invention by the youth of the nation—in spite of the fact that the discovery of wireless telegraphy was made by Marconi when a boy just out of his teens."

The manifesto contained a very able analysis of the situation.[1]

This was typical of protests in newspapers and periodicals of that period. The fact that every great invention in the history of wireless

[1] Wireless Age, January, 1919. Pp. 24-26.

and radio had been made by private individuals—no Government employee in Navy or Army having contributed a single great improvement—could not fail to influence the public in a contest over the Alexander Bill.

Sec. 94. Navy Department Vainly Supports Measure.

The National Wireless Association had organized a powerful opposition to the Alexander Bill prior to the date of the Congressional hearing in December, 1918. Although expert opinion of legislative matters had at first conceded passage of the measure, yet by this time even the Navy Department had become dubious of success of the measure. Secretary Daniels, nevertheless, put up a gallant fight for its passage. "We strongly believe," he declared, "that having demonstrated during the war the excellent service and the necessity of unified ownership, we should not lose the advantage of it in peace."

Secretary Daniels pointed out that the Navy "is so well prepared to undertake this work and to carry it on that we would lose very much by dissipating it and opening the use of radio communication again to rival companies."

Congressman Green of Massachusetts quizzed the Secretary on whether or not the bill aimed at accomplishing a "government monopoly, contrary to any control that we hoped for years to establish under the Sherman Anti-Trust Law" and also whether such action might not set the Navy Department up in "commercial business." Other Congressmen joined in the attack. Mr. Daniels sought to mollify the opposition by pointing out that a clause of the bill would permit the Secretary of the Navy to issue special licenses in emergencies. This explanation was received with the more or less derisive comment that private interests would never be able to convince the Navy Department of the existence of an emergency.

The opposition made such effective thrusts at the bill that Secretary Daniels was constrained to alter some of the provisions of the measure. Captain Todd, Director of Naval Communications, later took up the cudgels in behalf of the Alexander Bill as amended by Secretary Daniels. Congressional critics, however, hammered the speaker effectively. Congressman Green declared, among other pithy observations:

"I am of the opinion that it is too much to ask the people of America to punish the people of America by restraining all their abilities and opportunities and all their hopes and expectations. You have to have some place of opportunity that young men can in the future get into, because they cannot get into the Navy, because the Navy will not increase as it has during the war, and the Navy bottles up and keeps for itself the opportunities and keeps everybody out."

The chief speakers in opposition to the measure were Edward J. Nally, Vice-President and General Manager of the Marconi Wireless Telegraph Company of America, and Hiram Percy Maxim, President of the American Radio Relay League. The hearings closed on the legislation December 19, 1918. On January 16, 1919, the Committee, by unanimous vote, laid the bill on the table in response to a resolution offered by Congressman William B. Bankhead of Alabama.

Sec. 95. Marconi Interests Again Seek to Buy Alexanderson Alternator.

President Wilson's European trip may have had bearing upon the inability of the Secretary of the Navy to win favorable action on the project of Government ownership of wireless stations. The emphatic rejection of the measure by the Committee had reassured wireless enthusiasts that pre-war freedom of operation was only a matter of time. Obviously until a treaty of peace could be agreed upon by the nations lately at war, the President could not be expected to revoke his order that had put all wireless matters under Government control. Since long-range planning was necessary in preparation to supply the expected demand for wireless equipment when once the ban should be lifted, we find the officials of electrical manufacturing companies busily engaged in preparation. Each of them had prospered from wartime patronage of the Federal Government. Now that the war was over this patronage had virtually ceased. Not only had wartime prosperity vanished on November 11, 1918, but the Navy Department presently announced that it would no longer shoulder responsibility for patent infringements.

The case of the General Electric Company was typical, although undoubtedly more grave than the problems that beset the smaller concerns. The General Electric Company had been turning out expensive equipment such as the Alexanderson Alternator. The Armistice had suddenly cut off war patronage. With wireless stations still in government handcuffs the situation was critical. The company would shortly be obliged to dismiss many skilled employees.

In an early state of America's participation, the company had loaned a 50 kilowatt Alexanderson Alternator for use in trans-Atlantic tests at the Marconi station at New Brunswick, N. J. Experiments soon gave such encouraging results that a two hundred kilowatt alternator was installed in the fall of 1917. This marvel of science promptly demonstrated its ability to fulfill all the claims made for it by its inventor. It was a case of bread cast upon the waters, for just as the officials of the company were in the doldrums over continuing to manufacture this expensive machine, familiar figures reappeared at the office of Owen D. Young in March, 1919—Sidney S. J. Steadman,

General Counsel for the British Marconi Company, and Edward J. Nally.[2]

Four years previously, as already noted, Marconi interests had sought to purchase the Alexanderson Alternator. Steadman was now back to revive the long-dormant negotiations. The British Marconi Company had prospered mightily during the war. It was now embarked upon the ambitious project of attempting to dominate wireless communications throughout the world. The company needed the Alexanderson Alternator and needed it very much.

Steadman had come prepared to place an initial order for twenty-four alternators at $127,000 apiece—ten for the British Marconi Company and fourteen for the American branch. Other orders were to follow. Since this proposal came like sunshine breaking through dark clouds it is probable that it might have been accepted by the General Electric Company, except for the fact that the offer was coupled with conditions. The Marconi interests desired exclusive rights to the American device.

Mr. Young was too astute a man to overlook the implications in such a transaction. Then, too, he and other officials of the General Electric Company were well aware that some holders of important mechanical devices in America, such as the telephone and shoe machinery patents, had prospered heavily by retaining ownership in the devices and letting them out on a rental or royalty plan. The General Electric Company accordingly made a counter proposal that it supply the alternators on a royalty basis. This was an unexpected development. The Marconi interests had no desire to pay royalty on the machines. Negotiations continued from day to day. Mr. Nally finally came forward with a suggestion that the Marconi Company buy the machines outright and pay $1,000,000 bonus in lieu of royalty on a certain number of machines.

Sec. 96. The Navy Department Objects to Sale of Alternator.

Thus negotiations stood when the General Electric Company re-

2 Edward J. Nally was born in Philadelphia, April 11, 1859. Parental poverty due to the loss of eyesight of his father rendered necessary the going to work at a tender age. He was a cash boy at eight years old. At fifteen he was working as a Western Union messenger boy at St. Louis when given a place as office boy for the man who later became President of the Company. Young Nally rose rapidly in Western Union service. In 1890 he became Assistant General Superintendent of the Postal Telegraph-Cable Company with headquarters in Chicago. In 1892 he became General Superintendent of the Western Division with jurisdiction over lines and offices in twenty-two States. In 1906 he was transferred to New York as Vice-President, later being elected General Manager. In 1913 he resigned to accept the position of Vice-President and General Manager of the Marconi Wireless Telegraph Company of America. Mr. Nally organized the company for commercial service and prior to America's entrance into the World War had done much to prepare for world-wide commercial wireless service.

ceived from the Navy Department a letter requesting the professional services of Ernst F. W. Alexanderson to make a report on a speed-control system for the high-frequency alternator that had been installed in the Sayville, L. I., station. This development introduced a new element into the general picture of sale of the alternator, an element of such importance that Mr. Young was called upon to answer it personally. Franklin D. Roosevelt, future President of the United States, was then Acting Secretary of the Navy during the absence of Secretary Daniels at the Peace Conference. To Mr. Roosevelt Owen D. Young addressed a letter on March 29, 1919, advising him of the desire of the General Electric Company to co-operate with the Navy Department to the fullest extent compatible with its own commercial interests.

Mr. Young's letter recited the dealings that the General Electric Company had had with the Government for sale and installation of wireless equipment, but called attention to the fact that the company was then in the midst of negotiations with the British and American Marconi Companies "for sale to them of a substantial number of our high-power radio equipments with the necessary accessories, of which the above-mentioned devices are a part, including a license to those two companies to utilize our system commercially on a royalty basis."

This letter produced immediate reactions in Washington. Mr. Roosevelt naturally referred it to the appropriate department and it apparently came into the hands of Captain Hooper on or before April 3, 1919. "When I heard of this impending deal," [3] wrote Hooper in a feature article for *Radio Broadcast*, June, 1922, "I became convinced that the whole future of American radio communications was involved, and it was my conviction that the Government's established radio policy would fail utterly if any deal was made which would give the British Marconi Company the sole rights to these patents or would give them a chance to get the first output of this modern apparatus from the General Electric Company's factories, because if they acquired the apparatus and had time to place it in service, no other radio company could catch up with them and it would be impossible to interest American business men in the establishment of a strictly American commercial radio company, owing to the tremendous power which the British Marconi Company would have acquired."

Commander E. H. Loftin, U.S.N., was a wireless-minded navy man who saw at an early date the necessity of safeguarding American con-

[3] Since the U. S. Navy was then in charge of cable communications, news of the deal may have come from interchange of cable messages on the subject but coincidence of date indicates the Young letter as the source of information.

trol of wireless communications. He has thus explained his own part in events leading to the formation of RCA: [4]

"On joining in service with Captain Hooper after arriving in the United States immediately following the Armistice, I told him that because of matters I had encountered in connection with the trans-Atlantic communication to our forces in Europe I considered that something should be done to put future operation of radio in the United States in American hands in view of the prospects then existing of it going into alien hands. Captain Hooper immediately told me that this situation had also been the subject of such thought on his part, and we then put our heads together as to how to accomplish it. By that time we had seized all United States patent rights of all kinds then held by the German 'Telefunken' Company and its Sayville, Long Island, radio station, and purchased the Poulsen arc patents to prevent them going into the hands of the British Marconi Company then negotiating for said Poulsen patents. As a result, we narrowed our thought down to the General Electric Company as being the most appropriate of the well-financed electrical companies in the United States."

To continue with the Hooper recital:

"The situation appeared to require immediate action, and, obviously, some degree of secrecy was essential. On April 3, 1919, Admiral Bullard had but three days before arrived in Washington and taken up his new duties as Director of Naval Communications, but as yet had had no opportunity to familiarize himself with the situation when the writer, accompanied by Commander George C. Sweet, U.S.N., now retired, went to him and laid the whole situation before him with recommendations that a conference be held with the directors of the General Electric Company. As a result of this conference, it was decided at once to get in touch with the General Electric Company by long distance phone with a view to arranging a conference in which the entire matter could be laid before the directors of the company from the Navy's point of view."

It is evident from the foregoing recital of fact that Captain Stanford C. Hooper is entitled to much more credit than he has received for his part in checkmating the sale of the Alexanderson Alternator to the British Marconi Company.

In the article referred to Hooper makes this very modest claim: "The writer claims no credit for the result achieved other than having made the original suggestion that the time seemed opportune to bring about its accomplishment. After the negotiations were gotten under

[4] Memoranda furnished by E. S. Purington of the Hammond Research Corporation.

way the necessary details were handled by those within whose province those details came."

Owen D. Young himself, while stoutly maintaining that Admiral Bullard stated at the conference in New York that President Wilson had sent him, stated to the editors of *Radio Broadcast* after the appearance of the June, 1922, article by Commander Hooper that it was indeed Hooper who "spurred on Admiral Bullard in his negotiations with the General Electric Company. . . . The original thought, the initiative and the persistent pushing were Hooper's and he should have full credit for them." [4a]

Obviously there was no time to lose. On April 4, 1919, the day following the long distance telephone call from Commander Hooper, Mr. Roosevelt wrote a brief and urgent reply inviting officials of the General Electric Company to come to Washington for a conference on the following Friday, April 11. One very significant sentence in the Roosevelt letter demonstrated how thoroughly the Navy Department was aroused over the attempt of the Marconi interests to purchase the Alexanderson Alternators. "Due to the various ramifications of this subject," he wrote, "it is requested that before reaching any final agreement with the Marconi Companies, you confer with representatives of the department."

Both Mr. Roosevelt and Admiral Bullard must have realized that the General Electric Company would be under no legal obligation to heed this request, since the Navy Department had no right to interfere with a legitimate business transaction, especially one that was already far advanced. Thus we may account for the fact that Admiral Bullard, without waiting for the hoped-for conference in Washington, set for April 11, attended a personal conference in New York City.

There was formerly some uncertainty about the date of that first historic meeting. Owen D. Young declared in his testimony before the Senate Committee on January 11, 1921, that the meeting occurred on April 5th. Commander Hooper sets the date as April 7th,[4b] whereas the records of the General Electric Company demonstrate that the

---

[4a] Radio Broadcast, July, 1922. In a conference with the author in June, 1938, Mr. Young declared that Admiral Bullard explained President Wilson's part in the affair not in the open conference but privately during a lull in the conference of April 8, 1919. At the moment there was uncertainty as to what action the directors might take. The naval officer called Mr. Young aside and imparted the information as a state secret, saying that President Wilson was deeply concerned over the matter of checkmating British domination of wireless and had given him, as Director of Naval Communications special instructions with reference to American control of the Alexanderson Alternator. For diplomatic reasons the head of the nation could not openly show his hand in the matter.

[4b] Radio Broadcast, June 1922, p. 131.

meeting between Admiral Bullard and the Board of Directors of the General Electric Company occurred on April 8, 1919.

In the United States "Naval Institute Proceedings" of October, 1923, Admiral Bullard made the following statement:

"In early April, 1919, the writer had just returned from a war detail in Europe, and had assumed the duties of Director of Naval Communications. . . . The fact that the General Electric Company was negotiating with the English Marconi Company for a sale of a number of Alexanderson machines was brought to my official notice a few days after my arrival in my office, and immediately sensing the great advantage that would be placed in the hands of foreigners by the successful conclusion of this transaction, I tried at once to prevent it. I had continually in mind the cable situation, and its control by foreign interests and was determined that if possible this new form of international communication should remain in the hands of American citizens, particularly so as so many American engineers had provided the most valuable inventions in the radio world."

Sec. 97. Admiral Bullard Calls on Owen D. Young.

The story of Admiral Bullard's first visit to the office of Owen D. Young in April, 1919, has been written many times. In a conference with the author on February 5, 1937, Mr. Young gave an interesting version of the historic meeting:

"Admiral Bullard and Commander S. C. Hooper," he said, "came to my office, and Admiral Bullard said that he had just come from Paris, at the direction of the President, to see me and talk with me about radio.

"He said that the President had reached the conclusion, as a result of his experience in Paris, that there were three dominating factors in international relations—international transportation, international communication, and petroleum—and that the influence which a country exercised in international affairs would be largely dependent upon their position of dominance in these three activities; that Britain obviously had the lead and the experience in international transportation—it would be difficult if not impossible to equal her position in that field; in international communications she had acquired the practical domination of the cable system of the world; but that there was an apparent opportunity for the United States to challenge her in international communications through the use of radio; of course as to petroleum we already held a position of dominance. The result of American dominance in radio would have been a fairly equal stand-off between the U. S. and Great Britain—the U. S. having the edge in petroleum, Britain in shipping, with communications divided—cables to Britain and wireless to the U. S.

"Admiral Bullard said that the President requested me to undertake the job of mobilizing the resources of the nation in radio. It was obvious that we had to mobilize everything we had, otherwise any of our international neighbors could weaken us tremendously by picking out one little thing. The whole picture puzzle had to be put together as a whole in order to get an effective national instrument.

"At this time Mr. A. G. Davis was working with Mr. Steadman of the Marconi Company, who had come over here again, and the General Electric Company was about to conclude an agreement to sell about five million dollars worth of apparatus, with everything settled except the amount of royalty payments to be made to us on the basis of so much per word transmitted via the alternators. By this time we were not content merely to sell the apparatus—we wanted a royalty on traffic in addition. At this stage we were asked not to sell the Alexanderson Alternator to either the British or the American Marconi Companies—and there were no other prospective customers for that kind of apparatus.

"I asked Admiral Bullard what impressed President Wilson about radio. He said the President had been deeply impressed by the ability to receive all over Europe messages sent from this side—particularly the fact of the broadcast (i.e., by radio telegraphy) across all international boundaries from this country by the Alexanderson Alternator of his own 'Fourteen Points'. Bullard said he had been into some of the Balkan states and there found school children learning the Fourteen Points as they would learn their catechism—made possible by the Alexanderson Alternator at New Brunswick, New Jersey, which, defying all censorship, was stimulating in everybody everywhere a deep anxiety that the war should end."

Sec. 98. Bullard Persuades General Electric to Refuse Marconi Company.

The main conference, held on April 8, 1919, was attended by the following officials of the General Electric Company: Edwin W. Rice, Jr., President of the company, Owen D. Young, Albert G. Davis, Charles W. Stone and Edward P. Edwards. Charles A. Coffin, Chairman of the Board, was engrossed in other matters in an adjoining office but after Admiral Bullard's private message to Owen D. Young the latter went to Mr. Coffin and conferred with him, after which he sat in at the conference with the Naval officials. Admiral Bullard was accompanied by Commander Stanford C. Hooper.

The crucial moment of the conference came when Admiral Bullard spoke up bluntly for an all-American monopoly of radio communications, arguing that a sale of the Alexanderson and other devices to the Marconi interests would be "to fix in British hands a substantial monopoly of world communication." [4d] To this sentiment as an ab-

[4d] See Owen D. Young's testimony before Committee on Interstate Commerce, Jan. 11, 1921.

stract proposition the officials of the General Electric Company readily agreed, declaring that nothing would please them better than to deal with an American company but it was a fact that no wireless or radio company of American origin was then in a position to purchase these expensive alternators.

They reminded their visitors that during the war they had co-operated with the Government in every possible way but now that the war had terminated the General Electric Company had been left in a most unfortunate dilemma. The expensive manufacturing plant and a large organization of skilled operatives must immediately suspend operations unless the alternators could be sold. The stockholders of the company would have a right to complain if for any reason, however patriotic, the officials of the General Electric Company should refuse to sell their product to a customer who was eager to purchase the same.[4e]

Admiral Bullard was too level-headed a man to fail to grasp the force of this argument. The corporation had a heavy investment, with many stockholders whose rights would certainly be sacrificed if the company were to refuse to deal with their only possible customer. The officials argued that unless the United States Government were to carry on the business of wireless communications there would be no way of preventing the Marconi interests from building up a monopoly in this field. They reminded the Admiral that the Poulsen Arc transmitter, not controlled by General Electric, was on the market, hence a refusal to sell the Alexanderson device might not accomplish the desired result.

Admiral Bullard's eloquent appeal to their patriotism at length prevailed. It was voted to break off negotiations with the Marconi interests, whereupon Charles A. Coffin, Chairman of the Board, exclaimed:

"Now we can start afresh. We will not put this machine in the hands of foreigners without some regulation and control. But what shall we do? We have no other customers for it." [4f]

[4e] Owen D. Young thus explained the matter in testimony before the Senate Committee, Jan. 11, 1921. "In his characteristic, forceful and convincing way, Admiral Bullard elaborated these points and asked the officers and directors of the General Electric Company, as patriotic American citizens, not to part with their rights to foreign countries and thereby possibly sacrifice and certainly impair the possibility of establishing an American radio communications company, powerful enough to meet the competition of other radio interests of the world. The officers of the General Electric Company pointed out to Admiral Bullard that the business of the company was to develop electrical apparatus and to sell to its normal customers; that a very large amount of money had been spent in this particular development and that the associated Marconi companies were practically the only large possible purchasers of this apparatus."

[4f] See interview with Admiral Bullard in *Wireless Age*, Feb. 1921.

HARRY P. DAVIS
Vice-President Westinghouse Company
to whom KDKA owes its origin.

DR. FRANK CONRAD
Assistant Chief Engineer Westinghouse
Co., "Father of Radio Broadcasting."

OTTO S. SCHAIRER
Director Plant Development, Westinghouse Company; now Vice-President RCA.

Admiral Bullard had no illusions as to the attitude of the Congress toward government ownership of wireless communications. The conclusion was inevitable that if British interests were to be checkmated in this matter a powerful American company must at once be organized.

The Director of Naval Communications now brought forward the staggering proposal that the General Electric Company itself take the lead in forming such a company. Mr. Young pointed out that his organization was engaged in the manufacturing and selling of electrical apparatus and that they were not interested in the communications field; that they knew nothing about it and were not ambitious to engage in wireless communications. Admiral Bullard insisted, however, that if they were to sponsor such a company it would greatly strengthen their own position as manufacturers of electrical equipment, since it would provide them with a customer and a steady market for their expensive equipment.

This argument could not fail to capture the imagination of such a far-seeing man as Owen D. Young. Before this preliminary conference adjourned Mr. Coffin and Mr. Young had agreed that if difficulties could be ironed out and government co-operation could be secured the General Electric Company might properly launch such an American-owned communications corporation. Mr. Albert G. Davis, head of the Patent Department of the General Electric Company, concurred in this idea. Thus one of the truly great semi-patriotic public utilities of the United States had its inception almost exactly two years after the United States officially embarked in the World War.

Sec. 99. Owen D. Young Undertakes a Difficult Task.

The conditions then confronting Owen D. Young and his associates were of a most complex character. Wireless communication was still entirely in the hands of the Federal Government under its wartime powers. Until the official signing of the peace treaty the nation would remain technically at war. It was well known that Secretary of the Navy Daniels was still a militant advocate of government ownership of wireless communications. It was an open secret that he would make a further attempt to persuade the Congress to adopt his public ownership plan. The fact, however, that President Wilson had sent Admiral Bullard to confer with the officials of the General Electric Company about setting up private control of wireless indicated that he at least had abandoned hope of government ownership of this industry. Assuming, then, that the government would return commercial wireless stations to their owners in due time the task confronting Mr. Young and his associates was truly colossal.

To begin with, the American Marconi Company already had a strangle hold on the business of wireless communications in America. For any group, however soundly supported financially, to start from scratch and attempt to overcome such an adversary might well lead to ruinous competition. There were conditions, however, that complicated matters for the Marconi interests. Most important of all was the fact that responsible officials of the United States Government had decided that if national security were to be served no foreign-controlled corporation could be permitted to dominate wireless communications of the nation.

Another circumstance operated against the Marconi people. The Alexanderson Alternator and the Poulsen Arc, the only types of sending apparatus, except a French invention, that were highly efficient, were the products of American manufacturers. Without one or the other of these machines the Marconi stations would be at great disadvantage.

The patent situation was the greatest obstacle of all. During the war, as previously observed, the Government under its wartime powers had virtually pooled the patents of American inventors by informing them that if rights were considered infringed they should take their grievance to the Court of Claims. The patents were still in the Government bag, but with the official closing of the war the rival manufacturers would be entitled to assert all property rights in patents held by them. The mischief was that no one manufacturer had a complete system. The vacuum tube, for instance, involved patents originally issued to Fleming, deForest, Arnold, Langmuir and others. This was typical of other patent complications. The Marconi companies had purchased the rights of certain inventors; the General Electric Company held very important patents such as the Alexanderson Alternator; but the Westinghouse Electric and Manufacturing Company was also strongly entrenched in the same field. It was later to acquire the heterodyne device of Fessenden and the Armstrong "feed back" improvement on deForest's audion tube. A fourth holder of parts of the great jig-saw puzzle of patent control was the United Fruit Company with its crystal detector and the other patents controlled by it. Each of the four companies held portions without which the puzzle could not be fitted together, but since they were more or less bitter rivals, in litigation with each other except during the war period, the task of bringing their interests together in one company was an appalling one. Owen D. Young has thus described the situation then existing:

"It was utterly impossible for anybody to do anything in radio, any one person or group or company at that time. The Westinghouse

Company, the American Tel. & Tel. Company, the United Fruit Company, and the General Electric Company all had patents but nobody had patents enough to make a system. And so there was a complete stalemate." [5]

Yet Owen D. Young, at the conference with Admiral Bullard, undertook to clear up the tangle and to create a great American radio corporation.

Sec. 100. The General Electric Company Offers to Purchase Marconi Interests.

Inasmuch as the United States Government had very effectively pooled the patent resources of the rival companies during the war and had not yet released its control over wireless patents it was natural that Mr. Young and his associates should have endeavored to work out a plan in which the Government could be a quasi partner. Since the idea of an American company had originated with officials of navy communications, Mr. Young's first thought was to proceed under a contract between the Navy Department and the General Electric Company, thus to give the undertaking a semi-official character.

A contract was accordingly drawn up in which it was provided among other things that a representative of the Navy Department should sit on the Board of Directors of the new company. Admiral Bullard and Acting Secretary of the Navy Franklin D. Roosevelt were heartily in accord with the plan. Secretary of the Navy Daniels was to return from France in a few weeks. Official action on so important a matter could not well be taken until the return of Mr. Daniels. The most that Mr. Young and navy officials could do in the interval was to work out details of the scheme.

It was not until May 25th that the plan could officially come before Secretary Daniels. At this conference in Washington Mr. Young laid before the Secretary of the Navy the plans thus far formulated to carry out the suggestions of Admiral Bullard. Mr. Daniels admitted that these plans were logical in view of the request from the Navy Department but expressed his disapproval on the ground that the proposed communications corporation would be in effect a giant monopoly—a trust, and Mr. Daniels abhorred trusts. Owen D. Young countered by pointing out that a cable monopoly already existed in favor of Great Britain and that the only hope of checkmating Britain's domination of all communications, cable and wireless, rested in the possibility of establishing a great wireless corporation owned and controlled by American citizens. He stated his belief that a monopoly is

[5] Testimony of Owen D. Young before Committee on Interstate Commerce, U. S. Senate, December 9, 1929.

objectionable whenever it may fairly be said to control a product or service but not otherwise. Judged by this standard the proposed radio corporation could not offend the most ardent opponents of trusts, since it could only prove a competitor of the cable monopoly already held by Great Britain. The United States, Mr. Young declared, would no longer be at the mercy of a British monopoly but instead would be in a position to force that monopoly to lower its cable rates. He pointed out also that in the natural course of events cable and wireless would be competitors for business—hence each a check upon the other. Because of this fact the proposed wireless corporation, while apparently a monopoly, would not possess the dangerous characteristics of a trust.

Half convinced, Secretary Daniels suggested that Mr. Young consult Senator Henry Cabot Lodge, then a powerful figure in foreign relations, to get his views in the matter. Daniels finally declared that he proposed to try once more to convince the Congress of the advisability of government ownership of wireless transmissions, but should he be unsuccessful he would accept the Young plan as a necessary evil.

Senator Lodge was promptly consulted and proved to be wholeheartedly in favor of the plan. Government ownership of utilities during the war had convinced the Senator that it would be extremely unwise to embark in government ownership of wireless communications. Mr. Lodge promised all possible co-operation with Owen D. Young.

The officials of the General Electric Company realized the futility of waiting for government co-operation. They believed that radio stations would be returned to their owners within a few weeks. If the alluring plan were to be launched it must be done without delay. Secretary Daniels was thereupon notified by Mr. Young that his associates proposed to explore the possibilities of consolidating rival wireless interests in a private communications company. He informed the Secretary that the new company, if and when formed, would insert a provision in its by-laws making a permanent guarantee that control of the proposed corporation would rest in American hands. A further proviso would be inserted in the by-laws for membership in their board of directors of a representative of the Navy Department.

The American Marconi officials had by this time been sounded out on the proposition of outright purchase by the proposed corporation of the entire physical assets of the American Marconi Company. Evidently these officials already saw the handwriting on the wall— government opposition to foreign ownership of wireless communications and possible government ownership, or, failing in that, a government-favored new corporation that might shortly be able to offer ruinous competition to the Marconi Company.

The General Electric Company, having heretofore been engaged in manufacturing equipment, had no communications experts. It was not only good diplomacy but sound business as well to offer to the responsible officials of the American Marconi Company employment of the same nature with the new corporation, should the consolidation be effected. This was precisely the strategy adopted by Mr. Young. The directors of the American Marconi Company were willing to dispose of their interests to the General Electric Company, provided the parent company with its large financial interests in the American Company could be prevailed upon to sell its holdings. Thus the first barrier was cleared, but there remained the more difficult task of persuading the British Marconi Company to sell its stock holdings and at a reasonable figure.

Sec. 101. Attempts to Persuade British Marconi Company.

Having decided upon a course of action the officials of the General Electric Company were in a quandary as to the method of approaching the Marconi officials in England for the sale of their holdings. Obviously there was one man eminently qualified to act as negotiator in their behalf—Edward J. Nally, Vice-President and General Manager of the American Marconi Company. Mr. Nally had already expressed positive conviction that the purchase of British interests was the only means of safeguarding the rights of American Marconi stockholders. Mr. Nally realized that as an aftermath of war a fatal misunderstanding had grown up in the popular mind as to the true nature of the American Marconi Company. It was generally regarded as a mere branch of the British Marconi Company—its policies dictated by Britain, its ownership largely in British hands. As a matter of fact, the American Marconi Company had always been largely an American-owned corporation, nearly all of its active directors being loyal citizens of the United States. Its policies, however, were undoubtedly in accord with those of the parent company.

The U. S. Navy Department was hostile to it as an alien concern. Popular prejudice was against it. The corporation was doomed unless it could be reorganized under a new name. The General Electric Company had offered the only means of salvation—this Mr. Nally well knew. When approached with the suggestion that he go to England to persuade the British Marconi officials to sell their stock Mr. Nally was frankly concerned. He realized that it would prove a long and arduous task—that the outcome might be adverse. Duty to his own stockholders and an earnest belief that the new project was highly meritorious led him at length to agree to undertake the mission if his own directors would authorize him to do so.

It was of course necessary for the General Electric Company to

choose an official representative to accompany Mr. Nally on this momentous mission. The choice fell upon Albert G. Davis, Vice-President in charge of the Patent Department—a man of shrewd judgment
whose legal training could match the British negotiators. Mr. Davis
had no illusions as to the nature of the task confronting Mr. Nally
and himself—a task doubly difficult because only a few weeks before
the British Marconi Company had been rebuffed in an attempt to purchase the Alexanderson device. The American negotiators well knew
that the proud Britons would regard their mission as colossal Yankee
nerve.

Before sailing from New York Mr. Davis was given every possible
aid by his associates. That he would eventually be obliged to pay
millions of dollars to the British company in General Electric's behalf
was realized by all. The situation was thoroughly canvassed and when
Mr. Davis embarked he was armed with complete authority to make
terms in the great international transaction.

The two men sailed for England in June 1919. Since the formation
of an American wireless communications company hinged upon the
issue of their mission there was little of definite nature that could be
done in the matter in the United States. Reports from Mr. Davis soon
justified all the gloomy forebodings that had been entertained by the
officials of the General Electric Company. British pride had been
touched—national interests were involved—Britain's long domination
of communications of the world was challenged. All this would require
time for reflection and debate. The fact that the American Government
was determined to prevent the alleged foreign domination of American wireless was of course the most telling argument that Mr. Nally
could bring to bear upon the directors of the British Marconi Company. Weeks passed in weary negotiations.

In the meantime there was much agitation in Congress over the
continuance of wartime powers of the President. In July, 1919, a resolution was passed ordering the return to private ownership of telephones, telegraphs and cables. This resolution was signed by President
Wilson, July 11, 1919.

Mr. Young and his associates soon realized that tentative action
must be taken with respect to the American Marconi Company if
prejudicial delay were to be avoided after the negotiations in England
should be concluded. According to the "Report of the Federal Trade
Commission on the Radio Industry" filed with the House of Representatives, December 1, 1923, the following action was then taken:

"After due notice to the Secretary of the Navy of its intention the
General Electric Company undertook negotiations with the American
interests in the American Marconi Company. An agreement was made,

contingent on the General Electric Company being able to purchase the British interests, whereby the new radio company was to acquire the property, patents, good will and business of the American Marconi Company and to pay therefor, with its preferred stock at par, to the extent of the value of the tangible property actually turned over, and pay for the patents, good will and business with the common stock of no par value. The General Electric Company also agreed to contribute something over $3,000,000 to the new enterprise, for which it was to take preferred stock of the new company at par, and the General Electric Company would turn in its patents and those developed during the next twenty-five years in the radio field for common stock of no par value."

The first public announcement of the new project was probably a news story in the New York *Times* of September 4, 1919, from which we quote:

"The General Electric Company, it is understood, will become a stockholder in the company when the deal is arranged but it is asserted positively that the wireless company will in no sense be a subsidiary of the General Electric. The latter became interested through its having developed the Alexanderson Alternator which was installed at the New Brunswick station of the Marconi Company. This type gained high approval from the Navy Department.

"The financial details of the negotiations and the plans for reorganization if the deal is completed could not be learned yesterday. It is understood, however, that if reorganization is undertaken American capital will back the enterprise, so that control will rest absolutely in this country.

". . . The original capitalization of the American Company was $6,650,000, the 66,500 shares having a par value of $100. In 1910 the par value of the shares was decreased to $25 making the capitalization $1,662,500 and in 1910 the capitalization was increased to $10,000,000 and the par value of the shares reduced to $5."

Sec. 102. An International Victory.

The great day came at last when Mr. Nally could report to his associates on this side of the Atlantic the complete success of the English mission. Two months of diplomacy, of argument and persuasion were now crowned with the reluctant consent of the British Marconi Company, on September 5, 1919, to sell its American interests. Inasmuch as 364,826 shares of the American Marconi stock were then in British hands the transaction involved millions of dollars.

In September, 1919, Mr. Davis and E. J. Nally returned to New York in triumph. The British shares were deposited in the vaults of the General Electric Company. The way was now clear for the formation of an all-American corporation which its promoters had already decided to call "The Radio Corporation of America." The only cloud on the horizon was the fact that Secretary of the Navy Daniels had carried out his threat to make a final attempt to induce the Congress to assent to government ownership of wireless communications.

On July 19th the persistent Secretary of the Navy had prepared documents to be submitted to the Congress, including two proposed bills aimed to accomplish the object so close to Mr. Daniels' heart. These proposed bills had now been deposited in the legislative hopper. Few informed persons expected that the Congress would reverse its action of the previous year. The bitter controversy that was then raging between the President and certain members of the Senate over the League of Nations issue naturally decreased the chances of the several public ownership bills now pending in the Congress. Another circumstance militated against the success of the Daniels' campaign—public ownership of railroads and other utilities during the war was generally conceded to have been wasteful and ineffective. For this reason few people could enthuse over the prospect of government ownership of wireless communications. Amateur wireless enthusiasts all over the nation were again in battle array against the measures. Under these circumstances the General Electric Company could with reasonable assurance press forward with plans for launching the Radio Corporation of America.

CHAPTER
ELEVEN

Beginnings of Radio Corporation of America

Section 103. Radio Corporation of America Is Launched.

ON OCTOBER 17, 1919, the Radio Corporation of America was granted a charter under the corporation laws of the State of Delaware. There was a clause in the charter providing that not more than twenty per cent of the Radio Corporation stock might be held by aliens as voting stock. The first organization meeting was held on October 21, 1919, at Wilmington, Del. The incorporators named in the charter set in motion the legal processes through which all giant corporations must pass before a permanent organization can be set up. Certain directors were named at this first meeting. On the following day a meeting of this temporary board was held. In the minutes of this meeting of October 22, 1919, there appears a very significant letter addressed to the new corporation and signed by Owen D. Young as Vice-President of the General Electric Company. The letter recites that the General Electric Company, in anticipation of the formation of the Radio Corporation of America, has formulated plans "by which the corporation may obtain an advantageous agreement with Marconi's Wireless Telegraph Company, Ltd., for the conduct of international radio business with other countries and in South America and also an agreement with Marconi Wireless Telegraph Company of America for the purchase of certain of its assets for consideration which is deemed advantageous. Copies of these two proposed agreements are submitted herewith."

The letter [1] recited the expenditures that the General Electric Company had made in behalf of the Radio Corporation. Then came a proposal that the new corporation issue to the General Electric Company the amounts of preferred and common stock that were actually authorized in the main agreement, so-called, to which attention will be directed shortly.

It should be noted in passing, however, that these vital documents, produced from the archives of the Radio Corporation in response to a Congressional inquiry, reflect nothing but credit upon the officials of the General Electric Company. While senatorial sneers were at one time leveled at Owen D. Young's alleged patriotic motives in organizing the Radio Corporation of America, the documents themselves should be sufficient vindication. It is probable that in the history of corporate organizing there can be found but few instances where promoters have taken such chances and have expended such vast sums only to present an accounting with a simple request that stock be issued sufficient to cover those expenditures. Granted that the General Electric Company was in the act of creating a customer from whom it might expect profitable business thereafter, yet this fact would not have restrained the cupidity of ordinary men when issuing stock of

[1] See Appendix, Exhibit "A."

problematical value in payment for cash expenditures. That these men acted with the motives that they professed in days when patriotism was still a vital force in the land is obvious.

Sec. 104. Merger of American Marconi and RCA.

On October 22, 1919, a preliminary agreement was signed, the General Electric Company and the American Marconi Company being the high contracting parties. Since the Marconi stockholders had not yet formally voted upon the merger it became necessary to bring the matter to an issue immediately. The chief feature of this covenant of October 22nd was an agreement by the American Marconi Company to use its best efforts to persuade its stockholders to exchange Marconi stock for that of the Radio Corporation of America.[2] In the recitals of the proposed main agreement [3] it was disclosed that the General Electric Company had already paid to the Radio Corporation $287,262 and had transferred valuable rights and privileges to the same corporation. The General Electric Company had also agreed to make certain payments to the British Marconi Company. It had purchased a very large block of shares (364,826) in the American Marconi Company from British investors. In return for this munificent sponsorship of the great venture the Radio Corporation issued to the General Electric Company 135,174 shares of preferred stock at a par value of $675,870 and two million shares of common stock without par value.

The recitals of the proposed main agreement set forth definitely that "no other shares of the Radio Corporation have been issued or have been agreed to be issued, except as set forth in the said General Electric-Radio Main Agreement." Thus Owen D. Young's brain child was going forth into the world with frank and open credentials that bear the imprint of Mr. Young's lucid style.

The chief commitments of the American Marconi Company were as follows:

"The Marconi Company agrees to recommend to and urge upon its

[2] On the very day that this agreement was signed, October 22, 1919, John W. Griggs, President of the Marconi Company, issued to the stockholders of the company an eight-page recital of facts coupled with a plea that they exchange their Marconi stock for that of the Radio Corporation. A significant passage in the recital is as follows: "We have found that there exists on the part of the officials of the Government a very strong and irremovable objection to your Company because of the stock interest held therein by the British Company. This objection is shared by the members of Congress to a considerable extent. Consequently your Company has found itself greatly embarrassed in carrying out its plans for an extensive trans-oceanic traffic, and unless this British Marconi interest in your Company is eliminated your President and Board of Directors believe it will not be possible to proceed with success to the resumption of its preparations for a world-wide service when its stations shall be returned to it, as they will be in the near future."

[3] See Appendix Exhibit "B" for Copy of Preliminary Agreement.

stockholders to consent to and approve the execution by the Marconi Company of a certain agreement with the Radio Corporation of America . . . known as the Marconi-Radio Main Agreement, a copy of which is hereto attached, and agrees that as soon as such consent or approval can be obtained it will formally execute and deliver the said agreement with its exhibits to the Radio Corporation simultaneously with the execution and delivery by the Radio Corporation."

Farther on in the Preliminary Agreement was the following provision:

"The Marconi Company agrees forthwith after receiving the shares of common stock referred to in the said Main Agreement to take action which shall have the effect of distributing these shares of common stock among its stockholders in proportion to their holdings, and it further agrees that it will make a similar distribution when it shall receive preferred stock of the Radio Corporation in payment for Marconi Assets. And it further agrees at least as often as the end of each year when it shall have received further stock of the Radio Corporation under any provision of the Marconi-Radio Main Agreement [4] or otherwise to take action which shall have the effect of distributing such further stock so received; it being the intent of this agreement that all preferred and common stock of the Radio Corporation received by the Marconi Company shall be forthwith distributed to stockholders of the Marconi Company."

Thus the Radio Corporation had pledged two million shares of common stock and two million shares of preferred stock for the intangible assets, for the wireless stations, the physical equipment, the patent rights and the good will of the Marconi Company. The value of all these properties was estimated at $9,500,000, subject, however, to appraisal and adjustment.

At a meeting of the board of directors held on November 14, 1919, it was voted to fix the capital stock at ten million shares, five million of preferred stock with a par value of $5 a share and five million shares of common stock without par value. When the usual legal formalities had been completed, arrangements were made for the first meeting of the stockholders of the corporation. This meeting was held November 20, 1919. The Main Agreement (see Appendix, Exhibit "C") was now executed. Temporary directors and officers now withdrew and the permanent board was thereupon elected by the stockholders. Eight directors were chosen, four who had been on the board of the American Marconi Company and an equal number of General Electric representatives. The Board of Directors was composed as follows: Edward

[4] The Main Agreement will be found in the Appendix, Exhibit "C". In addition to the two million shares to be exchanged with stockholders it provided for payment of two million shares of preferred stock for Marconi assets, provided the net value of such assets should be found on appraisal to be worth $9,500,000, or a reduced number of shares if the value proved less.

J. Nally, former Vice-President, American Marconi Company; Edwin W. Rice, Jr., President, General Electric Company; John W. Griggs, former Attorney-General of the United States, former Governor of New Jersey, former President, American Marconi Company; Owen D. Young, Vice-President, General Electric Company; James R. Sheffield, law firm, Sheffield & Betts, former director, American Marconi Company; Albert G. Davis, Vice-President, General Electric Company; Gordon Abbott, director, General Electric Company; Edward W. Harden, former director, American Marconi Company.

Edward J. Nally now became President of the Radio Corporation and Owen D. Young chairman of the Board of Directors. C. J. Ross, former Secretary of the American Marconi Company, became the first Secretary of the Radio Corporation. The way was now paved for the carrying into effect of the ambitious plans on which Owen D. Young had been working for months past, by which he sought to consolidate the wireless facilities of the nation—to put together the "jig-saw puzzle" of conflicting interests in this great field.

The American Marconi Company on the 20th day of November, 1919, became officially merged with the Radio Corporation of America. To be sure, the corporation continued to exist for legal purposes thereafter in order to wind up its affairs, yet on this date it ceased to function as a communications corporation and RCA stepped into its shoes. Officers and operating personnel as well as the physical assets of the old company now were part and parcel of the new organization.

Sec. 105. The First Cross-Licensing Agreement.

The rapidity with which Mr. Young worked in these hectic days of organization is evidenced by the fact that on the very day when the merger of RCA and the American Marconi Company occurred, the first of the famous cross-licensing agreements was executed. As will be pointed out hereafter the cross-licensing idea—much criticized at a later time for its monopolistic features—did not originate with Owen D. Young. Its real author was apparently Captain Hooper, of the Navy Communications, who had urged it upon his superiors, and who in turn had urged it upon the General Electric Company and RCA, later confirming the same by a formal letter under date of January 5, 1920. The cross-licensing agreement was drafted by A. G. Davis, Vice-President of the General Electric Company, the contracting parties being RCA and the General Electric Company. Since this agreement was to serve as the model for future cross-licensing agreements it is deemed of sufficient importance to be included in the Appendix to this volume.[5]

[5] See Appendix, Exhibit "D."

This license agreement of November 20, 1919, established the rights of the Radio Corporation in the inventions and patents held by the General Electric Company as well as reciprocal rights of the General Electric Company in present or future inventions and patents which the Radio Corporation might own. By the terms of the agreement it was to continue operative for a period of twenty-five years. The importance of this new corporate device cannot be overestimated. True it had all the earmarks of monopoly—the tying of great corporations together in a network of reciprocal agreements. No one could have been more keenly aware of this than Mr. Young himself, yet it was obviously the only way of consolidating the conflicting interests in inventions and patents whereby a great national communications system could hope to function.

It will be remembered that Mr. Young had made definite overtures to the United States Government to participate in the creation and oversight of the Radio Corporation of America. As previously related, Secretary of the Navy Josephus Daniels had declined to approve such a plan, being intent upon his pet project of government ownership and operation of wireless communications. At least four bills were already in the Congressional docket providing for government ownership. While there was every prospect of defeat of the measures the new corporation nevertheless inserted in its by-laws the following provision:

"The corporation may permit a representative of the Government of the United States the right of discussion and presentation in the board of the Government's views and interests concerning matters coming before the board."

Thus was redeemed the pledge made to the Secretary of the Navy by Owen D. Young in his letter of June, 1919, announcing that he and his associates were about to undertake a mobilization of the wireless resources of the nation.

Sec. 106. Problems Confronting RCA.

Having effected a corporate organization, it became necessary to take over the radio stations and physical assets of the American Marconi Company. This was a task of great importance, since it vested in the Radio Corporation of America ownership and management of virtually all the commercial high power wireless stations in the United States. This task would have been much more difficult except for the fact that Edward J. Nally, former Vice-President and General Manager of the American Marconi Company, had been elected President of the Radio Corporation of America. His long experience as an executive and his intimate knowledge of the problems of wireless communications were assets of great value to the youthful corporation. Then, too, the fact that change of ownership of the wireless stations did not result in a change of personnel—the Marconi organization being taken over intact under the oversight of its former general manager—was a most fortunate circumstance.

To be sure, there were those in the Navy Department who disapproved the selection of Mr. Nally as President of RCA. Their opposition was based upon the fact that Nally had so long been connected with the Marconi interests that they feared a continuation of British influence, if not in legal ownership then in matter of policies of administration. Events were to demonstrate how groundless were these fears.

The new corporation had acquired ownership of all the far-flung activities of the American Marconi Company, including the Wireless Press, a New York Corporation; the Marconi Telegraph Cable Company, Inc. (New York); Marconi Telegraph Cable Company, Inc. (Massachusetts); Marconi Telegraph Cable Company, Inc. (Illinois) and three-eighths of the stock of the Pan-American Wireless Telegraph & Telephone Company of Delaware.

Mr. Young and his associates realized keenly the magnitude of the problems confronting the youthful corporation. If it were to function effectively, it must establish traffic agreements with foreign wireless companies for international transmission of messages. Here was a field that required diplomacy and business sagacity of high degree. To this task they addressed themselves with a broad vision and thoroughness that left nothing to be desired.

Unsolved technical problems also confronted them. Even before the World War, as we have previously observed, amateur stations and commercial as well had created virtual chaos of wireless interference. The United States Congress had been obliged to provide for the licensing of sending stations and the assignment of definite wave frequencies for such stations. Now that the war was over and new stations would soon be in operation everywhere, the problem of wavelength regulation assumed enormous proportions. Of what use would be all this expenditure for the Marconi assets if chaos in wireless transmission should ensue!

As an illustration of the concern with which the leading electrical engineers of the country regarded the situation we have but to refer to a startling speech reported in *Wireless Age* of December, 1919. Ernst F. W. Alexanderson, the inventor of the far-famed alternator, in an address at Schenectady declared that the ether waves would soon be as crowded as Fifth Avenue. He pointed out the limited range of wave channels and declared that nearly half of the inter-ocean wave lengths were already pre-empted by the few stations in operation.

Marconi Congratulates Alexanderson at the General Electric plant after inspection of Alexanderson Alternator.

ABOARD THE "ELETTRA"
Left to right: Owen D. Young, Guglielmo Marconi, and Edward J. Nally.

Although the Alexanderson Alternator had made possible the tuning of stations within one per cent of each other, the outlook was exceedingly serious.

Sec. 107. RCA Invites Government Participation.

While the plans of RCA were naturally shrouded in mystery during the first weeks of its existence, yet by January 1, 1920, publicity began to appear concerning its activities. In the January number of *Wireless Age* was to be found the announcement of the completed acquisition of the American Marconi Company's assets and the ambitious plans of the corporation to develop a great chain of commercial wireless stations. The election of Edward J. Nally as President of RCA was regarded by wireless enthusiasts as a sufficient guarantee that the new corporation had taken over the Marconi organization intact and was adequately equipped for international wireless activities.

Among the advantages flowing from the RCA-Marconi consolidation was the fact that Roy A. Weagant, who had been chief engineer in the employ of the Marconi Company, came to RCA.

Elmer E. Bucher, former Chief Inspector of the Marconi Company, also came to RCA as Commercial Engineer in charge of sales. Ernst F. W. Alexanderson was named Chief Engineer of the new company. On January 2, 1920, Weagant assigned (for a royalty agreement that might total $200,000) the valuable patents on Weagant inventions in radio fields—an important addition to RCA's technical assets.

By January 1st the company was in a position to go forward with its ambitious communications program. As an evidence of its desire to be a truly all-American utility company, the board of directors now authorized its president to carry out the promise made to the Secretary of the Navy by Owen D. Young during the preceding June. The letter written by Mr. Nally at this time is of such historic interest that it is reproduced herewith in full:

"January 3, 1920.
"The President,
The White House,
Washington, D. C.
Sir:
"The Radio Corporation of America is a corporation formed for the purpose, among other things, of engaging in international communication, an undertaking which is today attracting the keen attention of both the public and our Government.

"There is now pending in the House of Representatives a bill (H.R. 10831) relating to the matter. In the Senate a subcommittee of the Committee on Naval Affairs has also considered a great deal a proposed bill, which was prepared at the subcommittee's request by experts of the Navy and which appears in the printed report of the sub-committee's hearings, beginning on page 261 in Part II, Sixty-sixth Congress, first session.

"This proposed act, among other measures to protect against control of this business by foreign companies and against the granting to aliens of licenses to operate stations, provides (p. 264 of said printed report) that certain restrictions of the law shall not apply to those corporations whose by-laws provide, among other things, for the attendance and hearing at stockholders' and directors' meetings of 'a representative of the Secretary of the Navy, of or above the rank of captain.'

"I, of course, cannot predict the ultimate disposition of this matter by Congress, but meanwhile I beg to state that it is the desire of the Radio Corporation of America to consider the interests of the public, and we therefore invite suggestions which the Government may wish to present at our meetings.

"To such end the following has been inserted in the by-laws of the corporation, namely:

'The corporation may permit a representative of the Government of the United States the right of discussion and presentation in the board of the Government's views and interests concerning matters coming before the board.'

"Accordingly, on behalf of the Radio Corporation of America, I respectfully request that you appoint a representative to attend the stockholders' and directors' meetings of such corporation, with the right of discussion and presentation of the Government's views and interests concerning matters coming before the directors and stockholders.

"As to the importance of this matter I beg to suggest that full information may no doubt be had from Admiral Bullard, Director of Naval Communications. He has made an exhaustive study of the subject; has had wide experience, and has been most zealous in the protection of American radio interests. I feel confident that he will fully appreciate the advisability of the Government's prompt consideration of and action in this matter.

Respectfully,

(Signed) E. J. NALLY, President." [6]

Sec. 108. Navy Department Approves Cross-Licensing of Patent Rights.

Because the Radio Corporation of America was later bitterly assailed for the alleged illegal monopoly arising from its cross-licensing covenants whereby a number of manufacturers of electrical devices pooled their patent rights it is interesting to note the origin of the idea. It did not originate with Owen D. Young nor with anyone con-

[6] Extract from Hearings before the Committee on Interstate Commerce, United States Senate, 71st Congress, 2nd Session on S. 6, December 9, 10, 12, 13, 14, 16 and 17, 1929).

nected with RCA but with officials of the Navy Department itself. Captain Stanford C. Hooper, one of the most astute and far-seeing naval officials having to do with wireless communications, thus described the inception of the idea while testifying before the Senate Committee on Interstate Commerce in December, 1929:

"Captain Hooper: That cross-license system came about as follows: During the war when we bought radio equipment in the Navy Department we had to sign a patent release, because none of the companies nor the Navy knew who owned patents, and it was a very much mixed-up thing. After the war we did not want to continue that system, because we were afraid that we were getting in pretty deep. I myself had charge of the radio division of the Navy Department at that time, which handled all purchases of materials for that work, and I wrote a letter to the companies that owned these patents—or rather I should say that I drafted a letter which my superior signed—and appealed to them to get together and make some arrangement, so that the Navy could buy radio equipment without having to take the patent responsibility. I pointed out to them that ships, passenger ships and all kinds of ships, could not buy the modern radio equipment necessary for safety of life at sea unless some arrangement was made. Now, that letter was the start, indirectly, I might say, of this cross-licensing system. After they received that letter the companies took the matter up and decided among themselves that the only thing they could do was to get together and exchange licenses, so that they could sell the equipment. Otherwise it would have been a matter of years and years and much litigation, before either the Navy or steamships could have bought modern radio sets.

Senator Dill: But that was a separate agreement and a separate act from the mere acquiring of the patents of the General Electric Company, to keep them from going to the British Company?

Captain Hooper: Yes, sir; that was entirely separate.

Senator Dill: And the Navy was not directly responsible for that, and did not create that and advise that being done, as they did the original matter which you mentioned a while ago, did they?

Captain Hooper: What the Navy did was this, two things: On the one hand, we were working on this patent thing, trying to get some way devised whereby we could buy radio equipment without having to take the patent responsibility; and we suggested that the companies get together and work it out in some way."

The letter to which Captain Hooper refers was dated January 5, 1920, and was signed by A. J. Hepburn, Acting Chief of the Bureau of Steam Engineering of the United States Navy. It was addressed separately to the General Electric Company and the American Telephone & Telegraph Company. The text was as follows:

"Gentlemen:

"Referring to numerous recent conferences in connection with the radio patent situation and particularly that phase involving vacuum tubes, the bureau has constantly held the point of view that all interests will be best served through some agreement between the several holders of permanent patents whereby the market can be freely supplied with tubes, and has endeavored to point out with concrete examples for practical consideration.

"In this connection, the bureau wishes to invite your attention to the recent tendency of the merchant marine to adopt continuous wave apparatus in their ship installations, the bureau itself having arranged for equipping many vessels of the Shipping Board with such sets. Such installations will create a demand for vacuum tubes in receivers, and this bureau believes it particularly desirable, especially from a point of view of safety at sea, that all ships be able to procure without difficulty vacuum tubes, these being the only satisfactory detectors for receiving continuous waves.

"Today ships are cruising on the high seas with only continuous wave-transmitting equipment except for short ranges when interrupted continuous waves are used. Due to the peculiar patent conditions which have prevented the marketing of tubes to the public, such vessels are not able to communicate with greatest efficiency except with the shore and, therefore, in case of distress it inevitably follows that the lives of crews and passengers are imperiled beyond reasonable necessity.

"In the past the reasons for desiring some arrangement have been largely because of monetary considerations. Now, the situation has become such that it is a public necessity that such arrangement be made without further delay, and this letter may be considered as an appeal, for the good of the public, for a remedy to the situation.

"It is hoped this additional information will have its weight in bringing about a speedy understanding in the patent situation which the bureau considers so desirable.

"A similar letter is being addressed to the American Telephone & Telegraph Company, New York City."

Sec. 109. President Wilson Appoints Admiral Bullard to Act with RCA.

It is now well known that President Woodrow Wilson in January, 1920, was gravely ill from a cerebral hemorrhage sustained during his speaking tour in behalf of the League of Nations in the autumn of 1919. Joseph P. Tumulty, Secretary to the President, sent a polite acknowledgment of the RCA letter of January 5, 1920. It would be brought to the attention of President Wilson. There is mute evidence in the government archives that the stricken statesman retained such a lively interest in wireless transmission that he indeed gave personal attention to the matter.

Obviously his first reaction had been to send it to the Navy Department for suggestions as to the proper official to represent the Government at meetings of the board of directors of the Radio Corporation of America. The following letters, the second one personally annotated by President Wilson, were produced in the Senate investigation of the alleged monopoly by the Radio Corporation of America in December, 1929:

First Letter

"Navy Department,
Washington, January 12, 1920.

"Mr. E. J. Nally,
Radio Corporation of America,
New York, N. Y.

"My dear Mr. Nally:

"With reference to your letter of January 3, 1920, inclosing the letter which you addressed to the President of the United States, I beg to inform you that the President referred the letter to the Secretary of the Navy. The Secretary of the Navy has written to the President, nominating and recommending that I be appointed by the President to attend the stockholders' and directors' meetings of the Radio Corporation of America, in order that I may present and discuss informally the Government's views and interests concerning matters pertaining to radio communication coming before the directors and stockholders of said corporation.

"I hope that the matter will receive the President's consideration, and that it will not be long before I am able to co-operate directly with your company.

"Sincerely yours,
(Signed) W. H. G. BULLARD,

Rear Admiral, United States Navy
Director of Naval Communications."

Second Letter

"Navy Department,
Washington, January 12, 1920.

"The President,
The White House,
Washington, D. C.

"My dear Mr. President:

"With reference to the letter addressed to you by the Radio Corporation of America, relative to the appointment of a naval officer of or above the rank of captain in the regular Navy, to attend the stockholders' and directors' meetings of such corporation, I have the honor to nominate Rear Admiral W. H. G. Bullard, United States Navy, the Director of Naval Communications.

"It is recommended that Rear Admiral W. H. G. Bullard be appointed by the President to attend the stockholders'. and directors' meetings of the Radio Corporation of America, as requested by them, in order that he may present and discuss informally the Government's views and interests concerning matters pertaining to radio communication coming before the directors and stockholders of said corporation.

"It is considered very important that the functions of naval communication service be protected as much as possible inasmuch as the Navy must provide for extensive trans-oceanic communications in order to maintain communications with the fleets. A great many technical problems in trans-oceanic radio communication require cooperation between the interests involved; and therefore, it is very necessary for the Navy Department to solve these communication problems as they arise, and before harm is done by expenditures of funds.

"The Radio Corporation of America is an American company, and should, in the future, have an influential part in the communication system between the United States and foreign countries. It is important that they understand the mission of the Navy in maintaining an efficient trans-oceanic communication system.

"In addition, the Government is interested that the control of the Radio Corporation of America remain in the hands of American citizens.

"The letter from the Radio Corporation of America addressed to the President of the United States is returned herewith.

Sincerely and respectfully yours,
(Signed) THOS. WASHINGTON, Acting.

The White House,
January 14, 1920.

Approved. (Signed) WOODROW WILSON.

On the last day of February, 1920, the United States Government returned all high power stations to their owners. Thus the Radio Corporation of America was in position to carry into effect its long-meditated plans of operation. On March 1st, from the New Brunswick station, RCA transmitted its first commercial messages to England. Although the cable rate was twenty-five cents a word, the rate established for wireless messages was fixed at seventeen cents a word. On the same day wireless communication was established with Norway at a corresponding reduction in rates—twenty-four cents as against a cable rate of thirty-five cents a word.

When the Radio Corporation of America took over the business of the American Marconi Company in the autumn of 1919, David Sarnoff was commercial manager of that corporation. Upon the merger Mr. Sarnoff became commercial manager of RCA. It is apparent that he had abundant faith in his "Radio Music Box" idea and that in the winter of 1920, months before broadcasting began at East Pittsburgh, he revived the idea by laying the same before Owen D. Young, chairman of the board of General Electric Company and RCA. On March 3, 1920, Mr. E. W. Rice, Jr., the President of the General Electric Company, requested Mr. Sarnoff to submit an estimate of prospective radio business based upon his "Music Box" idea. A significant portion of that reply is as follows:

"The 'Radio Music Box' proposition (regarding which I reported to Mr. Nally in 1916 and to Mr. Owen D. Young on January 31, 1920) requires considerable experimentation and development; but, having given the matter much thought, I feel confident in expressing the opinion that the problems involved can be met. With reasonable speed in design and development, a commercial product can be placed on the market within a year or so.

"Should this plan materialize it would seem reasonable to expect sales of one million (1,000,000) 'Radio Music Boxes' within a period of three years. Roughly estimating the selling price at $75 per set, $75,000,000 can be expected. This may be divided approximately as follows:

1st Yr.—100,000 Radio Music Boxes	$7,500,000
2nd Yr.—300,000 Radio Music Boxes	22,500,000
3rd Yr.—600,000 Radio Music Boxes	45,000,000
Total...............	$75,000,000" *

* It is interesting to note that the RCA'S actual cash returns on sales of "Radio Music Boxes" for home sets for the first three years of the radio boom were as follows:

1st year......	1922	....	$11,000,000
2nd year......	1923	....	22,500,000
3rd year......	1924	....	50,000,000
	Total	....	$83,500,000

CHAPTER
TWELVE

Westinghouse Company Inaugurates Radio Broadcasting

190

Section 110. Westinghouse Company Decides to Compete with RCA.

THE CHIEF RIVAL in the electrical and manufacturing field of the General Electric Company for many years had been the Westinghouse Electric and Manufacturing Company of Pittsburgh, Pennsylvania. It has previously been noted that the latter company, like the General Electric Company, had been engaged in war work for the Allies as well as for our own Government. Laboratories of both companies had been very busy during the four years of war, experimenting, testing and perfecting various types of apparatus suitable for wireless transmission. While the General Electric Company had developed vacuum tubes, its greatest achievement had been the expensive sending apparatus known as the Alexanderson Alternator. The Westinghouse Company, on the other hand, had made great progress in the development of wireless transmitters and receivers. At the close of the war its plants were geared for production of wireless equipment for which there was no longer a stable market.

Like its rival in Schenectady, the Pittsburgh firm found itself hard hit by the sudden ending of the World War. Like its rival also, it had never contemplated entering into the field of wireless communications. As we have seen, it required the eloquence of an Admiral of the United States Navy to turn the thoughts of the General Electric Company to the possibilities of communications as a separate enterprise. No Admiral came to the Westinghouse camp to stir its chieftains to action. None was needed, for when news of the launching of the Radio Corporation of America reached the ears of Otto S. Schairer,[1] then newly appointed to the position of Director of Patent Development, he undertook an investigation of what, if anything, Westinghouse might do to maintain its status as a great electrical manufacturer. Mr. Schairer was already convinced that unless Westinghouse kept abreast of the new development in wireless transmission it would be at a great disadvantage. He made a report to his own department and also to the management of Westinghouse recommending immediate purchase of strategic patents as a means of establishing a trading position in relation to RCA. He did not advocate an attempt to wrest control of wireless communications from RCA but simply that Westinghouse, in self-defense, should adopt a policy of what might be termed in modern parlance "muscling in." Thus he hoped that his own company might oblige its rivals to recognize its claims to permanent participation in the manufacture of electrical devices.

[1] Now Vice-President of RCA having charge of patents. Mr. Schairer entered the employ of Westinghouse in 1902 as an engineering apprentice. From 1904 to 1919 he was assistant Patent Attorney. He studied law nights and was admitted to the Pennsylvania bar in 1912. From 1919 to 1926 he was Director of Patent Development; from 1926 to 1929 he was manager of the Patent Dept. of Westinghouse. He came to RCA in 1929 and was made Vice-President in 1930.

This report was adopted by the management of the Westinghouse Company and agents were sent out to reconnoiter the field. Fortunately for Westinghouse, the more or less defunct enterprise originally launched by Reginald A. Fessenden had its headquarters in Pittsburgh. It will be remembered that Fessenden had been financed in all his experimentation by two Pittsburgh financiers, Thomas H. Given and Hay Walker, Jr. These men had spent millions of dollars in the effort with no reward to themselves, but they had conferred enormous benefit upon the future radio industry. Fessenden had invented the alternator which Ernst F. W. Alexanderson had recently perfected and which was now one of the chief assets of Westinghouse's rival, the General Electric Company. The Heterodyne Receiving System and the rotary spark-gap device were still owned by the International Radio Telegraph Company, which was the successor of Fessenden's original National Electric Signalling Company. International Radio Telegraph Company had kept alive during the war, but was now faced with ruin because of lack of customers.

Such was its condition when an official of the Westinghouse Company, in the winter of 1919–20, approached with a suggestion that Westinghouse would be willing to purchase the Fessenden radio patents held by International. The officers of the latter company flatly refused to consider the proposal, asserting that for years they had contemplated re-entering the business of wireless communications in which Fessenden had vainly struggled for success. With perfected apparatus they believed that they might hope to win where the great inventor had failed.

This rebuff apparently set the Westinghouse people to thinking along new lines. Their rival had taken over the American Marconi Company and had formed the Radio Corporation of America. Why should they not form an alliance with the International Radio Telegraph Company, a company with a high-sounding name and with some experience in wireless communications? Taking a leaf out of Owen D. Young's book, they resolved to follow the same procedure that had brought such brilliant success to General Electric Company.

Again they approached the International Radio Telegraph Company, this time holding out the alluring bait of cross-licenses and financial backing that would enable the company to realize its dream of international wireless communications. Samuel M. Kintner, president of International, was too astute a business man to permit such an opportunity to escape. With financial backing, he believed that his company could offer genuine competition to the ambitious Radio Corporation of America. He informed the Westinghouse representative that a final decision in the matter must rest with the stockholders of his company—and the further fact that all of the stock was owned by the estate of Thomas Hartley Given.

Given, it will be remembered, had bought out the interests of his partner Walker, the two having been the only stockholders in Fessenden's venture. The circumstance of stock ownership in one family was fortunate indeed. General Electric Company had been obliged to deal with Marconi stockholders on both sides of the Atlantic.

Sec. III. The International Radio Telegraph Company Formed.

Martha A. Given, widow of the late financier, and the other beneficiaries of his will, were apparently not anxious to sell their stock in the company, or possibly the Westinghouse people did not offer to purchase the same. The proposal of financial backing, however, was most alluring. Inasmuch as the International Radio Telegraph Company had assets and interests not connected with the business of communications, it was decided to form a new corporation. Since the present name was exactly suited to their purpose the lawyers of Westinghouse and International hit upon the device well known in the legal fraternity of a slight alteration in the title. Since the official name of the present corporation was "International Radio Telegraph Company," the name of the new corporation could be "The International Radio Telegraph Company." This was decided upon and on May 22, 1920, (still following the procedure of General Electric) a "General Agreement" was officially signed.

In the recitals of this agreement it appeared that the capital stock of the old corporation had a par value of $2,500,000. In the new set-up the stockholders of the original company received 12,500 shares of 7% preferred stock (with a par value of $1,250,000) and 125,000 shares of no par value. Inasmuch as 125,000 shares of no par value issued to the Westinghouse Company were to cost the latter $2,500,000, it will be seen that the stockholders of International made a very good bargain for themselves by exchanging their stock—an apparent profit of $1,250,-000. Besides that they retained accrued rights under the original corporation. This transaction indicates that the Westinghouse people were very anxious to acquire a communications company to be used as a lever in prying open the gate that the young corporation was then endeavoring to close in the wireless field.

One of the features of the agreement was that the stock to be issued in the name of the Westinghouse Company was to be deposited in escrow with the Union Trust Company of Pittsburgh to be delivered as rapidly as paid for, all payments to be completed within two years.

After the signing of the preliminary agreement the attorneys for the parties at once set to work to organize the new corporation. This was obviously accomplished before June 21, 1920, since on that date a "General Agreement" was executed between "The International Radio Telegraph Company" and the Westinghouse Electric and Manufacturing Company in which was the following recital of facts:

"Whereas The International Company has been incorporated in accordance with all the terms of an agreement dated the 22nd day of May A.D. 1920."

The new agreement was in fact the fulfillment of pledges made in the preliminary agreement. The Westinghouse Company formally subscribed for the agreed 125,000 shares of stock. Other details were arranged as set forth in the previous agreement.

Thus far the Westinghouse Company had followed the course pursued by Owen D. Young. The corporation to operate a wireless communications system had been created. Here the analogy ceased, because the Radio Corporation of America was actually able to function, whereas The International Radio was powerless to follow its example because it lacked several of the essentials of a complete system. It had no efficient transmitter. The Fessenden 500-cycle spark device was their nearest approach to the necessary instrument. Experiments by the Navy Department during the war had demonstrated that the Fessenden machine was inferior to the Poulsen Arc and of course much inferior to the Alexanderson Alternator. One of the tasks of International would be to purchase, if possible, a more effective transmitter. Another was to endeavor to arrange with wireless companies abroad for exchange of international messages. A third problem was to endeavor to arrange with the United States Government for licenses to use patents owned by the Government. We will presently see how International fared in these several endeavors.

Sec. 112. RCA Makes Alliance with American Telephone & Telegraph Company.

On May 4, 1920, the Radio Corporation of America held its first annual meeting. Owen D. Young was elected Chairman of the Board and Edward J. Nally, President of the Corporation. Although RCA was now vigorously functioning, the officials realized that they were by no means secure against competition. The recent action of the Westinghouse Company had challenged RCA, yet the latter company was now almost ready to announce a great triumph. The powerful American Telephone & Telegraph Company, with its great network of land communication lines, could have been a much more potent rival than the Westinghouse group. For weeks Owen D. Young had been busy with plans and negotiations looking to a business alliance between American Telephone and RCA.

On July 1, 1920, a cross-license agreement between the General

Electric Company and the American Telephone & Telegraph Company was signed. The agreement covered a great variety of situations in which one company might grant exclusive or non-exclusive licenses to use patents or inventions owned by the other. It covered all phases of manufacture and sale of electrical apparatus. In short, it accomplished the purpose of fitting another section into the jig-saw puzzle that Owen D. Young was so busily putting together.

On the same day a so-called "extension agreement" was signed in which four parties were involved—General Electric, Telephone Company, RCA and Western Electric Company. The gist of the preamble to this agreement was that the first two parties desired to extend their agreement to include RCA and the Western Electric Company. It was really a cross-licensing contract by which each party acquired rights with certain limitations to utilize patents held by any of the four.

The significance of the transaction lies in the fact that the Western Electric Company and the American Telephone & Telegraph Company were owners of the deForest audion and other valuable patents, thus bringing to RCA the right to utilize these inventions in connection with the ambitious program that its officials were mapping out. In truth it may be said that Owen D. Young and his associates were building better than they realized. Unknown to them and unforeseen by even the wisest electrical engineers, certain experiments then being conducted in Pittsburgh were about to usher in a new era in which these audion patents were to become priceless to their owners and the term radio to acquire a new and distinctive meaning.

In the agreements with A. T. & T. Company and Western Electric, as in others of its kind, the Radio Corporation was made the exclusive selling agency for all broadcast receiving sets that were to be manufactured for public sale by members of the group. Before the completion of the cross-licensing campaign RCA was in this way to acquire exclusive selling rights for the General Electric Company; the Westinghouse Company; the American Tel. & Tel. Company; the Western Electric Company; the United Fruit Company and the Wireless Specialty Apparatus Company, each of whom held important radio apparatus patents and some of whom manufactured the same in large quantities. This does not mean that jobbing houses throughout the nation that were already selling General Electric and Westinghouse products were to be superseded. On the contrary they were automatically to become jobbers for RCA, the wholesale merchandising agency for the allied corporations.

Sec. 113. International Radio Checkmated by RCA.

In early summer of 1920, the newly formed International Radio Telegraph Company sent its president, Samuel M. Kintner, abroad on

the important mission of contacting wireless companies of European
nations in an effort to arrange satisfactory traffic agreements by which
commercial wireless messages might be exchanged in trans-Atlantic
communication. In this mission Mr. Kintner was to encounter undreamed-of difficulties. The astute gentlemen who had launched the
Radio Corporation of America had six months before made iron-clad
agreements with the far-flung British Marconi System. They had made
similar exclusive agreements with every other important wireless system of European nations. In Germany alone did Mr. Kintner receive
the dubious satisfaction of a promise that if his company were to erect
a wireless station in the United States capable of trans-Atlantic communication the German stations would give International Radio the
same commercial advantages already accorded to the Radio Corporation of America. The bitterness of this defeat must have been quite
overwhelming to the ambitious president of The International Radio
Telegraph Company. The very name of his company would be a mis-
nomer now that international wireless traffic arrangements were found
to be impossible.

But far greater issues were involved than the chagrin and embarrassment of the officials of The International Radio Telegraph Company. The great Westinghouse Electric and Manufacturing Company,
godfather of the new enterprise, had at the same time suffered a
disastrous defeat. Its traditional rival, the General Electric Company,
had completely outmaneuvered it in the field of world-wireless transmission. The Westinghouse people had already invested large sums in
the venture and had pledged their company to a minimum expenditure of two and a half million dollars. Imagine the rage in Pittsburgh
at the stunning news of the collapse of Mr. Kintner's overseas mission!

It is true that their new company, The International Radio, could
still function in the western hemisphere even though it could never hope
to rival RCA in trans-Atlantic communications. Men of mettle such
as the late H. P. Davis, Vice-President of Westinghouse Electric, Guy
E. Tripp, Chairman of the Board of Westinghouse, Charles A. Terry,
another Vice-President, and their associates do not tamely accept defeat. On the contrary they usually make energetic efforts to minimize
their losses and to seize every possible opportunity to build up a
counter-offensive against victorious rivals.

In the meantime, however, before hearing from Kintner's mission
abroad, the chieftains of Westinghouse took counsel together to discover, if possible, fields which they might hope to occupy in advance
of the prodigious campaign of RCA. It was well known that the
Federal Government was co-operating with RCA in its efforts to establish an all-American wireless service of international dimensions.
Shrewdly believing, however, that the traditional fear of monopoly

might still operate in government circles, the plan of seeking licenses to use government-owned wireless patents was agitated.

Sec. 114. Valiant in Defeat.

To the delight of the representatives of International Radio they soon discovered that in Washington was one field in which they had not been checkmated by RCA. The Navy Department, disappointed in its hopes for government ownership of wireless communications, was by no means wedded to RCA. Certainly they had government-owned patents, and plenty of them!

The Poulsen patents, including the famous arc transmitter that some experts declared equal in efficiency to the Alexanderson Alternator, were government-owned. All in all there were more than one hundred and forty wireless patents in government control. On August 5, 1920, The International Radio Telegraph Company entered into an agreement with the United States Government whereby it secured a license to use any or all of these patents. To be sure, International Radio was unable to persuade the Government to give them an exclusive license, so there was nothing to prevent RCA from making a similar license agreement. It was a guaranty, however, that International Radio could completely equip any wireless stations that it might establish.

In the meantime Westinghouse itself, under Mr. Schairer's leadership, was reaching out to gather up whatever of value in wireless transmission had thus far escaped the persuasions of the General Electric Company or its potent infant—RCA. It so happened that the Armstrong-Pupin patents, then recognized as of great value in the transmission and reception of wireless messages, were still privately owned. It was true that the Armstrong "feed back" device was in litigation with deForest but electrical engineers acclaimed it as vastly superior to anything of the kind yet devised.

On October 5, 1920, Westinghouse decided to buy a thirty-day option on the Armstrong-Pupin patents. The astute Mr. Schairer had concluded a brilliant campaign by which his company had acquired strategic trading advantages. RCA would be obliged to negotiate with Westinghouse in order to avoid complications. On November 4th the Armstrong option was exercised. The price to be paid was to be $335,000 at all events, but $535,000 if interference litigation on the "feed back" patent should be decided in Armstrong's favor.

By the familiar cross-licensing procedure The International Radio Telegraph Company was presently entitled to the benefit of these numerous patent rights. The Westinghouse Company also found itself more securely entrenched in the manufacturing field. Thus out of defeat had been snatched a partial victory. The Westinghouse Company had grim satisfaction, even after learning of Kintner's defeat in his European mission, in the knowledge that they had beaten RCA in one skirmish.

Unable to compete in a world arena, the Westinghouse Company and its brain-child were of necessity confined to a narrow sector. Wisely they decided to make the most of their opportunities by brightening up their particular corner. From this decision was indirectly to result the radio broadcasting industry of today. Up to 1920 the word "radio" had been applied very casually to wireless transmission of electrical impulses. The very names "Radio Corporation of America" and "International Radio Telegraph" illustrate that fact, since at the time they were adopted no one dreamed that the almost forgotten pioneer work of Fessenden and deForest in broadcasting grand opera would ever lead to one of the world's truly great industries—radio broadcasting. The manner in which the Westinghouse Electric and Manufacturing Company long brooded the golden egg and then unexpectedly hatched it into a chicken very much alive and tremendously prolific deserves special attention.

In discussing Westinghouse's predicament, in a lecture given in 1928, H. P. Davis, its Vice-President, made the following illuminating reference to the beginnings of radio broadcasting:

"The International Radio Telegraph Company owned and operated several ship-to-shore stations, and was a pioneer in this field. The operation and development of this service immediately became a part of Westinghouse's activities.

"A large sum of money expended for control of The International Radio Telegraph Company emphasized in our minds the necessity for developing our new acquisition into a service which would broaden, popularize, and commercialize radio to a greater extent than existed at that time, in order to earn some return on this investment as well as to keep the radio organization together.

"In seeking a revenue-returning service, the thought occurred to broadcast a news service regularly from our ship-to-shore stations to the ships. This thought was followed up, but nothing was accomplished because of the negative reaction obtained from those organizations which we desired to supply with this news service. However, the thought of accomplishing something which would realize the service referred to still persisted in our minds."

Thus again we find the spirit of valor in face of frustration of hope working for the blessing of mankind. Fortunately for Westinghouse its chief investigator in the field of wireless telephony had by this time developed a persistence in his quest that was now the ruling passion of his life. That man was Dr. Frank Conrad.

EARLY CARBON MICROPHONE
Used with de Forest wireless telephone
sets installed on vessels of the United
States Navy during the world cruise
of 1908.

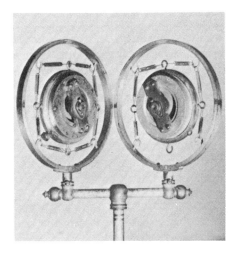

DYNAMIC MICROPHONE   CARBON MICROPHONE—DUO TYPE

Sec. 115. The Radio Dream Becomes a Reality at Pittsburgh.

In an earlier chapter it has been noted that during the war the Westinghouse Company had undertaken intensive research in wireless telephony. Dr. Frank Conrad was the engineer in charge of this work. His first interest in wireless is said to have arisen in 1912 from a desire to check his watch with the Arlington time signals. He built a small receiving set to enable him to get first-hand information.[2] The toy became an object of experimental interest that led to a profound knowledge of radio technique. He was now seeking to develop a wireless telephone transmitter. It was necessary to test his experimental apparatus over a distance of several miles. Two experimental stations were maintained, one at the Westinghouse plant and the other on the upper floor of Dr. Conrad's garage four or five miles distant. As the quest became more intriguing Dr. Conrad kept late hours at his home station—tinkering, testing, adjusting—until he had succeeded in producing desired results. Now that the war was over and amateur stations were again in operation, some of them using vacuum tubes, Dr. Conrad relicensed his station 8XK in April, 1920, and presently had the satisfaction of discovering that his broadcasts were being picked up in the neighborhood. Conrad soon had a circle of amateurs who were in frequent communication with him by wireless.

Tiring of talking to the group, he finally resorted to phonograph records as a means of entertaining his growing public. By the summer of 1920 his listener response was becoming a bit troublesome. Letters and telephone calls were coming in, many of them making odd requests, such as that on a certain hour of the evening he broadcast in order that the listening amateur might entertain his friends with this latest marvel of science.

In sheer self-defense Dr. Conrad finally announced that at 7:30 o'clock on Wednesday and Saturday evenings he would broadcast for two hours. This required the use of fresh phonograph records for each broadcast. Dr. Conrad could not afford so expensive a luxury by outright purchase, so he contrived to borrow records from a local phonograph dealer. This canny merchant, the first commercial advertiser on the air, made the not unreasonable request that his store be mentioned as the source of supply. To the delight of the dealer he soon discovered that listeners were buying far more of the records used by Dr. Conrad than any other on sale.

The obliging scientist naturally grew weary of his self-imposed task but his two young sons, Francis and Crawford Conrad, were eager to assist in so delightful a pastime.[3] They announced their programs with

2 *Literary Digest,* March 13, 1937—a story of Dr. Frank Conrad.
3 *Ibid.*

gusto. They introduced local talent. The circle of listeners grew apace. The demand for radio sets increased locally and finally an enterprising department store in Pittsburgh inserted advertisements in the local papers announcing a supply of radio sets for those who desired to listen to the Conrad programs.

The Conrad family now occupied the position of public benefactors, yet it was the position of entertainers who receive nothing but glory as their reward. A growing clientele was listening to their phonograph and conversational broadcasts—a clientele that was demanding more and more of entertainment from the pioneer broadcasting studio in the upper story of the Conrad garage. The only persons who were reaping reward were the local mechanics and the department stores that dealt in radio sets. Indirectly, however, the Westinghouse Company was beginning to experience a boom in gadgets that went into the assembling of the small home sets with which the people were listening. These were the battery sets, unwieldy and crude when compared with the compact and artistic household radios of this Year of Grace 1938.

Sec. 116. Westinghouse Decides to Build a Radio Broadcasting Station.

To the late Harry P. Davis, Vice-President of the Westinghouse Electric and Manufacturing Company, belongs the credit of being the first official of a great electrical manufacturing plant to glimpse the possibilities of radio broadcasting on a commercial plane. In an address at the Graduate School of Business Administration of Harvard University in 1927–28 Mr. Davis thus explained his sudden interest in radio:

"During this period Dr. Conrad had continued in his experiments with the station at his home and had greatly improved his radio telephone transmitter. Following the date on which government restrictions were removed from radio stations, Dr. Conrad quite regularly had operated this radio telephone transmitter to send out interesting programs of one kind or another, and to such an extent that people with receiving sets became sufficiently interested to listen to his station.

"The program material available to him was largely phonograph records, although there were some talks, baseball, and football scores. The station, whose letters had been changed, was then designated as 8XK and was known as one of the best amateur stations in the country.

"We were watching this activity very closely. In the early part of the following year the thought came which led to the initiation of a regular broadcast service. An advertisement of a local department store in a Pittsburgh newspaper, calling attention to a stock of radio receivers which could be used to receive the programs sent out by Dr.

Conrad, caused the thought to come to me that the efforts that were then being made to develop radio telephony as a confidential means of communication were wrong, and that instead its field was really one of wide publicity, in fact, the only means of instantaneous collective communication ever devised. Right in our grasp, therefore, we had that service which we had been thinking about and endeavoring to formulate.

"Here was an idea of limitless opportunity if it could be 'put across.' A little study of this thought developed great possibilities. It was felt that there was something that would make a new public service of a kind certain to create epochal changes in the then accepted everyday affairs, quite as vital as had been the introduction of the telephone and telegraph, or the application of electricity to lighting and to power. We became convinced that we had in our hands in this idea the instrument that would prove to be the greatest and most direct means of mass communication and mass education that had ever appeared. The natural fascination of its mystery, coupled with its ability to annihilate distance, would attract, interest, and open many avenues to bring happiness into human lives. It was obviously a form of service of universal application, that could be rendered without favor and without price to millions eager for its benefits.

"Resulting from this was my decision to install a broadcasting station at East Pittsburgh and to initiate this service. This decision, made in 1920, created the present huge radio industry. Not until fall, however, was the equipment ready for operation. In the interim, I had occasion to hold many interesting and now really historical conferences to plan our undertaking in such a way that our vision of service and opportunity might be realized to its fullest extent.

"Dr. Frank Conrad, Assistant Chief Engineer, Mr. J. C. McQuiston, General Advertising Manager, Mr. S. M. Kintner, manager of the Research Department, Mr. O. S. Schairer, manager of the Patent Department, Mr. L. W. Chubb, manager of the Radio Engineering Department, and Mr. M. C. Rypinski, of the Sales Department—all of the Westinghouse Electric and Manufacturing Company—participated in these conferences, and it was their experience, advice, constant faith, and loyal efforts in the undertaking and the developments that followed that carried the project to success."

Sec. 117. Station KDKA Broadcasts 1920 Election Returns.

The year 1920 was a year of great beginnings in wireless transmission. Strangely enough, in this twelvemonth, radio as we know it today was born, yet months before that great event the scientific world was stirred by the almost incredible announcement of television which is today, after eighteen years of experimentation, still in its swaddling clothes. In England H. Grinnell Matthews was experimenting hopefully in this field.[4] His claims, it is true, were regarded with skepticism

4 *Wireless Age,* August, 1920.

by American electrical engineers, but a month later a Danish inventor succeeded in transmitting pictures by wireless. A Copenhagen newspaper actually published two photographs transmitted in this manner.[5]

During the summer of 1920 the Radio Corporation of America made substantial progress in its campaign for world coverage in wireless transmission. Edward J. Nally, President of RCA, returned to America September 6, 1920, having concluded important business with reference to traffic relations with European wireless companies.[6] This task had been lightened by the fact that the British Marconi Company already held contracts of long standing for traffic relations with the principal countries of Europe. The alliance between the British and American companies naturally paved the way for Mr. Nally, who had formerly been an official of standing in the Marconi councils. His chief task had been to arrange for traffic exchange with Germany. The contract with the proper German officials was signed on August 10, 1920. Elmer E. Bucher, long associated with the American Marconi Company, was appointed a commercial engineer of RCA in September, 1920.

In the previous section Mr. Davis' story of the inception of the idea of establishing a radio station in East Pittsburgh has been set forth. Fortunately we have an additional bit of information. Samuel M. Kintner, the chief co-worker of Dr. Conrad, gives us the following dramatic version:

"Their advertisement in the Pittsburgh *Sun* on the evening of September 29, 1920 caught the eye of Mr. H. P. Davis, Vice-President of Westinghouse. The next day he called together his little 'radio cabinet,' consisting of Dr. Frank Conrad, L. W. Chubb, O. S. Schairer, and your speaker. He told of reading the Horne advertisement and made the suggestion that the Westinghouse Company erect a station at East Pittsburgh and operate it every night on an advertised program, so that people would acquire the habit of listening to it just as they do of reading a newspaper. He said, 'If there is sufficient interest to justify a department store in advertising radio sets for sale on an uncertain plan of permanence, I believe there would be a sufficient interest to justify the expense of rendering a regular service—looking to the sale of sets and the advertising of the Westinghouse Company for our returns.' Mr. Davis asked us whether we could get the station in operation by November 2nd, in time to report the Harding-Cox election. We, of course, said 'Yes,' and Dr. Conrad, assisted by D. G. Little, did most of the work in completing the installation." [7]

Mr. Davis had counted upon being able to broadcast the national

[5] *Wireless Age*, September, 1920.
[6] *Ibid.*, October, 1920.
[7] *Proceedings of Institute of Radio Engineers*, December 1932.

election returns of November 2, 1920, as a fitting program to inaugurate the service. Local newspapers had been enlisted in a plan to publicize the broadcast, yet added to the worries of setting up the station had been the fear that a mere handful of people—local amateurs only—would hear the broadcast. It was essential, if Vice-President Davis were to justify the expenditure of corporation funds, that the first broadcast should reach an influential audience. This thought no doubt led to the adoption of an expedient that can best be described in Mr. Davis' own words.

"A broadcasting station," he declared, "is a rather useless enterprise unless there is someone to listen to it. Here was an innovation, and even though advertised, few then, other than possibly some of the amateurs who had receiving sets, could listen to us. To meet this situation we had a number of simple receiving outfits manufactured. These we distributed among friends and to several of the officers of the company. Thus was the first broadcast-audience drafted." [8]

On October 27, 1920, the new station was licensed by the Department of Commerce and assigned the historic call letters KDKA. In preparation for the ambitious attempt it was decided to set up the station on the top of the tallest building in the Westinghouse plant, which was located in a valley, with hills rising around it. Obviously some sort of shelter must be provided for the transmitter, as well as to protect the mechanics and the announcer. In this pioneer stage there seemed no reason why all broadcasting activities could not be conducted in the same room. While Dr. Conrad and his assistants were feverishly at work setting up the mechanical apparatus of the station, carpenters erected a tiny penthouse on the roof—and such a penthouse! Mr. Davis described it as "a rough box affair on the roof."

A photograph taken on that historic November 2, 1920, discloses that the penthouse was built of matched sheathing. It boasted at least two windows. The transmitter was in the corner between the windows, and was flanked by table-like desks, set against the walls on two sides. The engineer sat before the transmitter and the announcer was stationed close by. The microphone seems to have been much like an old-fashioned telephone set with a box-like arrangement behind the mouthpiece. The hastily constructed station had two 50-watt oscillators and four 50-watt modulators.

Headphones were worn by the engineer and the reporters, two of whom were present during the broadcast. So hurriedly had the work been rushed to completion that there had been little opportunity to test the sending apparatus before the evening of election day. On the night of November 1st it was tried out but the results were unsatis-

[8] *The Radio Industry* (lectures at Harvard Univ.), p. 197.

factory. Adjustments were made next day. Dr. Frank Conrad was very nervous over the prospect, so nervous in fact that he rushed home to his own garage-station 8XK and remained there during the broadcast—"standing by" to pick up the program in case anything should go wrong in the new station.

Fortunately, however, all went well in the "penthouse." Dispatches from all over the nation were pouring in at the editorial rooms of the *Pittsburgh Post* and thence were relayed by telephone to the radio station. Each bulletin was broadcast as it came in. From five hundred to a thousand listeners, equipped with earphones or gathered in stores, were enabled to hear the election returns. They knew that Warren G. Harding had been elected President of the United States. The news had come to them from the evening sky—a thrill never to be forgotten. The sensation in the public press created by this marvelous demonstration of wireless telephony set in motion a movement that eventually encircled the globe.

The term "broadcast" was soon to become a household word in America. To be sure the more awkward expression "broadcasted" was to be found for a time even in technical magazines but the more grammatical term at length prevailed. Instead of saying "The fight was broadcasted over Station ———" American journalists gradually adopted the simple form "The fight was broadcast by Station ———."

CHAPTER
THIRTEEN

Pioneer Days in Radio Broadcasting

Sec. 118. Who is Entitled to Priority—KDKA or WWJ.

IT HAS BEEN OBSERVED in the progress of this historical narrative that great discoveries and great inventions are usually the result of a quest in which various contestants have struggled toward the common goal. Radio broadcasting is no exception to this rule. A station operated by the *Detroit News,* WWJ, is alleged to have antedated KDKA in broadcasting news. It is claimed that on August 31, 1920, a radiophone program was put on the air from an alleged *Detroit News* wireless telephone station and that the service thus inaugurated was continued on a regular schedule thereafter. If this can be substantiated then KDKA, unless it have other claims to priority, would yield its crown to Station WWJ, the lineal successor of this early beginning.

The fact is, however, that KDKA was the lineal successor of the Westinghouse experimental station that Dr. Frank Conrad had operated on a schedule for a long time prior to the opening of KDKA. Moreover, if we consult the records of the Department of Commerce as contained in the monthly *Radio Service Bulletin* we discover that Station WWJ was not on the list of licensed stations until June, 1922, although there was an earlier station listed in the name of the *Detroit News* and labeled WBL, November 1, 1921. Assuming that WWJ is entitled to the November, 1921, date we find that KDKA antedates it a full year as a regularly licensed radio broadcasting station and if we consider the alleged date of the experimental station as August 31, 1920, we find that the Westinghouse experimental radiophone antedates that by many months. Dr. Frank Conrad's celebrated experimental Station 8XK was first listed in the monthly bulletin of the Department of Commerce August 1, 1916. It was relicensed with the same call letters after the war and was on the list published in the bulletin of May 1, 1920. Singularly enough, no station, either experimental or regular, appears in the name of the *Detroit News* until November 1, 1921.

In support of the claim of priority it is alleged that the *Detroit News,* prior to the establishing of Station WBL in 1921, maintained an amateur station whose call letters were 8MK. The author has examined with great care the back numbers of the *Radio Service Bulletin* prior to November 1, 1921, and is unable to discover any such station, despite the fact that other experimental stations in Detroit not affiliated with the *Detroit News* are in the listings. The claim is also made that a station 8CS was listed in the name of an employee of the *Detroit News.* Strangly enough, this station is not listed in the *Radio Service Bulletin.* Inasmuch as the *Bulletin* was the official publication of the Department of Commerce, the failure to list either of these experimental stations would indicate that the claim of priority advanced in behalf of WWJ is based upon imperfect recollection rather than upon facts susceptible of proof.

Further evidence on the point confirmatory of this conclusion of fact was obtained for the author by Wayne L. Randall, Director of Publicity of the National Broadcasting Company. At the author's request, Mr. Randall wrote to Col. Patterson, Assistant Secretary of Commerce, and received a report under date of July 16, 1938, signed by Alexander V. Dye, Director of the Bureau of Foreign and Domestic Commerce, from which the following is a quotation:

"The early records of these amateur stations were listed under the heading of 'Radio Service' by the Bureau of Navigation, Department of Commerce, in a publication entitled, *Amateur Radio Stations of the United States of America*. In this bulletin, published June 30, 1921, on page 156, Station 8CS is listed as belonging to W. J. Scripps, of 3664 Trumbull Avenue, Detroit, Mich., and as having a capacity of 20 watts.

"In the same volume on page 160, there appears the name Radio News and Music Company, Inc. of Detroit, Mich., as the operator of Station 8MK with a power of 1000 watts. Whether this is a station established by the *Detroit News* is not evident."

The report confirms the date given by the author for the first listing of WBL, November, 1921, and states that the name was changed to WWJ in March, 1922. As previously noted, this change did not appear in the *Radio Service Bulletin* until June, 1922.

Now that official records have demonstrated that Station 8CS (operated by W. J. Scripps, now manager of WWJ) was first listed in a bulletin published June 30, 1921, whereas KDKA was listed eight months earlier, we may safely conclude that the Pittsburgh station is entitled to priority on that score alone. But as previously indicated, KDKA could claim Dr. Conrad's experimental station as its origin and go back to August 1, 1916. It would seem therefore that WWJ's claim to priority is disproved on all counts.

Sec. 118a. Station KDKA Broadcasts from a Tent.

Immediately after its successful performance on election night, November 2, 1920, KDKA established an evening broadcasting schedule that ran until 9:30 P.M. Its program was at first not unlike that of Dr. Conrad's amateur station—largely drawn from phonograph records. The astute H. P. Davis, the godfather of this new form of public entertainment, soon perceived that mere phonograph music over the air could never stimulate growth of the industry. People would not buy expensive radio sets in order to listen to phonograph records that they themselves might play on their own phonograph. No indeed, something more vital must be provided.

Band music—broadcast from an actual concert—was a logical idea. Westinghouse already had an excellent band. Mr. Davis resolved to utilize the Westinghouse band. A difficulty, however, was at once encountered. The rude penthouse on the roof was only large enough for the operators. Dr. Conrad believed that an auditorium could be utilized as a broadcasting studio. An auditorium of East Pittsburgh soon became the headquarters of Station KDKA but complaints from the radio audience began to pour in. There were disconcerting echoes and distortion in the broadcasts. The pioneers had encountered that bug-a-boo of early broadcasting—resonance! Try as they might the auditorium was unsatisfactory for band music.

In desperation they took the band out-of-doors and lo! the broadcast improved amazingly. Back went the studio to the roof-top for out-of-doors band concerts. Stormy weather, however, made necessary a large tent to shelter the musicians. The tent worked admirably—no resonance was encountered. Thus during the Spring and Summer of 1921 Station KDKA lived its life like a true pioneer—in a tent!

This first broadcasting station was now equipped with a 100-watt transmitter, a mere toy in comparison to the present-day equipment of radio broadcasting stations. It was, however, much more powerful than amateur stations of the locality. Amateurs had hitherto had the air to themselves but now that KDKA was on the air every evening amateurs were seriously inconvenienced. A virtual feud speedily developed. Since the average amateur was equipped with a spark set, he was not without the means of retaliation. The Westinghouse band may have produced true harmony within its tent on the roof-top but squeals and squeaks and sudden thunder from amateur sharpshooters all too often accompanied the Westinghouse music in its circuit of the upper air. The receiving sets that were being offered to the public in the pioneering days of KDKA have thus been described by George H. Clark, Historian of RCA:

"These receivers had but a single circuit, for the Westinghouse designers figured that reception in the home must be simplified down to the utmost, if home-folks who could not even replace a burned-out fuse were to be able to operate the devices. No 'forest of knobs' here; no complicated table of settings; merely one circuit and one handle to vary it. I can recall the personal scorn with which this single circuit receiver was viewed by 'old-style' radio engineers, i.e., myself, for it was held that this was going back to the days of 1900. But later, we . . . I . . . realized that the new transmitters were so much more sharply tuned than the old spark sledge-hammers that a single circuit receiver was in 1921 actually workable! Little by little, actual use showed that for handling by people who knew nothing of radio's technicalities the single circuit was just what had been needed. It was a bold psychological move in the struggle to bring radio out of the attic into the sitting-room, and it worked. How well it worked I can realize today, as I stroll home from the office at seven P.M. and find that, as I pass house after house, I am never out of touch with what Amos is saying to Andy."

Sec. 119. RCA Absorbs International Radio Telegraph Company.

It will be remembered that the agreement between The International Radio Telegraph Company and the Westinghouse Company had called for the payment of $2,500,000 for certain shares of stock, complete payment to be made within two years. This agreement had been entered into on June 21, 1920. A year had now elapsed—a year of disappointment. The International Radio had discovered that it could never be international in fact—that the Radio Corporation of America had already acquired almost everything worth-while. It was true that The International Radio had made certain successful raids on patents not already captured by RCA, but such successes as they had gained were like guerilla operations of a defeated army—small comfort to the commanders of the defeated host.

To make matters more disheartening the Westinghouse sponsors had held back on their promises of funds. Their agreement gave them two years in which to pay $2,500,000. Very well, they would take their time. For twelve months the International stock had remained in escrow, or nearly all of it, for in June, 1921, only $300,000 of Westinghouse money had been paid over to the agents of The International Radio Telegraph Company. As previously noted, the Westinghouse officials were in reality using the communications corporation as a pawn in a contest for industrial equality.

It should be noted that Station KDKA, that was already attracting the attention of the scientific world, was owned and operated by Westinghouse Electric and Manufacturing Company. The International Radio could not claim any credit for this achievement. It is small wonder under these depressing circumstances that The International Radio should have been in a mood to surrender to the Radio Corporation of America. Surrender it did—and with the blessings of Westinghouse, since we find the following significant facts, unearthed by the Senate investigation of the merger of RCA and International.

On June 30, 1921, a sales agreement was drawn up between International and RCA,[1] yet the same was not formally executed and delivered until August 8th following. On the same day that the sales agreement was drawn, June 30, 1921, the Radio Corporation concluded a cross-licensing agreement [2] with the Westinghouse Company

[1] See Appendix, Exhibit "E."
[2] See Appendix, Exhibit, "F."

in which the RCA-International Radio merger was ratified. All the patent rights so laboriously acquired by Westinghouse were cross-licensed to RCA. Thus the last sections of Owen D. Young's famed jig-saw puzzle were at length fitted into place. On the dizzy heights of Olympus the financial gods had completed transactions that were to cost headaches to Senate investigators and wholesale heartburnings in various quarters.

No fair-minded person could question the necessity of following the consolidation tactics that Mr. Young had outlined. Critics maintained, however, that they had done the job altogether too thoroughly, had set up a complete and iron-clad monopoly of wireless transmission. Senate investigations will be set forth in the progress of this recital.

Sec. 120. Pioneering in Radio Program Building.

Since Station KDKA had been preceded by more than a year of continuous operation of Dr. Conrad's experimental station it was naturally in a position to blaze the trail for all other radio stations. After all, a radio audience needs to get beyond the novelty stage of broadcasting before the influence of its desires can be of much value to the managers of a radio broadcasting station. A phenomenon of the times no doubt aided Station KDKA immeasurably. The radio listeners were then so impressed by the magic of being able to capture voices and music from the air that they wrote letters freely. Anything and everything in a broadcast program affecting them favorably or unfavorably was sure to be commented upon in this fan mail. Thus those in charge of programs were kept on their toes, so to speak, to please, to enthuse the unseen audience out there in radio-land.

In December, 1920, the Westinghouse station in Pittsburgh, under the progressive administration of its station manager J. C. McQuisten, and Vice-President Davis, decided to undertake the hazardous venture of broadcasting a church service. They reasoned that if Lee deForest had succeeded in broadcasting grand opera ten years previously, at a time when broadcasting instruments were much inferior to their own equipment, there should be no question of the feasibility of their project. The U. S. Signal Corps had broadcast services of Trinity Church, Washington, D. C., August 24, 1919.[3]

It so happened that one of the Westinghouse engineers was a member of the choir of the Calvary Episcopal Church of Pittsburgh. The rector of the church, Dr. E. J. VanEtten, was consulted. Fortunately he proved to be a progressive man, broad of vision and impressed by the possibilities of radio broadcasting. He gladly consented to the plan. The date of the initiation of the service was fixed for Sunday, January 2, 1921.

[3] Private records, RCA.

Three microphones were installed in the church auditorium in order that organ, choir and clergyman might equally be served. The broadcast went over splendidly, making so favorable an impression upon the radio audience that it became a regular Sunday feature of Station KDKA. Thus the way was opened for church broadcasts that have continued to this day, the custom spreading to other radio stations, when other stations were inaugurated, which was still months in the future at the time of this first church broadcast.

Another significant bit of pioneering under the leadership of J. C. McQuisten was done by Station KDKA during those days when it was the only commercial station on the air. It so happened that Herbert Hoover had then newly returned from Europe with a record of humanitarian service that had made him one of the sought-after public characters of the age. Pittsburgh citizens, in common with those of other great American cities, were making an intensive drive to raise money for European relief. A dinner was arranged at the Duquesne Club in Pittsburgh, for January 15, 1921. Mr. Hoover was invited to attend. To the joy of all concerned he accepted the invitation.

With a keen appreciation of the public interest in Hoover's expected speech, the officials of the radio station arranged to broadcast the speaking program. Thus for the first time the future President of the United States faced a radio microphone at the Pittsburgh dinner. Radio listeners of the vicinity then made their first acquaintance with that deep monotone, with its rolling "r-rs," that characterize the Hoover voice. Hoover was never a dynamic radio speaker. At the beginning of his experience before the microphone his merits were largely his vast reputation. Listeners were hearing the voice of the world-famous Herbert Hoover, who so capably had administered relief to the stricken people in war-torn Europe.

Hoover was the first of many famous people to make their first radio appearances over Station KDKA. On February 18, 1921, Alice M. Robertson, Congressman-elect from Oklahoma, the first of her sex to be elected to Congress, appeared before the Pittsburgh Press Club. Col. Theodore Roosevelt, Jr., was the other speaker on this same program. A veritable procession of dignitaries came to Pittsburgh that winter. Three members of the Harding Cabinet, Mellon, Davis and Weeks, were speakers whose remarks were broadcast by KDKA. The greatest orator of his day, William Jennings Bryan, made his first appearance before a microphone at Pittsburgh during these days of radio pioneering.

Sec. 121. Beginnings of Sports Broadcasts.

The first boxing event to be broadcast occurred April 11, 1921, in the Motor Square Garden in Pittsburgh, a minor event but significant because of the ambitious attempt to report a blow-by-blow description. Johnny Ray and Johnny Dundee were the contending parties. On August 4-6, 1921, KDKA was to report the Davis Cup matches, an important tennis meet. On August 5, 1921, it was to broadcast a play-by-play description of a national league baseball game.

Before these latter events, however, comes the most fantastic of all radio beginnings, a radio station created for the occasion, to broadcast a world's heavyweight championship prize fight. Jack Dempsey, the colorful Manassa Mauler, was being challenged for the heavyweight crown by one Georges Carpentier, the champion of France. Carpentier himself was a glamorous figure in sporting and theatrical circles. America and France were thus to meet in the squared circle. This particular circle was to be established in Jersey City. David Sarnoff, formerly of the American Marconi Company and now recently elected to the post of General Manager of the Radio Corporation of America,[4] conceived the brilliant idea of broadcasting this great international event. KDKA in Pittsburgh, Pennsylvania, was then the only commercial radio broadcasting station in the land. It was too far from Jersey City to be of any use. Besides RCA had no claim upon it.

Nothing daunted, Mr. Sarnoff called Major J. Andrew White, the resourceful editor of *Wireless Age,* and requested him to arrange for broadcasting the fight. White in turn called Harry Walker and J. O. Smith, radio technicians, to assist in the fantastic attempt. Fortunately for the trio, they soon discovered that the General Electric Company had just completed a transmitter intended for the United States Navy but had not yet delivered it. Major White succeeded in borrowing the transmitter.

Time was short and so the persuasive Major White went to the officials of the Lackawanna Railroad and wheedled them into permitting him to suspend an aerial between two of their experimental train wireless towers in Hoboken. It so happened that in the railroad yard was a galvanized iron shack sacred to Pullman porters. Here the porters were wont to dress for their routine duties. No white men were allowed in this holy of holies, at least that was their belief, but a man named White now invaded their dressing room. He did so, moreover, with express permission of the Railroad Company. Not only did he invade the place—he and his companions carted in a fearsome collection of radio equipment. This equipment occupied an unconscionable amount of space.

The indignant porters threatened the trio with violence. They promised to demolish the apparatus. Since radio bulbs, wires and switches are decidedly vulnerable it became necessary to guard the

4 At a meeting of the Board of Directors, April 29, 1921.

stuff night and day. Smith even slept beside the set in the beleaguered shack. The fight was scheduled for July 2, 1921.

All night long and until four o'clock in the morning of July 2nd the three men tested and adjusted their apparatus. Their subsequent experiences have been thus described:

"Then, instead of going to bed, Walker and White went to the arena to set up the microphone at the ringside. Having surrendered their tickets at the gate they could not leave the enclosure. They had nothing to eat. They sat and smoked and worried. Intermittent showers dampened their clothes and skin. Their spirits were already dampened. When the sun finally rose the heat, mingled with the dampness, caused what is popularly known as humidity. Steam rose from the arena and themselves. Smith was at the transmitter in Hoboken. Finally the arena began to fill, became crowded, the hour arrived and the fight was on. White had not thought how he was going to announce it. He had no time to think. Only time to worry. At first he could not start. But being an amateur boxer, he soon became lost in the enthusiasm of the occasion, and keeping his eye glued to the fighters, announced in the ready, clear, natural style that marks the man who knows whereof he speaks. One eye he kept on the fighters. The other on a thermos bottle of ice water. He never drank therefrom. The holder of the bottle misunderstood his wild beseechings.

"Between rounds, Smith at the transmitter telephoned back to White his OK of the transmission. Smith too was having his troubles. Standing close to the transmitter, he was partially blind for days afterwards from the glaring tubes. The equipment was not built for continuous service with the power that was being used. It became hotter and hotter. In the middle of the last round, having been on the air more than four hours, one tube exploded. Smith pulled the base from the socket and quickly inserted a new one. After the final signing off he went to the hospital to have the palms of his burned hands bandaged. Before the end of the fight the transmitter had begun to smoke and shortly after the finish of the program it resolved itself into a rather molten mass. Two hundred thousand persons heard the fight." [5]

George H. Clark thus comments on the broadcasting of the Dempsey-Carpentier fight:

"WJY was installed, in a hurry, at the D. L. & W. terminal in Hoboken, so that RCA could broadcast the Dempsey-Carpentier boxing match for the heavyweight championship of the world, which took place at Boyle's Forty Acres, in Jersey City. The antenna was strung between a steel tower and the clock tower of the Lackawanna

[5] *This Thing Called Broadcasting*, pp. 210, 211.

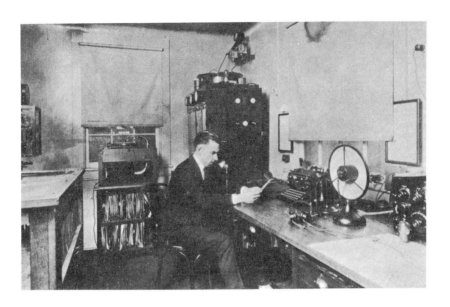

STATION KDKA
Interior of Station KDKA in its early days.

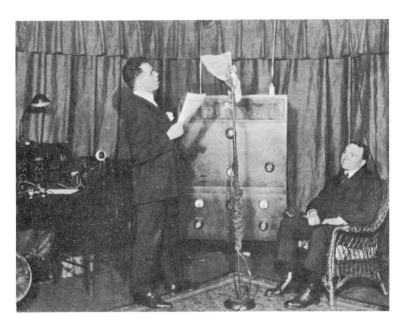

STATION WDY
View of interior of the station at Roselle Park, N. J.

terminal, this steel tower having been used some years previous in tests of train-radio by the railroad company. The wave length used was sixteen hundred meters, and the General Electric Company's 3½ k.w. base station set which was used as transmitter radiated fifteen amperes.

"This broadcasting stunt was staged for the American Committee for Devastated France, and the Navy Club of the United States. The latter organization, as shown by a pamphlet describing the forthcoming broadcast, was headed by no less illustrious a personage than our country's President of today. The fight itself was under the management of Tex Rickard. The National Amateur Wireless Association, whose president was Guglielmo Marconi, was asked to take care of the reception and the loudspeaker installations at various halls, theaters, sporting clubs, Elks, Masonic and K. of C. club-houses, and other public meeting places. About one hundred such gatherings were arranged, the proceeds from the admissions to be divided equally between the two beneficiating clubs. Participating amateurs received certificates signed by Tex Rickard, Georges Carpentier, Jack Dempsey, Miss Anne Morgan, and Franklin D. Roosevelt.

"Remote control was not in the picture in those days, hence it was necessary for the 'sports announcer' at the ringside to describe the fight over an A. T. & T. private wire to the radio station, where it was typed directly from the telephone and handed to the radiophone operator. Major J. Andrew White, 'radio's pioneer impresario,' was the ringside announcer, and J. O. Smith was the second-hand describer whose voice was heard by the three hundred thousand 'ear-witnesses' to the fight. The event was a tremendous success, scientifically, having been heard as far away as Florida, but financially it benefitted the two club organizations in name only."

Sec. 122. Westinghouse Opens Station WBZ.

The success of the radio broadcasting station at Pittsburgh naturally suggested to the Westinghouse officials the idea of opening other broadcasting stations. In the summer of 1921 plans were formulated for stations in the New York City area and at Springfield, Massachusetts. Records of the Department of Commerce disclose that Station WJZ at Newark, New Jersey, was listed as a new station June 1, 1921 whereas Station WBZ in Springfield was first listed October 1, 1921. These listings do not mean that the stations went into operation in the order of their licensing by the Department of Commerce. As a matter of fact, Station WBZ went on the air in September, 1921, some days in advance of Station WJZ. A curious legend has grown up that WBZ was the first radio broadcasting station to be licensed by the Government. In 1930, in response to an inquiry by the National Broadcasting Company, an official of the Department of Commerce, confused by the fact that a new classification of such stations was not adopted until September, 1921, erroneously stated that the first four stations to be licensed were in the following order:

Name	Owner
(1) WBZ, Springfield, Mass.	Westinghouse
(2) WDY, Aldene, N. J.	RCA
(3) WJZ, Newark, N. J.	Westinghouse
(4) KDKA, Pittsburgh, Pa.	Westinghouse

The truth, however, appears in the listings month by month as published by the Department of Commerce. The bound volumes of these reports in the Library of the National Broadcasting Company have been checked by the author and yield the following facts:

Name	Owner	Date First Listed
(1) KDKA	Westinghouse	November 1, 1920
(2) WJZ	Westinghouse	June 1, 1921
(3) WDY	RCA	October 1, 1921
(4) WBZ	Westinghouse	October 1, 1921

While WBZ and WDY appear on the same list it was apparently the custom of the Department of Commerce to list stations in the order of their registration rather than alphabetically. For this reason WBZ would appear to be entitled to fourth place rather than first, a conclusion which the author regrets for the very personal reason that for five years, 1929 to 1934, he was a guest speaker every week in the studios of WBZ and entertains very warm affection for this pioneer radio station.

While Station KDKA was still in its tent studio on the roof-top in East Pittsburgh, a dramatic event was to demonstrate that tents in exposed positions are not to be relied upon. One day in this very autumn when high gales were rife, the operators of Station KDKA arrived to discover that their studio had blown down during the night. With a heavy gale still running there was nothing for the operators to do but retreat into the interior of the building. Having had experience with resonance in the auditorium and finding it again here the desperate pioneers tried a truly desperate expedient. They pitched the tent within the room. It worked as well as it had on the roof. The demon resonance had been foiled. The first satisfactory indoor broadcasting studio had been devised. Westinghouse engineers had discovered how to conquer echoes and resonance—or at least had taken the first step in that direction.

It is not likely that tents were used in their new radio stations in other cities, since their engineers soon discovered that to drape the interior of a studio with lowly burlap, later to be rechristened "monks' cloth," was to accomplish all that a tent could do to combat resonance. Thus sack-cloth in broadcasting studios became the symbol not of groveling penance but of triumph over a bug-a-boo of radio listeners.

Sec. 123. Westinghouse Establishes Station WJZ.

High in the list of potent pioneers was Station WJZ, which was on the list of licensed stations June 1, 1921, but did not actually go on the air until October 1, 1921. Because of its geographic location, in Newark, New Jersey, but a short distance from the great theatrical district of New York City, Station WJZ was destined to become the most important of all Westinghouse stations.

The inauguration of Station WJZ was simple indeed. No one had yet glimpsed the true mission of radio. The art was still at the stage when any program at all seemed marvelous to the listener. That the human voice could be understood and that music, even of a "canned" variety, could be captured from thin air was so wonderful to listeners in the New York City area that they were not at first so exacting as KDKA's listeners had become.

Dr. William H. Easton had been selected by Westinghouse as the impresario of this station. "I remember the opening of WJZ very well," Dr. Easton later declared.[6] "The program feature was the reading of bulletins on a World Series game which were secured from the Newark *Sunday Call*. A group of us sat in an office in Newark, where there was a piece of apparatus that represented a radio receiver and which nearly filled the room. If I am not mistaken, it took two men to keep the receiver working. There was one pair of earphones, and each of us listened, in turn, to the thin voice in the phone and were thrilled to think it was coming from a distance of at least a half mile."

We have yet another bit of authentic evidence of pioneer days at WJZ which was typical of 1921 radio broadcasting. The station was located at the Westinghouse meter factory in Newark. The decision to open a station in the New York area was evidently a speedy one.

"When word came from Pittsburgh ordering the installation of a radio telephone for mass communication," writes Goldsmith, "the problems were placed in the hands of a mechanical engineer and efficiency expert, Charles B. Popenoe,[7] who was later to become Treasurer of the National Broadcasting Company until the time of his death in

6 Goldsmith and Lescarboura—*This Thing Called Broadcasting*, 1930, p. 23.
7 Charles B. Popenoe was born in Dayton, Ohio, December 21, 1887. He was trained for the profession of mechanical engineer at the University of Texas (Class of 1912). His first construction job was with the Department of Public Works, State of Ohio, after winning a captain's commission in the World War, but not getting overseas. He entered the employ of the Westinghouse Company in 1919. He became manager of Station WJZ in 1921 and when the station was taken over by RCA in 1923 continued as manager of the Broadcast Division.

1928. Long on ideas but short on funds, it remained for 'Pope,' as he was affectionately known, to squeeze out the necessary space for the WJZ studio. A cloakroom proved the best solution, whereupon the coats were crowded up a bit and a space about ten feet wide by perhaps eighteen feet long, became available. This was the original WJZ studio. The transmitting equipment was installed in a shack on the roof, with the necessary lines and signaling system between transmitter and studio." [8]

In a manuscript, apparently written in 1926, now in the files of the National Broadcasting Company, Charles B. Popenoe has described the studio as follows:

"It was now decided to establish a studio, and half of the ladies' rest room of the Newark works was set aside for the purpose, making a space some thirty feet long by fifteen feet wide. Microphones were installed, the necessary wiring from these instruments to the roof, a control panel placed in order to keep announcers and operators in direct communication, and the room draped in a dark red material not only to add to its appearance, but to subdue any echo noticeable. A few pieces of furniture were secured and a piano rented of the Griffith Piano Company in Newark."

The first microphone of WJZ has been described as in form of a "tomato can" suspended from a stand probably improvised from the familiar music stand used by orchestras. The amplifier used in the first studio was a weird contraption mounted upon a rubber-wheeled truck. The truck was indeed essential. The collection of batteries and the amplifier base with its thick copper-covered cable made the apparatus very heavy. Vacuum tubes, switches and gadgets made the instrument much more impressive to the uninitiated than the second-hand grand piano that Mr. Popenoe had thoughtfully installed.

In order to make the studio as impressive as possible the floor was spread with old rugs. The walls were draped in red cloth and rugs. An ancient table with a telephone thereon completed the equipment of Studio WJZ during its first months of operation.

The Westinghouse Company apparently recognized home talent, so to speak, in setting up its station. Mr. Popenoe in the MS already quoted quite frankly admits that he knew nothing about radio when assigned to the new station.

"The writer of this article," he declared, "was a supervisor in the Newark Works Organization, reporting directly to the superintendent, Mr. H. E. Miller, and was selected by this gentleman to take charge of all station matters as manager, and carry on the station, co-operating

[8] *This Thing Called Broadcasting*, p. 26.

with the engineer, Mr. Blitziotis (an old Belgian Marconi expert). The writer, a mechanical engineer by profession, knew little of broadcasting, but felt that it was a new position no one had ever held before, and that he was as well qualified as any other man for the duty.

". . . Just prior to the establishment of this studio T. H. Cowan had been taken from one of the Testing Departments and made the first announcer, Mr. George Blitziotis being the engineer and operator in the roof station. Mr. Cowan did the announcing, arranged the programs of recordings and made himself generally useful. This was in September and October, 1921."

Since WJZ was the first radio broadcasting station to be erected in the near vicinity of New York City, it was hoped that the wealth of talent in the metropolis would enable Program Manager Popenoe to provide with ease all-star programs. Newark, however, was not then as accessible as it is today. Despite the fact that the radio had undeniable drawing power, traffic congestion and distance soon dampened the ardor of artists of stage and concert halls. The situation was further complicated by the fact that no funds were available to pay even modest fees to visiting artists. Their services were necessarily gratuitous. This explains why at an early date WJZ established a New York City studio. The story of this pick-up studio is to be found in the Popenoe MS, p. 19:

"Early in February 1922, it was decided to install a broadcasting studio in the Waldorf-Astoria Hotel, New York City. Two twisted pairs of Western Union wires were installed between the hotel and the Newark station and from that date on little of our broadcasting was done in Newark. The Waldorf studio grew famous and was very popular with all our artists as it saved them the long tedious ride to the Newark studio."

Sec. 124. RCA Builds a Radio Station.

The license dates of the pioneer radio stations, as already observed, demonstrate that the Radio Corporation of America did not intend to permit the Westinghouse people to have the radio broadcasting field to themselves. Their own temporary station in Jersey City had been for reporting the prize fight—a station for a day merely. Its success, however, had inoculated RCA with the idea of a permanent radio broadcasting station. In casting about for a location the officials finally fixed upon Roselle Park, New Jersey, sixteen miles west of New York City. The General Electric factory was considered an ideal site for the new station. The transmitter used to broadcast the Dempsey-Carpentier fight was moved to Roselle Park and a group of electrical engineers was presently at work upon the antenna and broadcasting equipment.

Apparently a great deal of repair work was necessary because the station, licensed September 19th, was not ready to go on the air until December 14, 1921, as Station WDY.[8a]

The program manager and guiding spirit was Major J. Andrew White, whose reporting of the Dempsey-Carpentier fight weeks before was still the talk of the sporting world. Major White was the founder and editor of *Wireless Age* which had recently been taken over by RCA. He was a colorful figure in those days, a man destined to play many parts in the development of radio.

Major White was undoubtedly the best-known man in this new industry. He had been in the forefront as a champion of amateur wireless operators for many years. He was known to leaders in theatrical and sporting circles. His reporting of the Dempsey fight had made him a public character. In short, he was apparently the ideal choice for the important post of director of RCA's first venture into the field of commercial radio broadcasting. Radio needed to be rescued from phonograph records and mediocre amateur talent. Major White was in a position to attract to the microphones of WDY talent of high degree, except for the fact that sixteen miles of distance from the Great White Way was a distinct disadvantage.[9]

George H. Clark has preserved for us some of the memories of WDY's short and hectic career:

"Then came the sound of broken glass, as the Man in the Room dropped in through the broken skylight. This was, of course, a burlesque of the Man in the Moon bedtime stories told nightly by WJZ of Newark. The Man in the Room greeted his children and then turned over the microphone to a voice from the Milky Way, 'where bedtime stories twinkled, undimmed by those thrilling time signals.' He then told of the Ginger Ale Man, and of the Bandman with a Bag of Beans, one for every good little boy and girl. No wonder that the newspapers related that the program was 'full of Christmas spirit.'

"But it was on Friday evening that WDY, 'that cute castle of cordiality' excelled itself. That was 'Radio Party' night, when theatrical stars-from Broadway gave their all, without money but with benefit

[8a] The first program was broadcast from 9:15 to 10:15 .P.M., December 14th. The artists were Louis Brean, piano solo; Harry Howard, popular songs; Jack Cook, vaudeville entertainer; Nat Saunders, comedian—Geo. H. Clark MS.

[9] An interesting anecdote has been handed down of Eddie Cantor's introduction to radio. It occurred at Station WDY. The banjo-eyed comedian was nervous when he approached the microphone. Then when his best jokes evoked no ripples of mirth Cantor fell into a sort of panic. He continued to the end of the program, however, but before leaving the microphone expressed his doubt that anyone had actually heard his broadcast. Then he flung the challenge into the ether for anyone who had heard him to send him a dime to be donated to some charity. The shower of dimes that came to him through the mail convinced the doubting Cantor that radio broadcasting actually had an extensive listening public.

—New York *Sun*, March 3, 1934.

of dinner and wine, for radio. Never were these programs announced in advance, chiefly because the program director never knew, until the moment of going on the air, who would be his performing guests of the evening, and even then he wasn't always sure. Despite the handicaps of transportation, temperature and temperament, the program always went on the air and stayed on. During one of these Friday evening specials, on February tenth of 1922 it was, Eddie Cantor was the leader of the 'gang.' I wish I had heard J. O. Smith leading the chorus of 'We Want Cantor.'

"There were serious events, as well. Dr. Richard Strauss, 'the world's greatest living musician,' gave a recital on December 22, 1921, piano-player rolls prepared by him especially for this occasion providing the music from WDY. It was planned originally to have Mme. Elisabeth Schumann sing, in the Knabe studios in New York City, to the accompaniment provided by WDY, via receiver and loudspeaker, but an electric motor in the building interfered, so this interesting stunt failed. On another program, Sigmund Kentner, twelve-year-old xylophonist, was the feature. Paul Godley, amateur and professional radio man all in one, gave a talk on trans-Atlantic reception on January 25, 1922, telling of his experiences on the Scottish moors, receiving signals from American amateur stations, under the auspices of the A.R.R.L. There was no lack of program material, serious or gay.

"Perhaps a few words of description of the station itself, 'which abounds in chic and cozy atmosphere,' would not be amiss. The studio, which was located in the station building, was a hexagonal-shaped little room, artistically finished with draperies of blue and gold. A large hanging lamp in the center of the room was reflected in the bright colors of the oriental rugs, the wicker furniture, the red glow of the electric heaters. On one side of the room was a Knabe-Ampico piano, and opposite it stood an Edison Re-creation phonograph. No pick-up mikes were visible, until one looked closer and noticed a tiny disc suspended by a thin wire. The general appearance of the studio was gay and friendly.

"In the foyer hung a large map of the United States, with colored tacks indicating reports of reception. Eastern Canada and Cuba were the up and down limits, and westward the station reached as far as Omaha. This was not bad for five hundred watts at 360 meters.

"Coming to crude technical data, the transmitter was rated at 1000 watts C.W., 500 watts 'phone. Four 250-watt tubes were used, two as voice modulators and two as oscillators. A 50-watt tube served as voice amplifier. A multiple tuned antenna swung above, from the old Marconi towers. The antenna current varied between eight and ten amperes. This was the equipment which drew the rating of 'giant broadcasting station' from the press of the day!"

Sec. 125. Trials of a Metropolitan Radio Station.

Miss Vaughn de Leath, one of the early favorites of radio—the "original Radio girl" of 1916—began her career at WJZ in 1921.

The operators at Station WJZ, eager for talent, were soon to discover that not all talent that offered itself freely could safely be utilized. The art had not reached the stage where the manuscript of a speech could be required in advance of delivery. Armed with a few notes an orator might extemporize to an alarming degree. Cranks and propagandists saw in this new vehicle something far more potent than a soap box in a public square. They came to WJZ and some of them got on the air. Of course, it was always possible for horrified operators to throw the switch and stop broadcasting even though the impassioned orator might continue to vociferate until exhausted. To cut a speaker off the air was an unseemly termination of broadcasting and so Mr. Popenoe and his technicians at WJZ worked out a plan that soon became universal among radio stations. The operator, in his shack on the roof, later in a nearby control room, was provided with an emergency microphone and a phonograph. He could break in with an announcement of a musical number, then turn on the phonograph.

It may well be that experience with cranks was not the only reason for this important innovation. An incident that occurred in 1922 will sufficiently illustrate how a radio studio in those early days might be blanketed with unseemly noise. The story is taken from Goldsmith and Lescarboura's book, *This Thing Called Broadcasting*.

"Of small dimensions, the WJZ studio became unbearably warm in the summer days of 1922, so much so that its window, facing on a fire escape, was kept open. No elaborate air-conditioning system, providing ample cooled air strained free of any possible external sounds, was available in those days, such as we now have in the National Broadcasting Company and the Columbia System studios. Broadcasters then took chances with a world of noise.

"It was a particularly warm evening. One of the authors was in the studio at the time, waiting for his cue to go on the air. A soprano was doing her utmost before the microphone. Suddenly, without warning, there was the most uncanny howling and screeching and spitting. We turned hurriedly to the window, where two fat tom cats were competing with science and art. An instant later, the cats dashed into the studio and completed their duet before the microphone. They stole the show. The soprano's efforts were momentarily upset. Pandemonium reigned. And finally, the calm 'ACN,' in a businesslike manner, announced the next piece without word of explanation.

"Sixteen telephone calls were received within the next fifteen minutes. Five hundred letters flowed in during the next day or two. Newspapers pestered for information regarding the unearthly noises that had emanated from WJZ. All of which was explained at length to the interested public, and two tom cats scored a permanent place in broadcasting history." [10]

[10] *This Thing Called Broadcasting*, p. 29.

An incident related in the same book concerning WJZ's early experiences in broadcasting vocal music illustrates how much there was to learn in the technique of this new field.

"During the actual broadcasting the announcer usually wore a pair of headphones connected to a crystal detector receiving set. In this manner, he could judge how the program feature was going out over the air. The microphone was generally placed and replaced several times during the broadcast, so as to pick up the voice or music under the best possible conditions. In those days, no control room operator was at hand to watch a volume indicator and to make the necessary allowances for fortissimo or pianissimo passages.

"We recall, too, how easy it was to paralyze the undefended microphone. The occasion was the initial appearance of a great operatic singer, Madame Johanna Gadski, in the ground floor studio of WJZ. It was a gala affair. Various officials of the Westinghouse organization were garbed in evening clothes to welcome the prominent one to the studio, and the announcers and operators were in their formal attire. Well, Madame Gadski, renowned for her powerful voice, sang a number of selections. Evidently she believed that the louder she sang the more homes were permeated with her voice. We did not see the radio operator, who presided at the controls up on the roof of the factory building, but as likely as not he was frantic, trying to keep circuit breakers and fuses from blowing out. Suffice it to state that the amiable 'ACN,' rushing back and forth from his crystal set monitor booth to the microphone, kept moving the 'mike' away from the singer until he had it as far away as the liberal studio dimensions would permit. What a contrast with today, when the monitor operator, seated in an adjoining booth and gazing into the studio through a double plate glass window, could regulate the pick-up of the microphone and signal the announcer for any necessary change of position. But of course there had to be a beginning, as in everything else." [11]

In the late autumn of 1921, according to recollections of Charles B. Popenoe written five years after the happening, an exciting event occurred in the WJZ studio—a fire that threatened for a few hectic minutes not only to destroy the studio but also to cause extensive damage to the building. A photographer was in the studio at 10 o'clock one evening taking a flashlight picture. In those days flashlight-powder, in a tray held aloft by an attendant, was fired to illuminate the scene. In a studio with overhead drapery the explosion could prove very dangerous, as the horrified attendants discovered when the draperies caught fire. In spite of all efforts the draperies were destroyed, the furniture was ruined and the piano was rendered useless. By the following evening, however, new draperies had been hung, new furniture installed and a new piano provided.

[11] *This Thing Called Broadcasting*, pp. 30, 31.

Station WJZ was fortunate in attracting the interest of officials of
the Aeolian Company, of New York City. They loaned to the station
a Weber-Duo-Art grand piano and a Vocalion for the playing of records. Not only that but in November and December, 1921, the Aeolian
staff sent to the Newark studio such famous pianists as Percy Grainger
and vocalists of world renown. John Charles Thomas, May Peterson,
Marie Sundelius, Madame Gadski and others sang to the WJZ microphone.[12] "Literary vespers" were established. A daily children's hour
from 7 to 7:30 P.M. became a feature of the station. Orchestral music
and humorous speeches were regularly on the WJZ program.

[12] Popenoe MS, NBC Library.

CHAPTER
FOURTEEN

Owen D. Young and South American Wireless

Section 126. British Marconi Company Confer with RCA Concerning South America.

ALTHOUGH THE YOUTHFUL RADIO CORPORATION had made a strong beginning in establishing itself as an international power in wireless transmission, thus justifying the faith of Admiral Bullard and other naval officials, yet a great uncharted domain existed in the Western Hemisphere. To be sure, the United Fruit Company, now allied with RCA, had wireless stations in the West Indies and Central America, yet South America had no great wireless stations. In the original agreement between the British Marconi Company and RCA there had been a clause (Clause 7) that contemplated the development of a complete system of wireless transmission for South America.

Although the British Marconi Company was then in a position to begin operations in that region, yet the RCA agreement was such that neither corporation could act without the other. RCA had too many domestic problems at first to warrant expansion into foreign fields.

In November, 1920, Godfrey C. Isaacs, chief executive of the British Marconi Company, paid a visit to America. During this visit he discussed with the officials of RCA this matter of unfinished business. On September 5, 1919, when the original pact had been signed, the Marconi executives had been keen to establish a high power wireless station in the Argentine—in fact to do the like in other strategic locations in South America. There had been a tentative agreement between British and American negotiators that the South American territory should be exploited on a 50-50 basis. This clause in the contract brought back by Nally and Davis had caused considerable embarrassment to Owen D. Young and his associates, since it violated the spirit of their compact with the United States Government that in all its activities RCA should be controlled by American citizens. The pact for control of South American trade was accordingly revised.

The original agreement had called for the completion of the Argentine station within three years. Mr. Isaacs was concerned over the fact that more than a year had elapsed since the agreement had been signed and yet nothing had been done to forward the South American project. In the meantime, German wireless interests had formed a German-controlled corporation in Buenos Aires and were already arranging for the speedy erection of a wireless station. Should this station be completed and service with Europe inaugurated, it would place both the British Marconi Company and RCA in an embarrassing position.

It is understandable why RCA, with its great and pressing domestic problems and its imperative financial needs, had neglected the South American situation. The impatience of the long-established British Company at having its empire-building plans held up by its American ally is likewise easy to understand. At a conference with Owen D. Young during the American visit it was agreed that the situation was now so complicated that it was no longer possible for the two corporations to exploit South American wireless to the exclusion of the Germans. In fact it now seemed advisable to invite the French wireless company to participate in the proposed deal. Thus they might hope to convert the German station now in process in Buenos Aires into an internationally controlled station. It was agreed that Isaacs, upon his return to England, would endeavor to arrange a conference or conferences with the French and German interests in which representatives of RCA might participate.

Sec. 127. French and Germans Invited to Enter Consortium.

Such conferences were arranged and Edward J. Nally and Gerard Swope represented the Radio Corporation. A tentative agreement was arrived at whereby each of the four wireless monopolies should share equally in the South American venture. The Germans, however, could not bind themselves to the agreement because, having organized a wireless company in Buenos Aires, it was needful to confer with that corporation. This would require months of negotiation—a delay at which Godfrey C. Isaacs naturally chafed. Mr. Nally's group, on the other hand, probably welcomed the delay because of great problems still unsolved in the United States.

Some weeks subsequent to the return of President Nally to New York the managing-director of the German-Argentine Company arrived in Europe and a new conference was arranged in Holland. Mr. Nally was notified of this meeting but was unable to sail in time to attend the conference. The conference was held pending the arrival of Mr. Nally and it was found that all parties were in substantial agreement.[1] An adjournment was taken and the President of RCA was advised by cable that the conferees were holding themselves in readiness to reassemble upon summons of Mr. Isaacs. Mr. Nally thereupon fixed the date when he might be expected to arrive in Europe.

It seems that clause seven in the original agreement between the British Marconi Company and RCA had not only offended the principle of American control of communications but was also contrary to the laws of Delaware, and RCA was a Delaware corporation. Mr. Nally's delay in sailing had been influenced no doubt by the desire of the directors of the corporation to have time to draft the terms under which they would be willing to enter into the South American consortium.

This new draft differed in certain material particulars from the ten-

[1] This information gleaned from a letter from Godfrey Isaacs to RCA under date of July 12, 1921.

tative pact that had been agreed upon at the earlier parley. Mr. Nally carried the draft of this new proposal with him. When he called upon Mr. Isaacs in advance of the meeting of the representatives of the wireless companies and submitted the same, the British tycoon was filled with consternation and chagrin. He refused to accept it and charged the American corporation with having presented an ultimatum. So bitter was his resentment that no action was taken on the American proposals. Mr. Nally eventually returned to the United States.

Sec. 128. British Marconi's Ultimatum and RCA's Rejoinder.

Such was the state of affairs in the latter part of July, 1921, when a letter reached New York from Godfrey Isaacs, addressed to the President of the Radio Corporation of America. It had been written in London, July 12th. It was in effect an ultimatum to the American corporation. It recited the facts from the British viewpoint. A portion of the letter was as follows:

"Apart altogether, therefore, from our objection to your legal right to call upon us to enter into this new agreement, the entering into it at this stage would have rendered the completion of the negotiations with the French and Germans impracticable.

"Further, it is too late, today, to contemplate erecting stations independently of the French and Germans on account of the delay which has enabled the Germans to obtain so great an advantage over us. There is still another more serious consideration as relying on the terms of the consortium which has been approved in principle; the French, much against their will, have refrained from erecting the station under their concession and any breaking away by us from the negotiations at this stage would involve a grave breach of faith on our part to which we are not prepared to lay ourselves open."

The letter ended with the following declaration of purpose:

"There appears to us to be but one practical business course open to us and that is to carry through the consortium to which all parties have agreed in principle and from which we should be sorry to see the Radio Corporation retire at the eleventh hour."

The Isaacs message created somewhat of a sensation in the RCA executive offices. Although the board of directors had postponed action on the South American matter they had no idea of abandoning the project. To have permitted European wireless companies to exploit South American territory without lifting a hand would be to fail in one of the professed objectives of RCA—America for Americans. Obviously something must be done to checkmate the British Marconi Company. In this emergency the board of directors of RCA turned to

Owen D. Young—their diplomat, man of action, engineer of corporate relations.

Mr. Young, with characteristic astuteness, at once dispatched a radiogram to Mr. Isaacs—a radiogram that displays masterly strategy. The British letter may have been intended as an ultimatum, but the response of Mr. Young met challenge with challenge. Not only that, but instead of dealing merely with the challenger Mr. Young went over his head to the Germans and French as will be seen from the following:

"AUGUST 11, 1921.

"YOUR FORMAL LETTER TWELFTH RADIO CORPORATION HAS BEEN REFERRED TO ME BY BOARD OF DIRECTORS (STOP) THIS MESSAGE IS NOT TO BE CONSIDERED AS A REPLY TO THAT LETTER BECAUSE PERSONALLY I DESIRE TO APPROACH THE MATTER CONSTRUCTIVELY FREE FROM THE RESTRAINTS WHICH SOME PORTIONS OF YOUR LETTER SEEM TO IMPOSE (STOP) THE REAL QUESTION IS WHETHER YOUR COMPANY AND MINE DESIRE TO CARRY OUT THE SPIRIT OF THE CO-OPERATIVE ARRANGEMENT WHICH YOU DISCUSSED WITH ME IN NEW YORK LAST NOVEMBER AND LATER WITH NALLY AND SWOPE IN LONDON (STOP) I UNDERSTOOD THAT WE WERE THEN IN AGREEMENT AS TO FUNDAMENTALS AND YOUR LETTER OF THE TWELFTH SEEMS TO CONFIRM THAT VIEW (STOP) IF YOU WISH TO DEAL WITH THE MATTER IN THE SPIRIT ABOVE OUTLINED I SHOULD BE GLAD TO MEET YOU FIRST IN LONDON AND IMMEDIATELY THEREAFTER THE GERMANS AND FRENCH WITH YOU AT SOME CONVENIENT PLACE ON THE CONTINENT (STOP) I AM NOTIFYING FRENCH AND GERMANS DIRECT OF MY WILLINGNESS TO ATTEND SUCH CONFERENCE AND I WOULD APPRECIATE HAVING THE TIME AND PLACE FIXED BEFORE I SAIL (STOP) AS PERSONAL MATTER APPRECIATE EARLY REPLY IN ORDER THAT MY PLANS FOR THE NEXT FEW WEEKS MAY BE PROMPTLY MADE (STOP) IF THIS SUGGESTION IS NOT ACCEPTABLE TO YOU I WILL FORMALLY REPLY TO YOUR LETTER OF THE TWELFTH

YOUNG"

Godfrey Isaacs was evidently taken by surprise at this vigorous rejoinder. In an obvious attempt to placate Mr. Young he dispatched the following by radio:

"LONDON, AUGUST 12, 1921.

"YOUNG

"I AM VERY PLEASED TO RECEIVE YOUR TELEGRAM YESTERDAY REGRETTING ONLY THAT ANY THOUGHT WITH YOU SHOULD HAVE INSPIRED THE LAST SENTENCE OF YOUR MESSAGE. (STOP) I CAN ASSURE YOU MY COMPANY'S DESIRE TO CO-OPERATE WITH YOURS AS CLOSELY AND AS WIDELY AS POSSIBLE HAS NOT CHANGED. (STOP) I SHALL BE VERY PLEASED TO SEE YOU. (STOP) IMMEDIATELY UPON HEARING FROM YOU EARLIEST POSSIBLE DATE

HERBERT HOOVER
Who as Secretary of Commerce rendered invaluable aid to the struggling
new science of Radio Broadcasting.

OF YOUR ARRIVAL I WILL AT ONCE FIX MEETING AT CONVENIENT PLACE ON
CONTINENT WITH FRENCH AND GERMANS AS YOU PROPOSE. (STOP) HOPING
YOU CONTEMPLATE SAILING NOT LATER THAN AUGUST EIGHTEENTH OTHER-
WISE ARGENTINE REPRESENTATIVE WILL HAVE SAILED AND DR. SHAPIRA
WILL BE ON HOLIDAY.

ISAACS."

To this message Mr. Young sent the following laconic response:

"NEW YORK, AUGUST 15, 1921.

"ISAACS

EXPANSE

LONDON

"NALLY ELWOOD AND I SAIL AQUITANIA TWENTY THIRD ASSUME THIS
DATE WILL BE CONVENIENT FOR YOU (STOP) HOPE IT WILL NOT INCON-
VENIENCE DOCTOR SHAPIRA AND THAT ARGENTINE DIRECTOR WILL WAIT

YOUNG"

Sec. 129. Owen D. Young Sails on Momentous Mission.

This exchange of radiograms marked the first round in one of the
most momentous international controversies ever handled by private
individuals. The mighty Godfrey Isaacs, chief executive of the world-
girdling British Marconi Company, brother of the great Lord Reading, had challenged Owen D. Young to a single combat in which
should be decided whether Great Britain or the United States of
America should dominate world-wide wireless transmission. Mr. Young
had accepted the challenge and had wisely stipulated that the two
gladiators should meet on the Continent rather than upon English soil.

Owen D. Young was still an unknown so far as international controversies were concerned. To be sure he had marshaled the forces
that had captured the American Marconi Company, but the wily British tycoon no doubt accounted for this fact on the theory that the influence of the United States Government had been behind the movement to wrest control of American wireless from his company—hence
that Owen D. Young's achievement had been overrated. The hour had
now come when Isaacs believed that he would demonstrate to the
American novice how little the latter could accomplish in a world
arena against a champion like himself. Isaacs was set upon regaining
for Great Britain in 1921 what it had lost in 1919. It must be remembered that Americans were then regarded in Europe as the most gul-
lible, the most easily hoodwinked people of the earth, for had we not
been as clay in the hands of British potters in the shaping of our national policies in the late war? Atrocity stories and propaganda that
had smelled to high heaven had been fed to us. War missions from

England had flattered and cajoled us into a crusade to make the world safe for democracy. Then, too, our President Wilson, reputedly one of the most profound thinkers in American life, had been completely outgeneraled by Lloyd George and other British statesmen at the Peace Conference. Small wonder, therefore, that Godfrey Isaacs, like the giant of fable, muttered "fe-fi-fo-fum" at the prospect of annihilating little Jack, who in this case happened to be Owen D. Young.

What Isaacs did not then appreciate, even though he had met Mr. Young in New York in the fall of 1920, was that this Yankee lawyer was far different from Woodrow Wilson. President Wilson was the cocksure pedagogue who could "tell the world." Owen D. Young was modest and unassuming—even shy, yet possessing a world vision. He could drive toward his goal with an outward meekness that deceived his enemies. He was a man of ideals, yet not an idealist, a man of vision who was not visionary. Such was the antagonist that Godfrey Isaacs was to meet in the arena at Paris.

On August 23, 1921, Owen D. Young, accompanied by Edward J. Nally, and John W. Elwood, President and Secretary respectively of the Radio Corporation of America, sailed from New York on the momentous mission. Quiet days on shipboard, free from the distractions of conferences and problems of a giant corporation, gave Owen D. Young opportunity to perfect his plans. Well he knew that his great adversary, a veteran in international manipulations, with a brother high in the councils of the British Empire and with the interests of that Empire deeply involved, was an antagonist with whom he could take no chances. Mr. Young was familiar with the history of British imperialism. He knew that commercial penetration and domination rather than force of arms had given Britain her pre-eminence in world affairs. Isaacs was the spearhead in this campaign of Great Britain's commercial diplomacy. He must, therefore, be prepared for every subtlety of movement, every strategy, every subterfuge that Godfrey Isaacs and the best brains of the British Empire could devise for his undoing.

Mr. Young was well aware that the British Marconi interests, through a 25 per cent stock ownership in the French wireless monopoly, virtually controlled its policies. He knew that in this four-nation conference he could count in advance upon the united opposition of Great Britain and France. His only possible ally would be discredited Germany, and that was the real secret of Mr. Young's eagerness that Germany be included in the Paris conference. So far as votes were concerned, it was apparent that the best that Mr. Young might hope for in any clash of national interests would be a deadlock. Why, then, the formalities of an international commercial conference?

The answer to this question lies in two important considerations—

first, that the Radio Corporation of America had already ousted Britain from North America and had begun a penetration of South American wireless transmissions; secondly, Mr. Young's own undisclosed plans, which, if successfully executed, might result in victory for the American corporation. The ocean voyage on the eve of battle was, therefore, a godsend to the champion of the Radio Corporation of America. Quietly the three Americans had departed from New York. Quietly they landed in France and proceeded to the Ritz Hotel in Paris, their appointed rendezvous. Isaacs and Steadman were there to represent the British Marconi Company. The French wireless corporation was likewise represented by two delegates, but where were the representatives of the Telefunken Corporation? Mr. Young was informed that Germans, the enemies of France, might not be admitted to French territory, whereupon he raised indignant protest. It was pointed out that Germany no longer possessed colonies, that Germany had ceased to be a world power, and that this defeated and discredited nation was not really a factor in the international scene. The United States, the British Empire and France were all that counted anyway. All this did not move Owen D. Young from his plan of campaign. He needed the Germans, needed them beyond words, yet in voicing his demands he fell back onto the familiar idealism of Woodrow Wilson. The vanquished enemy must sit at the council table if only for the gesture of healing the wounds of war. He pictured the dramatic possibilities of the event—La Belle France holding out the olive branch to the bloody Hun. Godfrey Isaacs, no doubt, rejoiced at this evidence of softhearted idealism on the part of his American antagonist. There could be no harm in the plan, he whispered to his French allies—humor the visionary American! Isaacs thereupon joined Mr. Young in a petition to the French Government for a permit that would enable the German delegates to come to Paris for the conference. The permit was granted. Thus Owen D. Young won the first skirmish in the great campaign.

Sec. 130. The Four-Nation Conference Begins.

In due time the German representatives arrived at the Ritz. Mr. Young and Mr. Nally greeted them warmly. Isaacs and Steadman were stiffly polite. The French delegates would not greet them at all, except with dagger-glances and an obviously suppressed desire to hiss "name of a pig." The formalities of the opening of the conference being completed—the inevitable speech-making and preliminary sparring concluded—the real business of the conference began. Since Mr. Young had successfully led the way for the consolidation of conflicting interests in America, it was natural that he should have been called upon to give the highlights of that consolidation and its cross-licensing features. The analogy to the international situation confronting them was obvious. If the inventions of all wireless engineers, present and future, of the four nations could be pooled, Mr. Young argued, the result would be advantageous to all. He proposed an international radio circuit.

These suggestions, as their author expected, aroused the delegates of Britain and France. The British Empire with its family of nations —Canada, India, Africa, Australia, British Guiana, British mandates and concessions in all parts of the world—Mr. Isaacs declared, could enter into an arrangement such as this only on condition that the territorial pre-eminence of the British Empire be recognized. Clearly the old British policy of spheres of influence was uppermost in the mind of the President of the British Marconi Company. France, like a true ally of Britain, agreed with this contention.

Owen D. Young pointed out that the development of wireless transmission had in no way been influenced by territorial considerations. The great Marconi himself was an Italian, and Italy was not even represented at this council table. Back of Marconi was the German scientist Hertz, the real discoverer of wireless phenomena. Tracing the development of the wireless industry, he pointed out that the United States had done more than all the rest of the world to make wireless telegraphy an effective international agency for the blessing of mankind.

Thus began a dramatic and soul-stirring contest in which Owen D. Young and Godfrey Isaacs faced each other in virtual single combat. Each had the certain support of a natural ally—Mr. Young of the German delegation and Isaacs of the French. During hectic days they argued and declaimed. By pre-arrangement Young and Isaacs took turns at presiding over the council table with its eight embattled delegates.

After days of argument the most that had been accomplished was that the British Marconi Company should be free from competition within the territorial limits of the British Empire; the United States within its own territories, and France within its geographic boundaries —which was no progress at all, since this principle had been conceded at the beginning. The real battle raged over South America. By this time Mr. Young had made clear that the American delegation would insist upon the spirit of the Monroe Doctrine in all aspects of wireless domination of American territory. He had proposed, in order to avoid duplication of wireless stations, that an international partnership be formed, with the wireless companies of Great Britain, United States, France and Germany as the high contracting parties.

When Isaacs raised the question of relative interests in this proposed partnership Mr. Young had replied that no relative interests could be considered—share and share alike must be the rule. Radio Corporation of America, British Marconi, French Wireless and German Telefunken would share expenses and profits of operation. Young proposed, moreover, the drawing up of an international trust agreement with two trustees to represent each national group and a neutral chairman of the governing body—some eminent American who had no relation whatever to the wireless industry.

There was challenge in this proposal—a challenge that provoked fresh floods of oratory. To the delight of Mr. Isaacs, the German delegates now came out against the American plan. They had bitter reasons for believing that in such a combination they could count upon being outvoted or deadlocked in every conflict of policy. Mr. Young had foreseen this development. He was ready with a solution. Let the neutral chairman have a power of veto over any vote that seemed to him unfair to the minority!

Sec. 131. The Germans Walk Out of Conference—Young's Strategy.

After the adjournment of this very stormy session the German delegates came to Mr. Young privately and declared that they had attended the conference more as observers than as delegates clothed with power to bind the Telefunken Corporation. They had already reached the limits of their powers. In view of the hostile attitude of England and France, they now proposed that the Radio Corporation of America disregard them entirely and make cross-licensing agreements with the Telefunken Corporation. Secretly pleased at this development, Mr. Young pointed out to the Germans that a four party agreement would forestall costly competition of clashing national interests. He, therefore, urged them to refrain from an open break in the conference until another effort could be made to effect an international consortium. It was agreed that the German delegates would present their views to the conference and try for an adjournment until they could receive instructions from Berlin.

On the following day the German delegates met with the others as before. They had no sooner voiced the request for adjournment than the French, always suspicious of their late antagonists in the great war, denounced the suggestion as a mere subterfuge—a Hun trick. A spirited retort on the part of the Teutonic delegates led to a violent debate. The dramatic moment arrived when the flushed and excited Germans declared that it had been folly to hope that they might ever expect justice from French or English. Their spokesman ended by inviting the American delegates to come with them to Berlin, where they could be sure that they might conclude traffic agreements with the Telefunken Corporation. Before the British and French had recovered from their surprise at this turn of affairs the Germans had gathered up their papers and bags and had stalked angrily from the room. Owen D. Young, a master of strategy, now made a neat speech in which he expressed sympathy with the departed delegates and hinted darkly that because of the clashing viewpoints he was inclined to consider seriously a separate pact with the Germans.

A crisis had been reached. Isaacs and his associates saw with alarm that with the Germans entrenched in the Argentine and the ambitious RCA supported by a national tradition intent upon keeping Europeans at a distance, their own chances of commercial advantage would be foreclosed. It would never do for the Telefunken Corporation to make a separate alliance with the Radio Corporation. In addition to the territorial monopoly that would undoubtedly be theirs they could also command the bulk of the inventive genius of the age. No, it would never do—and so, as Mr. Young had hoped, they begged him not to make a separate pact with the Germans. He replied with withering logic that he seemed to be wasting his time in Paris, hence that there could be no harm in going to Berlin, where there was a prospect of a definite alliance.

Isaacs and his companions realized that concessions were in order. They agreed to the formation of the proposed international trust in the manner suggested. Owen D. Young insisted, however, that the neutral chairman be an American—and that he, moreover, should have veto power over any agreements or votes that might seem to him unfair to any minority. Since the American delegation was adamant on the proposition, Isaacs and his fellow delegates eventually surrendered. Young in his turn stipulated that he would not make a separate pact with the Germans. On the contrary he would accompany them to Berlin and strive with might and main to persuade the Telefunken Corporation to agree to the four power pact. This he did, and after a strenuous week in the German capital returned to Paris with the Telefunken envoys prepared to sign the pact. Thomas Nelson Perkins, of Boston, a lawyer who had been associated with Young in earlier days, was named as the chairman of the commission that was to administer the wireless trust.

Before the conference adjourned the delegates had worked out the details of operation. Each of the four contracting parties was to contribute equally to the funds needed for the erection of wireless stations in South America. They were to share and share alike in expenses and in earnings of the international partnership. It is probable that in the history of international commercial controversies no American ever achieved a more overwhelming victory than did Owen D. Young in the Paris Conference of August and September, 1921.

Sec. 132. The Four-Power Pact and Its Significance.

The objects sought to be attained by the compact into which the four companies entered were stated in the agreement in the following language:

"Whereas all four companies own or control various patents and inventions in and for the Republics of South America; and

"Whereas the French, German, British, and American companies have each, directly or through associated companies, obtained one or more concessions in South American Republics to construct and operate stations for long distance wireless communication, and each has such a concession in the Argentine and has incurred substantial expenses under such concessions; and

"Whereas it is realized that the construction of a number of stations for long distance communication in substantially the same locality in South America, as, for instance, in the Argentine, would be economically unsound and contrary to the interests of the commercial and general public as involving a wasteful use of the relatively small number of bands of wave lengths available for the wireless communications of the world, and as involving also a total expenditure out of all proportion to the volume of traffic which can reasonably be expected; and

"Whereas the parties accordingly desire to co-operate in the establishment and operation of such a number of such stations in the South American Republics as may be necessary for the handling of the external communication in the best and most efficient manner.

"Under this agreement an assignment was made by the various parties involved to nine trustees who are delegated to carry out the provisions of the agreement. Each of the four concerns are to appoint two trustees and the ninth, who is to act as chairman, is to be appointed by the American company and is to be an American citizen. The important provisions of the agreement are as follows:

1. All concessions owned or acquired by the four parties up to September 1, 1945, in the South American Republics relating or applicable to communication to points outside of South America, but not including ship-to-shore traffic, are assigned to the trustees.

2. Exclusive divisible and transferable licenses to use (but not to make and sell) apparatus, devices, and systems under all patent rights now owned or to be acquired by the four parties.

3. Each of the parties covenants with each of the other and the trustees that it will not directly or indirectly engage in the business of radio communication in the South American Republics, except through the subsidiary companies provided for or the trustees.

4. All companies associated with or which may be hereafter formed or acquired by the four concerns are to be bound by the agreement.

5. It shall be the endeavor of the trustees to divide the total traffic between the four parties equally.

6. The formation of subsidiary companies (to be known as the National Companies) for the purpose of conducting the communication business in the Argentine and Brazil.

"The *second agreement* between these four parties was entered into on the same day as the first agreement, and which is supplementary thereto, relates principally to the transfer of the rights of the various parties involved in South American countries to the trustees. The important provisions of this agreement are as follows:

1. The retention of the stock of the Marconi Wireless Telegraphy Company of the River Plate, which is the property of the British company, the Pan-American Wireless Telegraph & Telephone Company, which is owned by the American company, the French Argentine Company, and the Trans Radio Argentina, owned by the German company, only until such time as their patent rights and concessions in the South American fields have been transferred to the trustees.

2. The organization of the Argentine National Company, which shall take over the stock of the Trans Radio Argentina, the German concern, and a division of the stock of the new company so that the share of all four companies shall be equal.

3. The reorganization of the Companhia Radio Telegraphia Brazileira, which is to be known as the Brazilian National Company, whose stock is to be held equally by the four companies.

4. Concessions for communication from and to Venezuela are transferred by the French and British companies subject to the rights of the Compagnie Française des Cables Telegraphiques.

5. Provisions for purchase of the British station at Bogotá, Colombia, and the German station at Cartagena, Colombia, subject to the rights granted the United Fruit Company in Colombia by the Radio Corporation.

6. Provisions for an enlargement of territory which would include the Central American countries but would except European possessions, Cuba, Porto Rico, and other possessions of the United States.

7. The trustees are given power to make agreements with the United Fruit Company regarding the exchange of traffic and also, if necessary, for the exchange of patent rights held by the trustees."

It will be observed that each of the four parties granted all external wireless communication rights in the South American territory to a board of trustees to be held for the four parties in equal shares. The significant feature of the compact or consortium from the American angle was that the Radio Corporation of America, through Owen D. Young's adroit bargaining, was in the driver's seat. Not only did it have equal powers and equal representation with the other three parties but it had the right to name the ninth trustee—the chairman of the board. This chairman, as previously noted, was not a mere presiding officer with a right to break a tie vote. No indeed, he had the power to veto the action of the majority whenever he might consider that their action had been unfair to any minority. Thus the principle of the Monroe Doctrine was carried into the field of communications in the Western Hemisphere. It gave American interests effective leadership. Thus Great Britain in this four-power pact surrendered its last hope of regaining a dominating position in wireless communications in the Western Hemisphere.

CHAPTER
FIFTEEN

Radio's Great Era of Expansion

Section 133. Radio Boom Sweeps Nation.

THE ADVENT OF RADIO BROADCASTING created one of the most extraordinary booms in the history of the American people. From all over the United States orders for equipment for prospective radio broadcasting stations came pouring in to the manufacturers of such apparatus. The unexplainable part of it is that no one at that time, except the manufacturers, had any reasonable prospect of monetary gain. No one knew how radio could earn any money for the owner of a station unless such owner chanced to be a dealer in radio supplies. That there were staggering expenses—upwards of fifty thousand dollars even for a modest station—did not seem to dampen the ardor of would-be broadcasters.

It required months, however, to cope with the avalanche of orders. It was not until mid-winter of 1922 that the national craze developed in full force. The *Radio Service* bulletins issued monthly by the United States Department of Commerce bear eloquent testimony to the impressive nature of the boom.

August	1,	1921	Two new stations
September	1,	1921	Nine new stations
October	1,	1921	Twelve new stations
November	1,	1921	Six new stations
December	1,	1921	Three new stations
January	1,	1922	Twenty-six new stations
February	1,	1922	Fourteen new stations
March	1,	1922	Twenty-seven new stations
April	1,	1922	Eighty-eight new stations
May	1,	1922	Ninety-nine new stations

A list of radio stations existing in May, 1922, will be found in the Appendix (See Exhibit "G").

Periodicals of the period reflect in graphic manner the sudden expansion of the radio industry. In the first issue of *Radio Broadcast,* May, 1922, we find the following editorial comment:

"The rate of increase in the number of people who spend at least a part of their evening in listening in is almost incomprehensible. To those who have recently tried to purchase receiving equipment, some idea of this increase has undoubtedly occurred, as they stood perhaps in the fourth or fifth row at the radio counter waiting their turn only to be told when they finally reached the counter that they might place an order and it would be filled when possible. . . . The movement is probably not even yet at its height. It is still growing in some kind of geometrical progression. . . . It seems quite likely that before the movement has reached its height, before the market for receiving apparatus becomes approximately saturated, there will be at least five million receiving sets in this country."

The editorial sentiments above quoted were ably seconded in a special story in the same issue of *Radio Broadcast:*

"The manufacturers of radio receivers and accessories," writes Parkhurst Whitney, "are in much the situation that munition makers were when the war broke. They are suddenly confronted with a tremendous and imperative demand for apparatus. It is a matter of several months at best to arrange for the quantity production of radio receiving apparatus if the type to be manufactured were settled, but the types are no more settled than were the types of airplanes in the war. The manufacturing companies are, therefore, confronted with carrying on their experimental work, devising new types and at the same time producing the best they can in such quantity as they can, and they must do all this while building up their organizations, working out their policies and keeping an eye on the Government so that they can keep in accord with its regulations."

A human interest yarn that appeared in *This Thing Called Broadcasting* is an excellent illustration of the absurd reasons that lay behind some of the attempts to open radio stations:

"The story is told of a young man who approached the Federal Radio Inspector for a license at a time when the air was overcrowded with broadcasters frantically endeavoring to make themselves heard above the din of the modern Tower of Babel.

"Said the young man to the inspector, 'I want a license to broadcast.'

"Said the inspector to the young man, 'Do you know the cost of going into broadcasting these days, with the elaborate studios, microphones, amplifiers, transmitters and so on? Why, it costs at least fifty thousand dollars to install a station worthy of a place on the air.'

" 'Oh, that's all right,' said the young man. 'I have the fifty thousand dollars and then some. All I want is a license so I can go ahead. I have the site bought on the Palisades, opposite the heart of New York City, so as to blanket the New Yorkers.' . . .

"The inspector, still hoping to discourage the petitioner, asked, 'But what will you do for programs? You see, it's one thing to have a broadcasting station and quite another to have something to broadcast so that listeners-in will be satisfied.'

"Whereupon the young man solved the growing mystery. 'You see, Inspector, it's this way: I have a girl friend who has a marvelous voice. She's dying to go on the air. I'd do anything for her. So I want to put up this station so she may go on the air every day if she likes.'

"The inspector was weak at the knees. There seemed to be no discouraging this young man. Ah! Another idea:

" 'Why not have the young lady broadcast through existing stations, instead of putting all that investment into a station just for such a purpose?'

"And the young man came back: '*Well,* she has tried the various broadcasting stations but not one of them recognizes real singing.'

"Fortunately the youthful swain never constructed the station, although at the time it was not in the power of the inspector to refuse a license to any American citizen of good standing." [1]

The first broadcasting of church services in the New York City area probably occurred at Station WJZ. We find the following account in the Popenoe MS at page 9:

"Early in January, 1922, we inaugurated the first radio chapel service, from 3:00 to 3:45 P.M. each Sunday afternoon. The Rev. George P. Dougherty of Christ Episcopal Church, Glen Ridge, N. J., conducted the first service, this gentleman previously having extended a Christmas eve message in 1921 to the public most successfully. These services were a great success . . . all denominations being asked to take part."

The first stage-show ever broadcast went on the air February 19, 1922, over Station WJZ—Ed Wynn's "The Perfect Fool." In the light of subsequent events and Ed Wynn's later mastery of radio technique it is interesting to note the great comedian's first reaction to the microphone. Had the broadcast been picked up from the theater there would probably have been little difficulty, but the affair was staged in a broadcasting studio. *Radio Broadcast* thus describes the incident:

"Ed Wynn approached the microphone gingerly. He looked at it suspiciously. The time came for him to perform. As with all professionals, he was a trifle nervous. The nervousness, however, wore off, but Wynn was appalled by the silence. He had told some of his best stories and had not even heard a snicker.

"Wet with perspiration, he turned to the announcer.

" 'I can't do anything,' he said.

"The announcer quickly assembled all the people from around the studio. Electricians in shirt sleeves, scrub-women with their skirts tucked up, telephone operators, and artists who were billed later on the program, were invited to come into the studio-theater and enjoy the show. It was a strange audience, but their approbation turned the trick. With their giggles, guffaws, and shouts of merriment to encourage him, Wynn proceeded with the entertainment. He needed only the responsive sight of his hearers doubled over with laughter. Had he been a more frequent radio performer, he would have been able to imagine the fans in their homes, tuned in on his program and convulsed with mirth."

This experience with Ed Wynn was no doubt the forerunner of the later custom of permitting radio shows to have studio audiences. Paul

[1] *This Thing Called Broadcasting,* pp. 46-47.

Whiteman's first experience before the microphone of WJZ while it was still in Newark had been equally disconcerting, but the Wynn case was unique in that a studio audience was assembled on the spur of the moment.

In commenting on the Ed Wynn broadcast Raymond F. Guy, one of the engineers at WJZ at the time, has given the following amusing explanation of the "mike-fright" of veteran actors:

"Able to judge the effect of their endeavors by watching visible audiences, they were lost before the super-critical, all-seeing eye of the little microphone which must have appeared as an ogre pointing fiercely at them and crying, 'You are falling flat. Think of billions of people listening to you, watching for a mistake,' or perhaps, 'Nobody is listening to you. Don't you feel foolish? Why not stop?' "

Sec. 134. RCA Radio Station WDY Discontinued.

The Radio Corporation of America had opened Station WDY as an experimental station. It certainly accumulated experience at a rapid rate. At the very time when all the world seemed bent upon opening new radio stations RCA was discovering, as were all others who were trying the same experiment, that radio was a very expensive game. Unlike many others this corporation had the courage to face the facts and to act accordingly. RCA was closely allied, in a business way, with the Westinghouse Company, which was already pioneering extensively in radio fields. Since Westinghouse was a manufacturing company with a large corps of eminent engineers, it was exceptionally well qualified to discover and develop the most efficient type of radio receiving sets as well as radio broadcasting devices. For RCA to continue a losing venture with no reasonable prospect of accomplishing anything noteworthy was not a pleasing idea either to Edward J. Nally, President of the Corporation, or to Owen D. Young, Chairman of the Board of Directors.

It may well be that the vaudeville character of the programs that Major J. Andrew White was putting on the air did not set very well with the Board of Directors. "The station depended on extemporaneous announcement," writes George H. Clark, "and on spontaneously inspired artists to a very great extent. Partly because it was organized hurriedly and did not have time to work up a regular program fabric before going into operation. Partly because of the difficulty of getting talent to traverse the almost insuperable barrier between Broadway and the hinterland of Roselle Park. Once there, the rigors of a New Jersey winter had to be neutralized by a few pitifully overworked electric heaters. No wonder that portable heating had to be provided. No wonder that the announcements were made, to a great extent, on the spur of the moment. Full credit is due to Messrs. White and Smith for almost always having a room full of guests, in spite of all these difficulties."

Burlesque and good-natured joshing have attained a degree of popularity in recent years, especially on sponsored radio programs. No doubt the same type of entertainment emanating from Station WDY rendered it popular indeed with radio listeners of that day. The fact, however, that listeners paid nothing for the entertainment and really had no voice in determining the policy of RCA left the station to its fate. A development at this time, mid-winter, 1922, enabled RCA to retire gracefully from the field. It had just taken over the sale of broadcasting receivers and tubes manufactured by Westinghouse. RCA accordingly let it be known that it had decided to join forces with Westinghouse in developing an enlarged and powerful station at Newark.[3]

"The last program of WDY," writes George H. Clark in recording its epitaph, "was appropriately enough, a local one in part. The first radio dance ever given in Roselle was scheduled for February 24th in the Robert Gordon school, the dance music to be provided by WDY. This is the last recorded offering of the station on the air. WDY signed off for eternity.

"Roselle Park was, thus, only a transition station, almost the equivalent of a tryout of a Broadway play in the provinces. Its handicaps were many, but in overcoming them the RCA engineers learned many valuable things. There was the inaccessibility of the station, making it hard to obtain—and retain—entertainers. There was the variable condenser formed by freight trains of the Lehigh Valley and the C.R.R. of N. J., which, passing almost directly under the antenna, changed its capacity and made unescapable variations in the radiated output. Finally, there was the insulation problem, for these same engines coated the antenna insulators with carbon, making leakage and not insulation the major characteristic of the overhead system. It is a wonder that even two months of this was endured."

[3] *EXTRACT FROM MINUTES OF THE MEETING OF THE BOARD OF DIRECTORS*
RADIO CORPORATION OF AMERICA
APRIL 21, 1922.

"The General Manager submitted recommendation that the Radio Corporation share one-half of the expense of operation of the Westinghouse WJZ station at Newark from February 15th, 1922 and as long as the WJZ station continues to be operated on a partnership basis (which program is contemplated until the Radio Corporation completes its own station in New York City at which time it is planned to discontinue WJZ). The General Manager stated that the cost of operation from February 15th to February 28th was $1,461.01 and for the month of March the cost of operation was $2,897.09 (March figures subject to final check by the Westinghouse Company). On motion, duly made and seconded, the General Manager was authorized to pay one-half of the expense of the WJZ station, as recommended."

Sec. 135. Hunting for a New President of RCA.

During the winter of 1922, in the month of February, Edward J. Nally held a very important conference with Owen D. Young, who was now recognized as the guiding genius of the Radio Corporation of America. Mr. Nally confided to the chairman of the board that the trend of events in corporate affairs, especially into the field of sales of radio appliances, was a bit out of his line. All his life Mr. Nally had been engaged in communications. He had no enthusiasm for sales expansion, yet realized that the corporation's future prosperity probably lay in this direction. For this reason he was frankly of opinion that the welfare of RCA would be served by the selection of a new president who would be conversant with sales problems. Mr. Nally hoped that he might continue to direct the communications department of the corporation's activities. He suggested that if he could be re-elected President at the next stockholders' meeting Mr. Young might consider that he held the Nally resignation, to be acted upon whenever a successor could be chosen and Nally himself given a suitable communications assignment abroad in international affairs.

Mr. Young was thereupon confronted with the task of selecting a successor. It is characteristic of Owen D. Young that whenever attempting any important task he invariably formulates in his own mind or on paper those conditions or specifications under which he proposes to operate. In a letter to Mr. Nally dated October 25, 1922, Mr. Young thus comments on the nature of his task in searching for his successor in the presidency of RCA:

". . . Naturally, after my talk with you in February, I began to cast about for a man who might be qualified to act as your successor as President of the Radio Corporation. First of all, I tried to formulate in my own mind certain specifications which it would be desirable for the man to have. In a rough way, these specifications were as follows:

1st. He should be well known both nationally and internationally and he should have made such a place for himself as would enable him to speak with authority either to foreign Governments or to our own Government.

2nd. He should not have been previously identified with politics because that would mean party alignment and partisan reaction.

3rd. He should not have been identified with Wall Street and the money interests because it is important that the American people should accept the Radio Corporation as an organization for service to American interests both at home and abroad rather than as an organization primarily to make a profit for Wall Street interests.

4th. He should have had administrative experience and if possible business experience.

5th. He should be well known in Washington and in a position to appear before Committees of Congress and before the Departments and have his statements of facts accepted without question. It is particularly important in this connection that no one should be able to question his Americanism, such as they have done in several instances in the case of our international bankers.

6th. He should be a man of public position whom to attack would be bad politics rather than good politics.

"At first it seemed absolutely impossible to find a man who could comply with these specifications. I sought suggestions everywhere and passed under review many names quite regardless of whether, if satisfactory, the man could have been obtained. Naturally, I reviewed most of the men in prominent positions in America and it was most disappointing to find how universally they failed to meet the specifications. I then reviewed the specifications but felt that I could not change them."

The manner in which Mr. Young settled upon Gen. James G. Harbord is likewise characteristic. Harbord's name was first suggested by Newton D. Baker, recently Secretary of War. This recommendation might have moved a more impulsive man to action. Not so Owen D. Young. With all the caution of a truly great lawyer he canvassed the situation with others. He learned that General Pershing regarded Harbord so highly that when he himself accepted appointment as Chief of Staff of the United States Armies he did so on condition that Harbord be Deputy Chief of Staff and thus enabled to carry on executive duties while Pershing was away on important diplomatic missions in connection with complications remaining from the World War. General Charles G. Dawes was enthusiastic over Harbord's work in France. Business leaders such as Atterbury, Stettinius, and Swope, who knew Harbord's record, were alike generous in their praise of his ability. Of Young's first attempt, unsuccessful as it proved, to persuade General Harbord to accept the presidency of RCA we have the following account in his letter to Edward J. Nally:

". . . I, therefore, decided to have an interview with General Harbord, whom I had never personally met. I saw him in Washington sometime last spring and discussed the matter with him. He promised to consider it and to discuss it only with General Pershing, the Secretary of War, and General Dawes. I may say that I assumed the responsibility and so frankly stated to General Harbord of talking with him about the matter without having previously mentioned the subject to any member of our Board of Directors. I explained to him that it was necessary for me to start somewhere and that it hardly seemed to me wise or practical to bring his name before the Board without at least ascertaining first whether he would consider an offer if one were made. Some days later, I received a letter from General Harbord, which, I think, for the purpose of the record as well as your good understanding, I will quote in full as follows:

" 'I have decided that I cannot accept your very complimentary offer. I am deeply sensible to the splendid opportunity you open before me, and I realize that declining it at my age means that it will never come again and that for the remainder of my days I am condemning myself to the comparatively small remuneration and narrow horizon of the military service. But a man's duty is not done until it is all done, and the difficulties that now confront the Army; the hostility of the appropriating authority; the consequent worry and uneasiness that beset our whole personnel, seem to me to call for me to stand by even at this sacrifice. I have the confidence of the service, I am sure, and to set the example of quitting in the face of adverse conditions where I feel that I can be a steadying influence, even at such pecuniary advantage to myself, is something I cannot bring myself to do.

" 'I will not try to tell you how grateful I am to you for having given me my one great chance, nor how much I wish it could come to me a very few years later.'

"This letter, of course, ended further consideration of the matter and I wearily took up a new review but without success."

Sec. 136. The Department of Commerce Holds Radio Conference.

So serious did the problem of rapidly multiplying radio stations become that by mid-winter of 1922 President Warren G. Harding saw fit to instruct Secretary of Commerce Herbert Hoover to call a conference of manufacturers and broadcasters to convene in Washington. Congressman (later Senator) Wallace H. White, Jr., of Maine, represented the National Congress. Dr. S. W. Stratton, Chief of the Bureau of Standards, was chairman of the technical committee of the conference. Dr. Alfred N. Goldsmith and E. H. Armstrong, eminent inventors and engineers, were present as were Dr. Louis Cohen and Hiram Percy Maxim. The conference opened February 27, 1922, and continued its sessions until March 2nd.

In opening the Conference Secretary Hoover declared: "We have witnessed in the last four or five months one of the most astounding things that has come under my observation of American life. This Department estimates that today more than 600,000 (one estimate being 1,000,000) persons possess wireless telephone receiving sets, whereas there were less than fifty thousand such sets a year ago. We are indeed today upon the threshold of a new means of widespread communication of intelligence that has the most profound importance from the point of view of public education and public welfare."

There was one point upon which all delegates to the conference were unanimous—that the United States was in need of a definite radio policy. From that point onward, however, they violently disagreed. The commercial broadcasters complained of the irresponsible conduct of the radio amateurs. The amateurs stoutly retorted that the blame rested upon the selfish policies of the commercial broadcasters. Each faction loudly clamored for the regulation of the other, whereupon Secretary Hoover wittily observed that "this is one of the few instances where the country is unanimous in its desire for more regulation."

It was obvious to all that regulation must take the form of allocating channels of communication, or in other words, wave lengths that the various stations should be permitted to use. The laws of 1912 regulating wireless telegraphy were powerless to cope with the situation or to unsnarl the dreadful tangle which radio broadcasting was rapidly developing. The various governmental agencies now dependent upon radio had vital interest in this matter of regulation.

Colonel Griswold, the official delegate of the American Telephone and Telegraph Company, set forth the views of his company. Radio, he declared, has opened lines of communication between islands and mainland or in remote areas where no other means of rapid communication would be possible. Despite the fact that the Telephone Company was mainly interested in communication by wire the company was sufficiently interested in the possibilities of radio as supplementary to its lines to be contemplating opening an experimental radio station.

The Westinghouse Company, with four stations already in operation, was represented by L. R. Krumm. This gentleman made no secret of the fact that his company was in the broadcasting business to stimulate sales of its various radio appliances. When Secretary Hoover asked him if he did not fear reaching a saturation point in sales, Mr. Krumm replied, "I don't believe it. There is no saturation point on automobiles, for instance. We have found a steady increase in sales and we don't anticipate any drop if the quality of the broadcasting is maintained."

The refreshing frankness of the speaker at length got him into a hornets' nest when he declared that there were already far too many radio stations and expressed an opinion that fifteen stations could cover the nation.

The conference soon developed acrimonious aspects. Police departments were clamoring for special wave lengths for police calls and broadcasts. Newspaper publishers with radio stations had their special problems. The tendency of department stores to advertise over the air was denounced and defended. Manufacturers of radio equipment whose product failed to give adequate range or service were roundly censured. The alleged monopolistic tendencies of some manufacturers of radio equipment were paraded, as might have been expected from the nature of the gathering.

The conference accomplished several important results. The problem of amateur broadcasting was thoroughly aired. The commercial companies had an opportunity to present their views. Newspaper publishers had spoken their minds. Sympathetic co-operation by the government was assured. Best of all, the conference adopted definite recommendations, among which were the following:

"*Resolved,* That the Conference on Radio Telephony recommend that the radio laws be amended so as to give the Secretary of Commerce adequate legal authority for the effective control of—

(1) The establishment of all radio transmitting stations except amateur, experimental and governmental stations.

(2) The operation of non-governmental radio transmitting stations.
"*Resolved,* That it is the sense of the conference that radio communication is a public utility and as such should be regulated and controlled by the Federal Government in the public interest.
"*Resolved,* That the types of radio apparatus most effective in reducing interference should be made freely available to the public without restrictions."

Other recommendations were of a technical nature and demonstrate the earnestness and thought devoted to the problems in hand.

Sec. 137. Radio Manufacturers Swamped by Orders.

In March, 1922, the second annual Radio Show was held in New York City. The roof of the Pennsylvania Hotel had been selected as the site for the exhibition but the directors of the show were to discover too late that even if they had staged the affair in Madison Square Garden they could scarcely have accommodated the multitude who fought for admission. Thousands were turned away, but even so, many of those who got in were unable to see the exhibits because the exhibition room was so crowded that view was impossible. The exhibitors were distressed at their inability to display their products. The following extract from *Radio Notes* in the May, 1922, issue of *Radio Broadcast* is illuminating:

"All of which isn't exactly a criticism of the promoters of the show. Their past experience had led them to believe that the exhibition would attract the amateur chiefly; they were unprepared, as all branches of the radio industry were unprepared, for the sudden great development of interest in the art.

"Viewed as a whole, the show was noteworthy as indicating the belief of manufacturers in the permanency of broadcasting and the permanency of public interest. The tendency among producers of radio equipment is towards a compact receiving set in cabinet form which will take its place without criticism among the furnishings of the home. Loose ends, loose wires, are steadily being eliminated. The loud speakers generally didn't make an entirely satisfactory impression. Some were good, but there was much evidence of throat trouble; one of them was usually yowling regularly. Before the next show the manufacturers should be able to exhibit reliable loud speakers. Otherwise they had better be left at home."

A significant item in *Radio Notes* of the May, 1922, issue has to do with investigations being made by a French scientist with vacuum tubes in an effort to adapt them to use on an electric light circuit, thus to eliminate the use of storage batteries. The commenter reaches the conclusion "that it is perhaps best, after all, to be satisfied with storage battery operation."

The radio boom, beginning in the East, swept the central states and the Pacific Coast with surprising rapidity. The licensing of radio stations in the Western portion of the United States immediately took the lead in numbers of stations, despite the fact that possible listeners per station must be a mere fraction of the potential audience available for the more densely populated eastern states. The boom reached the western states in the winter of 1922. A writer in *Radio Broadcast* thus comments on the difficulty of procuring radio sets:

"But what amazed and perplexed us and still does, was that if we wanted anything in the radio line except copper wire and roofs to string our antennae on, we would have to go down on a waiting list as long as that of the Bohemian Club, and that we would be lucky to get service inside of three months. If we postponed action for three days, we went to find that the waiting list had quadrupled in length and that six months or maybe eight was the best we could hope for." [4]

Making due allowance for possible humorous exaggeration, the radio boom was an amazing phenomenon in the West, where long distances had always more or less isolated small communities from the outside world. The instinctive craving of mankind for amusement, for something to brighten the humdrum of life, was now to be had for the mere cost of a radio set. The author's own experience as a radio lecturer over a coast-to-coast network some years ago gave him special insight into what radio means to listeners in isolated places. "I am keeping bees in an abandoned lumber camp sole alone," wrote a man in the State of Washington. "Radio is my only comfort—it keeps me from going mad." "I am a shut in," wrote a Colorado lady, "bedrid-

[4] *Radio Broadcast,* June 1922, p. 158.

den for ten years and I can never hope to leave my bed again, but radio brings me the only joy that I know or can ever know."

These letters were typical of "fan mail" from the West and Southwest in the years 1930 to 1933. In 1922 radio must have seemed even more alluring to people who had never dreamed of such a marvel of science until it actually appeared.

"The average man on the street," wrote the Pacific Coast reporter, "had never more than vaguely heard of radio until two months ago. . . . All of a sudden it hit us. The first most of us saw of it, beyond random and rather dull newspaper and magazine accounts of developments, was in first page, first column headlines from New York, not over two months ago, proclaiming that the East had gone mad over radio. Within twelve hours the interest swept the coast." [5]

Not only had radio become a household necessity but it speedily invaded that universal vehicle of transportation, the automobile. Pictures are often more eloquent than words and certainly more revealing. We have but to behold in the June, 1922, issue of *Radio Broadcast* [6] the reproduction of a photograph of an ingenious Chicago high school lad who had installed a radio in his Ford car to understand the truth of this observation. There he sat in proud state, earphones clamped in place. Strangely enough, in the picture we also observe that the radio clamped to the seat beside him was equipped with one of those terrible first loud speakers. Its megaphone mouth was leveled upon him. Evidently the lad was taking no chances, for loud speakers were then very unreliable. They had throat trouble, if we may term it such. The lad was pioneering in two senses, since the loud speaker was still in the experimental stage and the automobile radio was not to emerge as a commercial success for nearly a decade.

Sec. 138. Who Will Pay the Bills of Broadcasting?

In the mad rush to open radio stations few who succeeded in doing so had apparently counted the cost of maintenance of the station. For a newspaper or a manufacturer of radio equipment or even for a department store there were obvious advertising returns to balance expenditures. For the ordinary radio impresario, however, there could be little but glory to be harvested.

To the thoughtful observer of the hectic scene and no doubt to the owner of a radio broadcasting station after it was fairly launched came the serious question of station finance. England was shortly to solve the problem by creating a government monopoly of broadcasting supported by an excise tax levied on each radio set annually, but such a solution was not even seriously considered in the United States. The

[5] *Radio Broadcast*, June 1922, p. 157.
[6] *Ibid.*, p. 159.

natural reaction first observable in the public press was that manufacturers should bear the cost of radio broadcasting.

There were serious difficulties about any such plan. Fly-by-night
manufacturers were turning out quantities of bootleg equipment and
selling the same to the detriment of the owners of radio patents. There
was no way of assessing the cost of broadcasting against them. Then,
too, legitimate manufacturers could not be expected to shoulder the
expense unless they were to be given a monopoly of the air—which was
unthinkable in individualistic America. No doubt advertising was
thought of even in early days of broadcasting but was dismissed as
impracticable. It may seem fantastic to the present generation but the
editor of *Radio Broadcast* in its very first issue came out squarely for
endowed radio stations.

"It would seem then," he wrote, "that the solution of the problem
will finally involve some different scheme of financing than that used
at present. There are various schemes possible, of which the most
attractive one, in so far as the general public is concerned, is the endowment of a station by a public-spirited citizen. This may sound at
present like a peculiar institution to endow, but it seems sure to come.
We have gymnasiums, athletic fields, libraries, museums, etc., endowed
and for what purpose? Evidently for the amusement and education of
the public. But it may be that in the early future the cheapest and
most efficient way of dispensing amusement and education may be by
radiophone.

"A powerful station in the vicinity of a large city like New York
would reach at present perhaps one or two hundred thousand persons.
. . . Such an audience would be impossible by any other scheme. A
lecturer can, at such a station, reach more people in one evening than
he could on the lecture platform in a year of speechmaking.

"The first cost and maintenance cost of a powerful station are not
prohibitive when compared to that of other institutions designed to do
as comprehensive a piece of work. Thus a powerful station could be
put up and operated at a cost less than a reasonable-sized library, and
there is no doubt that a properly conducted radio broadcasting station
can do at least as great an educational work as does the average
library. This is not to disparage the endowment of libraries but to
point out another way for the wealthy citizen to invest part of his
excess wealth for the public good. To one with vision of the probable
growth of radio communication, the endowment of such a station
should appeal strongly and there is much likelihood that many such
stations will be operating in the next twenty-five years."

The learned editor did not pause with a single suggestion for financing radio broadcasting. He discussed also the suggestion that had come
to him from some source that broadcasting stations be financed "by

contributions to a common fund, which would be controlled by an elected board."

This scheme he dismissed because he was enough of a philosopher to know that the average human being who could listen to radio programs whether he paid for them or not would naturally accept the benefit and forget the moral obligation.

As an evidence of the mental fog in which thoughtful observers of the radio scene were then groping the editor takes up the out and out socialistic scheme of municipal financing.

"A weird scheme this will undoubtedly appear to many," he writes, "but upon analysis it will be found not so strange, even to those who have no socialistic tendencies. In New York City, for example, large sums of money are spent annually in maintaining free public lectures, given on various topics of interest; the attendance at one of these lectures may average two or three hundred people. The same lecture delivered from a broadcasting station would be heard by several thousand people. Because of the diverse interests of such a large city as New York it would probably be necessary to operate two or three stations, from each of which different forms of amusement or educational lectures would be sent out. The cost of such a project would probably be less than that for the scheme at present used and the number of people who would benefit might be immeasurably greater." [7]

Sec. 139. Unsolved Problems of Radio.

Radio broadcasting in the spring of 1922 was still in a primitive stage. Every halftone published at that time and for a long period thereafter depicting a radio listener was sure to disclose the inconvenient earphones in operation. The faint whisper captured by crystal detectors required the earphone, which led to the ludicrous spectacle of a group of people, some equipped with "ear muffs" and others apparently awaiting their turn to listen in.

To be sure the advertising pages of leading periodicals now carried alluring advertising for ungainly trumpets labeled "Loud Speakers." Nevertheless, the editor of radio's leading periodical frankly admitted that they were a snare and a delusion.

"The small crystal sets," he writes, "requiring head sets do give fairly good reproduction provided that the transmitting station is functioning properly, but the wearing of a head set is not a pleasant way to spend an evening. When vacuum tube receiving sets are used, attached to amplifiers and loud speaking horns, there is generally a good deal of distortion. . . . Loud speaking receivers are at present very crude devices compared to what they may be; they nearly all give fair

[7] *Radio Broadcast*, May 1922, p. 4.

reproduction of music, but for speech they are somewhat lacking in performance. This is not an insuperable difficulty and a good loud speaker is almost sure soon to appear. Then the speech will be clearer than would be the case if the lecturer were in a hall and the listener were one of the audience; the lecture may be enjoyed by the whole family seated in easy chairs and if the lecturer proves to be tiresome the set will be returned to some other station offering a more attractive program." [8]

Interference in radio transmission was still one of the great unsolved problems of the industry. The difficulties experienced occasionally even in this year of grace 1938 are as nothing to the exasperating everyday interference encountered in pioneer days. Learned articles were being written on the subject by eminent electrical engineers such as John V. L. Hogan, Dr. Alfred N. Goldsmith, Paul F. Godley and others. Not only did these engineers write on the subject but the leading radio manufacturers were wrestling constantly with the problem.

Station WJZ at Newark, New Jersey, was doing notable work for the New York City area. The establishment of other nearby stations, however, produced the annoying phenomenon of interference that sometimes marred WJZ broadcasts. In Newark new stations were being opened. Stations WBS and WJZ were listed in April and Station WAAM in May, 1922. Station WOR was licensed in February, 1922. With five stations already in operation in Newark and more in contemplation in New York City the prospect was not at all pleasing. Multiplicity of stations might result in chaos unless ways of curing interference could be devised.

The American Telephone and Telegraph Company had hitherto confined itself to transmission by wire. Its technical engineers, however, had experimented considerably with vacuum tubes and were utilizing them in long distance wire-telephony. Since it was generally believed that vacuum tubes would inevitably play an important part in the future of radio broadcasting it was natural that engineers of the telephone company should have taken keen interest in the new science of radio broadcasting. The officials of the American Telephone and Telegraph Company were not slow to perceive in radio broadcasting an indirect benefit to their own industry. In early spring of 1922 it became known that the American Telephone and Telegraph Company would shortly open an experimental radio station in New York City. The top of one of New York's skyscrapers was to be utilized for the purpose. This station moreover was to embody the most advanced thought of the leading radio technicians of the nation.

Since this ambitious project of the American Telephone and Tele-

[8] *Radio Broadcast,* May 1922, p. 4.

graph Company was to lead the way to emancipation of radio broadcasting it deserves more than passing mention. To begin with, it is apparent that the editors even of magazines devoted to radio had no clear understanding in 1922 or later of the real motive of the Telephone Company in entering the broadcasting field. The company scorned publicity and hence editors were left to their own conjectures as to the meaning of the venture.

An eminent electrical engineer who was closely related to the venture has recently pointed out to the author that there was a significant covenant relating to wireless telephony that ran through the famous cross-licensing agreements of 1920 and 1921. Radio broadcasting in its true sense was not at the time of these agreements even glimpsed, but wireless telephony for point-to-point communication was already known to electrical engineers. Telephoning of messages for profit was considered by the great corporations that joined in the cross-licensing agreements to be the rightful domain of the American Telephone & Telegraph Company, just as wireless telegraphy was considered the exclusive province of the newly created Radio Corporation of America.

The covenant referred to first appears when the Telephone Company joined the group—in the license agreement concluded between the General Electric Company and the American Telephone & Telegraph Company July 1, 1920. The language was as follows:

4. "Wireless Telephony—(a) The Telephone Company grants to the General Company non-exclusive licenses in the field of wireless telephony for its own communication or for purposes of convenience, or to save expense in connection with its commercial operation of wireless telegraph systems but not for profit or for transmission of messages for the general public. . . .

(d) (2) "Non-exclusive licenses to establish and maintain transmitting stations for transmitting or broadcasting news, music and entertainment from a transmitting station to outlying points and licenses to make, use, sell and lease wireless telephone receiving apparatus for the reception of such news, music and entertainment so broadcasted."

On the same day that this agreement between the General Electric Company and the American Telephone and Telegraph Company was concluded the two companies made extension agreements with RCA and the Western Electric Company whereby the two latter corporations acquired reciprocal rights and assumed the obligations involved in the said cross-licensing agreement. When the Westinghouse Company came under the cross-licensing "tent" on June 30, 1921, the agreement containing the wireless telephony provision was enumerated as one of the numerous cross-licensing agreements in which it was to share.

So far as mutual agreements between powerful organizations could be said to have given the American Telephone and Telegraph Company a monopoly of wireless telephony for profit, the company now had the exclusive right to exploit radio broadcasting for public use. Thus, although each of the other great companies had the right to erect radio stations and to use them in disseminating news or entertainment or even to advertise their own products, they had no rights to sell time on the air. That right, by virtue of the cross-licensing agreements, was reserved to the American Telephone & Telegraph Company.

Now that virtual chaos was resulting from the building of radio stations the Telephone Company officials believed that the time had come for them to build a super-station that could be offered to the public on a toll basis similar to that of its long distance toll lines. Since this new type of mass transmission must inevitably cut into the Telephone Company's established business it was logical that the company should assert its rights to radio broadcasting to the exclusion at least of the other parties to the cross-licensing agreements.

Sec. 140. A Toll Station Planned by American Tel. & Tel. Company.

Perhaps unknown to *Radio Broadcast* and to other periodicals of the time the American Telephone Company had already formulated in writing plans of a far-reaching nature before news of the contemplated station got noised abroad. In the archives of the National Broadcasting Company there exists today a most significant document in the nature of a press release (possibly never issued) by the American Tel. & Tel. Company bearing the date of February 10, 1922. It reads in part as follows:

"A permit has been granted for the erection of a wireless telephone broadcasting station by the A. T. & T. Company on the roof of the twenty-four story operating building between Walker and Lispenard Streets. This building is 350 feet high and rises conspicuously above any other building in the immediate neighborhood. The steel towers supporting the antenna will be 100 feet high. . . . This wireless broadcasting station will be unique in many respects. This important radio distributing station is to be equipped with the latest developments of the Bell System, including the use of electrical filters and new methods, whereby, as the business grows, several wave-lengths can be sent out simultaneously from the same point, so that the receiving stations may listen at will to any one of the several services. It will be unique in another respect, because it will be the first radio station for telephone broadcasting which will provide a means of distribution and will handle the distribution of news, music and other programs on a commercial basis for such people as contract for this service."

The most surprising part of the announcement was the rather naive idea that it would be possible to conduct a broadcasting station in much the same manner as the Telephone Company was then maintaining toll service for customers desirous of sending long distance messages. The Company would soon learn that the analogy was not complete—that radio presented far different problems of maintenance and of operation. But let us examine further the announcement of February 10, 1922:

"The American Telephone & Telegraph Company will provide no program of its own, but provide the channels through which anyone with whom it makes a contract can send out its own programs. Just as the company leases its long distance wire facilities for the use of newspapers, banks and other concerns, so it will lease its radio telephone facilities and will not provide the matter which is sent out from this station. There have been many requests for such service, not only from newspapers and entertainment agencies, but also from department stores and a great variety of business houses who wish to utilize this means of distribution. . . . This is a new undertaking in the commercial use of radio telephony and if there appears a real field for such service . . . it will be followed as circumstances warrant by similar stations erected at important centers throughout the United States by the A. T. & T. Company. As these additional stations are erected, they can be connected by the toll and long distance wires of the Bell System so that from any central point, the same news, music or other program can be sent out simultaneously through all these stations by wire and wireless with the greatest possible economy and without interference. . . . The new line of business to be handled by this radio telephone broadcasting station will be in charge of the Long Lines Department of the A. T. & T. Company which is now engaged in solving the many problems both technical and commercial which arise in connection with this new kind of service."

Sec. 141. General Electric Company Founds Station WGY.

It was natural that the General Electric Company with its great manufacturing plant and its vital interest in the progress of the science of radio broadcasting should early have entered the radio lists.

"It was late in 1921," writes Goldsmith, "that G. E. engineers decided upon the installation and operation of a broadcast transmitter in order to study the problems of mass communication. A radio license was secured [9] and the letters WGY assigned to the 1500-watt transmitter that resembled a laboratory workbench with its disorderly accumulation of tubes and wires. Two 150-foot towers were placed on the roof of one of the factory buildings at Schenectady to support the antenna."

[9] In February 1922—on list of stations in *Radio Service Bulletin*, March 1, 1922.

WGY went on the air for its initial broadcast on the evening of February 20, 1922, with Martin P. Rice as manager. Mr. Rice had been the head of the publicity department of the General Electric Company, hence was well qualified to inaugurate a radio program that would have distinct publicity value. Under his able administration Station WGY at once took its place among the leading radio stations of the nation. Not only did WGY carry on the most careful of scientific experiments in broadcasting but it enlisted the co-operation of the public in matters of broadcast reception. Whenever alterations were made in broadcasting equipment listeners in distant places were asked to report on the volume and quality of the results. Since WGY began operation with a much more powerful transmitter than that used in other stations and at a time when there were but few stations on the air, it achieved truly marvelous results.

Under favorable atmospheric conditions the broadcasts from Station WGY were picked up on the Pacific Coast and even in Alaska. They likewise spanned the ocean and were heard in England.[10] A large staff of engineers were constantly employed to devise new and better methods of radio broadcasting. The quality of its program-offerings made WGY an especial favorite among radio listeners. There was in fact an element of rivalry among the early stations that proved highly advantageous to the new art of radio broadcasting. Music, both instrumental and vocal, was common to all such programs but there was a reaching out into new and untried fields.

Sec. 142. Station WJZ Broadcasts Mozart's Opera.

The ambitious Lee deForest, nearly a generation ahead of his time, had put grand opera on the air in the winter of 1910. The late lamented Station WDY, under the energetic Major J. Andrew White, had drawn upon theatrical talent from the Great White Way to enliven its radio programs. The officials of Station WJZ were resolved to perform some spectacular feat of an original character. It so happened in the winter of 1922 that an opera company that had been on tour for twenty-five weeks with Mozart's comic opera "The Impresario" returned to New York City. This was regarded as WJZ's opportunity to do some pioneering of a popular nature.

In these early months of Station WJZ's existence its staff was very small. Charles B. Popenoe was Program Manager of the Station. Dr. William H. Easton, who was in charge of the station when it was inaugurated, had apparently found his regular duties with the Westinghouse Company more to his liking and was no longer on the staff. Harry E. Miller, the assistant superintendent of the Westinghouse

10 *This Thing Called Broadcasting*, p. 35.

plant at Newark, was the real power behind the throne—the general manager of the Station.

Next in importance to Popenoe at this time was Thomas H. Cowan, who acted as talent scout, host to visiting celebrities and announcer of programs.

The third member of this original group was a very affable and intelligent colored porter, Alvin Simmons, destined to remain in this position through all the changes that came to Station WJZ and the National Broadcasting Company for fifteen years, until the fall of 1937. Al was popular with everybody from the very first. His cheerful smile and immaculate uniform became bywords at NBC.

There were three engineers or operators, George Blitziotis (chief operator), who, by the way, could not speak English; Raymond Guy and Harry E. Hiller.

At this time and for a year or two thereafter WJZ was operating on a part-time basis. The reason for this was at first voluntary but with the opening of Station WOR in March, 1922, Station WHN in April and Stations WAAM and WBS in May, 1922, it became necessary to share broadcasting time with them in order to avoid chaos on the air.

On March 15, 1922, at the time of the broadcast of Mozart's comic opera, "The Impresario," WJZ was already on a time-sharing basis. Fortunately for the student of history the story of WJZ's first operatic broadcast was written, and very well written, for the August, 1922, issue of *Radio Broadcast*. The author was a composer and director of the opera company—C. E. LeMessena. This contemporary word picture and its halftone illustrations are priceless contributions to the story of radio's pioneer days. Here we see the star of the cast, Percy Hemus, singing into the "tomato can" microphone—an elongated cylinder much more imposing than the conventional tomato tin—and a view of the cloth-draped studio itself.

"At Newark," reads the LeMessena story, "the recording took place in a small room about 10 by 40 feet [11] on the second floor of the Westinghouse plant. At one end is a grand piano. On one side is the electrical apparatus which conveys the message to the amplifying station on the roof. On the opposite side is the switch and a set of headphones, also a phonograph and an orchestrelle. In the center is the portable microphone into which the sound waves are directed. At the back of the room are chairs and tables for auditors and reporters. There have been several kinds of microphones employed, a platter disc, a cup and a cylindrical tube. The last named was in use at this time. It is about six inches in diameter, lined with felt, and is suspended from an adjustable tripod." Thus we have the most complete description of

---

[11] The length was exaggerated since we have the testimony of Dr. Easton that the studio was less than twenty feet long.

primitive broadcasting apparatus from the layman's viewpoint that the author has been able to discover.

Sec. 143. Broadcasting "The Impresario" at WJZ.

"The program for the evening," LeMessena writes, "has been announced through the press and by bulletin, and the thousands of radio fans are adjusting their headpieces at the scheduled hour. Of course they do not hear the voices of the singers or the tones of the instruments any more than they do over the ordinary telephone. They hear a reincarnation, a recreated voice and tone, because the original tones are not conveyed but first transformed into ethereal waves and then transformed back again by means of the many receiving outfits within range of the broadcasting station. This is what makes the whole thing so uncanny, mysterious and sensational. It is the thrill of thrills. . . . To talk or sing or play to an invisible audience of unknown proportions is sufficient to make the most seasoned opera star or concert artist quake. A new experience—a novel sensation, even to those who knew nought of awe or fear."

Before going on with the story it is necessary to explain that in the early years of broadcasting at WJZ it was the settled policy to do all announcing under the cloak of anonymity. Like the station itself the announcer had code letters assigned at the beginning of his service. ACN was the symbol for Thomas H. Cowan, A for announcer, C for Cowan, and N for Newark, to distinguish it from other Westinghouse stations. When Milton J. Cross joined the staff some months later the initial "C" could not be used for him so his middle letter was substituted. He became AJN. Bertha Brainard, who did some announcing for a time, was known as ABN.

"The company arrives," writes LeMessena "and is shown into the *sanctum sanctorum*. They take their places. The announcer explains that they are subject to certain radio traffic regulations, as other broadcasting stations are also operating and it would be discourteous to begin until the exact hour announced when the air lanes are free. . . . Movement is prohibited, whispering is little short of criminal and even too deep breathing is forbidden. The announcer cautions all regarding these details and asks if they are ready. With a final admonition of 'sh-h,' he closes the switch and then speaks into the microphone, while the members of the company stand silently by, with eyes dilated, enwrapped in a new experience. 'This is WJZ Station at Newark, N. J.' he begins, 'broadcasting Mozart's opera comique "The Impresario" under the direction of William Wade Hinshaw. Announcer ACN. I take pleasure in introducing Mr. Hinshaw.' Mr. Hinshaw silently slides into the position promptly vacated by ACN and addresses his audience. . . . Mr. Hinshaw proceeds to introduce the several artists by name, requesting them to speak and tell who they are and what characters they impersonate. This done, the signal was given to the pianist to proceed, and the opera is on. As each character appears, the singer steps forward, delivers his lines or sings, as the case may be, then retires to make way for the next, who takes up the thread immediately. When two or more are engaged in dialogue or ensemble musical numbers, the heads come together so that everybody may be recorded and no one be more prominent than another. At the end of an hour and a quarter, the company is ready to draw a long breath and a handkerchief, and relax. It is fun, but it is hard work, too."

This vivid and delightful picture of broadcasting at WJZ in March, 1922, deserves to go down in history as the reaction of seasoned veterans of the operatic stage to the newest marvel of science.

The success of this performance no doubt did much to fix in the minds of leaders in the entertainment field of the metropolitan area a wholesome respect for the possibilities of radio broadcasting. It certainly increased the activities of Station WJZ and rendered necessary the services of a clerical assistant. Miss Helen Guy, a sister of one of the engineers of the station, entered the employ of WJZ on April 27, 1922, the first woman so far as the records show to become a regular worker in a radio broadcasting station.[12] She was the first woman to announce radio programs on Station WJZ. Incidentally Miss Guy, now Mrs. R. L. Winget of West Orange, N. J., is still in the employ of the National Broadcasting Company after sixteen years of continuous service.

Station WJZ now deserved larger and more suitable quarters. Fortunately we have a description of the new studio in the Popenoe MS at page 11:

"It was not until June of 1922 that the new studio on the ground floor of the main building was completed. This was a room some 45 feet long by 30 feet wide, with double walls and windows to keep out all sound. Artificial ventilation was installed and to prevent echo, heavy French pleated draperies made of monks' cloth were hung loosely on the walls, reaching entirely from ceiling to floor. Heavy rugs were placed and expensive furniture of heavy, padded type was installed. This was a most artistic room and was the first real studio established for any of the few broadcasting stations of the country at that time."

[12] From Popenoe MS (1926).

"Probably one of the staff best acquainted with the program difficulties is Miss Helen Guy, the writer's secretary for a period of service dating from April 1922, to date, having sole charge of the program books, scheduling of events, petty cash and the thousand and one details of this nerve-racking job."

JOHN A. HOLMAN
Station Manager at WEAF when network broadcasting was developed.

SAMUEL L. ROSS
Became Program Manager and Musical Director Station WEAF August, 1922.

CHARLES B. POPENOE
Under whose capable management Station WJZ originated and developed.

W. E. HARKNESS
From A. T. & T. Company to Station Manager Station WEAF, November 1, 1922.

Sec. 144. The American Tel. & Tel. Company Enters Broadcasting Field.

Weeks before the scheduled opening of Station WBAY (later consolidated with Station WEAF) the leaders of the radio industry were keenly interested in the project. Nobody had yet discovered how to commercialize radio broadcasting and few there were who even entertained the thought that radio could ever be self-supporting. The decision of the powerful A. T. & T. Company to erect a broadcasting station was generally believed to be primarily in the interests of science, but, as previously indicated, the Company was pursuing a definite, although unannounced, commercial policy and expected to spend money freely in this new venture.

The transmitter of Station WBAY was designed and constructed for the station by engineers of the Western Electric Company, a subsidiary of the A. T. & T. Company. "The vacuum tubes used," writes the editor of *Radio Broadcast,* "have oxide coated filaments, such as were employed in the detecting tubes used so extensively by the Signal Corps during the war. The larger tubes, of which there are four, are of 250 watt rating, using 1600 volts in the plate circuit. An interesting detail in the construction of these tubes is the blackening of the plates to increase the radiation of heat; a black plate will radiate much more heat at a given temperature than a shiny one."

Not only was the new station to be equipped with the last word in transmitters but a new type of microphone was to be tested. A tightly stretched diaphragm of thin steel membrane was to be used, the membrane having a natural frequency far above that of the human voice.

"It is designed," writes the editor, "to give better reproduction of the consonant sounds than does the ordinary microphone transmitter. It is anticipated that only about forty per cent modulation will be employed, this comparatively weak modulation being used with the idea of keeping out the distortion of voice sounds that occurs if complete modulation is attempted."

The new station, moreover, was to try another revolutionary experiment. Instead of a heavily draped room for a broadcasting studio the new plan was to reduce echoes by using two-inches-thick sound absorbing material in the ceilings. The side walls were to be padded with thick felt. Thick carpeting was to cover the floor.

"This A. T. & T. station is being constructed, and is to be operated, purely as an experiment," conjectures the editor of *Radio Broadcasting* in a laudatory interpretation of the Telephone Company's unexplained new enterprise. "It had its inception in repeated demands for supplying broadcasting transmitting sets. . . . Evidently it would have been short-sighted policy to sell these equipments. The purchasers would soon find out they had white elephants on their hands. Such stations would evidently be installed for advertising, indirect, of course, but advertising, nevertheless. And if a dozen of them were to operate at once they would so jam the air that none of them could be received. With the idea of avoiding this situation and further to get first-hand information on the need and desirability of such broadcast advertising the A. T. & T. Company decided to erect and operate themselves a first-class station. . . . The operation of WBAY for a few months will probably furnish an answer to these questions. Whether the answer be yes or no the operation of this station (which will have such a program as not to interfere with WJZ) will be of benefit to the radio public because of the technical excellence of the station." [13]

Sec. 145. David Sarnoff Proposes High Power Short Wave Broadcasting.

David Sarnoff's uncanny ability to forecast future events was demonstrated afresh on August 2, 1922, when he prepared a special report for President Nally of RCA entitled "High Power Short Wave Broadcasting." In the course of this article he makes the following prophecy:

"Although it is purely a speculative statement and necessarily based on incomplete knowledge and information, yet it would not surprise me if in the next few years we find that a radio signal sent out on 100 meters with 100 or 200 k.w. of power will travel around the world and be received through the highly sensitive and delicate receiving instruments which are rapidly projecting themselves into the radio art, for example, the super-regenerative.

"It may well be that some day in the future we will signal and talk across the Atlantic and Pacific with short instead of long waves and if this should come true, the problems of static elimination and high speed operation would take on a new appearance, for it is well known one can signal on short waves at a rate of speed many times that possible on the longer waves, and static at the shorter wavelengths is not comparable to that on the long waves."

Even then Mr. Sarnoff was thinking of super-power broadcasting stations as a means of supplying the radio listeners of the nation with high quality programs free from interference of stations maintained at the expense of radio manufacturers.

Sec. 146. Brief Life of Station WBAY.

The much heralded Station WBAY, owned and operated by the American Tel. & Tel. Company, was first listed as a licensed station in the Department of Commerce *Radio Bulletin* for May 1, 1922. It was

[13] *Radio Broadcast*, July 1922, pp. 196, 197.

not ready to go on the air until July 25th of that year. Strangely enough another radio station, WEAF, was on the list of licensed stations June 1, 1922, and the Western Electric Company was its record owner. The fact is, however, that the Western Electric Company was a subsidiary of the A. T. & T. Company, hence both stations were controlled by the Telephone Company. WBAY was located at 24 Walker St., New York City, whereas Station WEAF was listed at 463 West St.

By the irony of fate the expensive towers and equipment of Station WBAY that had cost the engineers so much thought and the Telephone Company so much hard cash were to prove useless. On the roof of a twenty-four story steel skyscraper the station at once taught the engineers a lesson in radio construction—that the roof of a steel building was the worst place in the world on which to build the widely advertised best radio station in the world. To be sure, the Telephone Company had endeavored to avoid publicity, but the public press could not be muzzled. Here was something of momentous import going on within the City of New York itself, sponsored by the great A. T. & T. Company. *Radio Broadcast* for July, 1922, went into editorial ecstasies over the prospect of WBAY's opening. "By the time this is in press," the editorial began, "a new broadcasting station will be in operation, a station on the design of which probably more thought and talent has been expended than on any other in existence."

In the archives of the National Broadcasting Company is a press release, undated but obviously issued at the very time when Station WBAY was going on the air for its initial broadcast. This statement, it will be observed, is in strict conformity with the preliminary announcement by the A. T. & T. Company quoted in Section 140 under date of February 10, 1922. The company still apparently believed that the opening of a toll-broadcasting station was comparable to setting up a telephone central to which citizens would apply for the privilege of sending messages of an advertising nature.

"Anyone desiring to use these facilities for radio broadcasting should make arrangements with Mr. A. W. Drake, General Commercial Manager, Long Lines Department, Am. Tel. & Tel. Company, 195 Broadway, New York City. Mr. Drake can advise fully with reference to all particulars concerning the use of the station, including information as to the periods of operation and the charges thereof. He is also in a position to give helpful suggestions with reference to the arrangement of programs and the kind of subject matter which it is thought will be most acceptable to the radio audience.

"Coincident with the wave of enthusiasm on radio broadcasting of a few months ago, the A. T. & T. Company received a great number of requests from New York and vicinity for broadcasting equipment or broadcasting service. It soon became evident that it would be impossible for each of those who desired to broadcast to own and operate his own station. There should be only one, or at best only a few wave lengths available for such service and therefore it could be expected that only a very limited period of operation could be obtained from any one such station. Further it developed that a great number of people desired broadcasting facilities placed at their disposal but did not desire to bear the expense of owning and operating their own equipment.

"Recognizing these conditions and bearing in mind that broadcasting facilities should be provided for the general use of the public rather than for the few who might desire to own and operate stations, this Station, WBAY, has been established as an experiment in toll broadcasting. Its success or failure will depend upon the use of it made by those who employ its facilities. Those who broadcast will not receive general favor from the radio audience unless they broadcast programs of merit and of general interest."

Alas for the hopes of the Telephone Company and the public! The radio transmitter on the top of the twenty-four story steel structure worked so poorly that Station WBAY, instead of opening in a blaze of glory, opened with man-made static. The first program for this station went on the air at 4:30 P.M. July 25, 1922 on 360 meters. Edmund R. Taylor and Delro K. Martin enjoy the distinction of having been the engineers in charge of the transmitter on opening day. Fortunately the first daily log of WBAY has been preserved. It is entirely handwritten and between the program numbers the operator on watch has written certain ominous facts—notations of interference from other stations. WNY, a wireless station, was heard at the end of the first minute of broadcasting and at intervals throughout the program. At 5 P.M. Station WJZ came in with a bit of interference and so it went during the hectic hour and a half of the first program. The program was largely instrumental, no doubt some of it the inevitable phonographic records, the items being as follows:

4:32 P.M.	1. Polonaise
4:40	2. Ave Maria
4:44	3. On Wings of Song
4:49	4. Meditation de Thaïs
4:52	5. Love Scene—Strauss
4:58	6. Marseillaise
5:02	7. Choc de Boc
5:07	8. Carry me Back to Old Virginny
5:12	9. Rhapsody
5:21	10. Melody F—violin
5:25	11. March, National Emblem
5:28	Signing off.

It was fortunate indeed that the Telephone Company had a second string to its bow, so to speak, because the disconcerting experience on opening day caused serious misgivings as to the future of WBAY. The still incomplete equipment being erected at 463 West Street for station WEAF might yet prove the salvation of the venture. No steel skeleton was in the vast closet of the structure on West Street. It was simply a massive brick and stone building which even in the midst of a great city should be free from the annoyance encountered at Walker Street. Two days after Station WBAY opened there was another ominous entry of interference with other stations. WJZ came on the air ahead of schedule and "jammed us before we finished." The log of station WBAY shows that on July 28th the station encountered such severe static that it was obliged to suspend broadcasting and try an experiment with the antenna which unfortunately burned out the resisters. Other experiments were tried and static was finally eliminated. By August 1st, however, the engineers were beginning to realize that the chief trouble lay in the building itself, with its trunk lines of telephone cable and the volume of electrical activity in a building whose steel framework was so susceptible to interplay of electric currents.

On August 7th a mighty thunder shower brought matters to a head. Even the heavens disapproved of this radio station, it seemed, for it is recorded in the log of that day that Jove's thunderbolts made three direct hits at 24 Walker Street. Two bolts struck the broadcasting towers and the third found its mark in the inviting antenna. It is small wonder that WBAY's engineers decided definitely to abandon the towers and antenna at Walker Street as soon as the equipment at 463 West Street should be ready to go on the air.

On the last day of WBAY's independent existence the following typical program was put on at 24 Walker Street from 11 to 11:30 A.M. Station WBAY generously surrendered its time to WJZ "so that they could give a program re *S.S. Mauretania,* with artists sailing who have been on WJZ, bidding them au revoir". The entry concludes with the statement: "WJZ thanks WBAY over air". The half hour remaining until noon carried seven numbers in which piano and violin alternated. The record shows that the station was again on the air with piano and violin from 4:30 to 5:30 P.M.

Sec. 147. Am. Tel & Tel. Company Launches Station WEAF.

The program outlined as the final independent offering of Station WBAY was the product of its new Musical Director—Samuel Louis Ross. Since he was to serve in a similar capacity for Station WEAF during the years in which this great station blazed the trail for the commercial emancipation of radio broadcasting Mr. Ross deserves special mention. He was born in Waterbury, Conn., August 14, 1892. He was graduated from Cornell, Class of 1915 with Phi Beta Kappa honors. After graduation Mr. Ross entered musical fields. Since 1919 he had represented music publishers in contracting artists, hence was well known in the musical world. It so happened that in July, 1922, a representative of A. T. and T. Company approached the director of the American Society of Composers, Authors, and Publishers about permission to broadcast music controlled by this powerful organization. During this conference the Telephone Company representative told the director that he was searching for a man with the necessary contacts to act as director of programs at the new station, WEAF, scheduled to open in three or four weeks. The director of A.S.C.A.P. recommended Samuel L. Ross. Mr. Ross was promptly engaged but was informed at the outset that the position was of a temporary nature because the station itself was experimental in character. An announcer, Vischer A. Randall, and Miss Helen Hahn, studio assistant and hostess, were the only other employees when Mr. Ross assumed his duties on August 1, 1922.

At the time he was engaged Mr. Ross had been given to understand that he was to be Musical Director of Station WBAY. He had no sooner begun work, however, than difficulties with the transmitter at 24 Walker Street led to a change of plans that would bring Station WEAF into the combination.

Radio broadcasting was then in a very chaotic state, owing in part to the fact that stations were virtually on the same wave length, and even where variation was attempted the broadcasting apparatus was inadequate to maintain unvarying wave frequency. The art of manufacture of radio sets had not progressed to a point where it was possible to tune out undesired stations. The licensing authority, moreover, was powerless to assign wave lengths and frequencies to different stations in the same locality. In the New York area in the summer of 1922 the station had worked out a gentleman's agreement to share broadcasting hours according to a schedule mutually agreed upon. Stations WJZ, WJX, WOR and WWZ were already in the field, before Station WBAY went on the air. The broadcasting hours available to the new station were naturally limited.

This fact rendered the task of the program manager, or musical director as he was called at WBAY, less difficult than it was afterward to become. He needed but a small staff at first. The physical limitations of the offices themselves would not admit of much expansion. There was no stenographer at first, hence programs were written out in longhand throughout the month of August, 1922. By the middle of the month the scene was set for the opening of the new station or rather for the dedication of the transmitting apparatus at 463 West Street.

After the unfortunate experience at Walker Street the Telephone officials in charge of radio broadcasting activities were naturally averse to any public ceremony when the station first went on the air from the new transmitter at 463 West Street.

The transition occurred on Wednesday, Aug. 16, 1922. The log entry of that date is entirely technical, with no entries as to the musical program. There is simply the significant legend "WBAY transmitter closed. WBAY Studio broadcasting through WEAF." The transmitter at 463 West Street gave glorious results. On the second day of WEAF's existence (for under the rules of the Department of Commerce any broadcasting station using a transmitter was obliged to adopt the call letters of the transmitter) an ambitious program was put on the air. Not only did WEAF broadcast during the day but it also launched an evening program three hours in length, using live talent. Miss Helen Clark, contralto, and Henry Kirby Davies, tenor, were the featured artists. Charles Hart and Miss Esther Nelson also figured prominently among the guests who contributed their talents to this novel form of public entertainment.

Sec. 148. Radio Developments in Summer of 1922.

A development in the New York City area in the late summer of 1922 focused the attention of the nation on one of the greatest problems of radio-interference between radio stations. *Radio Broadcast* declared in its October, 1922, issue, under the editorial heading "War Between Broadcasting Stations":

"It was a foreordained fact that there would eventually be conflicts between various broadcasting stations, especially in the neighborhood of New York, where a large number of them have been installed. This recently came to pass. We have had the experience of listening to a jumble of signals of just the kind anticipated—dance music competing with a lecturer for the ear of the radio audience.

"From the press notices it appears that WJZ, the Radio Corporation-Westinghouse Station at Newark, has been using the 360-meter ether channel during what seems to certain other stations a disproportionately large share of the time, and has refused to agree with these other stations on what they think a reasonable division of hours. It is probably because of this attitude on the part of the Radio Corporation Station that the Radio Broadcasting Society has been organized recently, banding together broadcasting stations for the purpose of allotting them hours in what they regard as a reasonable division, with the idea of averting the kind of interference to which we have recently been treated. It seems that WJZ felt the ether should be unchallenged by later comers and it was not until the counsel for the Broadcasting Society had started action to have the license of WJZ revoked by the federal authorities that a temporary peace and agreement were made possible."

The editor discusses the crisis in radio affairs that was involved in the controversy and makes the following pertinent observation:

"It would be sheer nonsense to stop the operation of WJZ for one minute so that some dry goods store might send out a scratchy fox-trot phonograph record which is mixed up with a loud commutator hum and 'blocking' of overmodulated tubes. The time has gone by when the public should have to listen to such stuff, because there are stations which have been properly designed and to which it is a pleasure to listen. . . . The only criterion which must serve to guide in the allocation of hours is excellence of programme excellently produced."

Another important development in the upward march of radio was the formation of a national Radio Chamber of Commerce. This was an association of manufacturers of radio apparatus meeting in Washington to discuss problems then confronting the radio industry. The fact that Secretary of Commerce Herbert Hoover had a committee busily at work on the vexed questions of wave lengths, frequencies and how to regulate stations and prevent mutual interference, was another evidence that the nation was awakening to the vital significance of radio broadcasting.

WJZ first broadcast a blow-by-blow description of a prize fight July 27, 1922—the Leonard-Tendler fight. One of the first concerts picked up by this station was a band concert at Lewisohn Stadium, August 24, 1922.[14]

In the July, 1922, issue of the *Journal of the American Institute of Electrical Engineers,* Dr. Lowell of the Bureau of Standards, who had long been working on the hoped-for "lamp-socket device" for home sets, published a description of a radio receiving set in which the A and B batteries were entirely eliminated, the power coming from an ordinary lamp socket of the electric lighting circuit. That there was still a long way to go in the search for radio perfection is indicated by the fact that a crystal detector was still used, the engineers of the Bureau of Standards not yet having discovered a means of utilizing a vacuum tube in place of the humble crystal detector. The new type of radio still required two clumsy boxes to house its component parts. *Radio Broadcast* hopefully announced, in commenting on the latest development of radio science:

[14] *Program Sheets,* Station WJZ for 1922.

"Developments are being carried out in the tube laboratories, however, which will soon give us a tube of peculiar construction such that it may fill the place occupied by the crystal in this latest amplification circuit."

One of the notable events of the summer of 1922 was the visit of Guglielmo Marconi to the United States. He lectured before the Engineering Societies in New York City on June 20th. On July 9th with a party of special guests aboard his yacht *Elettra* he sailed up the Hudson River to Albany, whence he proceeded to Schenectady, where he met the scientists Steinmetz, Whitney, Langmuir, Coolidge, and Alexanderson. On July 10th Marconi spoke over Station WGY.

Sec. 149. *Westinghouse KYW Puts Chicago Opera on the Air.*

The radio boom struck Chicago in full force when the Westinghouse Station KYW was established on the roof of a downtown skyscraper in the winter of 1922. In opening their station, the officials of KYW made a very strategic move in inducing the glamorous opera star, Mary Garden, to co-operate in the affair. Miss Garden was the Director General of the Chicago Opera Company. Wealthy people had been subsidizing the performances of the company but were wearying of the task, as Miss Garden well knew. Her sense of the publicity value of radio led her to accept with enthusiasm the opportunity thus presented of bolstering the waning prestige of the Chicago institution. Announcement that the opera would be on the air was made some time in advance of the event. It is said that up to the time of the announcement not more than 1300 radio sets were in use in Chicago. Then began a mighty scramble for home radio outfits. This boom was not confined to Chicago but extended to the entire Middle West. By the end of the opera season 20,000 sets were in use in Chicago alone and radio dealers in the entire region were frantically endeavoring to supply the demand for home radio outfits.

The Chicago Opera Company reaped a glorious reward from the publicity of this first radio opera season. Station KYW built up a tremendous nightly audience. In fact the very popularity of the opera presented a difficult problem to the officials of the station when the opera season closed. The vast radio audience must be entertained. Having listened to the best of musical offerings, the public would scorn phonograph records or amateur live talent. A musical director and a staff of competent musicians were engaged. When the opera season closed KYW was ready to substitute a twelve hour broadcasting service of the most comprehensive type yet offered by any radio station in America.

Broadcasting began at 9:25 A.M. with the market quotations of the Chicago Board of Trade—information of vital importance to the Middle West. At half-hour intervals until the grain market closed at 1:20 P.M. the progress of the market was thus reported. Livestock quotations also became a feature of the daily broadcasts of Station KYW. Markets, however, lack universal appeal. News flashes, with happenings, local and nation-wide—even world-wide—are sure-fire hits in Chicago or anywhere else. Not even the "kiddies" were forgotten by the enterprising Chicago radio station. "The children come in for their share of the program at 7:15," writes a commentator in the October issue of *Radio Broadcast,* "when a bedtime story is sent out. Just as soon as the story has been told and the children have been tucked into bed, father and the boys are given a concise summary of the sports of the day, with particular emphasis on baseball.

"Then the real entertainment begins. KYW has tried to keep its evening musical programs up to the standard set by the Opera Company in the first months of Chicago broadcasting. To do so is good business. Audiences can't be held with second-rate stuff. Not all of the entertainment is on the artistic level of the opera, of course. The radio audience is heterogeneous. To send out nothing but highbrow music would be to discourage many listeners. But nothing amateurish is permitted. Jazz is mixed with the classic, but it must be accomplished jazz and there must not be too much of it."

Sunday afternoon chapel services were also instituted at KYW. So great became the popularity of this enterprising station that during the summer of 1922 new radio towers were erected, 495 feet high, in order to ensure greater radio service.

CHAPTER
SIXTEEN

Radio Broadcasting Grows Up

Section 150. Station WEAF Inaugurates Sponsored Programs.

NOW THAT RADIO BROADCASTING had so firmly established itself in American life everyone was happy except the unfortunate broadcaster who may have had no revenue-producing sideline being advertised by his broadcasts. Manufacturers of electrical equipment during the boom days no doubt found a radio station valuable as a spur to business. Department stores such as Bamberger and Wanamaker were likewise reaping financial returns. Newspaper-owned stations, however, were more or less unsatisfactory from the angle of increased revenue. In fact antagonism was already developing in newspaper circles because of broadcasting of news. Editors in general have always labored under the belief, discounted by many thoughtful observers, that the broadcasting of news discourages the purchase of newspapers.

The summer of 1922 was destined to witness the first typical solutions by the English people on the one hand and the citizens of the United States on the other.

"In Great Britain," writes the editor of *Radio Broadcast,* "no one is willing to do the broadcasting unless assured of some definite return. Consequently it is not surprising to learn that the British radio organizations which are to do the broadcasting have asked the Postmaster General not to license a receiving set unless made by a member of one of the broadcasting organizations. In this way the profits derived from the sale of radio receiving equipment would go to those who maintain the broadcasting services. Still another plan is to have the Postmaster General exact a modest fee for each receiving license, and then turn over a part of the receipts to the broadcasting organization." This latter suggestion, as will be seen hereafter, eventually resulted in the government-subsidized British broadcasting system.

Perhaps unknown to the learned editor when he wrote the above article an event had occurred in the City of New York that was to lead the way to a solution of the American problem. In the light of history this seemingly insignificant event that occurred in the office of Station WEAF at 24 Walker Street now bulks large in radio annals. The Telephone Company's resolve to operate a toll-broadcasting enterprise was now to produce results. The most amazing feature of the transaction is that it occurred exactly twelve days after WEAF went on the air for the first time. Had WJZ or any other of the older broadcasting stations of the New York area originated paid commercial advertising we might accept it as a natural development—an inevitable event. To have the twelve-day infant, Station WEAF, lead the way is on the surface of it nothing short of astounding to a public that was unaware that these other stations were not permitted to broadcast for hire.

If we examine further into the phenomenon we perceive that this new station with its clarity of tone and its last-minute scientific equipment was precisely the station to lead the way by attracting commercial advertisements. Let us now examine the facts in connection with this remarkable event.

In the summer of 1922 a real estate development was being conducted by the Queensborough Corporation at Jackson Heights in Long Island City. Newspaper advertising in considerable volume was going on. An enterprising employee in the commercial department of the Am. Tel. & Tel. Company, H. Clinton Smith, conceived the idea that the company's new radio station could do much to quicken sales in this development. Not only did he conceive the idea, but what is more to the point he sold a ten-minute period on the air to the Queensborough Corporation. Imagine the rejoicing at Station WEAF when this unexpected gift from the gods—an actual commercial account—was plopped into their laps. This rejoicing even extended to the engineering staff. In the operating log of Station WEAF for August 28, 1922 was this triumphant entry in the handwriting of the engineer, R. S. Fenimore, operating supervisor:

"5.00/5.10 Queensborough Corpn.
    "Our first customer."

Fortunately the text of this epoch-marking commercial sales talk is in the files of the National Broadcasting Company. It would today be termed institutional advertising rather than ballyhoo for the sale of lots. It was well written. It was interesting in its context. Vischer A. Randall, WEAF's first announcer, put the program on the air. A Mr. Blakewell was the speaker. The ideals of the great American novelist, Nathaniel Hawthorne, were the theme. Incidentally a section of the real estate development was named "Hawthorne Court." [1]

This historic bit of advertising was not for one occasion only. The log book of the station discloses the following interesting facts:

August 28, 1922	Queensborough	5.00-5.10 P.M.
" 29	"	4.50-5.07 P.M.
" 30	"	5.00-5.07 P.M.
" 31	"	4.58-5.09 P.M.
Sept. 1	"	4.58-5.09 P.M.

Thus it appears that the first commercial advertiser bought time on the air for five consecutive days. It is said that $100 for each sales talk was the price of the first venture in radio advertising. That this experiment proved advantageous to the real estate corporation is evidenced by the fact that the log of Station WEAF discloses that on September

[1] For the text of this broadcast see Appendix, Exhibit "H."

14th the Queensborough announcement was again broadcast from 7.58 to 8.05 in the evening. On September 21st Station WEAF had three commercials on the air:

Queensborough	7.55-8.06
Tidewater Oil	8.16-8.26
American Express	8.46-9.00

It is unfortunate that a change in operators in charge of Station WEAF's transmitter at the end of September, 1922, caused a discontinuance of program entries. No other source of authentic information has been discovered by the author by which it might be determined whether the experiment in radio advertising thus instituted continued regularly. With an additional item under date of September 28th showing the Queensborough announcement "7.49-7.59 P.M." the program records of advertising abruptly closed. We are fortunate, however, to have discovered the first three radio pioneers in the great procession of commercial advertisers on the air. Not that commercial broadcasting, in which sponsors sometimes overdo their business announcements, is an unmixed blessing, but the fact remains that it is commercial advertising that has developed radio broadcasting to its present excellence. Listeners have learned to endure the sponsor's spiel as the price they must pay for the rich blessing that comes to them from radio stations.

Early in October, 1922, Station WEAF acquired a human asset of great value—a young man who could sing admirably, who could announce a program as well as Thomas H. Cowan and who could play the piano in wonderful manner. Alone and unaided he could furnish the live talent for hours if visiting talent were unavailable. It is no wonder that Samuel L. Ross lost no time in adding Albert V. Llufrio to the staff of WEAF.

Sec. 151. World Series Baseball Games for 1922 Broadcast over WJZ.

Station WJZ was eleven months old in August 1922. Due to the persuasive activities of Thomas H. Cowan, its first announcer, the Newark studio had been supplied with talent of high order. Among the artists whom Cowan had lured to the WJZ microphone during the summer of 1922 was a young man who was destined to become one of the truly great figures of radio—Milton J. Cross. The young man was then attracting attention as a singer. His singing voice was ideal for radio broadcasting. His speaking voice likewise won acclaim from the radio audience. Young Cross first appeared as a tenor soloist on a WJZ program March 14th, 1922. He soon became a welcome guest at the Newark station and with every visit his interest in radio became more pronounced.

Another visitor to the WJZ studios during the early spring of 1922 was destined to become notable in radio history—Miss Bertha Brainard. When she decided to investigate the new industry in Newark with the idea of offering to represent the station as a booker of talent in New York City she was at first rebuffed. Having driven an ambulance in the Red Cross Motor Corps in New York City she was not easily discouraged. Perhaps the indulgent Al Simmons, porter, office boy and general handyman, looked the other way on this occasion. Miss Brainard got past him and invaded Mr. Popenoe's little office. Did the Program Manager repel the intruder? Not at all. He gave her a chance to go on the air in a radio program. For several months Miss Brainard made regular appearances before the WJZ microphone in a series known as "Broadcasting Broadway." Her first program was listed May 9, 1922, appearing twice a week thereafter. It was a sprightly review of such plays as were being offered currently in New York theaters. On August 28, 1922, Miss Brainard became a regular member of the WJZ staff as a booker of talent—the New York representative of the station.

In the meantime Milton J. Cross was facing a serious problem. A musical career had been his fixed ambition. Teachers and musical critics had assured him that with such a voice as was his he might become a great figure in grand opera. This new thing called radio broadcasting, however, was upsetting his plans. He was by nature a modest and unassuming youth, despite his six feet of height and his undeniable good looks—his natural qualification for heroic parts. Young Cross was more inclined to music for music's sake than for the glory of singing to an audience across the footlights. Radio afforded an opportunity to sing or speak without the trappings and artificiality so characteristic of grand opera, or the nervous tension of the concert hall. The microphone was becoming a friend to whom he could sing or talk with perfect ease. The lure of it was quite irresistible, for to Milton Cross the absurd tomato can was not what it seemed to others, but a glorious listening ear of science through which his voice might reach out to unseen homes and firesides over a radius of hundreds of miles.

The fact that Albert V. Llufrio at Station WEAF was an announcer and artist all in one no doubt had its effect upon the decision that Milton J. Cross made on October 20, 1922, when he joined the staff of WJZ and began his notable career as a radio announcer. From the beginning he combined both talents but in years to come it was to be his glorious speaking voice by which he was to be known and loved by millions of radio listeners. For more than fifteen years at this writing

DR. ALFRED N. GOLDSMITH
Radio engineer, who gave WJZ its first
network.

O. B. HANSON
From A. T. & T. to WEAF in 1923, now
a Vice-President of NBC.

MAJOR EDWIN H. ARMSTRONG
Whose contributions to radio broadcasting are of great importance.

the popularity of Milton J. Cross has continued as an enduring feature of radio. Other announcers have come and gone during the decade and a half but the first great radio announcer is still true to his first love. His announcing of operatic broadcasts as well as the RCA "Magic Key" program gives delight to present-day listeners.

It was perhaps inevitable that the American Telephone Company should sooner or later have come into conflict with the Westinghouse Company over questions of radio broadcasting. Telephony, whether by wire or wireless, was considered by A. T. & T. as its special province. It had entered the broadcasting field largely to develop the art as well as to protect its own interests. It was natural for it to regard the Westinghouse Company and others as trespassers on its special domain. This will perhaps account for its ungenerous, not to say hostile, attitude toward WJZ as disclosed by the Popenoe MS concerning early days at the station:

"In the early summer of 1922 by special concession," wrote Mr. Popenoe, "the New York Telephone Company supplied us with wires in order to broadcast the music of the New York Philharmonic Orchestra direct from the Lewisohn Stadium, New York City. . . . We had hoped that the Telephone Company would continue to lease us wires, but we were doomed to disappointment, as Mr. A. H. Griswold of that Company bluntly turned down our request for wires for use at the 1922 World's Series Games, the first ever broadcast. At that time the American Telephone & Telegraph Company were operating . . . WEAF. This fact no doubt accounted for their flat refusal.

"Needless to say we were disappointed, but recently L. R. Krumm, Superintendent of Radio Operators, had been succeeded by C. W. Horn in the same capacity and as Mr. Horn was well connected with the Western Union Company we decided to investigate their wire services. To our great satisfaction we found Mr. J. C. Williver, Vice-President of Western Union, willing to help us, and . . . their wires have been used for remote control work to hundreds of points since, some 500 miles of Western Union conducting cables now (1926) being in use in New York, besides 150 miles to Station WGY of the General Electric Company and 240 miles to WBZ at Boston. . . .

"To return to our story, the World's Series, 1922. We heaved a sigh of relief after ascertaining that Western Union wires could be used. Through the assistance of the New York *Tribune* and their famous sports writer, Mr. Grantland Rice, we did a one hundred per cent job of this broadcasting feature, besides securing a great deal of front page publicity from the *Tribune*."

The author had great difficulty in verifying this important event in broadcasting annals—the first of its kind in history. The program sheets of WJZ carried no entry of the games, although Raymond F.

Guy, engineer of WJZ, who did a part of the announcing, was positive that the games were broadcast as alleged by Mr. Popenoe. Charles W. Horn, who had been in charge of engineering for the Westinghouse stations, was likewise positive of the facts. In *Radio News* for December, 1922, at page 1066, we found the necessary proof—excellent snapshots of broadcasting the World's Series, with Grantland Rice at the microphone. Here then was an important bit of pioneering for Station WJZ!

Sec. 152. Strife Between Radio Stations Over Broadcast Hours.

Radio broadcasting in the autumn of 1922 was in a truly precarious condition. "Every month," writes the editor of *Radio Broadcast,* "sees a remarkable growth in the number of stations licensed for radio broadcasting. This might be taken as a sign of healthy growth of the new art, but a little reflection seems to point to the opposite conclusion. . . . It seems to us that a curb should be put upon the licensing of broadcasting stations or there will soon be country-wide troubles of the kind which recently occurred in New York—conflicts between the various stations for the most desirable hours and the resulting interference of signals between the several stations, which made listening in no pleasure. There are at present nearly 500 licensed broadcasting stations in the United States and this list is being augmented each week; in one week recently there were 26 new licenses issued." [2]

The mischief of the situation as previously indicated was that the art had not progressed to the point where stations could be tuned to different wave lengths and definite frequencies, nor were receiving sets capable of tuning out undesired stations. RCA under the influence of David Sarnoff had by this time definitely decided to enter the field of marketing of radio sets on an extensive scale and was even then setting up a nation-wide organization for distribution of radio sets. This was to lead to industrial warfare but it offered hope of superior radio equipment.

The Radio Corporation was already experiencing considerable difficulties over its status as sales agent for Westinghouse, General Electric, and A. T. & T. By the terms of its agreement it was obliged to place with the sponsoring manufacturers irrevocable orders for radio sets. These orders, moreover, were required to be placed many months in advance. Due to rapid development in the industry, however, RCA's competitors were able to bring out new models and last-minute improvements that might eclipse radio sets being offered to the public by RCA. Thus the Radio Corporation might find itself obliged to accept and pay for outmoded radio sets that would be exceedingly difficult to sell. RCA's obligation to pay for the sets was

2 Radio Broadcast, Nov. 1922, p. 3.

none the less imperative. As early as the autumn of 1922 an acute situation arose. It appears that Major Edwin H. Armstrong, then recently returned from Europe, called upon Elmer E. Bucher, in December, 1922, and discussed with him the radio situation. As Sales Manager of RCA, Mr. Bucher complained bitterly that his company was loaded up with radio sets that it was virtually impossible to sell. Knowing Armstrong's reputation as an inventor, Bucher appealed to him to devise a radio set that would be an improvement over any then on the market. To this suggestion Major Armstrong lent a willing ear and immediately set to work on the project. Nearly all stations were then on the 360-meter wave length, with the natural result that stations in the same area were driven to agree among themselves—if possible—for a division of broadcasting hours. The national Congress was reluctant to interfere with the situation. Our sturdy citizenry have invariably resented government interference in local matters and have a tendency to manifest that resentment at the polls. Congressman Wallace H. White, Jr., of Maine, however, had filed a radio bill in September, 1922, that embodied the recommendations of the Hoover Conference Committee of the previous winter.

"Lost in the mazes of congressional procedure," reports the November issue of *Radio Broadcast,* "there is a radio bill introduced in the House more than three months ago by Mr. White. This bill was intended by its framers to obviate the interference which, we firmly believe, is sure to occur soon. It gives Secretary Hoover more power over the control of radio than does the older radio law of 1912 and if the bill should be passed, the broadcasting situation might be remedied at once, by assigning to the various stations, which are close enough to interfere, widely different wave lengths. . . . This reapportionment of wave lengths would evidently react to improve the quality of the broadcasting stations. Suppose that one station, with poor transmission, sends out a wretched program on, say, 325 meters and another in the same neighborhood sends out an excellent one on 375 meters. With the usual broadcast procedure the announcers at both stations would, at the end of the program, ask for comments and suggestions from listeners. No one would have been listening on 325 meters, so no suggestions would be received and the owner of the station would soon find out that his signals were being sent to 'deaf' radio sets, sets which had purposely shut out his message. He would then have to improve his station or stop broadcasting.

"In the reapportionment, the longer wave lengths assigned to broadcasting should be given to the more powerful metropolitan stations, those which can afford better talent for their programs. More power can be radiated on the longer wave lengths than on the shorter ones, so the shorter ones should be kept for the small radio jobbers and newspapers whose programs will generally be only of local interest." [3]

Station WJZ now inaugurated its first grand opera broadcasts. The late Charles B. Popenoe thus described the series:

"Late in December of that year (1922) arrangements were made to broadcast a special series of grand opera performances direct from the old Manhattan Opera House, New York City, these performances afterward being moved to the Century Theatre. These performances were given by a German Company called the Wagnerian Opera Festival Company direct from Berlin, all the cast being German subjects. This was the first time grand opera had been broadcast in the East, although KYW, the Westinghouse station in Chicago, had broadcast many performances of the Chicago Grand Opera in that city in 1922. This broadcasting was most successful and the performances of *Die Meistersinger,* several of the *Ring Cycle, Der Freischütz, Tannhäuser, Parsifal* and several others were broadcast.

Sec. 153. General Harbord Decides to Accept Presidency of RCA.

After Gen. James G. Harbord had declined to accept Owen D. Young's tentative offer of the presidency of the Radio Corporation, Mr. Young continued his search for a suitable man to fill this responsible position. Men with the necessary qualifications and the essential background of experience were indeed rare beings. It would never do to take a chance on an unknown person, however great might be his natural qualifications for the task. Public relations problems were sure to be of major importance in the near future. In a nation so opposed by tradition and by sad experience to the building up of powerful monopolies there was bound to be misunderstanding of RCA status, though its officials might try endlessly to demonstrate fairness in public relations. This was fully understood by Mr. Young and his associates even before political Washington began to bestir itself against them. They knew that regardless of how they might declare by word and deed their desire to be fair to the public they could never escape the damning fact that RCA was by its very nature a monopoly. It was futile to point out to the public that it could not have functioned as an all-American communications corporation such as the Navy Department had urged them to establish unless the corporation had been in a position to dominate wireless transmission in the same way that Great Britain now dominated the cables. Whether in the hectic days of organizing the giant corporation the forces under Mr. Young's command had gone farther than necessary to accomplish their purpose was, of course, a matter of opinion, but they could be very sure that public opinion could easily be arrayed against them.

[3] *Radio Broadcast,* Nov. 1922, p. 4.

In Mr. Young's letter to Edward J. Nally of October 25, 1922, previously quoted, he had told the story of how Gen. Harbord, despite his earlier refusal, had been persuaded to accept the presidency of RCA. He wrote as follows:

"During the summer while General Harbord was abroad, I learned that there was a possibility of his changing his mind due to the great curtailment of the army program by Congress. This program particularly required substantial reduction in the personnel of the regular army. I understood that many of the older officers of the army felt that under these circumstances it was their duty to give way and make places for the younger men in whose generation war might come if it came at all. I had reason to think that General Harbord had also changed his point of view from that expressed in his letter to me. That is to say, instead of feeling it his duty to stay and administer the office of Chief of Staff, he had come to the conclusion that under the reduced program it was his duty to afford an opportunity for a younger man to assume the responsibility of that great office. General Harbord was abroad, however, and I could not discuss the matter with him. He returned to this country two or three days after the tragic accident to John. Consequently, I could not see him and did not see him before you left for Europe.

"After my return from the country about the 20th of September, I learned that the pressure was very great in the War Department on the officers holding the higher positions to decide whether or not they would stay with the Army or would retire. The Act of Congress required the reduction of the Army be effective on December 31 of this year, and naturally if a reorganization were to take place, the Secretary of War desired it to be settled, certainly as to the more important places, sufficiently in advance of that period so that he might perhaps persuade younger men who were contemplating retirement to remain and be promoted. Therefore, during the latter part of September, I asked some acquaintances of General Harbord to find out whether he would be sufficiently interested in the matter to warrant my presentation of his name to our Board of Directors. The reply came back that General Harbord would consider the matter if it could be presented to him promptly, otherwise he could not consider it because he felt it his duty to answer the pressing request for decision which he had from the Secretary of War.

". . . I finally concluded to talk with General Tripp about the matter, not for the purpose of having him share the responsibility for my decision but rather to ascertain whether he felt that General Harbord would make a desirable President for the Radio Corporation. If he felt that General Harbord would not, then it seemed to me I would be largely relieved from the responsibility of not bringing his name forward at this time and of losing him for all time. I found that General Tripp did not know General Harbord personally, or at least did not know him well, and he expressed some hesitation at first as to the advisability, generally speaking, of taking an Army Officer and putting him at the head of a great commercial and business undertaking. After I had explained to General Tripp my conversation with you in February, he said that he would undertake to make inquiries regarding General Harbord. This he did and he received such enthusiastic reports, especially from General Atterbury, that he came to the conclusion that General Harbord was a desirable man for the place. This, if anything, increased my feeling of responsibility to the Radio Corporation, and after prayerful consideration, I finally decided to present the whole matter frankly to the Board and let the Board assume the responsibility of the decision. This I did at the meeting of October 6. I frankly recited the entire story as I have tried to tell it to you in this letter. After it had been told, Mr. Harden stated that you had told him of your interview with me. We both felt and we stated to the Board that you probably would feel relieved to learn that promising steps could be taken to fill the office and if you were here you would undoubtedly approve our going forward with the interview with General Harbord.

". . . After full discussion, it was unanimously voted by the Board that I should be authorized to discuss the matter with General Harbord and see whether or not an arrangement could be made for him to become President. It was hoped and believed that if the arrangement could be made, no discussion of it with others outside the Board or public announcement would be required until after your return. This seemed to be important so that the whole matter might be done in a way which would be satisfactory to you.

"Some days later I had a talk with General Harbord in New York and after taking the matter under consideration, I received a letter from him under date of October 16, in which he signified his willingness to accept the position. Accordingly at the last meeting of the Board on October 20, I reported that fact and asked that General Tripp and Mr. Harden be appointed a Committee to act with me to arrange the terms and conditions under which General Harbord would come and to arrange with you for your position abroad along the lines indicated in our conversation in February. General Tripp and Mr. Harden both accepted and they saw and approved my radiogram to you above quoted and they have seen and approved this letter."

Sec. 154. The Historic WEAF–WNAC Network Experiment.

In the light of history a very significant event occurred in the Fall of 1922. The Telephone Company engineers decided to test the possibility of long distance telephone connection in radio transmission. A football game was to be played in Chicago on a certain day. By means of special transmitters and amplifiers located on the football field an oral description of the game, together with the cheering of the spectators, was delivered to a telephone cable circuit connected with the toll office of the Telephone Company in Chicago. This circuit was connected with the toll line to New York City. In Park Row in New York a truck in which a radio receiving set was installed had been equipped with a public address system. By this means it became possible for a street throng in New York City to hear a broadcast of a game actually being played in Chicago.[4] This experiment demonstrated the soundness of the principle later successfully employed in chain or network broadcasting.

The American Telephone Company was not slow to recognize that Station WEAF was an experiment of major importance. It required engineering talent of high order. W. E. Harkness of the Long Lines Department was assigned to the station November 1, 1922. He was to become the official station manager April 21, 1923, and was to continue in that capacity for a year or two. It is difficult to determine from fragmentary records the exact functions of the various officials of the growing enterprise in the fall of 1922. Samuel L. Ross was Musical Director; Vischer A. Randall, Studio Director; R. S. Fenimore, Operating Supervisor; Edmund R. Taylor, Assistant Plant Supervisor. George F. McClelland came to the station as commercial representative, November 15, 1922. The rapid development of sponsored programs during the next twelve months was due in large measure to the energy and enthusiasm of George F. McClelland, who was later to rise to the position of manager of the station. O. B. Hanson, a Long Lines engineer, is one of the few officials who have served continuously in radio since the winter of 1923. He is now Vice-President in Charge of Operations, National Broadcasting Company.

The first outcry against radio advertising was apparently touched off by the September, 1922, broadcasts of sponsored programs over Station WEAF. In the November number of *Radio Broadcast* appeared a feature article entitled "Should Radio Be Used For Advertising?" The author mentioned no station by name. He did not identify any program but he did say some particularly mean things about radio advertising. He disclosed, moreover, that advertising by dealers and others had been for some time a common practice.

"Anyone who doubts the reality, the imminence of the problem," he wrote, "has only to listen about him for plenty of evidence. Driblets of advertising, most of it indirect so far, to be sure, but still unmistakable, are floating through the ether every day. Concerts are seasoned here and there with a dash of advertising paprika. You can't miss it; every little classic number has a slogan all its own, if it is only the mere mention of the name—*and* the street address, *and* the phone number—of the music house which arranged the program. More of

[4] *Bell Telephone Quarterly*, April, 1934.

this sort of thing may be expected. And once the avalanche gets a good start, nothing short of an Act of Congress or a repetition of Noah's excitement will suffice to stop it."

There was much in this article—all demonstrating that the listening public expected to be entertained without rendering any return to the entertainers—without suffering even a wee bit for the cause. As yet the public in general did not realize that radio broadcasting must find some means of self-support or perish. Manufacturers of rado sets might have an incentive to broadcast until the radio boom should have passed its crest, but so soon as profits might be endangered by the expenses of broadcasting they too must close their radio stations. A tax upon radio sets, or radio advertising, were the only choices. Great Britain was to choose the former, the United States of America the latter alternative.

In the autumn of 1922 a radio broadcasting station was opened in Boston that was to assist in solving some of the great problems of radio. It was Station WNAC, first listed in the *Radio Service Bulletin* October 1, 1922. The Shepard Stores, for many years a flourishing dry goods institution of Boston, was the record owner. A branch of Shepard Stores in Providence, R. I., had already established Station WEAN in the latter city (first listed July 1, 1922). John Shepard, 3d, whose grandfather had been a founder of the Shepard Stores, was the member of the family who by common consent became responsible for the welfare of Station WNAC. In fact, the broadcasting activities were more or less a concession to the trend of the times. The mission of the station was to attract patronage to the store by the repeated announcement of station name and ownership. In short, radio broadcasting was regarded as a small appendage to a large and important greyhound. That the tail would ever become much more important than the dog was never dreamed of by the Shepard family—except perhaps by John Shepard, 3d, the dynamic scion of the family who literally ate, drank and slept immersed in thoughts of radio broadcasting.

Station WNAC had not been in operation more than a few weeks before the originality of mind of its director caused it to be joined with Station WEAF in a spectacular experiment. The engineers of A. T. & T. Company had already staged a pick-up over land wires from a Chicago football field to New York. It was now decided to link Station WEAF in New York with Station WNAC in Boston and endeavor to reproduce the New York program over the facilities of the Boston station. Fortunately there are in the archives of the National Broadcasting Company library in New York the official program sheets of Station WEAF from December, 1922, onward. Under date of January 4, 1923, we find the historic entry:

"7.55–8.00 P.M. Saxophone solo by Nathan Glanz
'Lovelight in Your Eyes'
Program to be broadcast jointly by WEAF and WNAC.
(The Shepard Stores, Boston) from Studio WEAF.
The two stations will be connected by special long distance telephone wires of the A. T. & T. Company."

Since this was the first time that chain or network broadcasting had ever been attempted, the engineers of the Telephone Company studied every phase of it with great interest.

The energetic John Shepard, 3d, with an instinct for the dramatic, had advertised the experiment in advance and had even arranged for the Massachusetts Bankers Association, then in session at the Copley Plaza Hotel, to listen in on the saxophone solo. Its reception at the Boston end of the line did not measure up to the quality of a local broadcast, yet it did satisfy the listeners that there were distinct possibilities in the new idea. Whether the network program continued beyond the scheduled five minutes does not appear from the record. A newspaper account of the exploit indicates that it extended to other features.

The *Bell Telephone Quarterly* for April, 1934, states that while the listening public "as a whole were well satisfied with the success of the experiment, the Telephone engineers who had conducted the affair were not. They knew that transmission over the wires linking the two radio stations could be bettered—and it would have to be bettered if the future of network broadcasting was to be assured. They knew that there was a vast difference between the transmission of speech, as in the case of regular telephone service, and the transmission of music over the same wires. They knew that, for the latter purpose, specially designed circuits would have to be used."

The Telephone Company officials at once perceived that to develop a satisfactory method of handling this type of "long lines" for the hooking up of radio stations for the simultaneous broadcasting of a featured program would prove highly advantageous to the company. Possessing a virtual monopoly of intercommunication, the business of special toll lines for broadcasting could speedily become an important source of revenue. Electrical engineers who had superintended the WEAF–WNAC experiment were given orders to bend every effort to the task of producing the special telephone cables essential to satisfactory results.

Sec. 155. Further Developments in Sponsored Programs at WEAF.

Reference has been made to the first sponsored programs over WEAF disclosed by the operator's log book, which unfortunately discontinued program entries after September 28, 1922. No other records apparently exist concerning the WEAF programs until December 8, 1922, a lapse of ten weeks. Mimeographed daily-program sheets beginning with December 8th are now to be found in bound volumes in the custody of Miss Frances Sprague, the Librarian of the National Broadcasting Company. The program sheet for December 8th contains the following significant entry:

"8.00 P.M. 'The Story of the Little Glass Slipper,' by Gimbel Bros., New York City."

This was a ten-minute program. There was no entry to indicate that it was a commercially sponsored program, yet we know that the firm of Gimbel Brothers was thereafter for many months WEAF's chief advertiser.

On December 13th is the following entry:

"7.45–7.55 P.M. 'The Sad Story of the Polar Bear' by Santa Claus from Wonderland at R. H. Macy & Company, New York City."

This also must have been a commercial program. Let us follow the program sheets for mute evidence of sponsored programs:

"December 14, 1922. 7.30–7.45 P.M. 'The Reindeer With a Hole in His Stocking' by Gimbel Bros., New York.

December 15, 1922. 7.50–8.00 P.M. 'Mother Goose Rhymes' by James A. Hearn & Son, Inc., New York City.

December 16, 1922. 7.45–8.00 P.M. 'Nine Little Dolls and Fairies' by Santa Claus from Wonderland at R. H. Macy & Company, New York City.

December 18, 1922. 7.45–8.00 P.M. 'My Clowns' by Santa Claus from Wonderland at R. H. Macy & Company, New York City.

December 19, 1922. 7.50 P.M. 'Mother Goose Rhymes' by James A. Hearn & Son, Inc., New York City.

December 21, 1922. 7.45–7.55 P.M. 'Christmas and the Snowman' by Santa Claus from Wonderland at R. H. Macy & Company, New York City.

8.10–8.20 'The Story of the Christmas Card' by the Greeting Card Association, New York City.

December 22, 1922. 7.50–8.00 P.M. 'Mother Goose Rhymes' by James A. Hearn & Son, Inc., New York.

December 23, 1922. 4.30–5.30 P.M. Dance program of popular music by the Jockey Club Orchestra, well-known phonograph recording artists (Note: This may have been a sustaining program but if not it is probably the first musical commercial broadcast.)

9.00–9.10 P.M. Latest popular hits played by the Phoebe Snow Orchestra, well-known dance artists, through the courtesy of A. H. Grebe & Company, Inc., Richmond Hill, L. I. (Note: This must have been a commercial, since the Grebe Company was a large manufacturer of radio appliances.)

December 29, 1922. 7.45 P.M. 'Insulation Facts Every Amateur Should Know' a talk by Mr. O. B. Carson of the American Hard Rubber Company, New York City.

December 30, 1922. 8.00 P.M. 'Advertising and its Relation to the Public' by W. H. Rankin Company, New York City.

January 7, 1923. 3.40–5.30 P.M. Bedford Branch Y.M.C.A.–Dr. S. Parkes Cadman. (Note: This was marked as a sponsored program. It continued regularly every Sunday for months.)

January 10, 1923. 7.30–7.45 P.M. 'The Story of the Haynes,' America's First Car, by the inventor himself—Elwood Haynes.

January 18, 1923. (In longhand at end of mimeographed program) 'National Surety Company.' "

The above are typical commercial programs.[5] Talks were apparently

[5] First Commercial Sponsors–Station WEAF as disclosed by Log of Station Aug. 28–Sept. 28, 1922 and daily program sheets from Dec. 8, 1922 to May 31, 1923.

Queensborough Corp., Aug. 28, 29, 30, 31, Sept. 1, 14, 21, 28.

Tidewater Oil, Sept. 21.

American Express, Sept. 21.

(No records have been found for period between Sept. 21 and Dec. 13.)

Gimbel Bros., Dec. 8, 14, 1922, Feb. 20, 27, 28, Mar. 1, 2, 3, 3, 4, 5, 6, 7, 8, 9, 10, 12, 14, 15, 15, 16, 17, 19, 20, 21, 22, 22, 23, 24, 24, 26, 26, 27, 28, 29, 30, 31, Apr. 2, 3, 4, 5, 6, 9, 10, 11, 12, 13, 14, 14, 16, 17, 18, 19, 20, 21, 21, 23, 24, 25, 26, 27, 28, 28, 30, May 1, 2, 3, 4, 5, 5, 7, 8, 9, 11, 12, 12, 14, 15, 16, 18, 19, 19, 21, 21, 22, 23, 25, 26, 26, 28, 29, 30, 31, 1923.

R. H. Macy & Co., Dec. 13, 16, 18, 21.

James A. Hearn, Dec. 15, 19, 22.

Greeting Card Assn., Dec. 21.

Jockey Club Orchestra, Dec. 23.

A. H. Grebe & Co., Inc., Dec. 23.

American Hard Rubber Co., Dec. 29.

W. H. Rankin Co., Dec. 30.

Bedford Y.M.C.A., Jan. 7, 1923.

Haynes Automobile Co., Jan. 10.

National Surety Co., Jan. 18, Feb. 17, Apr. 5, May 3.

Cold Storage Co., Jan. 24.

Metropolitan Life Ins., Jan. 27.

Industrial Extension Ins., Feb. 5, 19, 26, Mar. 5, 12, 19, 26, Apr. 2, 9, 16, 23.

American Bond & Mortgage, Feb. 6, Mar. 17, May 11.

Mitchell Rand Co., Feb. 7.

Gotham Silk Hosiery, Feb. 8.

Benjamin Bills (Investments), Feb. 9.

Goldwyn Picture Corp., Feb. 11.

I. Miller & Sons, Feb. 19.

Hodkinson Co. (movie talks), Feb. 28.

Wm. C. Duckham, Mar. 10.

Famous Players Lasky, Mar. 15.

California Prune & Apricot Growers, Mar. 19.

Davega Sporting Goods, Apr. 12, 19.

Browning King, Apr. 25, May 2, 9, 16, 30.

Lily Cup Co., Apr. 26.

Earl Carroll, May 4.

Phoenix Mutual Life Ins., May 18.

Corn Products Co., May 22.

D. W. Griffith, May 28.

Knit Underwear Mfgrs., May 31.

the chief reliance of advertisers. A legend that has gained wide circula-
tion credits the Browning King Company with having originated the
sponsored musical program. The daily record sheets of WEAF disclose
the fact that the commercial musical program was originated by
Gimbel Bros. of New York City on March 1, 1923, and was continued
by this firm in a noteworthy series of concerts and recitals for nearly
two months before Browning King began their famous "Wednesday
Night Dance" series, on April 25th, 1923.

Since the historian should be concerned with facts and not with
popular tradition it may be well to establish from the record how definite a title Gimbel Bros. have to the honor of having originated the
type of sponsored program that has continued to this day.

On March 1, 1923 the first musical program by Gimbel Bros. ran
from 4.00 to 4.30 P.M., and carried the following title:

"Musical Program broadcast direct from the Radio Exposition at
Gimbel Bros. New York Store."

Programs of similar nature continued on March 2nd, 3d, 6th, 7th,
8th, 9th and 10th, when the Exposition apparently closed.

The usual short program of talks was resumed for several days yet
Gimbel Brothers apparently received so much favorable reaction to
their musical experiment that they decided to adopt this medium as a
regular feature. On March 14th a half hour (4.00–4.30 P.M.) program
was broadcast from the store.

March 15, 1923 deserves to go down in history as a red letter day in
advertising annals.[5a] On that date Gimbel Bros. launched their first
9–10 P.M. musical program over WEAF. No details of the first historic
evening program are extant. It was perhaps similar to that of the
following. On March 17th we find the pioneer program that set the
style for future commercial broadcasts.

"Program by Gimbel Brothers' New York Store
9.00 P.M. Helen Bell Rush, soprano, in a number of popular songs.
Program: 'Lady of the Evening;' 'You Know You Belong to Somebody
Else;' 'Crinoline Days;' 'Coal Black Mammy.'
9.15 P.M. Frank Gage, Singer, Pianist and Trumpeter with Tech
Show (1923) of Mass. Inst. of Technology. Program Solos—'Happiness
Blues' (Tech Show '21), 'Troubles' (Tech Show '21); Trumpet Solo—
'Somewhere' (Tech Show '23).
9.30 P.M. Solos by Helen Bell Rush, Soprano. Program: 'Caro Nome'

[5a] It is worthy of note that on this same day—March 15, 1932—Station WJZ, not
to be outdone by its great rival, broadcast "Tannhäuser" from the Lexington Avenue Theatre, New York City, 7 to 7:30 P.M. On the following day, 7:30 to 8:30 P.M.
the Broadway Dance Orchestra was broadcast from WJZ. The rivalry between these
two stations was already very bitter indeed.

from Rigoletto (Verdi), 'Ah! Love but a Day' (Gilberte), 'Song of Ages' (Heller), 'Honey, Dat's All' (Van Alstyne).

9.45 P.M. Frank Gage, Singer, etc. Program: Piano Solo—'Down in Egypt' (Tech Show '20); Solo—Freedom (Tech Show '22); Piano Solo—'My Old Kentucky Home,' with variations."

The next hour-long program was given on March 22nd and consisted of a recital by Charles C. Hohman, Bass Baritone, from 9.00 to 9.30, when Lucille Chalfant, coloratura soprano, gave a recital of similar length. On March 24th the enterprising merchants had two programs—dance music from 4.00 to 4.30 and a variety program from 9.00 to 10.00 P.M.

Concerts, dance programs and recitals were tried alternately thereafter. Even the Paulist Choristers were inveigled into a two hour program for Gimbel Brothers on April 19, 1923.

The first Browning King program, April 25, 1923, came apparently at the end of an evening broadcast. The entry was written in longhand. The next dance program of this firm appeared May 2nd in the mimeographed record. Gimbel Brothers averaged about seven programs to one of Browning King. Dance music evidently made a great hit with the radio audience for on July 14th we find Gimbel Brothers broadcasting from 9.00 to 10.00 P.M. with a dance program followed by an hour of dance music staged by the American Tobacco Company—the celebrated "Lucky Strike Hour"—the first in a notable series. Gimbel Brothers had blazed the trail for successful commercial sponsorship. Soon all America was keeping time to dance orchestras that were being broadcast from Station WEAF.

Sec. 156. Progress in Solving Interference Problems.

Radio technicians were by this time investigating the possibility of combatting the growing bedlam on the air by experimenting with broadcasting on differing wave lengths. The original plan of 360 meters for all radio broadcasting stations had failed. Suppose other wave lengths were to be tried and local stations operated upon them? The question of how far apart the assignments must be was of course to be determined by a process of trial and error. The radio inspector for the second district, Arthur Batchelder, prior to December, 1922, had suggested that Station WGY at Schenectady, N. Y., try operating on 400 meters while Station WHAZ at Troy, New York, broadcast at the same time on the regular 360-meter plan.

In *Radio Broadcast*, December, 1922, appeared an announcement of the experiment with a request that listeners in the locality co-operate to check results by tuning in alternately on the two stations and reporting whether interference between the two was encountered. It was hoped thus to determine whether the plan would work.

"With good receiving sets in the hands of skilled operators," wrote the editor, "little interference should be encountered if the wave length difference is only twenty meters, instead of forty, as in the trials referred to above. But even if the forty-meter wave length difference between stations has to be allowed, enough separate ether channels will be opened to improve broadcasting greatly, if the radio bill referred to in our last issue, is finally passed by Congress." The measure referred to was the White Radio Bill that embodied the recommendations of the Hoover Conference.

Conflict between radio manufacturers was perhaps inevitable. Willful or innocent infringement of basic patents was sure to occur. An unusual situation arose in the fall of 1922 when the Wireless Specialty Apparatus Company, the owner of more than twenty patents on crystal receiving appliances, became defendant in an equity suit in the Supreme Court of New York. In order to discourage sale of crystal sets not manufactured by the defendant company it had been advertising that dealers handling crystal sets not made or licensed by it would be prosecuted. The advertisement contained the suggestion that all dealers should require the manufacturers of crystal sets to sign guarantees of protection against infringement. The suit was to compel the Wireless Specialty Apparatus Company to desist in advertising in this manner. The court decided that the Company had no right to give the impression that the buyer of a crystal set must investigate for himself, or get expert opinion on whether the set infringed one of the defendant's twenty-one patents. The Company was ordered to cease advertising in the manner described.

Crystal receiving sets, however, had already sustained a death blow in the announcement by RCA and its associated manufacturers that they had at last perfected the now famous vacuum tubes "UV 199" and "UV 201A." These tubes were equipped with special thoriated tungsten filaments and required less current than previous tubes. They were shortly to replace the crystal detector in radio sets.

Radio broadcasting, it seems, was not to be the exclusive function of the law-abiding elements of the community. The police had been in the forefront of the new science. Rum runners were then infesting coastal waters. Naturally they did not dare to communicate with land except by resort to coded messages. In the fall of 1922, for instance, the Steamer *Korona,* bearing Peruvian registration papers, sailed from New York with 400 drums of alcohol consigned to a port in Greece. Her radio began to send messages declaring that the steamer was having trouble with her pumps and her boiler. These reports, however, were later found to have been code messages to confederates who staged an alleged high-jacking. The cargo was unloaded and smuggled back into the United States, whereupon the *Korona* sailed to Bermuda and picked up a cargo of whisky which was delivered to confederates as before.

To balance the score, however, we have a new use of radio in the apprehension of criminals. The Police Department of New York City in 1922 equipped all district headquarters, station houses and police boats with receiving sets, so that radio alarms might be broadcast over land or water. The listening public now began to experience such thrilling interruptions as the following:

In the midst of a musical program of one of New York's popular broadcasting stations one day the music suddenly ceased and through the ether came the alarm that a jail break had just occurred. The police were warned that the convicts had fled in the direction of a neighboring village. Description of the men and the clothing that they were wearing was given so that not only might the police be set upon the trail but citizens might also be on the lookout for them. In this instance the criminals were recaptured within a few hours after their escape.[5b]

One of the earliest mentions of the so-called Condenser Microphones is to be found in a story in the December, 1922, *Radio Broadcast* telling of the achievements of the Wanamaker Station in Philadelphia—Station WOO. This station by using the new type of microphone was accomplishing what radio engineers had declared impossible—broadcasting organ music in a highly satisfactory manner.

Station KSD, established by the St. Louis *Post-Dispatch* June 26, 1922, was operating on a 400-meter wave length, said to have been the first 400-meter station. Before winter set in it had already been heard by listeners in forty-one states, a record that challenged the attention of the nation.

Station WJZ in Newark, the first great station of its kind, had now been in operation a full year. Because of the general excellence of its programs it was one of the most popular in the radio broadcasting field, having a coverage of the United States east of the Mississippi River.

The experiment that was now being tried of stations in the same area operating on 360 and 400 meters was the subject of much discussion at the December, 1922, meeting of the Institute of Radio Engineers. The engineers were enthusiastic over the success of the experiment. With properly designed receiving sets it was now possible to tune out either station while listening to the other, unless it happened that one were in close proximity to a station, in which case tuning out was still difficult to accomplish. Thousands of humble radio listeners, however, were bitterly disappointed to discover that their home-made

[5b] Radio Broadcast, December 1922, p. 95.

radio set or sets of inferior workmanship that they had purchased were incapable of tuning out either type of station.

Radio Broadcast thus comments on the situation:

"Now it is really time for the public to be educated in the elements of radio communication. Undoubtedly many people have invested in radio with no knowledge at all of what the set they bought had in it or what it was supposed to do, and these people will be much disappointed until they learn the capabilities of the apparatus. Some who have purchased cheap sets, poorly designed and inadequately constructed, will remain disappointed, but those having sets built by reliable concerns will find it the easiest thing in the world to adjust their apparatus so that either the 360 or the 400 meter program can be heard at will, with no interference from the other.

"The margin of 40 meters between stations will probably be cut in two before long, so that sets will have to tune signals only 20 meters apart. This will not be difficult with efficient apparatus. . . . It seems likely, however, that the public will soon be able to separate two signals differing by not more than ten meters; such a margin will provide sufficient channels for all demands likely to be made on the broadcasting service of the near future." [6]

Sec. 157. RCA and the Fateful Winter of 1923.

One of the most striking wireless developments of the Winter of 1923 was the fact that the Alexanderson Alternator that only three years before had been the reigning sensation of the scientific world was now itself to fall by the wayside in the upward march of science. The Radio Corporation of America had long been engaged in an ambitious project on Long Island, building what they called "Radio Central." The original idea had been to equip the Central with Alexanderson devices, but while the trans-Atlantic station was in process of construction technical advance in the manufacture of vacuum tubes had been so rapid that the General Electric Company was able to produce tubes of astonishing capacity. With tungsten filaments vacuum tubes were found to accomplish far-reaching results as transmitters of wireless waves. The first test of the new tubes is set down in *Milestones of RCA Progress* as having occurred October 15, 1922.

"An announcement of the Radio Corporation just given out," writes the editor of *Radio Broadcast* in January, 1923, "states that an experimental tube transmitter has been in successful operation for sixteen hours continuously, sending out sufficient power to transmit perfectly as far as Germany. Instead of the 200-k.w. alternator ordinarily used, six pliotrons, rated at 20-k.w. each, were used to generate the high frequency power required to excite the antenna. A 15,000 volt supply

[6] Radio Broadcast, January 1923, p. 180.

of continuous current power is required for the plate circuits of these tubes and here, also, the electron evaporation idea of Richardson is utilized. Two-electrode tubes, plate and filament only, are used as rectifiers, to change the high voltage alternating-current supply available at the station into suitable continuous-current power.

"The installation of these tubes is so simple and the operation so reliable that it seems safe to predict that the life of all other high frequency generators is already measured. The tubes used in this first large installation have about five thousand times the power of the small transmitter tubes used by amateur broadcasters, but the research men who are responsible for the development of these 20-k.w. tubes are ready to build tubes of 100-k.w. or even 1,000-k.w. whenever the demand for them will justify the expense involved."

Another great problem was now being attacked by RCA engineers —the properties of short waves as a means of radio transmission. Great progress was being made in developing nation-wide markets for RCA products—especially radio sets and really reliable loud speakers.

The Radio Corporation of America was itself undergoing internal changes due to the extraordinary development of the industry. Not only was it the dominating force in wireless communications in the Western Hemisphere but it was also the official sales agency of the powerful group of electrical manufacturing companies that was endeavoring to supply efficient radio sets to clamorous millions. For two years since it began operations Edward J. Nally had been the official pilot of the organization. He had brought to the company the great asset of intimate understanding of wireless telegraph communications —the fruits of many years as the General Manager of the Marconi Corporation of America. He had now built up a strong wireless operating staff. Wireless telegraph communication, however, as previously indicated, was only one of the many phases of the business activity of the Radio Corporation of America.

The change in Mr. Nally's relation to the Radio Corporation of America was announced in December, 1922. Unfortunately for the corporation, the brevity of tenure in the office of President by Mr. Nally had all the earmarks of the ruthless ousting of one who had served his turn. The directors could not very well take the public into their confidence, but the author has already pointed out that the private records of the chief actors in the transaction show that the change was made at Mr. Nally's urgent request and that he was given a new and responsible position for a term of years. The change of administration was to take effect on January 1, 1923.

CHAPTER
SEVENTEEN

Litigation and Rivalries

Section 158. RCA Attacked as an Unlawful Monopoly.

THE RADIO CORPORATION OF AMERICA had completed but three years of corporate life, yet in that brief period unbelievable developments had occurred. It is not too much to say that at the beginning no official of the company—except David Sarnoff—had really glimpsed the possibilities of radio broadcasting as a feature of RCA's activities. Yet broadcasting sets were now in such demand that RCA was unable to fill the flood of orders that came pouring in. Not only that but this very inability to meet the public demand was causing competitors to arise in a veritable army. Home manufacture of sets was likewise stimulated.

The new President of RCA, who took office January 1, 1923, was Major General James G. Harbord. General Harbord had been a Rough Rider in the Spanish-American War and Chief of Staff under General Pershing in the World War. In the Belleau Wood to Chateau Thierry fighting he had commanded the marine brigade of the Second Division. In 1918 he had been in command of the important department of supplies for the entire A.E.F. Unquestionably RCA had chosen a man of wide experience and great executive ability—a worthy successor to Edward J. Nally.

An event of great significance to the history of radio occurred in February, 1923, an event that necessarily became a closely guarded secret of RCA. For several months Major Edwin H. Armstrong had been working on a radio set of highly original design. He had combined his own ideas with those of another inventor, Harry Houck, and had produced what was later to be known as the Radiola Super-Heterodyne, a set that was destined to revolutionize the radio industry. This was the age of battery sets, and the Armstrong invention was equipped with batteries. It was, nevertheless, so uncanny in its selectivity and sensitiveness that it was possible to operate it without the use of an antenna. It appears that Armstrong first exhibited the device to the astute General Manager of RCA, David Sarnoff. Mr. Sarnoff had just concluded arrangements that involved ordering several million dollars' worth of an improved type of radio that had been devised by RCA engineers. He was so impressed by the Armstrong invention that he at once halted these negotiations, much to the disgust of Westinghouse and General Electric, who were all set for quantity production. It was necessary, however, to convince the Board of Directors of RCA. An interesting incident arose when Major Armstrong took his new radio set to Owen D. Young's apartment for a demonstration, Mr. Young being chairman of the Board of Directors of RCA. When Major Armstrong came out of the elevator he carried the radio in his arms—the radio in full operation with an opera program in progress. This was so astounding an achievement in radio technique that there was no hesitation about adopting the Armstrong device. Months must elapse, however, before the machine could be offered to the public. It was not until the following summer that RCA announced the new Super-Heterodyne radio set. Not until 1924 was it possible to offer the device to the public in a nation-wide market. To the foresight of Elmer E. Bucher in suggesting the idea and to the genius of Major Armstrong, was due one of the great achievements in the early years of RCA's career.

One of the great problems confronting RCA in the winter of 1923 was that of patent infringement. The Corporation owned or had exclusive licenses under practically all of the important radio patents then outstanding in the United States. It had a legal right to prevent unlicensed manufacturers from producing and selling radio equipment that involved RCA patents. The unforeseen demand for radio sets all over the nation had furnished opportunity for unscrupulous dealers and fly-by-night manufacturers to reap quick harvests to the detriment not only of RCA but also of the multitude who were unfortunate enough to have purchased "bootleg" equipment.

Faced with this dilemma, the board of directors of RCA authorized an appeal to the courts. The test case was apparently that brought against the A. H. Grebe Company, a well-known radio manufacturer, alleging infringement of five patents owned by the plaintiff corporation. An injunction was sought to restrain the Grebe Company from further manufacture of radio equipment involving the patents in question without a license to do so from RCA.

The significance of this suit was at once apparent. If the Grebe Company could be obliged to come under the RCA banner then radio manufacturers all over the United States could be obliged to do likewise. Few of these companies could view the case without dismal forebodings. Each of them had friends in Washington—friends in the Congress of the United States. Does this explain why the mighty hullabaloo at once arose over the iniquitous radio trust? Even the temperate *Radio Broadcast,* published by the conservative Doubleday, Page & Company, at once joined the hue and cry against RCA, as will be seen hereafter.

The embarrassment of a congressional investigation with the necessity of producing all the cross-licensing agreements incidental to the establishment of RCA must have been a severe blow to that great corporation. Seemingly the Congress of the United States is never so happy as when it can summon the great financiers of the nation before an inquisitorial committee. The press is even more joyous. Headlines and yet more headlines spur on congressional crusaders in every trust-busting campaign. The luckless Radio Corporation of America was certainly in a serious predicament. Every cross-licensing agreement in its vaults was at first glance seeming evidence of guilt. In vain Owen D. Young and his associates asserted the rectitude of their intentions in forming the great corporation. An international task undertaken at the urgent request of the Federal Government, they averred, should not subject them to attack from the legislative branch of the same government. The inquisitors retorted that the Federal Government had never contemplated the setting up of a monopoly and accused the founders of RCA of taking advantage of the request from the Navy Department to accomplish purposes of their own. RCA responded by producing evidence that they could not have accomplished the allotted task except by a pooling of patents, just as the Government had done in the World War, except that cross-licensing was their substitute for the war powers of the Government. Thus was begun the long and expensive contest between the Government and RCA that was destined to make headlines for years thereafter.

In the March, 1923, issue of *Radio Broadcast,* Editor Arthur H. Lynch joined the hue and cry with a sizzling editorial entitled "Monopolizing Production of Apparatus." This must have been a blow much like that of Brutus when Caesar was assailed by his erstwhile friends. That *Radio Broadcast,* supposedly familiar with all the alleged extenuating circumstances, could have raised its hand was truly a staggering development. In the course of the editorial Mr. Lynch declared:

"The A. H. Grebe Company, one of the better known radio manufacturers, is now being sued for infringement of five different patents owned by the Radio Corporation—patents issued to deForest, Langmuir, Lowenstein and Mathes over a period reaching from 1902 to 1922, these patents covering tubes and circuits for using tubes. Should the injunction which is sought by the Radio Corporation be granted, it seems that every manufacturer in the country would be put out of business—excepting, of course, the Radio Corporation itself. It seems that a monopoly of the most grinding sort is the object of this firm. ... To give some idea of the scope and nature of the injunction sought by the Radio Corporation, we quote a part of one sentence of the plaintiff's bill, as affecting the deForest patents. In one paragraph of the complaint on which the Radio Corporation bases its prayer to the Court, it appears that the defendant, A. H. Grebe Company, 'did unlawfully and wrongfully make . . . wireless receiving sets adapted, designed and intended for use in combination with, and useful only in combination with, vacuum detector and amplifier tubes. . . .'

"A radio set must necessarily be used in combination with a detector, crystal or tube, and evidently all radio apparatus, be it coil, condenser, or what-not is 'intended for use in combination with' either tube or crystal. Hence the owners of crystal and tube patents could control everything in the radio field."

Admitting that Editor Lynch made out a very strong case against RCA, it is only fair that President Harbord should be permitted to answer him. The gallant soldier newly come to his high position must have felt that he had walked into a second World War. The publication of this attack in the March, 1923, issue moved the General to reply in the same magazine two months later. Possibly the General's argument was at least edited by RCA's legal staff, because it is a very complete rejoinder and discusses the technicalities of patent law with a clarity that few laymen could hope to attain. After discussing the historical and patriotic aspects of the formation of the Radio Corporation of America he declared:

"It has made great outlay for research and development work in perfecting its own inventions, and to advance the radio art it has also been considered wise to acquire the inventions of others. In no other way could the various improvements and best features of the numerous inventions—no one of them adequate in itself—which are regarded as requisite to satisfactory radio service, have been assembled and made available for the public in any one line of apparatus. . . . Thus far, the public, and a few manufacturers and dealers—some legitimate, but many of them infringers—have profited from the development and production of radio apparatus. The stockholders of this corporation whose money and faith in the patent laws have contributed to the technical achievements largely responsible for progress made have not yet drawn a dollar of profit. . . .

"An infringer of patents has the advantage that he has no patent investment, no research to finance, no responsibility to the art. He can make a thing and sell it. If he makes a dollar profit it belongs to him until the courts take it away from him, which can only happen after a long litigation. The great concern which has made all this development possible, which has spent millions in clearing the road for American radio, has to earn something on what it spent in acquiring that pathway. Enforcement of its patent rights with the Federal Courts will help it to earn that something. If its rights are not as broad as it believes them to be the courts will say so. In its efforts to test its rights and find out just what they really are and to enforce them the Radio Corporation should have the sympathy of everyone who really wishes the good of the radio art."

There was much more to the letter—a strong defense indeed, yet to the unthinking public no amount of logic could halt the hue and cry against a corporation charged with being a trust. "Trust busting" is a popular American custom.

One of the most dramatic radio incidents of the spring of 1923 concerned a great pioneer of wireless transmission—the inventor of the Alexanderson Alternator. Dr. Alexanderson had a six-year-old son,

Verner. On April 30, 1923, the small boy was lured from his home by the promise of a glib stranger that he would give the youngster some rabbits. This was all that could be learned by the police. They believed that the boy had been kidnaped. At the end of three days the case was at a standstill. On the evening of the third day a man who was engaged as caretaker for summer cottages chanced to be listening in on his home-made radio set to a broadcast from Station WGY in Schenectady. An announcement was made of the kidnaping of young Verner Alexanderson with a description of the child. It occurred to the listener that the description fitted a small boy who had just been brought to one of the rental cottages in his charge. His suspicion aroused, the man contrived to visit the cottage and to get a good look at the kidnaped child. He later brought the sheriff to the spot and the Alexanderson boy was restored to his parents—thanks to radio broadcasting.

Sec. 159. Station WJZ Acquires a Sister and a New Home.

It has previously been pointed out that when RCA closed its station WDY in February, 1922, it had entered into a business agreement with Westinghouse Company for the joint operation of Station WJZ, sharing expenses equally. The first mention that we find of the station in the annual report of RCA is for the year ending December 31, 1922. The statement reads as follows:

"During the past year, your Corporation in co-operation with the Westinghouse Company has been operating a broadcasting station, WJZ, at Newark, N. J. Your Directors early in the year authorized the erection of broadcasting stations in New York and Washington. Your engineers designed plans and drew specifications for these stations and the construction work is now nearing completion. . . . The Station in New York will be erected on Aeolian Hall Building at 42nd Street near Fifth Avenue, in the heart of the City, and the Station in Washington will be located on the Riggs National Bank Building at 14th Street and Park Road, N.W."

This latter station was to be WRC, to be opened August 1, 1923. The New York City development now merits attention. We have already noted the serious handicap under which Station WJZ labored by reason of its original studio location. It had been difficult enough while radio was a novelty to persuade artists to journey to Newark for a brief appearance before the microphone without compensation. The opening of Station WEAF in New York City itself served to increase the talent difficulty for Station WJZ. Why should great artists travel to Newark when it was possible to broadcast nearby? The officials of WJZ soon found it imperative to have a New York City Studio. They wisely decided to operate in the heart of the city. Suitable quarters for an auxiliary studio were engaged at the Waldorf-Astoria. This bit of strategy gave WJZ a distinct advantage over its great rival, since the WEAF studio at 24 Walker Street was miles away from the theater district. Many important broadcasts were staged at the Waldorf-Astoria. A pick-up line to the Hotel Astor was also of great service to WJZ.

This was in keeping with plans of the directors of RCA to establish a broadcasting station in New York City. Why it should have required so great a period of time for the engineers to make ready the station at the Aeolian Building is whimsically explained by the engineer who had charge of operations at the time, Dr. Alfred N. Goldsmith, in a recent interview with the author. "The General Electric Company," he said, "was one of the owners of RCA. We couldn't very well go to our boss and tell him to hurry that equipment along. We simply had to be patient until the instruments were ready."

According to the annual report above quoted the station was authorized in commission for more than a year before it went into operation. Station WRC in Washington, moreover, experienced an even greater delay in going on the air. It is evident, however, that the corporation was intent upon equipping its stations with the very latest developments in radio art. It certainly expended great sums in fitting up its broadcasting equipment at Aeolian Hall. This building was near the Public Library and close by Times Square. Since the Radio Corporation of America was now an industrial giant it was natural that it should do things in the grand manner. Its headquarters for wireless activities had long been known as Radio Central. Perhaps this was why the new venture was named Radio Broadcast Central. Lofty radio towers crowned the skyscraper which was Aeolian Hall.

Station WJZ had heretofore been under the joint control of Westinghouse and RCA, but in the spring of 1923 a change of ownership occurred and WJZ became the property of RCA.

It is probable that the fable of the camel who was once permitted to put its head within the tent and presently took advantage of the privilege by entering its whole body, thereby ousting the owner, had its modern counterpart in this change of ownership. The author has been unable to discover any evidence that RCA ever paid the Westinghouse Company anything for its interest in WJZ. In fact it has positively been stated by one who was in a position to know that no payment was ever made and that the Westinghouse Company very reluctantly parted with its property in WJZ. It appears that RCA was set upon establishing in New York City a high grade radio broadcasting station as a stimulus to the industry and would have done so even if

WJZ had been retained by Westinghouse. Rather than carry the station alone at a heavy loss the Westinghouse Company made the best of a bad situation by withdrawing from ownership of WJZ.[1]

RCA's plans were decidedly ambitious. Not one station but two, to be housed in the same building! Station WJZ was to have a sister, WJY! The plan was to have WJZ operate on 455 meters, broadcasting music and entertainment of the lighter vein, whereas WJY was to operate on 405 meters and was intended to specialize in what might be termed "highbrow" broadcasting. Opera, classical music, lectures and the like were to be the offerings of the new station.

"At Aeolian Hall, where this super-station is located," wrote Pierre Boucheron in the July, 1923, *Radio Broadcast*, "WJZ and WJY are characterized as channels A and B respectively and each is equipped with two complete sets of equipment in order to prevent any break in the program being broadcasted, regardless of any mechanical trouble that may develop. There are two pick-up devices in each studio, as well as a system of dual wiring from the studio to the control station on the roof where two complete transmitters are used on each channel."

In addition to the above a permanent set of Western Union cables leading to the station came up Sixth Avenue from 14th Street as far as the Yankee Stadium. Permanent lines were run from the cable to the Waldorf-Astoria, Aeolian Hall and Town Hall. Short temporary lines were planned to pick up important meetings, at Hotel Astor and other places, at theaters and the like. It was a super-station indeed. Appropriately enough, an impressive ceremony was held on May 15, 1923, when the station was officially dedicated—or rather when the two stations WJZ and its newborn sister WJY were put on the air from the new towers on 42nd Street.

General Harbord, President of RCA, as a part of his dedicatory speech declared: "This station will gather from every part of New York City and from all available sources all that will instruct and entertain, and hurl it over millions of square miles of territory . . . the world's first national theater."

Owen D. Young, Chairman of the Board of RCA, was the chief speaker on this occasion. The breadth of vision of the great financier and his affection for RCA's radio offspring are illustrated by the following extract from his remarks:

[1] The late Charles B. Popenoe gives the Radio Corporation a clean bill of health —no crowding—no elbowing out of original owner.
"It had always been the understanding in the Westinghouse organization that as soon as the Radio Corporation of America would erect a super-station in New York City, that the original WJZ would close down and the broadcasting responsibility would be taken over from Westinghouse, and all broadcasting by the affiliated companies, Radio Corporation, Westinghouse, and General Electric in the New York City district would be done by the Radio Corporation."
Popenoe MS, p. 20.

"Broadcasting has appealed to the imagination as no other scientific development of the time. Its ultimate effect upon the educational, social, political, and religious life of our country and of the world is quite beyond our ability to prophesy.

"Already it is bringing to the farmer, market, weather, and crop reports as well as time signals, which cannot help but be of economic value. In remote communities, where the country parson is no longer in attendance at Sunday morning services, it is filling a great need in spiritual life. Its educational possibilities are being investigated by our foremost national and state educators. It is taking entertainment from the large centers to individual homes. To the blind and the sick it has unfolded a new and richer life. For the purpose of communication it has destroyed time and space." [2]

Coincident with the change to New York City RCA began preparations to permit advertisers to use the facilities of the stations, allowing them free time on the air but requiring them to pay the cost of programs of high quality. This was competition with WEAF of serious nature, since the latter station charged heavily for both time and program. New and more commodious quarters brought also additions to the staff of the station. A publicity man, Stuart Hawkins, was added at this time, as was also Angela Caramore.

We are indebted to a half-tone illustration in the April, 1923, issue of *Radio Broadcast* for authentic information as to the personnel of WJZ prior to the change from Newark, so far as announcers and operators were concerned. J. L. Watt and Milton J. Cross were the announcers; G. E. Blitziotis, chief operator and G. E. Oliver, P. W. Harrison, H. E. Hiller and Raymond F. Guy, operators.

Sec. 160. Station WEAF Acquires a New Home—and Graham McNamee.

A spirit of rivalry between Stations WEAF and WJZ was no doubt an inevitable consequence of competition for pre-eminence in radio in the New York City area. For nearly a year WJZ was the reigning wonder of the section despite the fact that it was located in Newark, which to New Yorkers was a very provincial place—"the sticks," so to speak. An undoubted blow to its pride was the successful opening of WEAF in the heart of the financial district of New York City. We have already observed WJZ's strategy of a studio in Times Square, followed by the grand opening of Radio Broadcast Central in the Aeolian Building.

Despite the fact that WEAF had been in its offices at Walker Street only a few months, the announcement in the winter of 1923 that its rival would soon be located in sumptuous quarters at the edge of the theatrical district stirred its officials to action. Additional space was

[2] *Radio Broadcast*, July 1923, p. 255.

needed at any rate. A change to the theatrical center would no doubt have been more pleasing to Samuel L. Ross and his associates who were competing with WJZ scouts for talent, yet the best that could be done under the circumstances was to move to 195 Broadway. This building was miles from the musical and entertainment center. Like 24 Walker Street, it was in the financial district. But 195 Broadway was the huge American Telephone & Telegraph Building—more impressive architecturally than Aeolian Hall.

The Telephone Company was evidently intent upon excelling the new studios being prepared for WJZ and WJY. A new wave length was obtained—492 meters. The large reception room at the new studio was tastefully and expensively decorated. One wall was hung with a rich tapestry. Paintings and paneling, artistic furniture and deep-napped carpeting were features of the room. There were two studios, a small one for singers and speakers and a large studio for bands and choral groups. An unusual feature of the installation and about the only one that did not prove a trail-blazing innovation was an announcer's booth between the two studios. This was a small sound-proof room in which the announcer could sit and command a view of either studio. By the use of loud speakers in each studio the announcer by "remote control" could introduce the artists or speakers. The use of two studios made it possible for an orchestra to set up, or for a speaker or singer to take his place at the microphone in the studio not on the air. The announcer's control box regulated the microphones. It was theoretically perfect but experience was to prove that announcers needed to be physically present in a studio with the performers when calling them to the microphone.

An amusing evidence of the rivalry that had grown up between the two stations exists in the fact that WEAF held its opening on the very day that Radio Broadcast Central was being dedicated. The Telephone Company had in fact so far overcome its aversion to publicity as to invite the public to visit the new studios. Strangely enough, this very "open house" brought to WEAF its first great announcer—Graham McNamee. The records of the Am. Tel. & Tel. Company show that McNamee first appeared on the payroll of the station May 21, 1923— six days after the opening of the station at 195 Broadway.

Mr. McNamee's own story of his first visit to a radio station would indicate that it must have occurred on the opening day or immediately thereafter. In an interview with the author Graham McNamee stated that up to the time of this memorable visit he had entertained a very poor opinion of radio. He had a friend who was a radio enthusiast "with a roomful of radio junk." On one or two occasions the friend had persuaded him to listen, but squeals and squawks had offended his ears. In May, 1923, however, while serving on a jury, McNamee was let off early one day. He walked down Broadway and when passing the Am. Tel. & Tel. Building an impulse came to him to visit the new radio station. In the reception room he met Samuel L. Ross, the Program Manager. This very friendly and magnetic young man soon learned that the visitor was a singer by profession—a juror by accident. Ross insisted upon giving McNamee an audition. It was not the singing voice of the visitor but his speaking voice that electrified Mr. Ross.

Thus an audition, begun as a mere gesture of friendliness, soon became a matter of excited bargaining. Ross needed another announcer. Llufrio was a star at WEAF. Ross was sure that he had made an even greater find. McNamee had a speaking voice that excelled any that Ross had ever heard in a microphone. Before the visitor left the office Ross had hired him to announce programs six evenings a week from 7.00 to 10.00 P.M. Since this arrangement did not interfere with his duties as a juror McNamee began work within a day or two. The fact that his name was on the payroll of May 21st demonstrates that he indeed reported for duty very promptly.

No greater asset could have been acquired by Station WEAF at this time than the dynamic and volatile McNamee. He was a singer, an entertainer, but above all he had a clarity of voice that captivated radio audiences. In this respect he was a match for Milton Cross of WJZ. But McNamee had a popular appeal that the rival announcer lacked. Cross was ideally qualified to broadcast the so-called "highbrow" program but McNamee became at once the announcer-extraordinary of "low-brow" broadcasts. A prize fight, a ball game and later the great football games found in Graham McNamee an interpreter who could project over the microphone the very spirit of the arena. Even the cadence of his voice as he watched and described what he saw communicated to the radio audience the emotions of the moment. Vast audiences were to hang upon his colorful words; to share his enthusiasms. His own genuine excitement when a knockdown was witnessed, when a baseball was clouted into the bleachers for a home run, or when a touchdown was scored, was carried over the air in a manner so compelling that listeners sometimes forgot their surroundings and cheered.

Thus Station WEAF introduced a new and vital factor in radio broadcasting—established the McNamee cult, so to speak. In the fifteen years since that date many announcers have aped Graham McNamee —many have come and gone, but like Milton J. Cross, Graham McNamee is still one of the great figures of the radio world.

Sec. 161. Dr. Conrad at KDKA Develops Short-Wave Broadcasting.

Station WEAF at an early stage of its career manifested a warm sympathy for educational programs. To be sure there were serious handicaps to be overcome before a frankly educational program could be made acceptable to a typical radio audience. Early in the spring of 1923 a program of lectures on music and literature began to find favor with WEAF listeners.

Dr. Frank Conrad, whose experiments at Pittsburgh had resulted in the establishment of Station KDKA—and radio broadcasting—was evidently a scientist who did not believe in resting on his laurels. Having scored one great success he presently turned his attention to the problem of short-wave broadcasting.[3] An appreciative article in the June, 1923, issue of *Radio Broadcast* thus heralds the amazing results of his latest experiments.

"The Westinghouse Company has been carrying on experiments with this method of broadcasting for the past year and has in that time been able to gather a great deal of useful data from these experiments. Frank Conrad, Assistant Chief Engineer of the Company, and well-known in the radio world because of his station, 8XK, is believed to be the man who first experimented with broadcasting on the very short wave lengths. Before Mr. Conrad got into the work, radio engineers had proved by mathematics that transmission on short waves was impracticable, but he had an idea that their calculations might not be correct, and decided to investigate for himself the possibilities of broadcasting effectively on wave lengths of 100 meters or lower. First he built a set to transmit on 100 meters and found by tests with an amateur operator in Boston that the 100 meter wave length was more selective and more efficient than even 360 meters. Mr. Conrad next arranged for a private telephone connection between Station KDKA and his home, about four miles distant, and by a special circuit arranged to receive programs from the studio circuit over his telephone line. He then connected this telephone line to his 100 meter transmitting set and sent out KDKA's programs simultaneously with the broadcasting on 360 meters.

"In Boston and other places it was reported that this transmission was stronger than the signals received directly from KDKA on 360 meters! This was true enough though his station was much less powerful than the one at East Pittsburgh." [4]

Once more Dr. Frank Conrad had blazed a new trail in a great field of science. Cold mathematics that had denied the possibility now stood confounded in the presence of a brilliant demonstration of the feasibility of short wave broadcasting. The Westinghouse radio engineers now set to work in the new field. It had already been discovered that in some portions of every section of the country there seemed to be areas

[3] By a coincidence Senatore Marconi was at this time conducting experiments in the same field aboard his floating radio laboratory on his private yacht, the *Elettra*.

[4] *Radio Broadcast*, June 1923, p. 120.

where radio reception is very poor. Cleveland, Ohio, for example, had never been able to pick up in satisfactory manner the broadcasts on 360 meters from KDKA despite the fact that much more distant places had no difficulty at all. Very well! The Westinghouse engineers would try out short wave broadcasting with Cleveland as a target.

A short wave relaying station for 100 meter signals with a loop antenna but eight feet square was set up inside the Cleveland Foundry on the shore of Lake Erie. KDKA signals were now heard in Cleveland in the same volume as local broadcasts. This experiment convinced the Westinghouse Company that short-wave broadcasting had great possibilities. Station KDKA's long antenna for broadcasting on 360 meters was 105 feet high and 200 feet long. Radio engineers of the station now set up a supplemental short-wave antenna for 100 meter broadcasting which was a mere toy in comparison to the other—35 feet high and 40 feet long.

Two very important discoveries had been made as early as the spring of 1923. Static seemed to have much less effect upon short wave than upon long wave reception. A second joyful discovery concerned the old bug-a-boo of ordinary broadcasting—the effect of daylight on radio transmission. It was well known that long wave radio transmission loves darkness but fades into a comparative whisper with the coming of daylight. Not so with short wave broadcasting. In fact, daylight transmission at 80 meters appeared to be materially better than at night.[5]

Sec. 162. Litigation and Threats of Litigation in Radio.

The spring of 1923 witnessed an important development with reference to the use of copyrighted music over the air. At an early stage of radio broadcasting development the American Society of Composers, Authors and Publishers had raised indignant protest against the indiscriminate use of their property by broadcasters. They contended that the copyright laws would be nullified if unauthorized persons could use copyrighted music or songs for public entertainment without recompense to the owner. Radio officials retorted that their work was experimental and carried on not only without profit but also at heavy expense. They had no funds from which to pay royalties to A.S.C.A.P. They contended, moreover, that they were really benefitting the owners by popularizing their products. A.S.C.A.P. officials quite naturally could not see the matter from this angle. They complained bitterly that the life-span of a popular song would be exceedingly brief if radio stations all over the nation could be permitted to wear it threadbare in a week or two as they were doing.

[5] *Radio Broadcast*, June 1923, p. 122.

No satisfactory solution being arrived at, A.S.C.A.P. appealed to the courts for protection. Broadcasting stations thereupon found themselves confronted with royalty payments or injunctions to prevent unauthorized use of copyrighted materials. Some stations like WJZ, still in Newark when matters came to a head, staged a boycott of popular music. Miss Bertha Brainard, then assistant program manager of WJZ, tried to get even with A.S.C.A.P. by booking talks on non-copyrighted music continuously for several days.[6] Station WEAF on the other hand had a fellow feeling for the luckless publishers of music, for had not the American Tel. & Tel. Company reserved to itself the exclusive right to sell time on the air only to have a great multitude of stations start selling radio advertising without so much as notice to the owners of WEAF? Much to the dismay of other stations and to radio men in general, Station WEAF, acknowledged as one of America's most influential radio stations, made peace with A.S.C.A.P.

The editor of *Radio Broadcast* became very much exercised over the situation as it existed when the July, 1923, issue was prepared.

"When a station can be shown to be on a paying basis," he wrote, "then it seems proper for music writers to collect as their share of the proceeds as much as seems reasonable, but to insist on large royalties while the game is in the experimental stage seems very much like killing the goose which might some day lay golden eggs for them."

After commenting upon the fact that RCA, one of the few companies that was reaping real returns from the radio industry by selling vast numbers of radio tubes, had taken a determined stand against A.S.C.A.P., he went on to discuss American Tel. & Tel.'s attitude.

"Their activities in the radio broadcasting field have proved so far a rather expensive proposition, yet they have come to some kind of an agreement with the Society of Composers, Authors and Publishers and tell their audience so every time they broadcast—tell it in phraseology which sounds as though it had been specified by counsel for the musicians. We think the public is rather 'fed up' with this Society and would enjoy some music without being informed of the copyrighter's existence."

Another development that presaged trouble for the broadcasting stations occurred at this time. Station WEAF being on the lookout for new fields to conquer, decided to broadcast a musical comedy directly from the stage of a New York theater. This exploit at once incurred the wrath of the Producing Managers' Association. In behalf of this Society no less a person than Arthur Hammerstein made the following warlike declaration:

[6] Private records of NBC.

" 'On behalf of the Producing Managers' Association I wish it to be understood that no music of any opera, musical comedy, or musical play produced by these Managers will be permitted to be broadcasted by radio or otherwise without the consent of the Producing Managers' Association. We give notice now that we shall hold to strict account-ability anyone who shall attempt to produce or broadcast any of our music or our works . . . in addition to which we shall attempt to hold, if it is found possible, any violators of our rights under the copyright laws of the country.'

"So it seems that the path of the broadcast station manager is beset with difficulties—wherever he turns for material he finds the counsel of somebody or other confronting him, with bills for royalties on one hand and an injunction on the other. In the meantime the public, the real beneficiaries, get it all for nothing." [7]

Litigation of a variety of forms had thus already been attracted to the infant industry of radio. The Government itself was beginning a far-reaching prosecution of the Radio Corporation of America for an alleged monopoly. RCA was seeking injunctions against manufacturers who were alleged to be infringing its patent rights. A.S.C.A.P. was on the warpath against broadcasting stations and threatening them with injunctions for using copyrighted music. Now the Producing Mana-gers' Association had joined the fray to prevent radio stations from broadcasting opera, musical comedies and the like. A mad world in-deed for radio, when we consider that the National Congress had not yet taken action to unsnarl the dreadful tangle of interference on the air by empowering the Secretary of Commerce to make traffic rules for the air lanes and to assign differing wave lengths to competing radio stations.

Sec. 163. Perilous Outlook for Radio Broadcasting.

In the interval since January 4th, when the WEAF–WNAC experi-ment in simultaneous or network broadcasting was attempted, the engi-neers of the Telephone Company had been wrestling with the problem of telephone cable as a carrier of the program from the station of origin. Westinghouse, as we have seen, was experimenting with short-wave. In July, 1923, there was genuine uncertainty as to which method might eventually link stations that desired to broadcast an identical program. That network or chain broadcasting was highly desirable had by this time been accepted by thoughtful observers.

"It is evident to any one who thinks much about the question," writes the editor of *Radio Broadcast*, "that in the final solution of the broadcasting problem a given program must be made to reach as

[7] *Radio Broadcast,* July 1923, p. 181.

PHILLIPS CARLIN
Announcer who became a radio executive.

MISS BERTHA BRAINARD
First Lady of Radio.

GRAHAM McNAMEE
Veteran sports announcer.

MILTON J. CROSS
Whose golden voice is loved by millions.

large an audience as possible. As the programs of the broadcasting stations improve, this fact will become increasingly apparent. For example, if an opera is being broadcasted from the Metropolitan Opera House in New York, the artists may be the finest in the world. Why then should people in other sections of the country who enjoy opera, have to listen to some mediocre program from a local station? Of course entirely apart from radio, this is actually the case today. We can't all go to the best opera and so we have to content ourselves with something less expensive and less artistic. But right here lies the great promise of radio—it need cost but little more to broadcast to a million listeners than to a thousand, so that the very best programs should be available to everyone. . . . It seems to us that the future of broadcasting is intimately connected with the establishment of a wire network covering the country and connected to the best broadcasting station in a given locality." [8]

The name of deForest, long missing from these pages, again reappears in the summer of 1923, in the announcement of the sale of the deForest Radio Telephone & Telegraph Company to a group of automobile manufacturers. The reorganization brought needed funds to the luckless company and incidentally to Lee deForest himself. He was retained as consulting engineer for the reorganized company for a period of ten years. The company was then manufacturing vacuum tubes. Under the new set-up it was hoped to raise the output to 2400 a day. DeForest was working upon a phono-film intended to be used in the field of talking movies, but this endeavor did not go into the transaction above indicated.

An interesting development in the controversy over copyright infringements came in July, 1923. The action of Station WJZ in boycotting popular songs had received the approval of its owners, the Radio Corporation of America. A group of music composers and publishers not affiliated with A.S.C.A.P. and known as Music Publishers' Association of the United States held a convention and received a report of a committee on broadcasting. This committee had been at work since November, 1922. A part of the report was as follows:

"We appreciate the fact that radio broadcasting is still in a chaotic and experimental stage, and that while ultimately it will have to be placed on a commercial basis if it is to develop its potentialities, nevertheless the commercial side of the broadcasting problem has not yet been solved. In view of these facts, and also because we desire to cooperate in developing the music possibilities of radio, we believe that we should allow the use of our copyrighted compositions for broadcasting without charge for the present and without prejudice in our rights."

[8] *Radio Broadcast,* July 1923, pp. 187-188.

This generous action of the Music Publishers' Association no doubt had a salutary effect upon the radio industry. It certainly demonstrated that one association, at least, had friendly feelings for the perplexed and groping pioneers of radio broadcasting.

Now that a full year of nation-wide radio broadcasting had been completed the summer of 1923 afforded an opportunity to cast up the accounts, so to speak. This was indeed a disturbing experience, since the studio ledgers of every station disclosed entries almost entirely in red ink. Fortunes had been squandered in the mad rush for fame and fortune in the radio "Klondike." Even during the early months of the industry an ominous story of disaster was being recorded each month —a list of broadcasting stations that had closed their doors. As early as December, 1922, the Department of Commerce reported the suspension of twenty stations for that month alone. With every succeeding month the casualty list had grown more appalling. Between March 19 and April 30, 1923, forty-two stations gave up their franchises. In the month of May there were twenty-six failures. June, 1923, saw fifty radio stations become silent. In July twenty-five franchises were surrendered. Thus in the period from March 19th to July 31st of this fateful year 143 radio stations went out of business.

The outlook for the entire industry was black indeed when the editor of *Radio Broadcast* wrote the despairing editorial from which we quote in part:

"There are scores, or even hundreds, of broadcasting stations which cannot continue in this fashion. Their future is not promising unless some source of revenue is found and found soon. This is especially true since the popular music writers have begun to insist on their royalty rights and want to collect money where there is none."

The editorial went on to discuss the latest development in defensive organization among radio men. They had already formed a Radio Chamber of Commerce but now a group of managers of broadcasting stations had gotten together to form the National Association of Broadcasters. This new organization had evidently inspired the editor to a desperate suggestion—that composers turn over their copyrighted compositions to the Association "for nothing." Weird as this suggestion may seem in this year of grace 1938 the editor nevertheless had a plausible argument to back it up.

He cited an incident of an author who had sold one of his compositions to a Chicago music publisher. The song was apparently a "dud" with no recorded sales until arrangements were made with a broadcasting studio to permit the author to sing his song over the radio. It made somewhat of a hit and had since enjoyed a good sale. Song and author by the magic of radio had been rescued from obscurity. Unfortunately, however, the author was affiliated with A.S.C.A.P., which now intervened and prevented him from singing his own song over stations that had failed to pay royalties to the Society. This meant virtual prohibition, since few radio stations were then paying anything to A.S.C.A.P. The editorial argued that radio advertising of songs was a benefit to composers and authors for which they should thank their lucky stars instead of demanding royalty payments for every rendition on the air.

Sec. 164. Network Broadcasting at Last.

Since January, 1923, the engineers of the American Tel. & Tel. Company had been struggling with the problem of special long lines for network broadcasting. The attempt on January 4th when WEAF and WNAC had been hooked up in a single broadcast, had convinced them that special high-efficiency cable was needful for this type of work. By June, 1923, they were hopeful that they had accomplished their task. They naturally desired a dramatic occasion for the trial of the new cable. Fortunately a meeting of the National Electric Light Association in New York City scheduled for early June gave them the desired opportunity to make the test in a grand way. Telephone lines connected Station WEAF with the following stations: WGY in Schenectady, N. Y.; KDKA in Pittsburgh, Pa. and KYW in Chicago, Ill. A special program originating in one of the sessions, presumably at a banquet of the National Electric Light Association, went out from Station WEAF on the evening of June 7, 1923. The success of the attempt was pronounced. It excited great interest in radio circles.

One of the results of this spectacular broadcast no doubt astounded even the officials of the American Tel. & Tel. Company, since it brought post haste to New York an eccentric millionaire, Col. Edward H. R. Green, a son of the still more eccentric Hetty Green. The Colonel was a radio enthusiast. He was one of the few persons in America who could afford the luxury of a private radio station. This station was located at Round Hills, South Dartmouth, Mass. Its call letters were WMAF. This station had been licensed for about a year having been first listed in the group licensed between August 11th and September 16th, 1922. Col. Green had long ago discovered that the talent problem of an isolated station was a very serious one.

So on a day in the early part of June, 1923, the eccentric millionaire surprised the officials of Station WEAF with a request that his station be linked up with the great New York City station so that his transmitter might broadcast the same program. Thus he hoped to rid himself of the talent problem. He would have the satisfaction, moreover, of broadcasting from his station a program equal to the best that radio could boast. To be sure, he was to encounter difficulty with sponsored programs that were now forming an integral part of WEAF's offerings on the air. No sponsor would pay for the dubious privilege of a broadcast over the South Dartmouth station. Col. Green met this situation like a philosopher. He would broadcast the sponsored programs, commercial plug and all, free of charge. Sustaining programs he would pay for at some fixed rate. Thus a rich man's whim established the first continuous hook-up of stations in radio history and incidentally gave the engineers of the Am. Tel. & Tel. just the experience they needed to perfect the type of telephone cable essential to network broadcasting.

The author experienced great difficulty in uncovering accurate information concerning this important development in radio history. Col. Green now being dead, the station abandoned and no living person appearing to have more than vague recollection of the facts, it was feared that the mystery would never be cleared. By great good fortune, however, when exploring a miscellaneous file in the archives of the National Broadcasting Company on April 30, 1938, the author discovered a typewritten memorandum obviously prepared for Col. Green and filed with the Am. Tel. & Tel. Company as a press release. It bears no date except a penciled memorandum "7/1" but it contains the very information for which the author had searched in vain for weeks. It reads as follows:

"Col. E. H. R. Green has made arrangements with the A. T. & T. Company to have furnished by wire telephone lines from New York high grade programs such as are broadcast through WEAF for broadcasting through his own station. Beginning July 1st (1923) therefore, Station WMAF, located at Round Hills, Mass., will make available from their studio to the hundreds of thousands who reside within a hundred miles of the station, as well as tens of thousands of people who spend their vacations in that part of the country, the same high grade of programs rendered at the great metropolitan stations.

"Col. Green is a real radio fan and his enthusiasm has led him to erect extensive laboratories at Round Hills. The broadcasting transmitter which will be used for these programs from New York is a 500 watt Western Electric transmitter similar to that being used by many of the most prominent stations of the country, including WEAF, etc.

"WMAF's schedule will be 4 to 5:30 P.M. and 7:30 to 10 P.M. each week day and from 3:30 to 5:15 P.M. and 7:15 to 10:00 P.M. on Sundays, Eastern Daylight Saving Time."

The significance of the WMAF experiment lies in the fact that unlike the mere temporary hook-up of stations where the lines are removed after a special broadcast, the line from WEAF to WMAF was permanent. In this respect it was the pioneer of all networks, since in the true network the installation is permanent. Thus Col. Green, the millionaire to whom expense meant nothing, aided materially in working out one of the great scientific achievements of modern times. Speaking of expense, John A. Holman, who in the following year became station manager of WEAF, gave the author the following whimsical side-light on Col. Green's character. Mr. Holman stated that whenever the A. T. & T. Company rendered a bill to Col. Green for services rendered under the contract the latter almost invariably disputed the bill. He would come to New York, hire an expensive suite in some "swanky" hotel, and send for Mr. Holman. Any concession, however trifling, always satisfied the eccentric millionaire. Feeling that he had won a great moral victory he would return to South Dartmouth, only to repeat the performance when the next bill came in.

CHAPTER
EIGHTEEN

Radio and the National Election of 1924

Section 166. Secretary Hoover Reassigns Broadcast Frequencies.

THE SUMMER OF 1923 witnessed other great developments in radio history. Not the least of these was the growing popularity of installment buying of radio sets. The American people were now recovering from World War privations and were entering into that era of expansion of credit that eventually led the nation into the great catastrophe of 1929. Good times had dawned. There was work for everyone who really desired it. The apparent certainty of a weekly wage was seized upon by clever salesmen in all fields of industry to convince people who were not presently able to purchase for cash that installment buying was the sensible and proper method of securing the luxuries as well as the necessities of life. A small down payment and a trifling sum per week was the siren song that caused the average American family to step blithely into debt. The main purpose of all installment buying is, of course, to stimulate industry. Radio was only one of many lines that prospered under the installment plan. Radio, in fact, was the reigning fad, a luxury rapidly ripening into a household necessity.

President Warren G. Harding might justly be termed our first Radio President. Radio broadcasting had its first impressive demonstration in reporting the Harding election returns. His inauguration was similarly reported. At intervals the new President had appeared before the microphone. In the summer of 1923 radio received a great impetus through the fact that President Harding delivered a series of important messages to the American people over the radio. One of the most significant events of the closing months of President Harding's life was his speech of June 21, 1923, in the Coliseum at St. Louis, Mo., which was carried by special wire to New York City and broadcast over Station WEAF. A few other radio stations participated in the broadcast of the President's speech—a tribute to the skill of radio engineers.

President Harding was a colorful figure. Despite the shameful manner in which some of his close friends abused his confidence and betrayed the American people, the President himself remained popular with the rank and file. The facts of his fateful journey to Alaska in the summer of 1923 are too well known to require repetition in this narrative. It so happened, however, that A. T. & T. officials decided to utilize the President's expected home-coming for a spectacular radio demonstration. The Harding itinerary called for a speech in San Francisco on July 31, 1923. In preparation for this event elaborate plans were laid. In the archives of the National Broadcasting Company the author has discovered a proposed press release—alas, never used, because Warren G. Harding was facing death on July 31st. His speechmaking career was over and on August 2nd he was to die. This sad memento—the unused press release—sets forth the plans for radio's most ambitious venture up to that date. There was to be a nation-wide broadcast of the expected speech by the President at San Francisco on July 31, 1923. A hookup of six stations was planned: KPO, San Francisco; WAOW, Omaha; WMAQ, Chicago; WEAF, New York; WCAP, Washington; WMAF, Round Hills, Mass.

Immediately upon the death of Warren G. Harding, Vice-President Calvin Coolidge quietly assumed office as Chief Executive of the Nation. There was no proper occasion during the balance of that summer for radio, the fledgling, to try its wings in a nation-wide flight. Fortunately the change in administration did not cause changes in the cabinet. Herbert Hoover, radio's great champion, remained in office as Secretary of Commerce. He was free to carry out a reform in radio designed to remedy the bedlam of interference that had so long existed in radio broadcasting.

Secretary Hoover had waited long and patiently for Congress to give him a formal mandate to act. The failure of the White Radio Bill in the recent session of Congress and the fact that no more authority could be expected than he already possessed led Secretary Hoover to take the bit in his teeth, so to speak. Nearly every radio executive in the land must have rejoiced when the edict went forth from Washington that a reassignment of wave lengths for broadcasting stations was to be put into effect.

"Apparently feeling that he already had sufficient authority, and that the situation was bad enough to warrant immediate action," writes the editor of *Radio Broadcast* in August, 1923, "the Secretary of Commerce, acting in accord with the opinion of radio experts and authorities of the country, has reassigned frequencies to practically all the broadcasting stations in the country and has done it so well that we no longer have any cause for complaint. Instead of the bedlam of noise to which we had become almost accustomed, there is practically no interference at all. With a good receiving set, one can go through the range of wave lengths assigned to broadcasting and pick up perhaps twenty stations with no appreciable interference. . . . Even the novice can eliminate practically all interference; and the concerts, ever improving in quality, are really worthwhile staying at home to hear. The finer passages are not spoiled by the whining beat note of a competing station, as they formerly were. With this reassignment of wave lengths, a big step has been taken in forwarding the interests of radio broadcasting. Considering the apparent ease with which it was accomplished, we wonder more than ever why the Department of Commerce delayed its good work so long."

Alas for the editor's fond hopes of a complete solution of the radio interference problem! The new system that worked so well for a while had no compelling basis of law. Unscrupulous and selfish individuals, as we shall see, were to undo Secretary Hoover's splendid work in behalf of the radio industry.

In the very next issue of the magazine it was regretfully admitted by the editor that he had been unduly optimistic. Indignant subscribers had set him right. The ordinary single circuit radio set was not capable of the selective tuning necessary to accomplish the results that the editor had described. This was especially true of the home-made sets, made of a few turns of wire on a box, equipped with a crude crystal detector. Even the manufactured set, unless of an improved model, was inadequate to give desired results. The need of junking such sets and of replacing them with the latest and best was, of course, obvious to thoughtful observers. Many of those who had clamored for sets in the height of the radio boom were naturally resentful over the fact that their investment was now of doubtful value. They clamored for a return to the system by which radio stations had used the same wave length and shared broadcasting hours. The upshot of the matter was that installment buying of radio sets was given fresh impetus by the reassignment of radio frequencies.

One of the significant events of the summer of 1923 so far as radio broadcasting is concerned was the announcement of the adaptation by Edwin H. Armstrong of his super-heterodyne device to home receiving sets. This device had been famous since war days in France when it was first used. The reputation of the inventor and the obvious need of some means by which the home set could be improved resulted in such congestion in the hall at Columbia University where the inventor was to demonstrate the device that hundreds were unable to gain admission. Experts at once acclaimed the invention as likely to revolutionize radio receiving systems.

Sec. 167. Station WEAF Sets Standard of Sports Announcing.

No summer season in America would be complete without its quota of sports. A President may die and another succeed him in office, yet baseball and football seemingly go on forever—so great is the passion of the American people for sporting events. The spectacle is the thing! Tens of thousands sit by and watch a game—yelling themselves hoarse in vicarious participation. Prior to the advent of radio, spectator-excitement was necessarily limited to those physically present. The new agency, however, enabled an ever-increasing radio audience to remain in their own homes or gather in street throngs hundreds of miles distant and share in the thrills of a closely fought game.

The first exciting event of the 1923 sports season was the heavyweight championship fight between Jess Willard and Luis Angel Firpo, which occurred on July 12, 1923. This contest was projected over the air by Station WEAF, and added to its growing prestige. Station WEAF was now reaping an unexpected harvest of popularity out of the very medium that had caused so much anxiety to radio experts—from sponsored programs. It is true that the pioneer programs of the commercial variety were a bit heavy and uninteresting. Sponsors who were paying real money for time on the air quite naturally felt that they must get their message across by direct appeals similar to newspaper and magazine advertising. Words and more words were in order, although the more astute of the advertisers soon realized that a talk must have human appeal. The advertising must be incidental and inoffensive—a mere garnish to the main dish.

Then came the Gimbel Brothers' epoch-marking broadcast of March 15, 1923, with an hour-long musical program. The idea had "clicked" with the radio audience. Soon Gimbel Brothers, Browning King and others were using the musical vehicle for advertising—using it deftly and effectively. On July 14, 1923, the American Tobacco Company joined the procession with its "Lucky Strike" radio show. On August 22, 1923, the Happiness Candy Company went on the air with the inimitable "Happiness Boys," Billy Jones and Ernie Hare, the first real comedians of radio. Clean comedy that sent a far-flung radio audience into gales of laughter was their specialty. WEAF had become a virtual theater of the air, a circumstance that plunged the nation into a great era of radio advertising. With or without right every broadcasting station, now that WEAF had blazed the trail, was endeavoring to offer sponsored programs.

The advertising situation probably came to a crisis during this very summer. The American Tel. & Tel. Company had reserved to itself the right to use its basic patents for toll-broadcasting. So far as RCA, General Electric and the Westinghouse corporations were concerned it might successfully have asserted its rights. But what could the Telephone Company do when all over the nation radio broadcasting stations were ignoring its suggestions that they be licensed by A. T. & T. to broadcast for hire? It was a splendid theory that a fee be exacted from all stations that might desire to broadcast for hire, yet like some other theories it did not work when confronted with the ugly facts of human nature. The average man will go as far as he can with impunity in any direction to which inclination or self-interest may lure him. Then he may fight for the advantage thus gained.

In view of the congressional investigation of the alleged monopoly by the Radio Corporation of America then pending, the officials of the Telephone Company doubtless hesitated about appealing to the courts for the enforcement of its supposed rights. Here was prima facie monopoly in a public utility field. A. T. & T. wisely refrained from hostilities.

The attorneys for the Telephone Company were no doubt fully

aware that agreements drawn up when radio broadcasting was undreamed of might be fatally defective if tested in the courts. They were
constrained to mark time even though squatters had taken possession
of their rights. As a face-saving gesture they offered to license toll
broadcasting for a small fee. If stations still ignored the invitation,
well, that was that! The Telephone Company continued to assert its
alleged rights, no doubt hoping by threats to accomplish what it did
not dare undertake by wholesale resort to the courts. The company
was not without financial rewards from radio broadcasting despite
the toll-broadcasting situation. It was also apparent that the growing
need of leased wires for chain broadcasting would eventually bring
revenue into the Telephone Company treasury. Incidentally Station
WEAF was on the way to financial success.

In justice to the company it should be pointed out that revenue
was only incidental to its broadcasting activities. It could have opened
or have acquired other stations than WEAF and WCAP had it desired to dominate radio advertising. As an evidence that its activities
were largely actuated by motives of scientific research and public
service we have the long series of experimentation in radio transmission and the company's efforts to extend the aid of the new science
to the cause of public enlightenment. Two notable instances of the
latter occurred during the 1923 season. The Capitol Theatre broadcasts by "Roxy and His Gang" began January 28, 1923—public entertainment of high order. On July 17, 1923, the first of a series of talks
on English Literature by Hoxie N. Fairchild, Supervisor of Home
Study Courses at Columbia University, went on the air over WEAF.
The great radio personality, Dr. Walter Damrosch, made his first radio
appearance at the WEAF studios October 29, 1923. He gave a lecture-
recital on Beethoven.

Turning again to sports events, we find Stations WEAF and WGY
joined by special wire to broadcast the World Series games in October
1923. The series began October 10th with "Bill" McGeehan, Sports
Editor of the New York *Herald,* as announcer. In view of later events
in radio broadcasting it is interesting to note that on page 150 of the
December, 1923, issue of *Radio Broadcast* is an excellent snapshot of
Editor McGeehan at the WEAF "pick-up" microphone, broadcasting
a play-by-play description of one of the World Series games while
beside him sat radio's future wizard of the microphone—Graham Mc-
Namee. Graham was small in those days, weighing but 128 pounds. He
had already had his first taste of radio glory—broadcasting a prize fight
between Harry Greb and Johnny Wilson. He had asked for the privilege of assisting in the World Series games, but there he sat as pensive
and useless as a Vice-President while another man did all the talking.

Graham McNamee's chance came, however, before the series ended. The program sheets of Station WEAF tell the following story:

October 10, 1923, 1:30 P.M. World Series—Bill McGeehan, Announcer.
October 11, 1923, 1:30 P.M. World Series—Bill McGeehan, Announcer.
October 12, 1923, 1:30 P.M. World Series—Bill McGeehan, Announcer.
October 13, 1923, 1:30 P.M. World Series—Graham McNamee, Announcer.
October 14, 1923, 1:30 P.M. World Series—Graham McNamee, Announcer.
October 15, 1923, 1:30 P.M. World Series—Graham McNamee, Announcer.
October 16, 1923, 1:30 P.M. World Series—Graham McNamee, Announcer.

Graham McNamee was now in a way to establish his reputation as an announcer. Hereafter in all great sporting events for years to come Station WEAF was to be represented at the microphone by the dynamic word painter, Graham McNamee.

Within a month McNamee's great team-mate at the sports microphone—Phillips Carlin—was to be added to the staff of WEAF. Carlin had been haunting the place for a long time—fascinated by radio and its possibilities. The fact that he had a remarkable speaking voice could not overcome the admitted handicap that he was not a singer, nor did he understand music—all of which were then considered essential in a radio announcer. His persistence, however, finally overcame the resistance of the genial Sam Ross, Program Manager. Phillips Carlin's name first appears on the payroll of WEAF November 12, 1923, as a part-time announcer.

His interest in sports and the fact that he too could paint word pictures of sporting events led him to be teamed with Graham McNamee. This pair could put so much genuine excitement into a broadcast, taking turns without loss of tempo, that they became team-mates in the great sporting events of the nation for many years to come, even after Phillips Carlin had become Program Manager of WEAF and later Eastern Program Manager of the National Broadcasting Company.

Sec. 168. President Coolidge and other Famous Radio Speakers.

November, 1923, was destined to be a great month in radio annals. David Lloyd George, the famous wartime Prime Minister of Great Britain, led the procession by a chain broadcast over WEAF, WCAP and WJAR. He was making a goodwill tour of the United States. Enterprising radio men found him a willing participant in a broadcast that was staged November 2, 1923. On the eve of Armistice Day, at 8:30 P.M., November 10th, the stricken chieftain of our own War Administration, Woodrow Wilson, broke his long silence to broadcast a ten-minute message to his fellow countrymen—the last important act of his life. His topic, appropriately enough, was "The Significance of Armistice Day."

The annual Army-Navy football game was broadcast on November 24th with Graham McNamee at the microphone. Again the popular announcer acquitted himself with distinction and radio broadcasting of sporting events reaped corresponding advantage.

The next important radio event was the ambitious attempt to exchange radio broadcasts with England on the night of November 25, 1923. The contest had originated with a suggestion of F. N. Doubleday, President of Doubleday, Page & Company, the publisher of *Radio Broadcast*. He had proposed a two-way telephone conversation—by radio—between the two great English-speaking countries. The idea found eager response on both sides of the Atlantic. No less than eight English broadcasting stations were to participate, while on this side of the ocean a large number of stations made ready for the tests. The week of November 25th was to be devoted to the great trans-Atlantic experiment.

Owen D. Young was chosen as the first American speaker. His speech was broadcast through Station WGY at 10 P.M. Sunday, November 25th. Other American speakers during the week were Secretary of State Charles Evans Hughes through WDAR; Governor Hyde of Missouri through KSD; Dr. Frank Conrad at KDKA; Henry Ford at WWI; Major General James G. Harbord, President of RCA, spoke in the concluding program from WGY, while Burton J. Hendrick, Associate Editor of *World's Work* spoke from WOR. It is interesting to note that nearly every English listener who reported having heard American stations listed Station WGY. Other stations that were heard in England were WOR, WHAZ, WMAF, KDKA, WNAV, WOO, WDAF, WJZ, WSY, WJAZ, WBAH, KSD, WFAA and WCAE.

On December 4, 1923, President Calvin Coolidge delivered his first message to the Congress. For the first time the people of the nation had an opportunity to take the measure of the remarkable man whom fate had so suddenly and unexpectedly elevated to the Presidency. His clear, incisive New England accent and the shrewd wisdom of his message created a profound impression upon the radio audience. Here was a man who for two and a half years had been hidden under the bushel of the Vice-Presidency suddenly emerging from obscurity and stepping into the national spotlight, with characteristic modesty, it is true, but as a master of the situation nevertheless. Calvin Coolidge had never been understood by official Washington. He had accepted a position that called for reticence and self-effacement, and his record as Vice-President had been unblemished in these particulars. It was refreshing to his countrymen and reassuring to the national tradition that he could now so suddenly become in fact as in name the Chief Magistrate of the United States.

It is probably true that radio played an exceedingly important part in the career of Calvin Coolidge. In six months the national election would be in its preliminary stages. In that brief time President Coolidge was so to impress himself upon the voters that no serious opposition to his re-election was to manifest itself. His first message, December 4, 1923, was, therefore, an event of great national significance. It is interesting to note that the following stations participated in a chain broadcast: WCAP, Washington; WEAF, New York; WJAR, Providence, R. I.; KSD, St. Louis, Mo.; WDAF, Kansas City, Mo.; WFAA, Dallas, Tex.

Millions of radio listeners tuned in on this historic broadcast. A whimsical sidelight on the affair was that radio listeners a thousand miles from Washington gleefully reported that the broadcast was so perfect that they could hear President Coolidge turn the pages of his manuscript. Radio stations and radio audiences were alike enthusiastic over the new President. Within six days Calvin Coolidge was induced to broadcast a second time—to broadcast his views on national issues. This broadcast originated in the White House at 8:30 P.M., December 10, 1923. The participating stations were WCAP, WEAF and WJAR.

Radio periodicals of December, 1923, reported hopefully upon the progress being made by radio engineers in short-wave broadcasting. "The work of Franklin and Marconi in England, and of the Westinghouse Company and the Bureau of Standards in this country," declared *Radio Broadcast,* "proves beyond doubt the feasibility of employing a range of frequencies at present used by no one. . . . This unused high-frequency band will permit the non-interfering operation of 150 channels. *This is six times as many channels as are today available for all our broadcasting,* if we allow the same separation of channels. Just think of it, these 150 channels would be so far apart that the beat-note between the two stations closest together in the series would be inaudible." [1]

The terms wave length, frequency, meters and kilocycles are more or less confusing to the uninitiated, yet the explanation is comparatively simple. If we realize that radio impulses, like those of sound, travel in waves spreading out in all directions, we have a basis of

[1] *Radio Broadcast,* December 1922, pp. 103-104.

understanding. Waves are long or short according to the nature of the sending apparatus, but all waves have a crest and a trough. The length of a wave may be determined by measuring from crest to crest. In passing through these motions from the time the wave leaves its norm until it has accomplished its crest and trough and has reached norm again for the next gyration, we may describe it as having completed its cycle. Then, since the electrical impulse, whether by short wave or long, travels at the speed of light—completely encircling the earth in one-eighth of a second—we may understand that the number of cycles per second will depend upon the length of the waves. Since the velocity of light is 300,000,000 meters a second it follows that if the wave length is three meters the frequency would be 100,000 kilocycles, since in radio parlance one thousand cycles is equal to a kilocycle. Short waves range from one meter to one hundred and fifty meters whereas long waves range between six hundred and twenty thousand meters in length. Thus we may readily see that the longest of these waves would have a frequency equal to 300,000,000 divided by 20,000, or 15 kilocycles, whereas the shortest in the long wave band would have a frequency of 500 kilocycles.

Sec. 169. Federal Trade Commission Reports on the Alleged RCA Monopoly.

On December 1, 1923, the long-expected report of the Federal Trade Commission was issued—347 pages long. This report contained the results of the investigation made by the Commission in response to a resolution passed by the fourth session of the Sixty-seventh Congress. No trust-busting crusade could have been more fully supplied with ammunition than was available to the National Congress when this monumental report came from the Government Printing Office. It was indeed a scholarly document—an invaluable compilation of historical material. Not only did it contain a detailed exposition of the historical background of the formation of the Radio Corporation of America ninety-four pages in extent, but in a lengthy appendix it offered documentary evidence of the original agreements and the later cross-licensing agreements between the General Electric Company and the other industrial giants who acted as godfathers for RCA. The whole story was there. No one could deny that the new corporation was in effect a monopoly of the most extreme type, yet in and out of Congress were those who contended that from the nature of things a monopoly was absolutely essential.

The report with admirable impartiality admitted that RCA was the direct result of an appeal to the General Electric Company by representatives of the Navy Department to form an all-American corporation to take over commercial wireless transmission of the nation. All this had occurred, however, during the Wilson Administration. A new party was now in power, a party not ordinarily hostile to big business. The exigencies of politics, with a national election in the offing, rendered the plight of RCA decidedly uncomfortable. Although the Trade Commission report studiously avoided conclusions as to the guilt of the accused, nevertheless the facts themselves were prima facie evidence of guilt. An occasional summing up of the evidence on a particular point was quite devastating, as witness the following excerpts:

"As shown above the Radio Corporation has acquired all the high-power stations in this country with the exception of those owned by the Government (Note: This refers to wireless telegraph stations in distinction from radio broadcasting stations—G.L.A.) and it has practically no competition in the radio communication field." [3]

"There is no question that the pooling of all the patents pertaining to vacuum tubes has resulted in giving the Radio Corporation and its affiliated companies a monopoly in the manufacture, sale, and use thereof. With such a monopoly, the Radio Corporation apparently has the power to stifle competition in the manufacture and sale of receiving sets, and prevent all radio apparatus from being used for commercial radio communication purposes." [4]

Enemies of RCA were naturally jubilant over this report of the Federal Trade Commission. To have the latter's most intimate agreements and trade secrets published to the world was indeed a matter of rejoicing both to politicians and rival manufacturers. Even *Radio Broadcast* indulged in verbal broadsides at the alleged iniquitous trust, from which we quote:

"This report is so thorough in its gathering of important facts not generally known in the radio field that it should have the widest publicity. Many items in the daily press, having to do with patent suits, trade agreements, shortage of tubes, etc., can be better understood in the light of this official report of present conditions in the industry. The Federal Trade Commission has no power to determine whether or not a monopoly exists in radio. It could merely collect the facts of the situation. . . . Practically no messages originating in foreign countries can be received in America except through the Radio Corporation. An interesting outcome of this situation in international radio was the decision of several of the more important daily newspapers and press services to be rid of this control. They decided to build a radio station of their own (Note: wireless, of course). But they couldn't

[3] Federal Trade Commission on Radio Industry, p. 52.
[4] *Radio Industry*, p. 69.

"ROXY"
Samuel J. Rothafel, one of the great pioneers in radio entertainment.

JOHN McCORMACK
The great Irish tenor who had "mike fright."

MISS VAUGHN DE LEATH
One of the first singers to attain popularity on the air—and still a favorite.

LUCREZIA BORI
Appeared with McCormack in early radio triumph of grand opera stars.

do it in the United States—so they went to Canada and erected their station in Nova Scotia. This station is now being operated independently of the Radio Corporation of America, by virtue of an agreement with the British Post Office.

"Here are some authoritative figures which show the tremendous growth of the radio industry. In 1921 the Radio Corporation furnished on order 112,500 tubes; in 1922, 1,583,021; and in 1923, at the rate given in the report, the sale of tubes will reach 4,000,000. This means that the radio public has invested about $24,000,000 in tubes alone, in a single year. We do not question these figures. But—isn't it time that more of the 'development cost' of the tube was charged off and the price adjusted more in accordance with the actual manufacturing cost?" [5]

The annual report of the Directors of RCA for the calendar year 1923 shows the sturdy independence of the Corporation in meeting this formidable attack. Convinced of the soundness of their position, they could write the following optimistic comment on the report of the Trade Commission:

"Though not pertinent to the report of operations for 1923, it will not have escaped your notice that the corporation has recently been made the object of a complaint by the Federal Trade Commission. The position of the corporation, with regard to this, has been that it welcomes the opportunity to make a complete review of its history, organization and policies to that body. As a matter of fact we have, during 1923, already opened our records, correspondence, files, minutes of the meetings of our Board of Directors, together with all our contracts and agreements to the representatives of the Federal Trade Commission. The Commission has reported the result of that survey to Congress in a report which is in main respects highly complimentary to the Radio Corporation. Your Directors are confident that when the investigation is fully completed and finally considered, the position of the Radio Corporation will be found to be entirely sound and proper."

Having had a liberal dose of undesired publicity in the Federal Trade Commission Report, it is no wonder that the corporations involved were reluctant to carry into the courts their own rivalries and dissensions. A bitter feud had already developed between the American Telephone Company on the one hand and the manufacturing group and RCA on the other over the interpretation of the famous cross-licensing agreement of July 1, 1920. Even before the Federal Trade Commission made its sensational report the parties were ready to take drastic action but to avoid publicity if possible. Obviously the

only type of legal action that could be safely taken under the circumstances was to resort to arbitration. On December 28, 1923, an arbitration agreement was drawn up between the warring factions. The
Telephone group comprised the American Tel. & Tel. Company and
the Western Electric Company, whereas the Radio Corporation group
included RCA, General Electric Company, the Westinghouse Company, the United Fruit Company, the Tropical Radio Telegraph
Company and the Wireless Specialty Apparatus Company. Roland W.
Boyden, a Boston lawyer, was chosen as referee of the dispute, which
was destined to be a prolonged and bitter contest.

In 1923 the Radio Corporation of America decided to undertake the
establishment of wireless communications with the Far East. It so happened that the Federal Telegraph Company of California had a more
or less moribund concession from the Chinese Government for the
erection of wireless stations in China. RCA concluded successful negotiations with the California company whereby the concession was to be
turned over to a new corporation for energetic development. In pursuance of this agreement the Federal Telegraph Company of Delaware
was formed. R. P. Schwerin, formerly President of the Pacific Mail, was
elected president of the Delaware corporation. John W. Elwood, who
had served the Radio Corporation as Secretary, became Vice-President
of the new corporation, January 1, 1924. The headquarters of the
Federal Telegraph Company of Delaware was presently established
in San Francisco.

The new corporation at once found itself in a sea of difficulties.
The Chinese authorities were notoriously dilatory in carrying out
their agreements. The fact that British, Dutch and Japanese interests
were endeavoring to checkmate American domination of communications in the Orient added to the problem. Years of difficulty and dis-
couragement were to cast a blight on this particular endeavor of RCA
to establish world-wide communications.

Sec. 170. Experiments in Financing Radio Stations.

One of the most extraordinary developments of radio in the winter
of 1924 was the formation of a committee of New York business men
to solicit funds from the radio audience for the hiring of high-class
radio talent. That men of affairs could have indulged in such a flight
of fancy is little short of amazing. The nation was full of broadcasting
stations yet this committee proposed to solicit funds to be applied to
high-class programs for WEAF. This station was to donate broadcasting time and all funds subscribed were to be applied to the
hiring of first class talent. The choice of WEAF was natural enough,
since its technical facilities were of high order and it was generally
recognized as a leader in program building. The fact, however, that

the average radio listener tunes in on various stations from hour to hour caused a divided allegiance that militated against the success of the plan of financial support for any one station. Why pay for that which was being offered free of charge? Then, too, a suspicion that such donations might indirectly benefit stockholders of A. T. & T. no doubt had its bearing upon the final issue. Appeals were made over WEAF and some donations came in. The results, however, were so very disappointing that all subscriptions are said to have been returned to the donors.

Another curious event in the history of radio has to do with President Calvin Coolidge and his speech on Washington's Birthday. The President was to speak in Washington. A radio station in Chicago desired to pick up the message by a leased wire, but the charge for the service was so great that the plan was abandoned. The Telephone Company is said to have demanded $2500, whereas the radio station had refused to pay more than $1000 for the service.

"Before condemning the Telephone Company for its apparently excessive charge for this service," writes *Radio Broadcast,* "it must be considered that the ordinary wire connection will not serve at all for such a purpose. Special lines and repeaters have to be taken out of regular service, have to be put through special tests and adjustments, all extraneous noises eliminated and a special staff of men, as well as spare lines, be kept in readiness in case the connection should fail. However large we may think the bid of $2500 for ten minutes' service may be, all of the related factors are not on the surface, and we feel that the Telephone Company is entitled to the benefit of any doubt there may be, when we consider the fine radio broadcast service they have given the public during the past year. Whatever may be the policy of their financial advisors, we do know the company makes a continual effort to improve broadcasting service. This has been a great benefit to the radio public—a public which so far has paid the Telephone Company nothing at all for the service." [6]

Short-wave experiments at KDKA had by this time aroused international co-operation of radio engineers. In September, 1923, the Metropolitan-Vickers Electrical Company of Manchester, England, came to an understanding with KDKA. The English station was to attempt to relay the Pittsburgh broadcasts to its British audience. KDKA was in fact testing out both long and short wave transmission. The Metropolitan-Vickers Company built a short wave station similar to that at KDKA. To the surprise of all concerned the 100-meter broadcasts crossed the Atlantic with greater clarity and power than the 326-meter wave length. Not only that but the short wave transmission enjoyed

[6] *Radio Broadcast,* May 1924, pp. 23-24.

greater freedom from static and did not have the tendency to fade out that was characteristic of the long wave broadcasts.

By January 1, 1924, KDKA's programs by short-wave were being rebroadcast to British listeners. During a single week the English station succeeded in relaying the Westinghouse program for an aggregate time of eighteen hours, whereas long wave signals were not capable of being rebroadcast more than two or three hours a week.

"Thus it may be claimed," *Radio Broadcast* declared, "that these experiments with the Westinghouse Company have increased the chances of American relaying probably about ten times." [7]

[7] *Radio Broadcast,* June 1924, p. 119.

CHAPTER
NINETEEN

The Struggle for Network Broadcasting

Section 171. The A. T. & T. Company Wins a Dubious Victory in Court.

AN INTERESTING DEVELOPMENT of the winter of 1924 was a test case brought by the American Telephone Company against Station WHN of Ridgewood, N. Y., for unlicensed radio broadcasting.

Threat-muttering had ceased to be a virtue when alleged outlaw stations could set up sponsored programs everywhere. The defiance of Station WHN had been particularly exasperating to the guardians of the rights of the stockholders of A. T. & T. They decided to take legal action. This suit was no sooner brought than cries of "monopoly control" began to be heard on all sides. So great became the clamor that Secretary of Commerce Herbert Hoover was at length drawn into the controversy. In a public expression of his views Mr. Hoover declared:

> "I can state emphatically that it would be most unfortunate for the people of this country to whom broadcasting has become an important incident of life if its control should come into the hands of any single corporation, individual or combination. It would be in principle the same as though the entire press of the country were so controlled. The effect would be identical whether this control arose under a patent monopoly or under any form of combination, and from the standpoint of the people's interest the question of whether or not the broadcasting is for profit is immaterial." [1]

Thus the A. T. & T. experienced something of the far-flung hostility that had assailed the Radio Corporation of America. Since the suit against WHN was a feeler to test the vexed question of whether the Telephone Company's patents entitled it to a right to license stations to operate there was cause enough for other stations to join the hue and cry. It mattered not to the public that the American Telephone Company was the legal owner of the patents covering broadcasting station equipment now being used even by the so-called outlaw stations. The fact that the Telephone Company was now granting licenses right and left to stations that applied for the privilege seemed to have no influence with the public mind. Here was an iniquitous trust jumping with hobnailed boots all over the little fellow—hence widespread clamor and ballyhoo.

Having started suit against WHN, however, the lawyers for the Telephone Company, supported by the directors of the company, pressed the case resolutely. They pointed out to the court that a fundamental issue of patent law was involved. Ever since the United States Government had first established the Patent Office it had been the law that the owner of a patent was entitled to legal protection against those who willfully infringe the aforesaid patent rights. Because A. T.

[1] *Radio Broadcast,* June 1924, p. 128.

& T. stood ready to license WHN on reasonable terms the lawyers contended that the court should order the offending station to comply with the law or cease broadcasting. Before the trial reached the stage where the judges would be called upon to render an official decision the lawyers for Station WHN, realizing no doubt that their case was hopeless despite the nation-wide clamor that they had stirred up, approached the lawyers of A. T. & T. with a suggestion of compromise.

Thus the test case was settled out of court. Protesting bitterly that the license agreement prohibited the licensee from using the station for revenue as WEAF was doing, Station WHN acknowledged the validity of the Telephone Company patents and signed the usual license agreement.[2]

The directors of A. T. & T. realized, however, that this vindication was no vindication at all so far as the public was concerned. The net result of the effort had been a distinct loss to the company. There could be no more victories of this kind. If a station could not thereafter be persuaded in private it would be unsafe to attempt to persuade it with all the world looking on. This no doubt accounts for the fact that so little was thereafter attempted in the courts against so-called outlaw stations.

Before leaving the topic it is only fair to the American Telephone Company to point out that its business ethics had been of very high order. When the great corporations got together in 1920 and "divided up the world" between them, radio broadcasting was unknown and virtually undreamed of. The A. T. & T. was allotted the field of station transmitting equipment, whereas the others either manufactured or sold (through RCA) radio receiving equipment. As the situation developed RCA, Westinghouse and General Electric were in position to sell all that they could produce. The Telephone Company on the other hand not only had a very limited field in which to work but with a self-restraint unusual among corporations it deliberately refused to sell transmitting equipment where the field was manifestly overcrowded or where the applicant evinced a desire to spread propaganda rather than to serve the public. It is true that this was a form of censorship that might be open to objection, but it nevertheless operated to reduce possible profits of the Telephone Company.

A comment by the editor of *Radio Broadcast* no doubt represented the milder type of journalistic opinion of the day:

"It is probably fortunate for the broadcast listener that this question is at present in the hands of the A. T. & T. Company. This gigantic corporation, with its hundreds of thousands of stockholders, is subject to all kinds of governmental inquiry because of its interstate character.

[2] *Radio Broadcast*, June 1924, p. 131.

And if there is anything this corporation does not want to start it is a popular demand for government ownership of the American Telephone system. . . . But the fact that WHN, by signing the agreement with the A. T. & T. Company, is not allowed to do any advertising for money, cannot well be classed as an oppressive measure, as the manager of WHN seems to regard it. We think that the interests of the radio public are being conserved when such stations are prohibited from broadcasting for direct monetary profit. Direct advertising by radio is highly questionable even when tried by so excellent a station as WEAF." [3]

Sec. 172. Station WEAF Gathers a Radio Network.

Station WJZ was the focal point in one of the greatest radio experiments ever attempted up to that time—a trans-Atlantic and transcontinental broadcast on March 7, 1924. The occasion was a banquet held in the ballroom of the Waldorf-Astoria in New York City by the Alumni of the Massachusetts Institute of Technology. The program was broadcast by WJZ with tap-off wires from the amplifier panel in the control room and carried by special lines to WGY. The program was there rebroadcast both by long and short wave transmission—short wave having trans-Atlantic coverage. KDKA picked up the program by short wave and relayed it to Station KFKX in Hastings, Nebraska. The latter station relayed the program to Station KGO in Oakland, California. Listeners in England and California were thus enabled to hear the program at virtually the same instant of time, so amazing was the speed of radio transmission.[4]

Opposition to advertising by radio was still deep-seated, even among those who occupied high positions in the industry. Station WJZ, now owned and operated by the Radio Corporation of America, was WEAF's chief rival for leadership among radio stations. David Sarnoff, then Vice-President and General Manager of RCA, in an address delivered in Chicago, stated the creed of the owners of WJZ. He believed that the multiplicity of radio stations was an unhealthy condition that would soon cure itself through lack of financial support. Broadcasting in the future, he predicted, would be carried on by a few super-stations supported by the industry itself "from returns on sales of radio apparatus." He then declared: "A fair method of determining the amount to be paid by each member, or portion of the industry, will be worked out and this will be based on a percentage of the sale price of the radio devices."

In reporting Mr. Sarnoff's speech the editor of *Radio Broadcast* added the following comment:

[3] *Radio Broadcast*, June 1924, p. 132.
[4] *World Wide Wireless*, April 1924, pp. 15, 16.

"Naturally, to the business man, this seems the logical solution. It is probably the simplest solution of the problem and possibly it will be the final one. A reasonable percentage on the sales profits in tubes, batteries, accessories, etc., will maintain a good many stations, even after the sale of new sets begins to fall off, and this falling off, by the way, is still a long way in the future." [5]

Mention has been made of the committee of New York business men who had attempted to solve the problem of program expense by appealing to the radio audience for contributions. The experiment had now been tried but with such disappointing results that subscriptions were returned to the few generous souls who had responded. A station in Kansas City, WHB, had tried the same experiment and had received slightly over $3,000—a gesture of appreciation or, in modern parlance, a token payment!

Samuel L. Rothafel, popularly known as "Roxy," was already making radio history. By the Spring of 1924 "Roxy and His Gang" had become so well known to radio audiences that a network of three stations—WEAF, WCAP and WJAR—broadcast his concert every Sunday night.

President Calvin Coolidge continued to be featured on the air. On February 12, 1924, he made a Lincoln's Day address that was regarded as the opening gun in his campaign for nomination as standard bearer of the Republican Party. WEAF and WJZ broadcast the program direct from the Grand Ballroom of the Waldorf-Astoria Hotel in New York City, where the banquet of the Republican National Club was held. Washington's Birthday likewise was the occasion for a Presidential broadcast, direct from the White House. On April 14th a Coolidge speech to the Daughters of the American Revolution was broadcast. On April 22nd he appeared at a convention of the Associated Press and his speech went out to the nation by radio. On May 10th an address on "Better Homes" by President Coolidge was broadcast from Washington. His Memorial Day speech, May 30, 1924, was broadcast over a network composed of Stations WEAF, WCAP and WJAR. These exercises were held at the Amphitheater at Arlington Memorial Cemetery.

Since 1924 was a year of the national election, radio naturally reflected the nation-wide interest in all phases of the expected contest. President Coolidge, by virtue of his position at the head of the Government as well as by reason of the sane and sensible manner in which he had conducted the office since Mr. Harding's death, was naturally far in the lead of possible contenders. The only threat to his nomination seemed to be in the known hostility of Senator Robert M. LaFol-

[5] *Radio Broadcast*, July 1924, p. 221.

lette. The Democratic Party, on the other hand, was sure to have an exciting time in choosing its standard bearer. William G. McAdoo, son-in-law of the late President Wilson and one of the outstanding members of the Wilson Cabinet, had a strong lead in a large field of candidates among whom were Governor Alfred E. Smith of New York and Senator Oscar Underwood of Alabama.

No extensive radio network existed at this time, although the A. T. & T. Company was rapidly clearing the way for such a development in broadcasting. On May 16, 1924, the Telephone Company in a press release declared with evident satisfaction that forty radio stations that had formerly been operating in disregard of the company's patent rights had recently applied for and had received licenses to operate. Although there was still more or less controversy over the allegation that licensees were being obliged to agree not to operate for profit, *Radio Broadcast* was informed by the Telephone Company that it had erred in giving credence to the report. In the August, 1924, number of the magazine the editor makes the following retraction:

"In the article in question it was stated that licensed stations were not allowed to broadcast for profit, one of the outlaw stations so claiming. It appears that this was in error, as the present form of licenses, some of which were sent to us, contain no such agreement."

Another uncertainty was cleared up by the letter from the company —uncertainty as to size of license fees. It had been alleged by critics of the Telephone Company that these fees were excessive and by company officials that they were so modest as to be negligible.

"The license fees," continues the editorial already quoted, "are from $500 to $3,000, depending upon the size of the station. They are paid but once. The fee may be paid in installments if so desired by the licensee. The license form seems reasonable enough . . . certainly no more than adequate to cover the various costly developments which the Telephone Company puts at the disposal of the licensee when he is operating one of their equipments."

President Coolidge's last appearance before the microphone prior to the assembling of the Republican National Convention was on June 6th at 9:30 P.M., when he and Chief Justice William H. Taft were the speakers at the annual congress of the Daughters of the American Revolution.

Preparations were now going forward for the opening of the Republican Convention in Cleveland, scheduled for June 10, 1924. A prepared statement now in the files of the National Broadcasting Company discloses the fact that the Telephone Company had connected its two operating stations, WEAF and WCAP, by special wires with twelve widely scattered cities, thus making available to radio stations in those cities the entire proceedings of the Cleveland Convention as well as the details of the Democratic Convention to open two weeks later.

"This will be the first occasion," the statement reads, "that a program will be supplied continuously to twelve cities, enabling stations at these points to broadcast such features of the Convention as they desire to make available to their respective radio audiences. . . . Microphones are being installed on the speakers' platform (Cleveland) with wires terminating in a control room on the rear of the platform. . . . An announcer will be in constant attendance with concise and vivid descriptions of the events taking place in the Convention Hall and explanations of the significance of what is going on. The announcer will introduce the various speakers so that the entire matter will be an interesting broadcasting program."

It was generally understood that WEAF's ace announcer, Graham McNamee, would cover both conventions, a prospect that brought satisfaction to hundreds of thousands of radio listeners who now found delight in McNamee's colorful performances at the microphone.

Sec. 173. Radio and the Political Conventions of 1924.

Station WJZ, however much it might have desired to imitate its great rival, was not in a position to form a real network of stations, since that was the exclusive province of the Long Lines Department of the A. T. & T. Company. Major J. Andrew White, WJZ's star announcer of robust events, was nevertheless able to represent two stations at the conventions, WJZ and WGY. This was a mere bagatelle, however, to the impressive list that were to broadcast the words of his young rival, Graham McNamee. Nineteen stations had signed up for the series. It was perhaps fortunate for McNamee that he was to have the experience of reporting the Republican Convention before attempting the tremendously stormy and protracted Democratic Convention in Madison Square Garden.

The Republican hosts gathered at Cleveland on June 10, 1924, for a three-day session. The Coolidge band-wagon had rolled across the nation with such effect that there was no real contest for the Presidency. Everybody expected that Calvin Coolidge would be the choice of the Convention. Never before, however, had the American people been privileged virtually to look in upon all the phases of a National Convention. Such was now their opportunity. With Graham McNamee and Major J. Andrew White on the sidelines to report in vivid and picturesque language the scene before them, announcing the speakers and permitting the audience to hear the impassioned oratory of the convention, it was a thrilling experience. Millions of radio listeners sat before their loud speakers or listened with earphones—

thrilled or enraged, depending upon their political faith, by what they heard.

The LaFollette delegation, small but militant, fought to inject certain liberal planks into the party platform. Failing in this, the way was of course clear for the LaFollette bolt and the attempt to set up a third party. Thus the radio audience had abundant human interest developments to keep them tuned-in until the nomination speeches were over and Calvin Coolidge had won, by the almost unanimous vote of the delegates, his expected nomination as standard bearer of the Republican Party. Three strenuous days of broadcasting brought the first great political convention to the radio audience.

The Democratic Convention with 1446 delegates assembled in Madison Square Garden, New York City, on June 24th for the most protracted session in the history of conventions. That it was to be a battle royal was anticipated by every delegate, yet when the nominating speeches were reached partisanship for candidates had developed such bitterness that even the delegates were appalled at the prospect. On the first ballot McAdoo received 431½ votes; Al Smith 241; Underwood 42½, with numerous other favorite sons trailing along, each with a small sector of votes. It is noteworthy that John W. Davis polled but 31 votes in the initial balloting. Ballot after ballot was taken. Day after day passed. One of the most spectacular features of the Convention was the clarion voice of the spokesman for Oscar Underwood's home State—"Alabama, twenty-four votes for Underwood." The repetition of this slogan in the ears of the radio audience day after day focused the attention of the nation, as no other one feature of the Convention could do, upon the significance of the contest being waged in Madison Square Garden.

Here for the first time was observed a new trend in political oratory. Democratic spellbinders could not fail to note that thunderous oratory, effective when directed at the assembly in the Convention Hall, might prove very disagreeable to millions of radio listeners. A burst of impassioned eloquence might blast the microphone and be rendered almost unintelligible to the vast invisible audience. A new technique was needed. *The Saturday Evening Post* of August 23, 1924, summed up the situation admirably in an editorial entitled "The Spellbinder and the Radio." It read in part as follows:

"The Democratic Convention was held in New York, but all America attended it. . . . It (radio) gives events of national importance a national audience. Incidentally, also it uncovered another benefit radio seems destined to bestow upon us, the debunking of present-day oratory and the setting up of higher standards in public speaking. . . . Orators up to the present have been getting by on purely adventitious aids. A good personality, a musical voice, a power of dramatic gesture have served to cover up baldness of thought and limping phraseology. . . . The radio is even more merciless than the printed report as a conveyor of oratory. . . . It is uncompromising and literal transmission. The listeners follow the speech with one sense only. There is nothing to distract their attention. They do not share in the excitement and movement of the meeting, nor does the personality of the speaker register with them. It is what he says and the words he uses in saying it that count with them. . . . Somehow the spread-eagle sort of thinking and all the familiar phrases and resources of the spellbinder sound very flat and stale over the air. Radio constitutes the severest test for speakers of the rough-and-ready, catch-as-catch-can school, and reputations are going to shrink badly now that the whole nation is listening in. Silver-tongued orators whose fame has been won before sympathetic audiences are going to scale down to their real stature when the verdict comes from radio audiences."

Fifteen days of oratory, of cheer-marathons, of marchings and countermarchings of delegates for this and that candidate, marked the sweltering contest that ended in the selection of a compromise candidate. William G. McAdoo reached his high point on the 69th ballot when he polled 530 votes. But he could not win, nor could Al Smith nor Oscar Underwood. John W. Davis was chosen on the 103d ballot!

Two national heroes had emerged from the grueling contest—U. S. Senator Thomas J. Walsh, the presiding officer of the convention, and Graham McNamee, the radio announcer whose picturesque descriptions of convention scenes and events went out over nineteen great radio broadcasting stations. Major J. Andrew White of WJZ also deserves honorable mention, but his radio audience was insignificant in comparison to the millions of radio listeners who were tuned to the McNamee broadcasts.

In the archives of the National Broadcasting Company is a typewritten statement by Graham McNamee that portrays in vivid manner his impressions at the close of the convention. The following is an extract:

"I wasn't overweight when I started announcing the convention and I lost eight valuable pounds in that little glass enclosed booth. . . . There was plenty of excitement and some of the things that happened will never be forgotten. One of them was that Smith demonstration featuring a four foot siren only three feet away which pumped several horsepower of noise into my ear. . . . 'Twenty-four votes for Oscar Underwood,' is still ringing in my ears. After hearing it more than a hundred times during those eventful fifteen days, I suppose I will be singing that in my sleep forever after. Another picture that remains indelibly stamped in my memory is that vast audience with attention focused on the thousands of delegates; their changing moods as they were roused to enthusiasm during the great demonstrations and their utter boredom as they took ballot after ballot without material change, and finally the relief that was shared no doubt by the radio audience when they finally did agree upon John W. Davis."

On July 4, 1924, the LaFollette Progressives met in a convention in Cleveland. The expected happened. Democrats and Republicans were denounced in words of burning eloquence. Senator LaFollette was nominated for President and Senator Burton K. Wheeler for Vice-President. The way was now clear for months of oratory from Maine to California. The conventions had served to confuse the country. Nobody knew how many Republican votes would go to LaFollette and nobody was rash enough to predict how the disappointed adherents of McAdoo, Smith and Underwood would react to John W. Davis, already publicly assailed as a corporation lawyer—attorney for Wall Street who had been chosen by delegates exhausted in body and soul and in a mood to choose anybody save the three real leaders of the party. LaFollette based his hopes of success in the relatively colorless personalities of Coolidge and Davis. The issue, he believed, was in the lap of the gods!

Sec. 174. Strife Among the Godfathers of RCA.

The summer of 1924 witnessed an interesting development in the relationship of the giant corporations that had collaborated in the setting up of the Radio Corporation of America. It is well known that each corporation in return for patent rights and privileges had received stock in RCA. This corporation, despite its great earnings, had not yet been able to pay dividends on its common stock and had paid but one dividend on the preferred stock.[6] It was now asserted that the A. T. & T. Company had disposed of its entire holdings of RCA stock,[7] which was construed to mean an intentional casting off of a distasteful alliance. Rumors of impending law suits between Westinghouse and A. T. & T., deForest Radio Telephone and Telegraph Company, and the General Electric Company over patent rights were given credence by *Radio Broadcast*. "The patent involved," writes the editor, "is one for 'an improvement in method and apparatus for pro-

[6] An interesting commentary on current trends was that although the Radio Corporation of America derived its chief sales profits from vacuum tubes, yet on August 5, 1924, it voluntarily reduced the price of Radiotrons to $4.00, making the second $1.00 reduction for the year. The price had been $6.00 but on January 11, 1924 it had been scaled down to $5.

[7] In the Federal Trade Commission investigation the Telephone Company asserted in its answer that on February 1, 1922 it began to sell its RCA common stock and by April 1, 1922 had disposed of the last of it; that on June 24, 1922 it began to sell its preferred stock, completing the sale by January 22, 1923.

ducing sustained electrical oscillations,' so evidently is one which may be seriously affected by the recent decision [8] of the oscillating triode in favor of deForest. If so more suits loom up in the foreground, for all of which the public pays." [9]

The fact that the Telephone Company had sold its radio stock was doubtless the outward manifestation of a growing conflict for supremacy in certain fields in which there were conflicting interests among the great corporations that had joined in creating RCA. Two basic ideas, aside from the need of an all-American communications corporation, had originally drawn General Electric, Westinghouse and the Telephone Company together into united action: first, the manifest necessity of a pooling of patents in order that each might be free to manufacture wireless and radio broadcasting appliances, and secondly, the need of a clearing house or sales agency for manufactured products. The Radio Corporation had been created to provide the sales agency and its birth and christening had been the occasion for the joining of hands of the great corporations in their famous cross-licensing agreements to which the newborn infant was admitted under the regency of the big three.

It had perhaps not occurred to the chieftains who had gathered around the cradle of RCA that the child, being a corporation and not subject to the laws of nature, might speedily develop adult characteristics. It might soon strain at the limitations placed upon it by the authors of its being. It might, for instance, desire to be more than a sales agency. It might chafe at its inability to manufacture radio appliances. It might aspire to complete freedom from the fetters in which it was born. That the youthful corporation, under the leadership of its ambitious General Manager, David Sarnoff, was urging its claims to greater fields of activity was an open secret. Every speech that Sarnoff made concerning super-power in radio broadcasting revealed a belief in the destiny of RCA. Later developments in the relation of RCA to its corporate godfathers indicate that internal friction in the council chamber must have developed even before A. T. & T. withdrew from stock ownership in Radio Corporation.

Sec. 175. Financial Support of Broadcasting.

The question of financial support of radio broadcasting was still a burning issue in the summer of 1924. The New York *Times* undertook to gather the opinions of leaders in radio broadcasting circles.

Herbert Hoover, Secretary of Commerce, who had courageously

[8] The suit referred to was the celebrated contest, seven years in the courts, between Armstrong and deForest over the so-called feed-back device and regenerative circuit. Armstrong took out the patent which was contested by deForest. Priority of invention was now awarded to deForest.

[9] *Radio Broadcast*, August 1924, p. 302.

dealt with the multifarious problems of radio since its birth, expressed opinion that broadcasting would continue to be supported by the industry but would eventually be organized into six or seven great national circuits. Each circuit would use simultaneously the finest talent available.

H. B. Thayer, President of the American Telephone & Telegraph Company that had solved its own problem by selling time over its broadcasting stations, was naturally reticent on this point. He expressed doubt as to the feasibility of a new plan then being agitated, of using specially modulated waves for which specially built sets, obtainable only from the broadcasting company, would be required. He believed that radio listeners would not take kindly to the idea, since the American people resented taxes, direct or indirect, for the support of radio programs.

David Sarnoff, Vice-President and General Manager of the Radio Corporation of America, now advocated outright endowment of radio broadcasting stations. He argued that because radio had reached the stage where it actually contributed much to the happiness of mankind it deserved endowment similar to that enjoyed by libraries, museums and educational institutions. Mr. Sarnoff believed that philanthropists would eventually come to the rescue of a hard-pressed industry.

Martin P. Rice, speaking for the General Electric Company, believed that broadcasting would eventually be supported by voluntary contributions or by licensing of individual radio sets.

Heywood Broun responded with language that demonstrated how thoroughly aroused the ponderous columnist was over the plight of the unpaid artist. His words are worthy of quotation—in part as follows:

"Until radio came along this sort of graft was beginning to diminish. Communities were beginning to realize that it was sheer nerve to ask anybody to speak, or read his poems, or tell a few funny stories without offering a fee, however small, in return. Then radio burst into the world and gall returned in its most noxious form. The broadcasters do not pay. Instead they offer the performer publicity. It is a highly depreciated currency. People who ought to know better yield to the lure."

The perennial topic of women announcers was still agitating the public mind. From the beginning of radio women had vied with men before the microphone both as artists and as announcers and commentators. The feeling was now quite general that however acceptable the female voice might be in song or dramatic parts, yet in ordinary talk the microphone-voice of women was much inferior to that of men. At the time it seemed somewhat of a mystery. Why a beautiful and pleasing speaking voice in ordinary conversation should lose its charm when projected over the air was a baffling phenomenon. Many listeners ascribed it to self-consciousness of the speaker and an attempt to put on a grand air which resulted in artificiality.

Dr. Alfred N. Goldsmith, eminent consulting engineer and one of the foremost radio pioneers, has recently explained to the author the conclusion that scientists have reached in this matter of voice distortion over the radio. Middle registers of voice vibration are found to go out over the air with perfect fidelity. This type of voice, as for example that of Graham McNamee, is ideally suited to radio broadcasting. A man with slow vocal vibrations—with a typical bass voice—is not at his best before the "mike." His voice is below the range of vibration suited to broadcasting. The woman's voice, on the other hand, is high-pitched and normally above this golden mean of true radio reproduction.

Sec. 176. Stations WEAF and WJZ Become Bitter Rivals.

A cause of friction developed in the summer of 1924 between the owners of WJZ and WEAF over the use of special wires to form a broadcasting network. WEAF was building up an impressive following by network connections with other stations, yet when WJZ sought to find an outlet for its own excellent programs in the same manner the American Telephone and Telegraph Company refused to grant the privilege or to supply the long lines essential to such a project. It is a known fact, however, that despite this prohibition WJZ actually effected a program union with WGY at the time of the National Conventions of 1924. Knowing that Dr. Alfred N. Goldsmith was one of the chief technicians of WJZ at the time, the author recently made inquiry of him as to how the feat was accomplished.

Dr. Goldsmith laughingly admitted that under his direction WJZ had stolen a march on its rival. Now that the truth may safely be told the facts are as follows: WJZ applied to the Western Union for a special line to Schenectady, N. Y., by which WGY and WJZ were hooked up for the convention broadcasts. This scheme worked so well that it was decided to do the like with Station WRC in Washington. Instead of approaching Western Union for a line to Washington, which would have given away the network project, WJZ applied to the Postal Telegraph Company for a line from Washington to a suburb of Philadelphia (Conshohocken) where a repeater station was established. From this point was a line to WJZ. Neither Postal Telegraph nor Western Union were at first aware that they were participating in a bold defiance of the powerful American Telephone Company's ban on network broadcasting by a competitor. Thus WJZ contrived to have WRC and WGY on a special network.

Since human nature is a constant factor in industrial relations it is easy to understand why a deep-seated animosity grew up between the employees of the rival stations. The staff at WEAF resented the alleged unfair tactics of the staff at WJZ. To permit advertising on the air was regarded as a violation of the rights of A. T. & T., but to permit it free of charge for time used was unfair competition—a striking below the belt, so to speak, for how could WEAF persuade merchants and others to pay for time and program cost when at WJZ they could get the same service at the mere cost of the program? The staff at WJZ, on the other hand, regarded the WEAF outfit as enemies to pure and undefiled radio journalism, which they themselves professed. The rival station was in their eyes a money-making organization, whereas their own station was a philanthropic, public service institution. Thus we may explain the growing up of the feud between these stations that was destined to persist even for years after they were combined under the common overlordship of the National Broadcasting Company.

Sec. 177. Presidential Campaigning by Radio.

The national election campaign of 1924 might have been more bitterly contested had not Calvin Coolidge been so clearly in the forefront of the race that rival candidates could not hope to win unless some unforeseen catastrophe should wreck the Republican bandwagon. Radio was already recognized as a potent political medium. It was now being freely used, although station managers were beginning to wail that somebody should pay the expenses of campaign broadcasts. The American Telephone & Telegraph Company was now in the process of creating a permanent network of stations. The wire installation between WEAF and WCAP was already permanent. WJAR, Providence, WGR, Buffalo, WCAE, Pittsburgh, and WGN, Chicago, were shortly to be connected by permanent wires with WEAF. A nation-wide service of the same nature was in contemplation. Since WEAF was already selling broadcast time and was now equipped for network sales on its temporary wire connections it was not troubled by the financial problem. It is probable, moreover, that the campaign was proving a stimulus to radio revenue. The A. T. and T. Company had expended large sums in developing facilities for network broadcasting. There seemed no logical reason why political parties, having campaign funds for other legitimate expenses, should not pay for radio time. Campaign managers were not slow to recognize this fact and to act accordingly. The very fact that time on the air was to be paid for out of the campaign chest had a salutary effect upon radio oratory. The political ranter, the mere word artist, had no place on the radio-speaking program. Men of brains, capable of presenting arguments clearly and effectively, were now at premium in campaign broadcasts. Thus the quality of campaign speeches that reached the voters by radio was of high order.

Those who have listened to the late President Coolidge in a radio address can readily understand why, entirely aside from his position as standard bearer of the party, he should have been given first place in the microphone battalions of the GOP in the summer of 1924. His speeches were few but they were impressive. There were no "fireside chats" nor direct appeals to the radio audience. Some great public meeting at which the President of the United States might appropriately appear as a guest speaker was the necessary background for a Coolidge broadcast. No such meeting could have been more timely than that which occurred in Washington on October 23, 1924, when the United States Chamber of Commerce was in convention. President Coolidge was the guest speaker on this occasion. A radio network of amazing proportions carried the Coolidge speech to the nation. The A. T. & T. Company had linked up twenty-two stations, coast to coast, on this historic occasion.

Because this was a landmark in radio history the stations participating in the broadcast deserve to be recorded in this connection. They were as follows:

Radio Stations Linked up for the Coolidge Speech at U. S. Chamber of Commerce at Washington—October 23, 1924.

Key Stations—WEAF		WCAP Washington	
WJAR	Providence	WMAF	So. Dartmouth
WEEI	Boston	WGR	Buffalo
WCAE	Pittsburgh	WDBH	Worcester
WGY	Schenectady	WSAI	Cincinnati
WGN	Chicago	WOC	Davenport
KSD	St. Louis	WDAF	Kansas City
WOAW	Omaha	KLZ	Denver
KLX	Oakland	KFOA	Seattle
KFI	Los Angeles	KHJ	Los Angeles
KPO	San Francisco	KGW	Portland, Ore.

The Coolidge radio voice had by this time won reluctant admiration even from such dyed-in-the-wool Democrats as Charles Michelson of the New York *World,* who wrote the following at about this time:

"Mr. Coolidge is no orator. There is a wire edge to his voice, due in some degree to the regular nasal twang of the thirty-third degree Yankee and in part to his meticulous enunciation of each syllable; but according to the professors of the new art, he has a perfect radio voice. The twang and shrillness disappear somewhere along the aerial, and he sounds through the ether with exact clearness as well as soft-

ness. Mr. Davis, on the contrary, has a voice which to the direct audi-
tor has that bell-like quality of resonance that doubles the quality of
his delightful rhetoric. Via radio, however, this muffles and fogs to
some extent. The radio was perfected just in time for Mr. Coolidge.
. . . Before an audience Davis glows, while the President always looks
unhappy whether he is or not. Under these circumstances, the radio
must be Mr. Coolidge's salvation. He doesn't look as if he had the
physique to stand the strain of an old-fashioned campaign—half a
dozen speeches a day and traveling every night for months—in the first
place, and in the second his hard, statistical, analytical method of
expression is scarcely calculated to counterbalance the unimpressive-
ness of his appearance. So the advent of radio must be listed as one
more item in the total of Coolidge luck or destiny or whatever it is
that seems to make things come right for him politically."

On election night the final radio chapter of the 1924 campaign was
written. Reports coming in from all parts of the nation were broadcast immediately to radio audiences everywhere—a contrast indeed to
the situation four years previously, when one lone broadcasting station
had flashed the news to a very limited group of listeners. Station
WEAF was now in position with its network of stations to entertain
a far-flung radio audience. The inimitable Will Rogers was at the
microphone with jokes and quips and homely philosophy to fill in
between election returns. All in all, it was a "radio election." The
Coolidge luck persisted. Davis of the Democratic hosts and LaFollette
of the Progressive party were overwhelmed at the polls. Coolidge and
Dawes were elected.

CHAPTER
TWENTY

Wave Lengths and Injunctions

Section 178. Renewed Agitation for Standard Wave Lengths.

SINCE THE ADVENT of radio broadcasting there had arisen bitter complaints, especially in the coastal regions, because of interference by wireless telegraphy. The spark devices used on shipboard were sending out signals within the broadcast range of radio sets. Dot and dash signals, powerful and persistent, were sure to come bursting into the most interesting of radio programs. Listeners raged at these unseemly interruptions. Even as far inland as Chicago, Atlantic shipping was causing untold annoyance. It was, of course, generally admitted that wireless communication between ships and the shore stations was absolutely necessary, yet there were those who claimed that spark transmitters were out of date and should be replaced by tube transmitters. The general manager of the Independent Wireless Telegraph Company, which then controlled the offending ships, disclaimed responsibility for the situation on the ground that the wave length assignment was too close to the broadcast channels being used by radio broadcasting stations. In response to the suggestion that spark transmitters be discarded in favor of tubes, he endeavored to shoulder blame upon the Radio Corporation of America.

"You ask," he wrote in response to the attack, "that the company change the apparatus at present employed to tube transmitters, but this is not possible owing to the prohibitive price asked for these transmitters." [1]

This development focused the attention of the radio industry upon the necessity of reassigning wave lengths in order that marine wireless communications might not interfere with radio broadcasting. This would, of course, require international action. The international wireless convention of 1912 at which the existing regulations had been adopted had not anticipated the radiophone or radio broadcasting. A new international convention was accordingly advocated.

The progress that had been made in radio science was strikingly illustrated by a report issued by the Bureau of Standards at this time. The report dealt with standard wave lengths and the records of the various radio broadcasting stations of the nation in adherence to assigned frequency. The Westinghouse engineers had won first honors in this respect. In fact, Westinghouse Station WBZ in Springfield, Mass., stood proudly at the head of the list. With an assigned frequency of 890 kilocycles this station during the period of the tests, since May 1924, had not deviated by even a fraction of a percent from 890 kilocycles. The station was, therefore, cited by the Bureau of Standards as a model for all other radio broadcasting stations.

The officials of the Radio Corporation of America were accused

[1] *Radio Broadcast,* November 1924, p. 33.

during the political campaign of having censored radio addresses of political orators. This led to a newspaper discussion of alleged censorship in radio broadcasting, an allegation which General Harbord, President of RCA, promptly denied.

"It is not at all the policy of RCA," he wrote, "to censor the political speeches of the accredited political representatives in the coming elections. . . . When we have asked for an advance copy of a scheduled broadcast speech it has been when the subject was of a commercial nature, or other than political, and with one of the ends in view, either when it was desired to give advance publicity to the speech or when it was desirable to make certain that the speech was of a nature at once acceptable to the listening public." [2]

That this rejoinder did not settle the vexed question of censorship is obvious. In various forms it has reappeared ever since. The public of today realizes more fully than it did in 1924 that radio stations have certain responsibilities, moral as well as legal, to exercise some control over what shall be permitted to go forth from their microphones. Just as newspapers are obliged to exercise discretion in what shall be printed in their columns, being held legally responsible for unlawful defamation, so radio stations, to a lesser degree perhaps, are chargeable with responsibility in the matter.

By this time radio sets were to be found in nearly every home in the land. In keeping with the spirit of the times, which looks very tolerantly upon those incarcerated for crime, an agitation was begun in 1924 to permit radio sets in prison cells. The fact that the Pennsylvania State Penitentiary had permitted prisoners to have radios was hailed as a great humanitarian triumph—until it was discovered that one of the prisoners had been receiving code messages from one of his pals outside the prison as to narcotic drugs being smuggled into the prison. The scheme had been working for some time until the warden discovered the conspiracy.[3]

Modern apartment houses were now conforming to the radio fad. Builders were already incorporating radio reception as a part of the service to be rendered to tenants. In fact this provision had been virtually forced upon landlords by the tendency of the tenants to erect makeshift antennae on the premises. Virtual wars were being engendered over radio rights, over amplifiers, loud speakers and the like.

Sec. 179. Third Radio Conference—October, 1924.

The Third Radio Conference was held in Washington in October, 1924. Like its predecessors, it was largely attended by leaders of the radio industry, each of whom was deeply concerned with the great

[2] *Radio Broadcast*, November 1924, p. 36.
[3] *Ibid.*, p. 37.

unsolved problems of radio broadcasting. Secretary Hoover had already experienced opposition to his wave length decree. He realized all too well that if the matter should ever be tested in the courts the decree might be declared invalid. It was a selfish group of broadcasters who might put their own desires above the common good that caused chief concern to the more thoughtful members of the industry. These leaders feared a return of wave-jumping and general chaos such as had reigned prior to the Hoover action in assigning wave lengths.

One of the most significant events in the conference was an address by David Sarnoff, Vice-President and General Manager of the Radio Corporation of America, in which he advocated a chain of super-power radio stations.

The net result of the conference has thus been summarized by *Radio Broadcast* of December, 1924:

"The amateurs are to be given a new series of wave-bands, somewhat lower than those to which they are at present entitled. They are to be permitted to operate continuously, for it is believed that such operation will in no way interfere with other services. The amateur showed his willingness to co-operate by volunteering to abolish the use of the spark transmitters and discouraging the use of oscillating receivers within the broadcast range. The latter is particularly important because it means that interference from squealing receivers will not exist so far as the amateur is concerned on the short waves to be used for re-broadcasting.

"Ship transmitting waves are to be pushed up beyond the broadcast zone, and thus another form of severe interference has been greatly reduced. A general revision of the licenses for various types of broadcasting stations will, it is believed, result in a great improvement in broadcasting conditions."

In discussing Mr. Sarnoff's proposal of super-power broadcasting stations in several parts of the country the editor reported a violent division of opinion. Many favored the idea and many opposed it. A compromise was finally arrived at by which the Secretary of Commerce was advised to issue licenses for experimental use of super-power—revocable if it should be found by experience that such stations might interfere with existing service. By super-power was meant 50 k.w. No one then dreamed of the present-day 500 k.w. broadcasting stations.

Short-wave broadcasting was still making great forward strides. It now appeared that the Westinghouse people had something more than a scientific reason for developing this new art. By its means they hoped to be able to establish chain broadcasting despite the A. T. & T. ban on leased wires. If a program could be broadcast by short wave and picked up for re-broadcasting at a distant station, this would solve the problem. Tests were being conducted with this object in view.

Station WGY of the General Electric Company was experimenting very successfully with short-wave broadcasting—exchanging messages with short-wave stations in England and other distant points, thus duplicating the record of pioneer KDKA.

Sec. 180. Opera Singers at Microphone.

The opening of a radio station had long ceased to be a novelty, but two stations opened in New York at about this time deserve mention. New York City itself opened a municipal broadcasting station, WNYC, in the fall of 1924. This action was severely criticized by *Radio Broadcast* on the ground that it was unfair to use the taxpayers' money to provide an agency for political propaganda for a mayor and his appointees.

"It may be used for propaganda of the most biased sort," declares the editor, "for unanswerable attacks on those servants of the public who happen to be of political faith different from that of the city's temporary ruler. . . . In New York the mayor uses the station whenever he will, speaking on any subject he cares to select. In case his policies are being attacked, he can at once prepare a brief (or pay someone else to prepare one that he may read) showing that he is 'supporting the interests of the people,' whereas all others represent the 'interests' and are seeking to rob 'the public.' If his opponents want to combat his perhaps unreliable statements, they may do so through the city's radio station but their remarks must be written, they must stick to their written notes and these must be sent to the mayor's office for censoring before the speech is delivered." [4]

The second station, WGBS, which opened October 26, 1924, was the property of Gimbel Brothers. Other department stores had opened radio stations but this station was opened by a store that had long advertised over the air, having been WEAF's chief customer in the early months of sponsored programs. Gimbel Brothers, as previously pointed out, originated the sponsored musical program in March, 1923. Evidently radio broadcasting had demonstrated great commercial value to the advertiser, since this firm had considered it important enough to build a station of its own.

December 31, 1924, marked the retirement of Edward J. Nally, the "grand old man" of wireless telegraphy, for on this date his resignation from active service with the Radio Corporation of America took effect. He had rounded out fifty years of activity in this great field, rising from the humble rank of messenger boy to the presidency of one of America's greatest corporations—RCA.

On January 1, 1925, a landmark in radio history was reached. Although a few of the great artists had already gone on the air, the atti-

[4] *Radio Broadcast*, Jan. 1925, p. 475.

tude of the stars of stage and concert hall had been one of aloofness toward radio. On this date, however, two of the outstanding singers of the day appeared before the microphone at Station WEAF—John McCormack and Lucrezia Bori of the Metropolitan Opera Company. John A. Holman, at that time station manager, tells an amusing story of the great Irish minstrel's nervousness before the microphone. He states that McCormack was so panicky that he insisted upon gripping Holman's hand all through the first period of his broadcast. Yet while the quartette was doing its turn McCormack rushed to the telephone and talked with his wife, who had been listening in. He returned all smiles and was thereafter as bold as a lion—his first songs having gone on the air gloriously.

Reference to the program sheets of Station WEAF discloses the details of this all-star program broadcast between 9 and 10 P.M. on New Year's evening, 1925. It was a "Victor Presentation" with the Victor Salon Orchestra under direction of Nathaniel Shilkret. McCormack's first song was "Out of the Dusk," followed by "Chanson Bohemienne." Miss Bori sang "La Paloma," "When Love Is Kind," and "Addio Del Passato," from "Traviata." Then came a duet by Miss Bori and Mr. McCormack, "Parigi o Cara" from "Traviata." After further orchestra numbers the program was concluded by John McCormack, singing "Marcheta" and "Mother Machree."

The famous Atwater Kent Radio Hour apparently originated on Thursday evening, January 22, 1925, over Station WEAF. We find a listing of "Atwater Kent" written in longhand at the end of the mimeographed program. On the following Thursday "The Atwater Kent Radio Artists" were on the regular program with an assignment of time from 9 to 10 P.M. By a coincidence on this same evening, 11 to 12 P.M., we find the first WEAF listing of "Ben Bernie and His Hotel Roosevelt Orchestra."

Sec. 181. The Coolidge Inaugural.

A very significant court decision involving radio was handed down by the U. S. District Court at Brooklyn, N. Y., on January 30, 1925. It was a libel suit in which *Radio Broadcast* was defendant. It seems that in the March, 1924, issue of the magazine an article had appeared in which a type of regenerative circuit was described as a "hodge-podge arrangement of coils and condensers and in no sense new." The manufacturer of the set was not only affronted by the criticism but because of it suffered damages. The jury decided that the criticism had been made honestly. The defendant was thereupon exonerated.

David Sarnoff's advocacy of establishing super-power radio broadcasting stations made at the Third Radio Conference continued to be agitated in radio circles for months thereafter. The fact of Mr. Sarnoff's relation to the powerful Radio Corporation of America, already feared and dreaded as a trust, literally caused the small radio station officials to quake at the thought of a super-station dominating the ether in which they were struggling to exist. It was admitted by all that a super-station with wide coverage could provide a better program than the small station could offer. This was no doubt one of the reasons for agitation—by those who feared comparison with their own humble radio offerings.

A new wave length allocation made by Secretary Hoover during the winter of 1925 failed to arouse enthusiasm. In fact even *Radio Broadcast* was inclined to question the necessity of some of the changes.

"Here are some examples of the new assignments," wrote the editor. "WEAF 491.5 meters, instead of 492; WGBS 315.6 meters, instead of 316; WJZ 405.2, instead of 405. The changes are so insignificant that just what is gained is not at all evident. Certainly no new channels have been created by such diminutive shifts from former wave lengths." Despite this criticism it is probable that Secretary Hoover had good reason for the changes, since to a man of his conservatism and engineering training, change for the mere sake of change would have been distasteful.

The inaugural of President Calvin Coolidge on March 4, 1925, was the occasion for the greatest radio triumph thus far recorded. Twenty-one stations from Boston to San Francisco operated under the banner of an A. T. & T. network. WJZ now had its three-station network in operation. WRC and WGY were joined with WJZ in the broadcast. It was estimated that fifteen million people listened directly to the voice of Calvin Coolidge on this occasion—a fact that staggered the imagination of thoughtful observers. Our far-flung democracy had at last found a means by which its duly elected Chief Executive could discuss great problems of the nation directly with all the people. It is true that this was a mere one-way discussion, since the voters must still register their opinions through their Congressmen and Senators, but the very fact that by the magic of radio the President himself could come into their homes and tell them of national problems could not fail to revivify personal interest of the common people in the affairs of government.

The success of the Coolidge inaugural from the standpoint of radio had the unexpected result of arousing discussion as to the desirability of broadcasting sessions of the National Congress. Even the editor of *Radio Broadcast* expressed himself in favor of the project, although he did not make it clear what would be done when both House and Senate were in session. His remarks were aimed at the Senate, as will be seen from the following:

"We hope that soon Congress will be forced to broadcast its activities. Verbose Senators may have their activities somewhat rationalized and sobered if they realize that secret chamber procedure is no longer available to them. Not very many of them would care to vote in the affirmative to increase their own salaries immediately after the President had outlined his economy program—that is, they wouldn't care to if they knew that a few million of their constituents were listening carefully to their words." [5]

Sec. 182. Wave Lengths and Injunctions.

Hotel Roosevelt, N. Y. C., was perhaps the first hotel to inaugurate "radio a la carte" for its guests. Actual radio sets were provided during the winter of 1925, each complete with portable receivers and self-contained loop antennae. The plan was to permit any guest in the hotel to have a radio in his room upon request. He would telephone to the service department for a radio set just as he might for a card table or ice water. Verily, radio was becoming a universal necessity in a changing world.

On Tuesday evening, March 31, 1925, a sustaining program of Grand Opera was inaugurated by Station WEAF. Five stations participated in the broadcast—WEAF, WWJ, WGR, WFI and WCAE. On the following Tuesday "Faust" was offered by the American Opera Ensemble with ten stations participating. So popular did the program become that by May 12, 1925, the ensemble had been officially named the "WEAF Grand Opera Company." It was under the direction of Cesare Sodero.

In the winter of 1925 an experiment in assigning wave lengths proved unsuccessful. Theretofore it had been the custom to assign wave channels 10 kilocycles apart, thereby providing 86 different channels. Secretary Hoover now attempted to reduce the kilocycles of separation to seven instead of ten, hoping thereby to increase the number of broadcast channels. This resulted in confusion and the attempt was abandoned. At that time there were 563 broadcasting stations in the United States—an uncomfortable multitude in view of the limited number of channels. Despite the fact that Secretary Hoover had already exceeded his legal authority by assigning wave lengths not provided for by existing law, he was roundly criticized in some quarters for not taking an even more arbitrary stand in the matter of granting or withholding broadcast licenses.

Hoover had been proceeding upon the democratic theory that all reputable applicants were equal before the law. He had issued licenses accordingly. A feeling was growing up, however, that the granting of

[5] *Radio Broadcast,* May 1925, p. 37.

licenses should hinge upon the public interest rather than on individual merit of the applicant.

"Many of our correspondents continually point out," wrote the editor of *Radio Broadcast,* "that the question Mr. Hoover has to ask himself is, do the listeners want this proposed station? If they don't want the station then the license should not be granted. We venture to suggest that a new applicant be obliged to accompany his request for a license by a petition signed by at least 100,000 people who live within, say 50 miles of the proposed station." This fantastic suggestion was evidently advanced in good faith. The editor perhaps did not reflect that until a station had demonstrated its qualities people of the locality could not be expected to join in a petition in its behalf. Such a scheme would have cut off the possibility of the licensing of new stations.

An extraordinary patent suit was reported by *Radio Broadcast* in May, 1925. It seems that years previously the deForest Company had given the Westinghouse Electric & Manufacturing Company a permit to manufacture deForest audion tubes. Not being equipped to manufacture delicate vacuum tubes the Westinghouse Company had turned the business over to a subsidiary—the Westinghouse Lamp Works. Tubes were being manufactured by the lamp works and delivered to the Radio Corporation of America for sale to the public. Just before the deForest patent expired his attorneys brought a bill in equity in the United States District Court in Wilmington, Delaware, asking for an injunction against RCA in connection with the sale of the tubes. To the surprise of everybody in the radio industry the court granted the injunction.[6] The court's reasoning is not reported but it must have been that while the parent company had a right to manufacture the tubes yet it could not delegate the right without permission of the deForest Company. It is interesting to note that during the year 1925 the Radio Corporation of America had made the following voluntary reductions in price of Radiotrons (vacuum tubes for radio sets): February 2 from $4 to $3; on August 1 from $3 to $2.50.

One of the most striking illustrations of the necessity of a Federal law for the regulation of broadcasting arose in Cincinnati during the winter of 1925. Two stations in that city were sharing the same wave length, owing to the shortage of available channels. After much squabbling over a proper division of broadcast hours they finally refused to co-operate further and each went on the air, thereby blasting and blanketing each other's programs. Repeated appeals to the Department of Commerce failed to move Secretary Hoover to interfere, for which he was taken to task by *Radio Broadcast.*

"One might well ask the Department how it did expect such dis-

6 *Radio Broadcast*—May 1925, p. 41.

putes to be settled," wrote the editor. "It is a strange idea of privilege and duty which consents to the issuance of broadcasting licenses to any who want them and then when trouble comes to the listening public as a result of the excessive number of stations, to turn one's back and let someone else settle the trouble—trouble directly due to the Department's freedom with its licenses. Who, we may well ask, does Mr. Hoover think will step in to straighten out such troubles between the various stations, if his Department thinks the task is too onerous?" [7]

Sec. 183. Marconi Reports on Beam Broadcasting.

Senatore Marconi had from time to time made announcements concerning the progress of his experiments in so-called "beam broadcasting." In the July, 1925, issue of Radio Broadcast appeared a feature article on the subject written by the great inventor himself. He described his own experiments in 1916 with short waves in combination with reflectors capable of directing the same in any direction. He traced the progress of his experiments to the previous year in which truly marvelous results with beam broadcasting were recorded.

"I tried the effect," he writes, "of still further decreasing the wave length, reducing it to 60, 47, and, finally, to 32 meters and I found that the opaqueness of space in the daytime diminished rapidly as the wave length decreased. During these tests, which were conducted in August and September of last year, the 92-meter wave could not be heard for many hours in Madeira—a distance of 1100 miles entirely over the sea. At Beyrouth, in the Mediterranean, the 32-meter waves were regularly received all day, although the distance was 2100 miles, practically all over mountainous land."

The forward march of science and man's triumphant conquest of distance are strikingly illustrated by this simple narrative from the pen of the man who in his youth had taken out the first patent involving wireless telegraphy. What tremendous strides had been made in less than three decades!

The spring of 1925 witnessed an interesting development, illustrative of the power of radio to endear radio performers to the unseen audience. On May 7th Godfrey Ludlow, violinist on the staff of WJZ, Keith McLeod, musical director and accompanist, together with Milton J. Cross, WJZ's famous announcer and singer, made a personal appearance at the Static Club. So great was the acclaim by the audience that the trio on May 16th gave a recital at Aeolian Hall for their radio friends. Hundreds were unable to gain entrance to the hall.[8]

A significant event occurred in the summer of 1925. "Roxy's Gang"

[7] Radio Broadcast, May 1925, p. 42.
[8] World Wide Wireless, June 1925, pp. 18, 19.

had made the name of the Capitol Theatre a household word in America, yet it was announced that "Roxy" was leaving Capitol Theatre to establish a theater of his own. "Roxy's" music had always won high praise from radio listeners, but his penchant for what the editor of *Radio Broadcast* labeled "drooling sentimentality" of presentation had caused friction not only with Station WEAF but also with the management of the theater.

"Mr. Rothafel deserves much credit," wrote the editor in commenting on the change, "for devising a genuinely new type of radio presentation, but why that presentation had to be constantly weighted with expressions of almost tearful sentiment and side remarks which somehow are invariably weightily saccharine—we could never understand." [9]

Major Bowes, the managing director of the theatre, was clearly faced with a serious dilemma when Roxy's departure became known. Capitol Theatre had long enjoyed radio pre-eminence. What would happen now that Roxy's Gang had moved elsewhere? It is probable that no one in radio circles, even including Major Bowes himself, had any idea at all that the managing director as "pinch-hitter" could ever duplicate Samuel L. Rothafel's popularity.[10] Major Bowes, the hard-headed executive with a somewhat harsh radio voice and a decidedly practical outlook upon life, was not at first considered what he shortly became —an outstanding radio personality. Major Bowes was on the program at WEAF as leader of the Capitol Gang for the first time July 19, 1925.

Sec. 184. Midsummer Events in 1925.

The Radio Corporation of America, in pursuance of David Sarnoff's plan of super-broadcasting, had for months been constructing in Bound Brook, N. J., one of the most powerful radio broadcasting stations ever erected. Its power was vastly superior to that employed at Station WJZ in New York City. The truth is that the Bound Brook transmitters were intended for Stations WJZ and WJY. Radio engi-

[9] *Radio Broadcast,* October 1925, p. 758.
[10] "Roxy" (Samuel L. Rothafel) was born July 9, 1882, in Stillwater, Minn. His parents moved to New York City when "Roxy" was twelve years old. In 1913 he became manager of Regent Theatre in New York City. In November 1922, he presented his first radio broadcast of the Capitol Theatre Gang, making an instant hit with the listening public. This program was continued each Sunday until July, 1925, when Roxy left Capitol to establish a theater of his own—"Roxy Theatre" on Seventh Ave. which was opened in March 1927. The theater did not prove a commercial success. When Radio City was built Roxy was selected by the Rockefeller interests to be the director of Radio City Music Hall—the largest theatre in the world with 6,200 seats. The theatre opened December 27, 1932, with a vast extravaganza of vaudeville which somehow did not "click" with the public. Roxy had a physical collapse and when he returned to his duties found that Music Hall had become a high class movie house. He attempted other theatrical ventures with indifferent success. His death from heart failure occurred in New York City, January 14, 1936.

neers were no longer laboring under the impression that studios and station needed to be in the same neighborhood. RCA had thus boldly ventured to separate studio and station by many miles. Since super-power could not well be used in congested New York City, the transmitter was located in the comparative isolation of Bound Brook, whereas the studios remained in Aeolian Hall. It was anticipated that so powerful a station would make it difficult for residents of Bound Brook to tune out WJZ in favor of any other station. RCA engineers, however, were already working on the problem in order that no unnecessary antagonism to their own station be developed in the neighborhood.

The expiration of the deForest three-electrode tube patent in February, 1925, had caused considerable confusion in the manufacturing field. Heretofore the owners of the patent could guarantee genuineness of their product and could label all three-electrode tubes manufactured by others not licensed under patent rights as "bootleg" tubes. Now that the invention was open to the public it was difficult indeed to distinguish between genuine and counterfeit. Added to this distressing condition was a dastardly custom of racketeering in used tubes that still possessed some life—selling them to the public as new. Discarded tubes carried off by the repairman or sent in good faith to the junk heap might reappear in cut-rate stores for sale to unsuspecting customers. Truly radio had its share of vandals preying upon the industry to the detriment alike of customers and honest manufacturers and dealers.

Still another disquieting development was revealed in July of this year—a development so flagrant that in reporting it the editor of *Radio Broadcast* headed the article "Crime of a Radio Manufacturer." The story is self-explanatory:

"Just as we had thought the single-circuit regenerative receiver was beginning to disappear from the market we learn from a most reliable source that an order for about one hundred thousand of these receivers is being put through the shops of one of the largest radio manufacturers. One hundred thousand more potential squealers from one manufacturer is a frightful stop to radio progress. This is no step forward in the march of radio. It looks as though this manufacturer was more interested in dividends than in the advancement of the art." [11]

In view of the feud that later developed between newspapers and radio broadcasters of news it is interesting to note that at the annual meeting of the Associated Press held in New York City in early summer of 1925 radio was emphatically endorsed by the gathering. By a

[11] *Radio Broadcast*, July 1925, p. 335.

vote of 130 to 10 the Associated Press decided to permit its dispatches to be used over radio channels whenever such items could be considered of transcendent importance.

The American Newspaper Publishers Association also at its annual meeting, held at about the same time, passed a similar vote. It is noteworthy, however, that the action of the publishers was coupled with a reservation refusing publicity to advertising programs. Because of its historical value we reproduce the resolution:

"Whereas, direct advertising by radio is likely to destroy the entertainment and educational value of broadcasting and result in the loss of the good-will of the public, therefore be it

"Resolved, that members of the A.N.P.A. refuse to publish free publicity in their news columns concerning programs consisting of direct advertising; also that they eliminate from program announcements the name of trade-marked merchandise or known products obviously used for advertising, and that newspaper broadcasters eliminate all talks which are broadcast for direct advertising purpose."

Sec. 185. Income From Radio Advertising.

The alleged income of radio broadcasting stations has always been a prolific topic of conjecture for reporters and journalists. To the youthful Radio Artists Association the matter was, of course, of vital importance. If radio stations were actually making money Radio Artists were determined to share in this prosperity. How much of fact and how much of sheer imagination was involved in early reports of radio profits is difficult to determine. Take, for instance, the allegation made at the 1925 summer meeting of the Radio Artists Association, that Station WHN then had a net income of $250,000 from advertising over the air. The station manager protested that the amount of net profit was grossly exaggerated. Station WFBH was also alleged to have a gross income of $90,000 as against an annual expense of $35,000. The manager of the station denied the truth of the report, declaring that the station's income was barely sufficient to meet its expenses.

It was a fact, however, that stations in the Telephone Company network made substantial charges for broadcasting time. In the summer of 1925 the schedule of rates was as follows:

WEAF, New York	$500 per hour
WEEI, Boston	250 " "
WJAR, Providence	" " "
WCCO	" " "
WOO	200 " "
WFI	" " "
WCAE	" " "

WGR	$200 per hour
WSAI	" " "
WWJ	" " "
WCAP, Washington	150 " "
WEAR	" " "
WOC	" " "

For the facilities of all these stations in a network commercial broadcast the charge was $2600 an hour, instead of $2900 if each were used individually.

Despite all efforts of David Sarnoff and other potent executives who were endeavoring to safeguard radio against the alleged pernicious trend toward commercial sponsorship the movement gained ground. The public, it is true, hated commercial "plugs" on the air. To have beautiful music preceded by an advertising spiel for cigarettes, for example, interrupted by an advertising spiel of similar nature and closed by cigarette persuasion, was exceedingly distasteful. The public love of music and entertainment, however, was actually triumphing over its aversion to advertising on the air. Radio listeners were learning to endure the one for the sake of the other—the thorn with the rose, so to speak. Mr. Sarnoff's eloquent appeals to philanthropy to deliver radio from the fatal allurement of cash across the counter was obviously a futile gesture. That he continued to do battle for the idea is because David Sarnoff is an indomitable fighter for any cause to which he sets his face—and his iron jaw.

The Victor Talking Machine Company, after vainly struggling against the radio tide for years, decided in the spring of 1925 to conform rather than perish. The company already had some of the very necessary elements of a successful radio program—an impressive galaxy of top-notch vocal artists as well as the Victor Orchestra, equal to the best. It will be remembered that John McCormack and Lucrezia Bori had already appeared with the Victor Orchestra and quartette on a radio program. This, no doubt, marked the beginning of the transition to radio broadcasting as an allied art. It was rumored in July, 1925, that the Victor Company had acquired patent rights to a loud speaker developed and patented in France. This speaker was said to be greatly superior to any type yet devised in the United States. In August the Victor Company definitely announced an alliance with the radio industry but expressly disclaimed intention of manufacturing radio sets. Instead, an arrangement was concluded with the Radio Corporation of America to have super-heterodyne sets built to be combined with the well-known Victor phonograph. The loud speaker was indeed of French origin. It was announced also that Victor artists would continue to appear on radio programs.

Sec. 186. Litigation, Deficits, Radio Depression.

It has been observed in the progress of this narrative that Dr. Lee deForest was many times involved in litigation over patents or inventions. Some of his rivals apparently regarded him and his company as objects of suspicion who must be kept under surveillance. The fact that he had recently won a seven-year contest over the Armstrong feed-back patent in which RCA had invested huge sums no doubt added to the bitterness that had grown up between the Radio Corporation and the deForest Company.

Not the least of the causes for bitterness was a suspicion on the part of the officials of RCA that the deForest Company was infringing certain patents relating to the manufacture of high-vacuum tubes. These patents involved the use of thoriated tungsten in the filament, the tube itself being evacuated by mercury vacuum pumps, both ideas having originated in the General Electric laboratories. Since RCA had the exclusive right of sale of radio appliances produced for commercial distribution by the General Electric Company, it was deeply concerned over the possibility of deForest infringement. Circumstantial evidence of such infringement existed in that deForest was producing vacuum tubes that apparently possessed the same characteristics as the Langmuir-Coolidge tubes. In manufacturing the tube the patented process called for the heating of the filament to a temperature higher than would be attained by it in actual use. This super-heating caused the impregnated thorium to come to the surface of the filament, thus giving it a special coating that rendered the tube highly efficient. The new deForest tube had this special characteristic. It also possessed a high-vacuum quality that raised the suspicion that the Langmuir mercury vacuum pump was being used in the manufacturing process.

It should be apparent that there is a great difference between a patented article and a patented process. In the former case the true and the spurious stand clearly revealed. They may be analyzed and compared—the products furnishing their own proof of infringement. A patented process, however, may be infringed with impunity if done in secret. Testimony of eye witnesses is essential. It was all very well to suspect deForest of wrongdoing, but to obtain evidence of his alleged infringement was quite another matter.

Under these exasperating circumstances some over-zealous employees of RCA took steps that presently led to very unfortunate publicity for the Radio Corporation. They crossed no-man's land, as it were, into the forbidden territory of the deForest plant. Their presence was discovered. The deForest officials promptly raised the welkin at the outrage. They instituted injunction proceedings to restrain RCA from further activity of this nature. The deForest Company was always adept at publicity and here was a marvelous opportunity to utilize publicity in industrial warfare. Headlines in the public press at once proclaimed the iniquity of RCA. When the court found that the story was true and enjoined the Radio Corporation from further prying, universal condemnation descended upon RCA.

The unfortunate part of the affair was that the officials of the great corporation took condemnation in silence, whereas in the very decision of the court was a clause that indicated how strong a defense they might have put up had they been more publicity-minded. *Radio Broadcast* reports the decision in the following language: "In the preliminary hearing, the Radio Corporation was enjoined from further spying on deForest but was granted permission to use for patent infringement purposes whatever pertinent information its spy system had already brought forth." [12]

When the court "granted permission to use for patent infringement purposes" evidence uncovered in the incident, this was equivalent to a decision that deForest was guilty of deliberate infringement of basic patents upon which RCA's nation-wide sales organization depended for continued prosperity. The net result of the incident was that the Radio Corporation was greatly injured in reputation. After a lapse of thirteen years the matter might be passed over as an unfortunate solitary instance of erroneous tactics in corporate warfare, except that critics of RCA still drag this particular skeleton from the closet whenever opportunity offers.

The author holds no brief for RCA, but in simple justice has endeavored to portray the true facts of the 1925 controversy. Granted that it was wrong for employees of the Radio Corporation to invade the deForest factory, yet when they actually discovered the very wrongdoing of which they had previously been unable to obtain proof it would seem that RCA was entitled to a bit of sympathy instead of condemnation. To excuse the counterfeiter because evidence against him was acquired without his permission and to raise hue and cry against his accuser could scarcely be more unjust than in this instance of the RCA-deForest publicity.

The evils of radio advertising had long been deplored by the public at large and various remedies had been suggested. The most spectacular attempt to cure the evil was announced by a publicity-loving Congressman who announced in September, 1925, that he was about to introduce a bill into Congress to abolish all advertising by radio. It is interesting to note that *Radio Broadcast,* that had published many editorials severely denouncing radio advertising, now came to the defense of the custom.

"We hasten to point out to him," the editorial reads, "that it would

[12] *Radio Broadcast,* September 1925, p. 599.

be wise to proceed slowly. The public will never get something for nothing and so if they are to get a good musical program without paying a cent for the artists, it will probably be necessary to listen to the name of the donor of the hour's entertainment. This indirect advertising, if well done, is not at all disagreeable. If Mr. Bloom is successful, he will legislate away our best radio entertainments." [13]

An interesting development in the fall of 1925 was a court action brought by the Citizens' Union of New York against the officials of the city, claiming that the establishing and maintaining of the municipal radio Station WNYC was a misuse of the city's funds. The ground alleged was that there was no authority in law for the expenditure of the taxpayers' money "for the broadcasting of political propaganda on behalf of the defendant or any other person or persons." It was alleged that the station was being used to praise and glorify the mayor and to make violent attacks upon any or all who might dare to criticize the administration. The Supreme Court Justice before whom the case was tried denied the petition, stating that it was within the discretion of the legislative body of the city and state to confine the use of the station to the administrative work of city officials or to permit a wider use. The attempt accordingly failed.[14]

To the surprise of the critics of the Radio Corporation who delighted in picturing it as a grasping monopoly draining the pockets of the people and waxing rich in the process, RCA reported a whopping deficit for the second quarter of 1925. For the second quarter of the year it had gone nearly $400,000 in the red.

"During the first quarter of this year," writes *Radio Broadcast,* "the earnings of the company were $15,229,923, which, with expenses of $13,301,594 left a comfortable surplus for dividends. But the second quarter showed earnings somewhat less than $4,600,000 and the expenses were nearly $5,000,000, leaving a deficit for the quarter of $391,053. This report shows the highly seasonal character of the radio business and serves to emphasize the fact that a company must have a good deal of financial reserve, or else carry on at the same time some other business which fills in the slack periods of the radio season." [15]

It was soon apparent that a genuine depression had struck radio broadcasting—a depression that bore heavily upon the hand-to-mouth independent stations. The pioneering period in its more primitive stage had passed more than a year before. The survival-of-the-fittest stage was now at its most acute phase. In keeping with its character as the most important sales agency in the field of radio sets RCA had encountered heavy buffeting. The key man in the great organization,

[13] *Radio Broadcast,* October 1925, p. 738.
[14] *Ibid.,* p. 740.
[15] *Ibid.,* p. 741.

however, was its Vice-President and General Manager, David Sarnoff. Ten years previously, when to his associates in the Marconi Company the idea had seemed a mere fantasy, David Sarnoff had unfolded his "Radio Music Box" scheme. The years had vindicated his prophecy. The music box of radio had become a thing of joy and service in countless American homes. In this respect the Sarnoff dream was now a reality, yet it needed more than an attractive radio set to put radio broadcasting on its feet. No one saw this more clearly than the far-seeing and energetic David Sarnoff. Radio entertainment of high order must somehow be provided by the industry. The Radio Corporation of America, at the risk of accusations of monopoly, must step into the broadcasting field in real earnest and attempt with strong hands to bring order out of chaos.

The Radio Corporation was not given to horn-blowing in advance of performance, choosing rather to let results speak for themselves. Very little was publicly known of the decision of the Corporation to build a super-power station at Bound Brook, N. J., but the work was progressing favorably and it was expected that by late fall the station would be in operation. This would be an initial step in a Napoleonic plan that David Sarnoff was then carrying "under his hat," so to speak.

Sec. 187. Dangerous Advice of Fourth Radio Conference.

The Westinghouse Company, in keeping with its position as the chief pioneer of modern radio broadcasting, was bending every effort to perfect its hoped-for short-wave system of linking stations in a true radio chain. For months Station KDKA had been carrying on experiments in conjunction with the Westinghouse station in Hastings, Nebraska, KFKX, in short-wave broadcasting. The purpose of the experiments, as previously pointed out, was to overcome, if possible, technical difficulties in broadcast relaying. This plan seemed to be a possible substitute for the long lines scheme of the American Telephone & Telegraph Company. Thus from rival camps independent efforts were being made to chart and claim the still unconquered realm of radio.

To this date the American Telephone Company had the lead on all its rivals. Through the medium of special long lines it had built up a very impressive network of stations. Not only that, but its key station WEAF was providing a high grade program for this ever-increasing network. A. T. & T. was apparently in a fair way to accomplish the very thing that David Sarnoff had long desired for RCA. The difficulty, however, was that the great Telephone Company was engaged in nation-wide activities with radio broadcasting only a side issue. There was apparently no man in their organization qualified to battle for radio dominion with the general manager of RCA. Sooner or later the two corporations must come to grips—or to a compromise in which David Sarnoff's leadership would be a vital factor in future developments.

From time immemorial mankind has celebrated great events or great achievements by holding banquets. The lure of good food, if not of liquid refreshments, is irresistible to most men. The great and mighty of the radio industry were not different from other men in this respect. Their annual meeting in the autumn of 1925 was climaxed by a notable banquet on the evening of September 16, 1925.

This dinner of the Radio Industries Group was broadcast from the Commodore Hotel and proved to be a notable success. Eleven broadcasting stations carried the program. Major J. Andrew White acted as the announcer for the occasion. Members of the Capitol Theatre Radio Family, the "Happiness Boys," Will Rogers, Rudy Weidoeft, Vincent Lopez and his orchestra, were in attendance. United States Senator Dill was one of the speakers,[16] bringing to the group some of the reactions of the National Congress to the problems of the radio industry. This was especially important to the delegates in view of the activities of the Federal Trade Commission.

On November 9th, 1925, the Bound Brook broadcasting equipment of WJZ was ready to transmit its first programs. Located thirty-five miles from New York City, it was connected with the New York studios by three pairs of land wires. RCA had at last accomplished the physical task—despite the American Telephone Company ban—of a genuine radio network. The Bound Brook transmitters were connected by wire lines not only with New York and Washington but also with Schenectady, Springfield, Rochester, Syracuse, Utica, Philadelphia, Baltimore and New Haven—ten broadcasting stations. The antenna at Bound Brook was of the "T" type cage construction, 220 feet high with a flat top 220 feet long. With a power of 50 kilowatts, or 50,000 watts, the station was capable of tremendous coverage.[17] Returns immediately came pouring in from far distant points, all of a highly complimentary nature.

Station WGY had by this time reported a similar experience in the operation of its high power program. In fact, for purposes of comparison, WGY had experimented with alternate use of 2½ k.w. and 50 k.w. Listener response indicated that the reception was immeasurably more satisfactory on the higher power. Despite dismal forebodings of interference by the super-stations, no complaint was registered either at WGY or WJZ, except from listeners in the near vicinity of the transmitters. It will be remembered that these tests were being made by the

16 *Radio Broadcast*, December 1925, p. 178.
17 *World Wide Wireless*, February 1926, p. 14.

two 50 k.w. stations to assist the Department of Commerce to determine a policy in regard to the licensing of high power stations.

The Fourth Radio Conference in the autumn of 1925 was regarded as especially important to the industry, since Secretary Hoover had virtually been forced to abandon his policy of issuing licenses to all applicants simply because the supply of radio channels had been exhausted. This was a dangerous situation because sooner or later some prospective operator would bring a test case challenging the present set-up of radio oversight.

The Hoover keynote speech at the conference was to the effect that the radio industry had better content itself with no government interference or help. Many people, he declared, were too ready to ask the Government to assume responsibility for problems that should be solved by private initiative.

"The one action of the conference which stands out more than any other," writes *Radio Broadcast,* "was the stand taken on the number of broadcasting stations. The opinion of the conferees was almost unanimous in favor of positively limiting the number of licenses issued. We have advocated the limitation of the number of stations for a long time and certainly it is gratifying to hear the voice of the conference so unanimous in settling this question. The conference recommended that the number of stations is not to be increased but actually is to be diminished. No new licenses are to be issued and those licenses which become forfeited because of disuse are not to be reissued to another station unless there is a demand from the public. The pleasing thing about this action is that the question was settled with the purpose of satisfying the radio listener instead of the station owner." [18]

The fatuous assurance in the above editorial that the question of station limitation had been settled by the conference is a striking illustration of how far afield even thoughtful people may drift. The early radio conferences in Washington had been regarded by all as mere voluntary gatherings of leaders of the industry for the purpose of advising Secretary Hoover. Now, forsooth, the Fourth Conference was settling things and causing editorial rejoicing, despite the fact that the conferees had no authority to settle anything. To be sure, there was an annual battle in Washington over proposed radio legislation but nothing ever came of it. Congressman White's perennial radio bills had always been rejected. The only genuine law on the subject was the wireless act of 1912—more than thirteen years out of date and having no provisions for the regulation of a great industry that did not arise until ten years after the bill was enacted into law. The distressing

[18] *Radio Broadcast,* February 1926, p. 431.

truth was that Secretary Hoover's splendid efforts to regulate radio broadcasting had no sound basis in law. He had been obliged to exercise legislative power that the Congress had neglected or refused to exercise or to delegate. Arbitrary action such as proposed by the Fourth Radio Conference, however desirable, could not fail sooner or later to precipitate a radio earthquake of nation-wide dimensions.

Sec. 188. End of the Pioneer Period of Broadcasting.

The trend was now unmistakably toward music of fine quality as a radio advertising lure. The Steinway Piano had long been one of America's truly great musical instruments. After seventy years of conspicuous success the company was in no mood to ignore the new vehicle of public entertainment and advertising—radio broadcasting. A genuine public sensation was created October 11, 1925, when it was announced over Station WJZ that the Steinway Company had completed arrangements for broadcasting a series of five radio concerts, to begin October 27th. The Philharmonic Orchestra of New York and the famous pianist Josef Hofmann were to share honors in the opening concert. Dr. Walter Damrosch was to appear on a later program as a pianist-conductor.

A very important announcement was made at about the same time by Atwater Kent. He announced that many Metropolitan opera stars had been signed for a series of broadcasts to be put out through WEAF and a chain of broadcasting stations beginning October 4, 1925. The WEAF Grand Opera Company, as it was originally labeled, was expected to furnish tabloid grand opera to a large group of stations. Thus the fifth year of radio broadcasts promised to mark a new high in excellence of programs.[19] The Atwater Kent Program could not fail to set a standard of quality that would command universal acclaim from the radio audience. That it became an instant success is now a matter of historical record. Thus Sunday evening concerts were given at 9:15 through WEAF, WCAP, WJAR, WEEI, WCAE, WSAI, WWJ, WOC, WCCO, WGR, WOO, KSD, WTAG. Reinald Werrenrath, Madame Louise Homer, and Toscha Seidel were among the first artists listed on the program.

The year 1926 was ushered in by an international radio program, the result of activities of the energetic David Sarnoff of RCA. As early as the summer of 1925 Mr. Sarnoff, abroad on a mission for the Radio Corporation, had concluded arrangements with officials of the British Broadcasting Company for an exchange of programs as soon as the contemplated super-power stations in America should be ready to function. A forty kilowatt station had been erected by the British Broadcasting Company at Daventry, about seventy-five miles from

[19] *Radio Broadcast*, November 1925, p. 33.

London. This station was designed to exchange messages with American stations. As a matter of fact, when the exchange of broadcasts occurred, the signals of the English station proved so faint that had they not been picked up by a short-wave station at Belfast, Maine, and relayed to New York they would not have been heard generally on this side of the Atlantic.

American broadcasts, on the other hand, were heard not only in the British Isles but also in France, Germany, Italy and in South American nations.

An ominous note was sounded in the January, 1926, issue of *Radio Broadcast* having to do with the Federal Trade Commission investigation of radio manufacturers. "The Radio Corporation is in for a thorough airing," the article begins. "The Corporation will have to convince the Federal Trade Commission of their fair and just treatment of competitors and the radio public in general. There are one or two unsavory reports of the corporation's activities still in our minds and it is to be hoped that no more will be brought to the light. The companies being investigated by the Federal Trade Commission in addition to the Radio Corporation are The General Electric Company; American Tel. & Tel. Company; Westinghouse Electric & Manufacturing Company; Western Electric Company; International Telegraph Company; the United Fruit Company; and the Wireless Specialty Company. The Federal Commission expects to bring out that a monopolistic trust exists in the radio field. It is possible that they will prove such to be the fact. That isn't the thing that really counts, however; the question is, has the trust (if such exists) been reasonable in the prices it has charged for its wares." [20]

Unknown to *Radio Broadcast* and unsuspected by the world at large, the year 1926 was to usher in a new era in radio broadcasting. The pioneering stage of a great industry had already passed. Hundreds and even thousands of would-be broadcasting tycoons had entered the field in the last four years. Every one of them had spent staggering sums to equip his radio station, only to discover that it cost thousands of dollars every month to maintain it. More than half of those who had tried this expensive gamble had been forced to quit it. Like the unlucky gambler, they had each lost everything. The lure of radio broadcasting, however, had been so great that for every broadcast owner who had quit there were others who were stepping hopefully into the mad circle. Not only were the ranks continually filled but at the end of four years there was a long waiting list of applicants for licenses to operate radio broadcasting stations. That this unhealthy excitement could not continue much longer was the conclusion of thoughtful men.

[20] *Radio Broadcast,* January 1926, p. 304.

Elmer E. Bucher, for many years the Sales Manager of the Radio Corporation of America, has admitted to the author that in those days he was extremely apprehensive of a collapse of the industry. That RCA, General Electric and Westinghouse Companies would be tremendously hard hit if and when the independent operators should suddenly develop a panic of bankruptcy and quit, was his settled conviction. Despite the fact that the great corporations had entertained illusions that they were the pillars of the radio industry Mr. Bucher, in his capacity as sales manager of RCA, realized that the widespread demand for home radio sets had been created not alone by the broadcasting stations maintained by the great electrical manufacturers but also by the multitude of unfortunates who were losing their shirts, so to speak, in operating independent or outlaw stations. They were creating demand for home sets in every hamlet in America. When the craze should pass, as it must soon pass, Mr. Bucher foresaw a collapse of the sales-structure of RCA with staggering losses for an industry geared to manufacture supplies for a market of temporary and artificial character.

This conviction was likewise forcing itself upon Owen D. Young and others in places of great responsibility in RCA and its associated corporations. How this great challenge was met and what inner convulsions occurred in the councils of the mighty is too long and too important a development to be set forth in the pages of this volume. To the task, however, the author will address himself in a second volume on radio.

Sec. 189. Conclusion.

At the close of the pioneer stage in January, 1926, we find the following unsolved problems: The National Congress had thus far refused to enact any laws for the regulation and control of broadcasting. The Department of Commerce under Secretary Hoover was still struggling to regulate radio broadcasting under the wireless communications law of 1912. Hoover's valiant attempts to follow the advice of the leaders of the industry by promulgating rules and regulations had now reached an impasse. All available broadcast channels had been assigned. Would-be broadcasters were already vainly clamoring for licenses to operate new stations. Ugly threats were already being made of forcing the issue into the courts. The entire radio world foresaw that the courts would be obliged to declare the Hoover rules and regulations invalid in law. In that event chaos in the air would be inevitable. Radio broadcasting was thus in danger of destroying itself by the mad scramble of selfish interests. Already there were instances of rival stations operating on the same frequency—destroying each other's

DAVID SARNOFF
Who rose from the humble position of office boy for the American Marconi Company to his present position as President of the Radio Corporation of America. By sheer merit and fighting ability commander-in-chief of the Radio Industry.

programs in an endurance contest that the Department of Commerce had no power to halt.

The question of who should pay the bills of radio broadcasting was still unsolved so far as it concerned the great corporations having to do with the radio industry. It is true that the American Telephone Company had apparently solved the problem by selling broadcast time to others for advertising purposes. The A. T. & T. Company had already built up a network of stations, yet less than two per cent of the broadcasting stations of the nation were in the Telephone Company control in this manner. Neither the General Electric, Westinghouse nor Radio Corporation had the unchallenged right to sell time on the air. In fact the Telephone Company, under the cross-licensing agreements as well as under patent rights claimant to overlordship of broadcasting for hire, was already at odds with its three former allies. David Sarnoff's advocacy of super-power stations and the actual establishment of some by RCA and the General Electric Company had apparently alarmed the Telephone Company. It resented the presence in the broadcasting field of the great manufacturing corporations. They should be content with their own sphere of activity without invading the telephonic communications field—thus reasoned the powerful A. T. & T.

The long contest begun in 1923 was now passing into its third stage. The arbitration between RCA and the Telephone Company had led to the redrafting of agreements between the corporations affiliated with RCA and now it was easy to foresee a battle of the giants to settle once for all these rival aspirations.

Who the leader would be in that future contest was not difficult to forecast. David Sarnoff, at thirty-five, was one of the most impressive figures in the radio industry. Having fought his way up from the ranks he had early learned to be self-reliant and to give himself unreservedly to any task to which he set his hand. Added to that, his uncanny foresight and his relentless pursuit of a goal made him a force to be reckoned with even among industrial tycoons of long experience. He had already demonstrated a positive genius for industrial negotiating, but the great test of his ability in this respect was yet to come. Another towering figure in the councils of radio was, of course, the Field Marshal who had created the industry—Owen D. Young. That there would be rivalry between him and Mr. Sarnoff was unthinkable for various reasons.

To begin with, Owen D. Young was a lawyer who had already won an international reputation because of his ability in conciliation of conflicting corporate interests and in marshaling the same in solid phalanx against foreign domination of wireless communications. The administration of communications would be entirely out of his line. David Sarnoff, on the other hand, had grown up in that industry. A two-fisted warrior who had fought every inch of the way from lowly newsboy to General Manager of the great corporation which Owen D. Young's organizing genius had created, Sarnoff was ideally equipped for leadership in the stormy days ahead. No one knew this better than Owen D. Young. Perhaps no one rejoiced more sincerely than did he in the fighting ability of the younger man. To David Sarnoff he had entrusted many important battles in his consolidation campaign. In each instance victory had resulted. Young was Sarnoff's sponsor—Sarnoff's friend in the councils of the mighty. Whenever a great task was to be performed, a task that required pertinacity and resourcefulness in the face of the enemy, David Sarnoff was Owen D. Young's inevitable choice. In days to come Young was even to call Sarnoff to Europe to assist in a great war-reparations crisis and Sarnoff was to justify in full measure the faith of his chief.

No, there could be no rivalry between these two men as to which should dominate the communications field. David Sarnoff was to assume the toga of leadership, but only after he should have out-generaled and outfought a succession of industrial giants. The story of that conflict, of its intrigues and schemings, its marchings and counter-marchings, its hand-to-hand battles, is a recital that cannot be included in the pages of the present volume. It will form the opening chapters of another volume.

APPENDIX

THE HAPPINESS BOYS	AL SIMMONS
"Jones and Hare," whose broadcasts on the Happiness candy program made radio history.	A radio pioneer who in humble capacity endeared himself to thousands of radio artists.

BROADCASTING THE GAME!
J. Andrew White in an early sports broadcast over WJZ.

EXHIBIT "A"

LETTER

OWEN D. YOUNG TO RADIO CORPORATION

(Letter undated but included in minutes of meeting of October 22, 1919)
"Radio Corporation of America:

"Dear Sirs: The General Electric Company, in anticipation of the formation of Radio Corporation of America (herein called the Corporation), has formulated plans by which the Corporation may obtain an advantageous agreement with Marconi's Wireless Telegraph Company, Limited, for the conduct of international radio business with other countries and in South America and also an agreement with Marconi Wireless Telegraph Company of America for the purchase of certain of its assets for consideration which is deemed advantageous. Copies of these two proposed agreements are submitted herewith.

"The General Electric Company to make possible the consummation of those two agreements (in addition to amounts expended by it in the acquisition of certain interests of the British Thomson-Houston Company which were deemed necessary to make possible the proposed agreement with Marconi's Wireless Telegraph Company Limited) must expend an amount largely in excess of $2,000,000 in the purchase by General Electric Company of the holdings of stock of Marconi's Wireless Telegraph Company Limited in Marconi Wireless Telegraph Company of America (amounting to a par amount in excess of $1,800,000).

"It is proposed that the Corporation shall issue to General Electric Company 135,174 shares of its preferred stock (to the par amount of $675,870) and 2,000,000 common shares of no par value in consideration (1) of the General Electric Company's expenditures above described on or before February 1, 1920, (2) of its obtaining for the Corporation the agreement with Marconi Wireless Telegraph Company of America above described and secure its approval by the Marconi Board of Directors and by a meeting of its stockholders and the transfer of its assets as therein described for the consideration therein stated on or before said date, (3) of its obtaining for the Corporation the execution by Marconi's Wireless Telegraph Company Limited of the agreement above described on or before said date, and (4) the payment by General Electric Company to the Corporation of $285,000 in cash whenever required by the Corporation.

"Such stock is to be authorized and issued by the Corporation as follows:

"Whenever the General Electric Company shall make payments of cash to the Corporation or prove to it cash expenditures by General Electric Company in accordance with the plan above outlined in purchase of shares of Marconi Wireless Telegraph Company of America it shall be forthwith entitled to receive preferred shares to an equal par amount or one common share for each $1 expended. The balance of stock to be issued to it shall be withheld until complete performance by it of its agreements herein.

"The General Electric Company will also enter into such arrangements with the Corporation as shall enable it to secure the manufacture by the General Electric Company of necessary apparatus and enable it to comply with its covenants in the agreements above described as to patents and licenses.

"It is understood that with the consent of the Corporation the terms of such agreements may be changed by mutual consent and that the dates of performance hereunder may likewise be extended.

Yours very truly,
GENERAL ELECTRIC COMPANY
By OWEN D. YOUNG, Vice-President."

375

EXHIBIT "B"

1. AGREEMENT OF MARCONI COMPANY TO URGE ITS STOCKHOLDERS TO APPROVE MAIN AGREEMENT

PRELIMINARY AGREEMENT

General Electric Company, a New York corporation, hereinafter referred to as the General Company, and Marconi Wireless Telegraph Company of America, a New Jersey corporation, hereinafter referred to as the Marconi Company, do hereby agree as follows:

All prior agreements between the parties (except a certain agreement delivered in escrow to L. F. H. Betts, Esq., and current agreements, orders and accounts for or with respect to the sale of apparatus, devices and supplies) are cancelled.

The Marconi Company agrees to recommend to and urge upon its stockholders to consent to and approve the execution by the Marconi Company of a certain agreement with the Radio Corporation of America (hereinafter referred to as the Radio Corporation) known as the Marconi-Radio Main Agreement, a copy of which is hereto attached, and agrees that as soon as such consent or approval can be obtained it will formally execute and deliver the said agreement with its exhibits to the Radio Corporation simultaneously with the execution and delivery by the Radio Corporation. The General Company agrees to cause the Radio Corporation simultaneously to execute and deliver the said agreement with its exhibits at any time after such consent or approval is obtained prior to January 1, 1920.

The Marconi Company agrees not to declare or pay any dividends to its stockholders prior to the execution and delivery of said Main Agreement or prior to January 1, 1920, whichever date is earliest.

The Main Agreement states the substance of the arrangement agreed upon. The matter of changes in form and procedure is left to counsel of the Marconi Company and the Radio Corporation to agree upon, the understanding being that if they propose a definite method for the union of the two interests, their recommendations shall be carried out.

As of the date of execution of the Marconi-Radio Main Agreement, the Marconi Company grants to the General Company an option, good until January 1, 1921, to lease the Marconi Company's factory at Aldene, New Jersey, as set forth in Exhibit C attached to the Main Agreement. The said lease shall run until January 1, 1945, but may be terminated by the General Company at any time on three months' notice and shall be terminated automatically if the Marconi Company transfers the said factory to the Radio Corporation. The rental shall be two thousand ($2,000) dollars a month, and at the same rate for any part of a month, plus taxes and reasonable insurance on said factory accruing during and with respect to the period for which the lease is operative.

The Marconi Company agrees forthwith after receiving the shares of common stock referred to in said Main Agreement to take action which shall have the effect of distributing these shares of common stock among its stockholders in proportion to their holdings, and it further agrees that it will make a similar distribution when it shall receive preferred stock of the Radio Corporation in payment for the Marconi assets. And it further agrees at least as often as the end of each year when it shall have received further stock of the Radio Corporation under any provision of the Marconi-Radio Main Agreement or otherwise to take action which shall have the effect of distributing such further stock so received; it being the intent of this agreement that all preferred and common stock of the Radio Corporation received by the Marconi Company shall be forthwith distributed to stockholders of the Marconi Company.

As of the execution of the Marconi-Radio Main Agreement the General Company releases and agrees to release the Marconi Company from all claims or demands which it has in respect to infringement of patents by the Marconi Company up to the date hereof. This release shall at the option of the Radio Corporation extend to and protect customers with respect to their use or resale of articles purchased from the Marconi Company prior to the date of the incorporation of the

Radio Corporation. As of the same date the Marconi Company grants and agrees to grant similar releases to the General Company under all its patents, such releases to extend to and protect the customers of the General Company in the use and resale of devices purchased from the General Company prior to said date and devices on order at said date, but such releases shall not extend to include any claims against the General Company which claims the United States has guaranteed or agreed to satisfy.

The releases above provided for shall take effect without further action of the parties, on the execution of the said Main Agreement.

In case it happens that at the time when the Marconi-Radio Main Agreement is executed the Marconi Company has in its possession any 200 kilowatt alternators with accessories the title to which is in the General Company the rights of the Marconi Company to the possession thereof shall forthwith cease and terminate. Such alternators with accessories shall become the property of the Radio Corporation and shall be regarded as part of the twelve (12) alternators with accessories sold by the General Company to the Radio Corporation and referred to in the General Electric-Radio Main Agreement.

In testimony whereof, the parties hereto have caused these presents to be executed and their corporate seals to be hereunto attached by their proper officers thereunto duly authorized at New York City this 22nd day of October 1919.

GENERAL ELECTRIC COMPANY

By OWEN D. YOUNG, Vice President.

Attest:

J. W. ELWOOD, Asst. Secretary.

Marconi Wireless Telegraph Company of America,

By EDWARD J. NALLY, Vice-President.

Attest:

C. J. ROSS, Secretary.

EXHIBIT "C"

2. MAIN AGREEMENT

Agreement dated this 20th day of November 1919, between Radio Corporation of America, a Delaware Corporation (herein called the "Radio Corporation") and Marconi Wireless Telegraph Company of America, a New Jersey Corporation (herein called the "Marconi Company").

RECITALS

1. The General Electric Company (a New York Corporation, hereinafter referred to as the General Company) has paid to the Radio Corporation two hundred eighty-seven thousand two hundred sixty-two dollars (287,262), and has entered into a contract with the Radio Corporation, dated November 1919, known as the "General Electric-Radio Main Agreement," whereby certain valuable rights and privileges are secured to the Radio Corporation. The General Company has further agreed to make certain payments to Marconi's Wireless Telegraph Company, Limited, a British Corporation, and to British Thomson-Houston Company, Limited, for the benefit of the Radio Corporation.

2. The Radio Corporation has issued to the General Company one hundred-thirty-five thousand one hundred seventy-four (135,174) shares of its preferred stock of a par value of six hundred seventy-five thousand eight hundred seventy dollars ($675,870) and two million (2,000,000) shares of its common stock. No other shares of the Radio Corporation have been issued or have been agreed to be issued, except as set forth in the said General Electric-Radio Main Agreement.

AGREEMENT

In consideration of the mutual promises, the parties agree as follows:

ARTICLE I—THE MARCONI ASSETS

1. It is desired that the Radio Corporation acquire all the assets of the Marconi Company, present and future, including its good will and business, rights of action,

patent rights, and all other rights and property to which it is now or may hereafter become entitled except the "reserved assets" hereinafter described and the factory at Aldene, New Jersey, and except an amount in cash, not exceeding five hundred thousand dollars ($500,000), sufficient to pay out of its surplus a dividend to its stockholders of twenty-five cents ($.25) per share. The assets to be acquired include a number of wireless stations, among which are the stations at—

New Brunswick, New Jersey
Belmar, New Jersey
Marion, Massachusetts
Chatham, Massachusetts
Bolinas, California
Marshall, California
Kahuku, Territory of Hawaii, and
Kokohead, Territory of Hawaii

and a number of concessions and contracts (domestic and foreign), patents, patent rights, applications, etc., in various countries, all the stock of the

Wireless Press, Inc., a New York corporation
Marconi Telegraph-Cable Company, a New York corporation
Marconi Telegraph-Cable Company, a New Jersey corporation
Marconi Telegraph-Cable Company, a Massachusetts corporation
Marconi Telegraph-Cable Company, an Illinois corporation

and three-eighths of the stock of the Pan-American Wireless Telegraph and Telephone Company, a Delaware Corporation. All claims and rights of action which the Marconi Company possesses being transferred by this present agreement to the Radio Corporation, it is understood and agreed that from such transfer there are reserved each and all of the claims or rights of action as follows, and that in any proceeding with respect thereto the Marconi Company may sue in its own name, joining the Radio Corporation as complainant if necessary. The claims or rights of action enumerated below are the "reserved assets" above referred to.

a. A claim against the United States Government arising from unlicensed use by and for the Government of the apparatus covered by the patents of the Marconi Company.

b. A claim now being determined in a suit pending in the United States District Court for the Southern District of New York, entitled Marconi Wireless Telegraph Company of America vs. Atlantic Communication Company, on the Fleming patent No. 803684.

c. A claim against the Alien Property Custodian and the Treasurer of the United States arising out of the creation of a trust fund out of moneys belonging to the Gesellschaft fur die Drahtlose Telegraphie, under section 9 of the "Trading with the Enemy Act" by reason of infringement of Fleming patent No. 803684 and Lodge patent No. 609154 and Marconi patent No. 763772.

d. A claim now being determined in a suit in the United States District Court for the Eastern District of New York entitled Marconi Wireless Telegraph Company of America vs. Atlantic Communication Company, on Lodge patent No. 609-154 and Marconi patent No. 763722.

e. A claim now being determined in a suit entitled Marconi Wireless Telegraph Company of America vs. Kilbourne & Clark Manufacturing Company, in the United States District Court for the Western District of Washington, on Marconi patent 763722.

f. A claim now being determined in a suit entitled Marconi Wireless Telegraph Company of America vs. de Forest Radio Telephone & Telegraph Company in the United States District Court for the Southern District of New York, on Fleming patent No. 803684.

g. A claim against the British Government arising from the commandeering, on the outbreak of the European War, of the British stations erected to communicate with the corresponding stations of the American company.

The seven foregoing claims are herein collectively referred to as the "reserved assets." All other assets of the Marconi Company which are to be acquired as herein collectively called the "Marconi assets."

Article II—Transfer of the Marconi Assets

1. The Marconi Company hereby transfers the Marconi assets to the Radio Corporation free and clear of all mortgages, liens, charges, and encumbrances and free of debt except current accounts payable. The Marconi Company further warrants its title to tangible physical assets referred to in the next two succeeding paragraphs hereof aggregating in value the par value of the preferred stock to be issued to it under such paragraphs, less five hundred thousand dollars ($500,000), the amount of the deficit below referred to.

2. The Marconi Company shall receive therefor two million (2,000,000) shares of the common stock of the Radio Corporation and two million (2,000,000) shares of preferred stock of the Radio Corporation, provided, however, that the Marconi assets so acquired (exclusive of patents, good will, and all other intangibles and deducting proper allowances for taxes and other accrued liabilities with respect to its operations up to date of transfer but including shares of the Pan-American Company at their actual cash cost to the Marconi Company) are of net value on a going concern basis in money or moneys worth of nine million five hundred thousand dollars ($9,500,000).

3. In case of disagreement as to such value the value is to be referred to arbitration. The arbitrators who are to be skilled appraisers or accountants are to be appointed one by E. J. Nally, one by the Radio Corporation, and the third by the two already chosen. In case of failure of the two arbitrators to choose a third arbitrator the third arbitrator shall be S. Roger Mitchell. In case such value as determined by the arbitrators amounts to less than nine million five hundred thousand dollars ($9,500,000), the Marconi Company shall receive two million (2,000,000) shares each of the common and preferred stock as above provided, but the amount of preferred stock to be issued in consideration for the "reserved assets" hereinafter provided for shall be reduced by an amount having a par value equal to the deficit, that is to say, the difference between the value of the assets as determined by the arbitrators and the sum of nine million five hundred thousand dollars ($9,500,000).

4. In addition the Marconi Company agrees to pay to the Radio Corporation the first five hundred thousand dollars ($500,000) (after making up the "deficit" if any) realized from the reserved assets, or alternatively to transfer to the Radio Corporation, prior to January 1, 1922, its factory at Aldene, New Jersey, as set forth in Exhibit C, hereto attached.

5. In determining the value of the Marconi assets no accounts shall be taken of the obligations or benefits of a certain contract dated the second day of September 1919, between Monsieur Emile Girardeau acting in behalf of the American Radio Company of New York and on behalf of the Compagnie Generale de Telegraphie sans Fils and Mr. Edward J. Nally acting on behalf of the American Marconi Company.

6. The Marconi Company warrants and agrees to keep its organization alive until the Radio Corporation shall in writing agree that it may be dissolved and the Marconi Company may at any time require the Radio Corporation to pay the expenses incurred thereafter in carrying out the foregoing agreement to keep its organization alive provided that at the same time the stockholders of the Marconi Company assign to the Radio Corporation a majority of the voting shares of the Marconi Company. The Marconi Company further agrees not to incur or obligate itself to incur any obligation or expense or make any payment except in accordance with an annual budget which shall have first been prepared by the Marconi Company and approved in writing by the Radio Corporation.

7. The Marconi Company agrees to prosecute at its own expense all the claims which are the "reserved assets" above described, and the Marconi Company agrees that all amounts received in cash by it at any time but after paying expenses for maintaining its corporate organization and the prosecution of such claims shall forthwith be paid to the Radio Corporation, and it is agreed that the Radio Corporation shall from time to time on such payments issue therefor preferred stock of

a par amount equal to the amount of cash so paid subject to the provisions of sections 3, 4 and 8 of this article, provided that when and if such par amount of preferred stock so delivered shall amount to five million dollars ($5,000,000) if the Aldene factory is transferred under section 4 of this article, or four million five hundred thousand dollars ($4,500,000), if it is not transferred, and in any case on December 31, 1930, regardless of the amount then issued, the Marconi Company shall forthwith assign to the Radio Corporation the reserved assets and all of them and all other assets which it then has without further compensation or consideration.

8. The Radio Corporation will advance such sums to the Marconi Company as may from time to time be reasonably necessary in the opinion of the counsel hereinafter mentioned to prosecute the claims or rights of action mentioned above as well as for the defense of any patent suits now pending against the Marconi Company or hereafter brought with reference to operations of the Marconi Company prior to the coming into effect hereof. In case any suit or suits against the Marconi Company with respect to operations of the Marconi Company prior to the coming into effect hereof are in the opinion of such counsel sufficiently serious to justify it, they may require the Radio Corporation to withhold preferred stock otherwise payable to the Marconi Company with respect to the "reserved assets" to such extent and for such period as may in their judgment be necessary for the Radio Corporation's protection. All amounts advanced, and all recoveries against the Marconi Company with respect to operations which it performed prior to the date hereof, shall be charged against and deducted from such reserved assets. The counsel shall be L. F. H. Betts and Albert G. Davis. In case they disagree they shall refer the matter to independent counsel.

ARTICLE III—GOVERNMENT RELATIONS

1. If the Radio Corporation issues two classes of common stock or classes of preferred stock, or both, one of which may and the other may not be voted if owned or controlled by aliens, the Marconi Company shall be entitled to the extent to which it is entitled to stock of the Radio Corporation to take enough of the first class mentioned (i.e., the class which may be voted if owned or controlled by aliens), to provide one share of such preferred stock and one share of such common stock (for each share of stock of the Marconi Company) for distribution to each of its alien stockholders of record as of the date of organization of the Radio Corporation insofar as and to the extent that the Radio Corporation issues a sufficient quantity of such stock for that purpose.

ARTICLE IV—CONDITION OF TRANSFER OF PATENTS

1. Inasmuch as the Marconi Company is not willing to turn over its patents, patent rights and licenses for any definite sum of money, but is willing to transfer such patents, patent rights, and licenses only for a considerable interest in the profits to be derived from the use by the Radio Corporation of such patents, patent rights and licenses, it is therefore understood and agreed that in the event of the taking over of the Radio Corporation by any superior authority all right, title and interest of the Radio Corporation in any patent, patent right or license herein granted or agreed to be granted by the Marconi Company to the Radio Corporation shall cease and shall be reassigned and shall revert to the Marconi Company as of the date of such taking over except to the extent provided below. If instead of taking over the Radio Corporation the Government takes over its radio stations in any field and/or territory, except in and for time of war or public danger, the same result shall follow so far as concerns that field and/or territory. But this action shall in no way affect the rights of Marconi's Wireless Telegraph Company, Limited, or of Shielton, Limited, as set forth in the "Radio Corporation and British Marconi Company Principal Agreement" nor shall it affect the rights of the General Company under Article II of the General Electric-Radio Corporation Main Agreement; such rights shall be reserved from any such reassignment by the Radio Corporation for the benefit of Marconi's Wireless Telegraph Company, Limited, or Shielton, Limited, and of the General Company respectively.

In testimony whereof, the parties hereto have caused these presents to be executed and their corporate seals to be hereunto affixed by their proper officers thereunto duly authorized at New York City the day and year first above written.

RADIO CORPORATION OF AMERICA

By EDWARD J. NALLY, President.

Attest:

C. J. Ross, Secretary.

Marconi Wireless Telegraph Company of America,

By JOHN W. GRIGGS, President.

Attest:

C. J. Ross, Secretary.

EXHIBIT "D"

LICENSE AGREEMENT—GENERAL ELECTRIC COMPANY AND RADIO CORPORATION OF AMERICA

Agreement made this 20th day of November, 1919, between General Electric Company, a New York corporation, hereinafter called the General Company, and Radio Corporation of America, a Delaware corporation hereafter referred to as the Radio Corporation.

RECITALS

A. The General Company has developed various inventions relating to, or applicable to, radio work and other communication work.

B. The General Company is under obligation to certain foreign companies to give them for their territory respectively exclusive rights to its various inventions and discoveries and to the business of selling General Electric products. Some of these companies are substantially controlled by the International General Electric Company, a New York corporation, hereinafter referred to as the International Company.

C. The Radio Corporation proposes to establish, maintain, and operate radio stations, and cable and wire lines and stations, and to deal in, lease, and maintain radio devices, and desires to utilize in such work the various inventions now controlled by the General Company and which may hereafter be controlled by it.

ARTICLE I—DEFINITIONS

1. Radio purposes is defined as the transmission or reception of communications, telegraphic, telephonic or other, by what are known as electromagnetic waves, but not by wire.

2. Radio devices are defined as comprising:

(a) Devices useful only in radio purposes.

(b) Devices especially adapted to radio purposes but capable of other uses, such, for example, as the Alexanderson alternator with accessories or the pliotron, except where the same are sold licensed only for uses other than radio uses, in which case the same are not to be regarded as radio devices hereunder.

3. The expression "devices" shall include apparatus, devices, systems, connections, and methods.

ARTICLE II—LICENSES

1. Reserving to itself and its controlled companies, present and future, respectively, personal licenses, transferable only to the successors to their business or part thereof and divisible only as their business is divided, to use for their own communication or other purposes for convenience or to save expense, but not for profit, the General Company hereby grants to the Radio Corporation an exclusive, divisible license to use and sell as well as a non-exclusive indivisible license to make only when, and to the extent that, the General Company is not in a position to supply the desired device with reasonable business promptness (the right to use and sell being limited to the use and sale of apparatus purchased from the General Company or with its written consent, so far as the General Company is from time to time in condition to supply the same with reasonable business promptness) for

radio purposes under all patents, applications for patents, inventions and rights or licenses under or in connection with patents which the General Company now owns or controls, or which it may acquire during the term hereof except those acquired by purchase and referred to below.

2. The General Company also grants to the Radio Corporation a nonexclusive nontransferable license to use, but not to make or sell (with the same limitations) for wire communication purposes under all patents, applications, inventions, rights, and licenses which it now owns or controls or which it may acquire during the term hereof by inventions of its employees.

3. For the purposes hereof the inventions, patents, and rights of the General Company are taken as including those of the International Company as well as following corporations, namely:

> Australian General Electric Company,
> China General Edison Company, Inc.,
> Compania General Electric do Brazil,
> South African General Electric Company, Ltd.,
> Cia. General Electric Sudamericana, Inc.,
> Mexican General Electric Company.

4. The Radio Corporation grants to the General Company the exclusive, divisible right to make and to sell radio devices to the Radio Corporation only as well as the exclusive divisible right to make, use, and sell devices other than radio devices, under all its patents and applications for patents, inventions, and rights, or licenses under or in connection with patents which the Radio Corporation now owns or controls, or which it may acquire during the term hereof except as far as is provided below in the case of certain such acquired by purchase. The Radio Corporation grants the General Company and its controlled companies, present and future, nonexclusive licenses transferable only to successors to their business or parts thereof, divisible only as their business is divided, to use for their own communication or other purposes for convenience or to save expense but not for profit under all the patents which the Radio Corporation now owns or controls or which it may acquire during the term hereof from the General Company or by inventions of its own employees or through contracts which it now has.

5. The said licenses are all to run for the terms for which the patents are or may be granted, reissued, or extended, and are subject to royalty only in so far as such royalties are payable to others by virtue of the contracts by which the party granting the licenses acquired or shall acquire the right to grant the same, and only at a rate not greater than that paid by such party.

6. Where in any case a party does not own or control a patent but has lawful power to grant rights or licenses thereunder to the other for part or all of its field or territory it shall do so subject to the conditions hereof.

7. In case the General Company shall acquire by purchase from others patents, patent applications, or rights or licenses under or in connection with patents, useful for or applicable to radio purposes or wire communication, and in case the Radio Corporation similarly acquires such patents, patent applications, or rights or licenses, the party making the acquisition will offer to the other to bring the same within the scope of this contract on payment of a fair proportion of the price actually paid or to be paid therefor. This shall not apply in the case of any patent, patent application, right or license secured by the Radio Corporation from or through the Marconi Wireless Telegraph Company of America, Marconi's Wireless Telegraph Company, Limited, Compagnie Generale de Telegraphie sans Fils, or others with whom the Radio Corporation may have relations similar to its actual or proposed relations with any of said companies; all such are to be treated as though they were not acquired by purchase.

8. The General Company has sold its inventions for certain countries to companies other than those mentioned in section 3 of this article. All covenants of the General Company with respect to such countries are subject to the present rights of the companies holding such inventions. As such rights revert to the General Company they shall pass under the operation of this contract without further consideration.

9. Each company agrees to continue the present practice of the General Company of requiring those employees considered likely to make inventions along this line of work to assign inventions to it; it being understood that each company shall use its best efforts to carry out this provision, but if due care and diligence are exercised neither company shall be liable in damages for failure to carry it out.

10. As soon as is reasonably possible after the filing by or on behalf of a party hereto of a United States patent application, rights to or under which should pass to the other party, the party filing the application shall transmit a copy thereof to the other party with a statement of its filing date and shall notify the other party of the countries foreign to the United States in which it has decided to file and will file applications to cover the invention of such application. The other party may then suggest that applications should be filed in additional foreign countries in which the first party has the right to file. If and so far as the first party does not within thirty (30) days after such suggestion agree to file in such other foreign countries the other party may file proper applications for protecting such invention in such other foreign countries, and take patents thereon in its own name at its own expense. Before either party intentionally drops an application or patent of any country, rights to or under which should pass to the other hereunder, it shall notify the other party in which case such other party may continue the prosecution of the application or continue the life of the patent in question at its own expense, being entitled in such case to an assignment thereof.

11. In case a right, application or patent is transferred by one party to the other in accordance with the provisions of section 10 of this article, the party with which such right, application or patent originated shall be entitled to its full rights thereunder as though such patent had originated with and had been taken out by the other party subject to any royalty or other payment required to be made to an outsider in accordance with this agreement.

12. The admission of validity implied in the acceptance of licenses and assignments hereunder is limited to the field and terms for which such licenses exist.

13. The General Company empowers the Radio Corporation to release the United States Government from any and all claims arising from past infringement by the Government of any radio patents which the General Company now owns or under which it has power to grant such release, provided, that this can be done in a contract otherwise satisfactory to the General Company.

Article III—Restrictions on Sales of Apparatus

1. The General Company agrees that it will not sell or dispose of any radio devices whatever covered by patents, rights under which are granted or agreed to be granted herein, for use in the United States except to fill orders now on hand, and except to the United States Government in cases where the Government insists on purchasing directly from the General Company (in which case the profits from such sales over the price of such devices to the Radio Corporation hereunder shall be paid to the Radio Corporation). The General Company further agrees that it will not sell or dispose of for use outside the United States any radio devices whatever covered by patents, rights under which are granted or agreed to be granted herein, except as it may be required to do so by existing contracts with others than the companies specifically named in section 3 of Article II hereof and except for its own use or for the use of the Radio Corporation. This reservation is not intended to enlarge the scope of the licenses granted in Article II hereof.

Article IV—Sale of Apparatus

1. The Radio Corporation agrees to purchase from the General Company all radio devices covered by patents, rights under which are granted or agreed to be granted herein, which the General Company is from time to time in a position to supply with reasonable business promptness for use in, or which are used in, the business and operation of the Radio Corporation and its licenses and customers.

2. The General Company agrees to produce or cause to be produced such patented devices of good quality, workmanship, and material with reasonable business promptness on the written order of the Radio Corporation.

3. The basis for determining the price charged by the General Company to the Radio Corporation shall be cost plus 20 per cent, except that for all articles complete in themselves which are purchased by the General Company from outside manufacturers and which form a necessary part of the complete device supplied by the General Company, the price charged by the General Company to the Radio Corporation shall be cost plus 10 per cent for handling charges.

4. The basis for determining cost shall be in accordance with the "Standard Accounting and Cost System for the Electrical Manufacturing Industry," as approved by the Federal Trade Commission, January 27, 1917.

5. Terms of payment shall conform to the standard terms of the General Company current at the time of placing the order.

6. If the Radio Corporation in any particular instance wishes the General Company to make a definite and firm price for such radio devices, and the General Company consents to make such firm price, such firm price upon acceptance by the Radio Corporation shall be substituted in such instance or instances for the cost plus 20 per cent arrangement above mentioned.

7. All prices mentioned above shall be f. o. b. factory.

8. Standard material not specifically designed for radio purposes is to be sold to the Radio Corporation at standard prices and on standard terms of payment but at the lowest price at which such standard material is sold in like quantities to any other customer of the General Company for use in the United States of America, and if at any time material, apparatus or supplies especially designed for radio purposes shall be sold by the General Company to its other customers for other uses than radio purposes in an amount greater than that taken by the Radio Corporation, the price at which such material, apparatus or supplies shall be sold to the Radio Corporation shall be the lowest price at which such material, apparatus or supplies are sold in like quantities to any other customer of the General Company for use in the United States of America. In determining such lowest price under this section 8 no account shall be taken of sales:

(1) To those corporations in which the General Company may own a substantial amount of stock;

(2) Where the General Company sells material on a schedule, such material is to be billed to the Radio Corporation according to such schedule;

(3) Where the General Company has a lawful contract not to sell material below a certain price, such material is not to be billed to the Radio Corporation for a less price;

(4) To the United States Government or any of its departments.

9. It is agreed that the Radio Corporation shall not resell patented articles except as a part of the radio system.

10. The Radio Corporation agrees not to lease, sell or dispose of devices bought of the General Company, where the General Company or one of the companies mentioned in section 3 of Article II hereof would not be free to sell such devices. It being understood that the rights of the Radio Corporation are only for radio purposes as above defined, the Radio Corporation agrees to use care not to enter with any patented device, process or system into the field of the General Company or to encourage or aid others to do so, and specifically that in selling radio devices it will use such precautions by contract of sale, restricted license notices, etc., as may be necessary or advisable to prevent its customers from acquiring (by purchase from it of devices or otherwise) licenses to use the same for purposes of which the Radio Corporation has no right to grant such licenses. The General Company agrees to observe similar precautions in selling apparatus and devices especially adapted to radio work but capable of other uses.

11. The General Company agrees to sell the Radio Corporation such patented communication devices as it may be in position to supply other than radio devices on the same terms, but only for the use of the Radio Corporation and not for resale or lease or other disposal and not exclusively.

Article V—Alexanderson Alternator

1. The Radio Corporation agrees to purchase from the General Company and the General Company agrees to sell and deliver f. o. b. factory to it, as fast as they can reasonably be constructed and prior to January 1, 1922, twelve (12) Alexanderson alternators complete with accessories, in accordance with specifications attached hereto and marked "Exhibit B" at the special price of one hundred twenty-seven thousand dollars ($127,000) apiece. Spare alternators or other incomplete spare equipments may be substituted at prices to be agreed upon provided that the total purchases hereunder aggregate in price the price of the twelve Alexanderson alternators with their accessories. In consideration for such agreement on the part of the General Company, the Radio Corporation agrees to issue and deliver to the General Company three hundred four thousand eight hundred (304,800) shares of its preferred stock, but subject to the provisions of Article VI hereof.

Article VI—Sale of Materials

1. The Radio Corporation proposes to purchase from the Marconi Wireless Telegraph Company of America, hereinafter referred to as the Marconi Company, all of its property used or useful in connection with its manufacturing business, except the factory at Aldene, New Jersey. In case this purchase is made the Radio Corporation agrees forthwith to sell and does sell the property so purchased to the General Company, such sale to take effect immediately on the purchase of the same by the Radio Corporation, including all drawings, blueprints, and material for manufacture and unfinished parts on hand or on order as of the date of the Radio Corporation's acquisition of the same, and any factory plants, tools, machinery, and dies which it may acquire from the Marconi Company, but not including the publishing plant of the Wireless Press, Inc., nor the building and real estate at Seattle, Washington, which latter will no longer be used for factory purposes. The accounts receivable are to be collected and the accounts payable are to be paid by the Radio Corporation.

2. The General Company agrees to pay for the property thus transferred by paying for the unfinished parts, work in progress and material on hand to be manufactured at actual cost of the same plus twenty per cent (20%), which amount is to be ascertained by two appraisers, one appointed by the General Company and one appointed by Mr. Edward J. Nally. In case they disagree the matter shall be referred to Mr. S. Roger Mitchell, or other public accountant satisfactory to both parties, whose decision shall be final.

3. In case the Radio Corporation shall acquire, prior to January 1, 1922, the factory plants, lands, etc., of the Marconi Company, at Aldene, New Jersey, as set forth in Exhibit C hereto attached, it agrees forthwith to sell the same to the General Company and the General Company agrees to buy the same for five hundred thousand dollars ($500,000).

4. The payments by the General Company to the Radio Corporation under this Article and deliveries of preferred stock to the General Company in payment for Alexanderson alternators and their accessories in accordance with Article V hereof, are to proceed as follows: At the time of taking over the unfinished parts, work in progress and material on hand, a special account is to be set up between the General Company and the Radio Corporation, in which account is to be charged against the General Company the value of such unfinished parts, work in progress and material on hand, ascertained as above; if and when, prior to January 1, 1922, the Radio Corporation acquires the Aldene factory and transfers it to the General Company, its price, five hundred thousand dollars ($500,000) is to be charged in the same account against the General Company. As and when the Alexanderson alternators and their accessories sold at the special price referred to above are shipped to the Radio Corporation, the price thereof is to be credited to the General Company on such account, until such credits aggregate one million five hundred twenty-four thousand dollars ($1,524,000). At any time when such account shows a balance in favor of the General Company the General Company may demand and shall then receive preferred stock of the Radio Corporation at par to any amount demanded not exceeding such credit balance, the par value of such stock to be charged to it in

such special account; and if at any time the balance of said account is in favor of the Radio Corporation, the General Company shall liquidate such balance by surrender to the Radio Corporation of preferred stock of the Radio Corporation of a par value equal to the amount of such balance. Such special account shall be entirely independent of all other accounts between the parties.

5. The Radio Corporation agrees to place forthwith with the General Company orders which will exhaust and consume said unfinished parts, work in progress and material; unfinished parts, work in progress and material not covered by such orders may be regarded by the appraisers as scrap in case the General Company shall find itself unable profitably to utilize the same.

6. The General Company agrees to fill the orders so to be placed on it and to bill the same to the Radio Corporation; in making up price of the articles so billed in accordance with Article IV hereof, the price of the unfinished parts, work in progress and material taken over and inventories shall be taken as the price actually paid for the same by the General Company as above set forth, the additional work and material being charged on the basis of Article IV hereof.

ARTICLE VII—EXPERT ADVICE AND TECHNICAL INFORMATION

1. The General Company agrees that it will from time to time permit the Radio Corporation to have and will assist it in obtaining full information concerning inventions, patents and the patent situation of the General Company in the radio field. The Radio Corporation engages reciprocally to do the same for the General Company.

2. The General Company agrees upon request to furnish the Radio Corporation suitable plans for buildings, lay-out of machinery, antennæ, etc., for use by the Radio Corporation hereunder, and if desired a man or men to supervise the construction and erection of such buildings, and the erection and installation of such machinery, etc., and also such other engineers and experienced men as the General Company can reasonably spare and the Radio Corporation may reasonably require in the organization, management, and development of the business of the Radio Corporation, and to give the Radio Corporation and those whom the Radio Corporation may designate from time to time all information in regard to technical and engineering but not manufacturing matters which it may possess from time to time and which the Radio Corporation may reasonably require for the conduct of its radio business hereunder, and further agrees to assist the Radio Corporation in every reasonable way to the end that the Radio Corporation shall have whenever needed, in its operations hereunder, the benefits of the widespread experience of the General Company. The Radio Corporation agrees to pay in each case the reasonable cost of furnishing such information and service, but not any part of the cost of acquiring the information except as the same may properly be charged as part of the development cost of apparatus which the General Company sells to the Radio Corporation.

3. Each party agrees to give the other at cost of supplying the same information and advice in connection with patent matters in its field.

4. The Radio Corporation agrees to give full information to the General Company on the same terms, and further agrees to afford the engineering representatives of the General Company the fullest possible facilities, consistent with the reasonable operation of the Radio Corporation, for experimenting and for developing and testing new apparatus, devices and inventions.

ARTICLE VIII—TERM AND TERMINATION

1. This agreement shall continue until January 1, 1945, at which date it shall expire. As soon as is reasonably practicable after that licenses shall be granted as provided above under all patents to issue on patent applications which are then or may hereafter be filed in any country on inventions made or conceived by employees of either company up to the date of termination.

2. The Radio Corporation shall after January 1, 1945, be licensed under all patents referred to in this agreement so far as the General Company now has or may hereafter acquire the right to grant such license to the extent necessary to enable it

to manufacture for its own use hereunder, but not for lease, resale, or other disposal, radio devices which it is unable to purchase of the General Company in accordance with the terms of Article IV hereof.

ARTICLE IX—FURTHER ASSURANCES

1. The parties agree to execute such further instruments as may reasonably be necessary for carrying out the purposes hereof.

ARTICLE X—CONTROLLED COMPANIES

1. This agreement shall be binding upon and inure to the benefit of the parties hereto and their successors and their controlled companies, present and future. The British Thomson-Houston Company, Limited, and the Tokyo Electric Company, Limited, shall not for the purposes hereof be regarded as controlled companies of the General Company.

ARTICLE XI

1. Inasmuch as the General Company is not willing to turn over its patents, patent rights, and licenses for any definite sum of money, but is willing to transfer such patents, patent rights, and licenses only for a considerable interest in the profits to be derived from the use by the Radio Corporation of such patents, patent rights, and licenses, it is therefore understood and agreed that in the event of the taking over of the Radio Corporation by any superior authority all right, title, and interest of the Radio Corporation in any patent, patent right, or license herein granted or agreed to be granted by the General Company to the Radio Corporation shall cease and shall be reassigned and shall revert to the General Company as of the date of such taking over except to the extent provided below. If instead of taking over the Radio Corporation the Government takes over its radio stations in any field and/or territory, except in and for time of war or public danger, the same result shall follow so far as concerns that field and/or territory. But this action shall in no way affect the rights of Marconi's Wireless Telegraph Company, Limited, or of Shielton, Limited, as set forth in the "Radio Corporation and British Marconi Company Principal Agreement"; such rights shall be reserved from any such reassignment by the Radio Corporation for the benefit of Marconi's Wireless Telegraph Company, Limited.

In testimony whereof the parties hereto have caused these presents to be executed and their corporate seals to be hereunto affixed by their proper officers thereunto duly authorized at New York City the day and year first above written.

GENERAL ELECTRIC COMPANY
By E. W. RICE, JR., President.

Attest:
J. W. ELWOOD, Asst. Secretary.

RADIO CORPORATION OF AMERICA
By FREDERICK C. BATES, President.

Attest:
CHARLES H. WHEELER, Secretary.

EXHIBIT "E"

SALES AGREEMENT

THE INTERNATIONAL RADIO TELEGRAPH COMPANY AND THE RADIO CORPORATION OF AMERICA

This agreement made this 30th day of June, 1921, between The International Radio Telegraph Company, a corporation of the State of Delaware, hereinafter called the "International Company," and the Radio Corporation of America, a corporation of the State of Delaware, hereinafter called the "Radio Corporation," Witnesseth:

That in consideration of mutual covenants and promises hereinafter contained, it is agreed:

388 APPENDIX

Section One. Subject to the exceptions hereinafter set forth the International Company hereby sells, assigns, grants and conveys all of its assets and liabilities (which liabilities as of the date hereof do not exceed one hundred thousand (100,-000) dollars), to the Radio Corporation, including its patent rights and licenses under patents, its leases and rights in leased property, its lands and real estate and especially including the right to receive and retain for its own use and benefit the sum of two million two hundred thousand (2,200,000) dollars payable by the Westinghouse Electric and Manufacturing Company to the International Company in accordance with the terms and provisions of an agreement dated June 21, 1920, between said companies, which sum is the unpaid balance of a subscription of two million five hundred thousand dollars ($2,500,000) in money made by the Westinghouse Electric & Manufacturing Company in consideration for the issuance to it of one hundred twenty-five thousand (125,000) shares of common stock, series A, of the International Company and the grant to it of certain other rights and privileges under the terms of the aforesaid agreement dated June 21, 1920. This sale, assignment, grant and conveyance, does not include—

(1) Any patent, patent rights or licenses in the following countries: Canada, United Kingdom of Great Britain and Ireland, and Japan, nor

(2) Any corporate franchise or shares of stock of the International Company, nor

(3) Any obligation of the International Company under the aforesaid agreement dated June 21, 1920, between it and the Westinghouse Electric & Manufacturing Company relative to the subscription and issuance of the stock of the International Company to the Westinghouse Electric & Manufacturing Company, nor

(4) Any nontransferable licenses under patents, such, for instance, as covered by an agreement dated August 5, 1920, between the International Company and the United States of America represented by the Secretary of the Navy (a copy of which agreement has been furnished to the Radio Corporation) pursuant to which certain licenses were exchanged, the license to the International Company being personal with the exception that it might be extended to the Westinghouse Electric & Manufacturing Company and such license having been heretofore granted.

Section Two. The International Company will, upon request of the Radio Corporation, make, execute, and deliver all such further special and particular deeds, conveyances, assignments, and other documents necessary to vest title in the Radio Corporation to any of the assets included within the sale, assignment, grant, and conveyance.

Section Three. The Radio Corporation contemporaneously with the execution of this agreement, and in consideration for the above sale, assignment, grant, and conveyance, has issued to the International Company, or its nominees, one million (1,000,000) shares of its preferred stock of the par value of five dollars ($5) each and one million (1,000,000) shares of its common stock without par value.

Section Four. Whereas the articles of incorporation of the International Company provide that no sale, lease or exchange of all of the property and assets of the International Company shall be made without the consent of a majority of the holders of stock of said company issued and outstanding having voting powers shall have authorized the board of directors of the International Company so to sell, lease or exchange all of the property and assets of said corporation, the International Company does hereby represent and declare that this contract and agreement has been authorized by the board of directors of the International Company by the written consent of a majority of the holders of stock of said company having voting powers and that attached hereto is a true copy of the resolution of the board of directors of the International Company authorizing this contract and agreement and an authorization signed by a majority of the holders of stock having voting powers issued and outstanding of the International Company authorizing and empowering the board of directors of said company to sell, lease, or exchange any part of all of the property and assets of the International Company upon such terms and conditions as the board of directors shall deem expedient and for the best interests of the corporation.

Section Five. The Radio Corporation hereby accepts the foregoing sale, assignment, grant and conveyance, and assumes and agrees to carry out all of the obligations, conditions, and contracts attached to all or any of the property sold, assigned, granted, and conveyed which the International Company is obligated to carry out, do and perform.

In witness whereof the respective parties have caused this agreement to be signed by their duly authorized officers and their respective corporation seals to be hereunto attached the day and year first above written.

THE INTERNATIONAL RADIO TELEGRAPH COMPANY

By (Signed) CALVERT TOWNLEY, Vice President.

Attest:

(Signed) WARREN H. JONES, Assistant Secretary. (SEAL)

RADIO CORPORATION OF AMERICA,

By (Signed) EDWARD J. NALLY, President.

Attest:

(Signed) LEWIS MacCONNACH, Assistant Secretary. (SEAL)

STATE OF NEW YORK, County of New York, ss.:

Be it remembered that on this 8th day of August 1921, before me personally came and appeared Calvert Townley, to me known, who executed the foregoing instrument as the vice president of the International Radio Telegraph Company, who being by me duly sworn did depose and say that he resides in New York, New York; that he is the vice president of the International Radio Telegraph Company, one of the corporations described in and which executed the above instrument; that he knows the seal of said corporation; that the seal affixed to said instrument is said corporate seal; that it was so affixed by order of the board of directors of The International Radio Telegraph Company and that he signed his name thereto by like order, and he duly acknowledged to me that he executed the same as his free and voluntary act and deed and as the free and voluntary act and deed of said corporation for the uses and purposes therein expressed and mentioned.

In witness whereof, I have hereunto set my hand and official seal the day and year last above written.

(Signed) C. WESLEY POMEROY, Notary Public.

RESOLUTION OF BOARD OF DIRECTORS OF THE INTERNATIONAL RADIO TELEGRAPH COMPANY, ADOPTED AT A MEETING HELD AUGUST 4TH, 1921

At a meeting of the board of directors of the International Radio Telegraph Company duly called and a majority of the board being present, the following preamble and resolution was unanimously agreed to, passed and adopted:

Whereas a majority of the holders of stock of this company issued and outstanding having voting powers have authorized this board by their written consent to sell, lease or exchange any part or all of the property and assets of this corporation including its good will and its corporate franchises upon such terms and conditions as the board of directors shall deem expedient and for the best interests of the corporation. Now, therefore, be it—

RESOLVED, That this board does hereby authorize the sale, assignment, grant, and conveyance to the Radio Corporation of America, a corporation organized under the laws of the State of Delaware, of certain of the property and assets of this company in accordance with the terms and conditions of the following proposed form of agreement:

(Here follows form of agreement in foregoing form)

FURTHER RESOLVED, That the proper officers of the Company be and they are hereby authorized and empowered to execute the foregoing agreement and such other deeds, conveyances, assignments and other documents as may be necessary to carry out the terms and provisions thereof.

STOCKHOLDERS' AUTHORIZATION

The undersigned, constituting the holders of a majority of the stock having voting powers issued and outstanding of the International Radio Telegraph Company, organized under the laws of the State of Delaware by a certificate filed June 12, 1920, do hereby authorize and empower the board of directors of said company at any meeting to sell, lease and exchange any part or all of the property and assets of the said company including its good will and its corporate franchises upon such terms and conditions as the board of directors shall deem expedient and for the best interests of the company.

Witnesses.

———— ————
———— ————

                                             ———— ————
                                             ———— ————
                                             ———— ————

EXHIBIT "F"

"ARMSTRONG AND PUPIN" AGREEMENT

1. LICENSE AGREEMENT—RADIO CORPORATION OF AMERICA, GENERAL ELECTRIC COMPANY, AND THE WESTINGHOUSE ELECTRIC & MANUFACTURING COMPANY

Agreement made this 30th day of June, nineteen hundred twenty-one, between the Westinghouse Electric and Manufacturing Company, a Pennsylvania corporation (hereinafter referred to as the Westinghouse Company), the Radio Corporation of America, a Delaware corporation (hereinafter referred to as the Radio Corporation), and the General Electric Company, a New York corporation (hereinafter referred to as the General Company).

The General Company has granted to the Radio Corporation, by an agreement known as agreement A, certain rights with respect to radio devices as defined in said agreement. The Westinghouse Company has granted to The International Radio Telegraph Company, a Delaware corporation (hereinafter called the International Company), by an agreement known as agreement D certain rights with respect to radio devices as defined in said agreement. The International Company has disposed of certain of its assets, good will, and business to the Radio Corporation. A certain agreement for the exchange of licenses in certain fields, known as agreement B, has been entered into between the General Company and the American Telephone and Telegraph Company, hereinafter referred to as the Telephone Company, and has by the operation of a certain agreement, known as agreement C, been extended in certain respects to the Western Electric Company, Inc., a New York corporation, and to the Radio Corporation. By a certain agreement, known as agreement E, between the Radio Corporation, the General Company, and the Westinghouse Company, certain rights are extended with reference to radio, and by an agreement, known as agreement F, between the General Company and the Westinghouse Company, provision is made for the exchange of certain licenses between those companies in certain fields of radio.

The rights extended to the Westinghouse Company by the General Company include certain rights derived and to be derived by it under agreement B.

The Telephone Company, by a letter known as agreement H, has ratified this extension and by agreement I the Westinghouse Company has extended to the Telephone Company rights in the Telephone Company's field under its patents.

The Westinghouse Company has entered into an agreement dated October 5, 1920, with E. H. Armstrong and M. I. Pupin, a copy of which is hereto attached and marked "Armstrong and Pupin Agreement."

The International Company, by an agreement dated May 12, 1920, with said E. H. Armstrong, has acquired a license under a certain patent and a certain prospective patent of said Armstrong referred to in said Armstrong and Pupin Agreement, and has agreed to pay to it certain royalties thereunder.

The Radio Corporation, by virtue of an agreement of April 28, 1916, with the said E. H. Armstrong, has acquired certain limited licenses on royalty under certain Armstrong patents.

The Westinghouse Company has paid to Armstrong and Pupin, under and in accordance with said Armstrong and Pupin agreement, the sum of eighty-five thousand dollars and has expended certain sums in litigation on Armstrong Patent No. 1113149 and in the prosecution of interferences in which the Armstrong Application No. 807388 is involved.

The agreements above referred to were entered into with the understanding that without some special consideration rights under the Armstrong patents should not pass from the Westinghouse Company to the other parties.

The expression "Armstrong patents" wherever used in this agreement means any and all patents and patent rights acquired or to be acquired under or by virtue of the said Armstrong and Pupin agreement, including as well patents foreign to the United States as those of the United States. The expressions "Armstrong United States patents" and "Armstrong foreign patents" refer respectively to said patents and patent rights for the United States of America, its Territories and possessions, and for countries foreign to the United States except the Dominion of Canada.

The expression "total cost" in connection with the Armstrong and Pupin agreement, includes not only the payments specifically called for in paragraphs 6, 7, and 8 of said Armstrong and Pupin agreement, as such payments are made respectively, but also the amounts which the Westinghouse Company has already paid and expended as above set forth and the cost of further prosecuting the Armstrong patent application, serial No. 807388, including the further cost of contesting in behalf of Armstrong all interferences in which it has been or shall be involved and the further cost of prosecuting the litigation now pending on the Armstrong Patent, 1113149, less any amounts paid or to be paid by the Telephone Company under agreement I.

The parties have agreed as follows:

1. The Westinghouse Company extends to the other parties hereto under the Armstrong patents rights as follows:

(a) To the Radio Corporation under the Armstrong United States and foreign patents of all countries the same rights for the same purposes which it extends to the Radio Corporation by agreement D as modified under its patents of the United States and certain foreign countries except the Dominion of Canada.

(b) To the General Company under the Armstrong United States patents the same rights for the same purposes which it agrees in agreements E and F to extend to the General Company under other United States patents.

2. The Radio Corporation agrees to pay to the Westinghouse Company two-thirds of the total cost of the Armstrong patents, as and when such costs are incurred by the Westinghouse Company.

3. The General Electric Company agrees to pay to the Westinghouse Company 10.5 per cent of the total cost of the Armstrong patents, as and when such costs are incurred by the Westinghouse Company.

4. The Westinghouse Company agrees that if rights are offered to it in accordance with paragraph 10 of the Armstrong and Pupin agreement it will not decline such rights without first consulting each of the other parties hereto and affording them all information to which it is itself entitled, and that if it decides not to purchase any invention or right in accordance with said paragraph 10, it will, at the request of either or any of the other parties hereto, purchase or negotiate for the purchase of rights in the fields of such other party or parties, in accordance with the desires of such other party or parties and for their benefit.

5. The Westinghouse Company further agrees that it will not discontinue the payments under the Armstrong and Pupin agreement, as paragraph 11 of said Armstrong and Pupin agreement provides that it may, without first consulting the other parties hereto, nor will it discontinue such payments if any or all of the parties requests that it should not do so. But if the Westinghouse Company wishes to discontinue such payments and any or all of the other parties desire that they should be continued, the Westinghouse Company may and shall then assign its rights under the said Armstrong and Pupin agreement to the other parties desiring that the agreement should be continued, such parties agreeing to make the future payments under such agreement in proportion to the value of the rights which they respectively receive, and in case of disagreement to arbitrate. In this event the rights under the Armstrong and Pupin agreement remaining with the Westinghouse Com-

pany shall be transferred to the General Company if it is one of the companies desiring that the agreement should be continued.

6. And the Westinghouse Company further agrees that in case it has opportunities to acquire other rights under said Armstrong and Pupin agreement, or in case it has occasion to decide upon dropping any other rights under said agreement, it will not act adversely to the acquisition or retention of such rights without consulting the other parties hereto before taking final action, and that in accordance with the general principles hereto it will in case it does not itself desire to exercise or retain such rights, exercise and retain them for the benefit of other parties hereto at their request and at their expense.

7. The Radio Corporation may at any time elect to withdraw from participation in and liability under the Armstrong and Pupin agreement, in which case it forfeits all its rights under the said agreements and under the Armstrong patents and all right to receive royalties thereunder. The agreement between the International Company and Armstrong and the agreement between Armstrong and the Radio Corporation, the operation of which agreements is suspended by this present agreement, will thereupon come into full force and effect, and in case the Radio Corporation withdraws from the Armstrong and Pupin agreement each of the other parties hereto shall have the right within one month thereafter to withdraw and to cease making payments under the Armstrong and Pupin agreement, and, further, either or both of the other companies concerned may cause the said agreement to be continued in force for its or their benefit. In such case the payments remaining to be made under the Armstrong and Pupin agreement are to be shared between the companies continuing in said agreement in proportion to the value of the rights which they respectively receive.

8. The Westinghouse Company agrees to pay to the Radio Corporation all sums heretofore collected by it as royalties under Armstrong licenses enumerated in the Armstrong and Pupin agreement. The Westinghouse Company agrees to distribute between the parties hereto all royalties hereafter collected by it under the said licenses and all sums received by it in any manner whatever under and in connection with the Armstrong and Pupin agreement as follows:

(a) In so far as they are received in connection with the manufacture, use, and sale of radio devices as defined in agreements A and D, they are to be paid to the Radio Corporation.

(b) In so far as they are received under United States patents and patent rights in connection with the field under which agreement F licenses are agreed to be exchanged between the Westinghouse Company and the General Company, they are to be divided in the proportions of 60 per cent to the General Company and 40 per cent to the Westinghouse Company.

(c) In so far as they are received in connection with the field and countries in respect to which the Westinghouse Company has not agreed to grant licenses to any of the parties hereto, they are to be retained by the Westinghouse Company.

The obligations of the parties as created in this present agreement and other agreements of even date herewith are such that no further manufacturing license in the radio field can be granted under the Armstrong patents except with the consent of the Radio Corporation and the two Manufacturing Companies. This being the case, it is agreed that such consent may be granted on terms agreed upon at the time and that in considering such matter the Manufacturing Companies are entitled with respect to all such future licenses to take into consideration the loss to them of manufacturing profits which will result from such grant.

Nothing contained in this paragraph shall require the Westinghouse Company to pay to any of the parties any portion of the contributions which the Radio and General Companies agree in this present agreement or the Telephone Company in agreement I has agreed to make to the payments under the Armstrong-Pupin agreement.

10. The Radio Corporation may proceed under the Armstrong patents against any infringement affecting its field of work, joining the Westinghouse Company as a party plaintiff, retaining the proceeds and damages recovered in such suits unless by special arrangement other parties contribute to the expenses of the suit in which case the profits and damages shall be shared as may then be determined.

In testimony whereof the parties hereto have caused these presents to be executed and their corporate seals to be hereunto affixed by their proper officers hereunto duly authorized at New York City, the day and year as first above written.

WESTINGHOUSE ELECTRIC & MANUFACTURING COMPANY,

By (Signed)   GUY E. TRIPP, Chairman.

Attest:

(Signed)   JAMES C. BENNETT, Secretary.

[SEAL.]

RADIO CORPORATION OF AMERICA,

By (Signed)   EDWARD J. NALLY, President.

Attest:

(Signed)   LEWIS MacCONNACH, Assistant Secretary.

[SEAL.]

GENERAL ELECTRIC COMPANY,

By (Signed)   ANSON W. BURCHARD, Vice President.

Attest:

(Signed)   J. W. ELWOOD, Assistant Secretary.   [SEAL.]

EXHIBIT "G"

from

RADIO SERVICE BULLETIN

Issued Monthly by Bureau of Navigation, Department of Commerce
Issue of May 1st, 1922

List of Stations Broadcasting Market or Weather Reports, and Music, Concerts, Lectures, etc.

Call Signal	Owner of Station	Location of Station	First Listed in Bulletin
KDKA	Westinghouse Electric & Manufacturing Co.	East Pittsburgh, Pa.	Nov. 1920
KDN	Leo J. Meyberg Co.	San Francisco, Calif.	Jan. 1922
KFC	Northern Radio & Electric Co.	Seattle, Wash.	Jan. 1922
KFI	Earl C. Anthony	Los Angeles, Calif.	May 1922
KFU	The Precision Shop	Gridley, Calif.	Mar. 1922
KFV	Foster-Bradbury Radio Store	Yakima, Wash.	Apr. 1922
KFZ	Doerr-Mitchell Electric Co.	Spokane, Wash.	Apr. 1922
KGB	Wm. A. Mullins Electric Co.	Tacoma, Wash.	Jan. 1922
KGC	Electric Lighting Supply Co.	Hollywood, Calif.	Jan. 1922
KGF	Pomona Fixture & Wiring Co.	Pomona, Calif.	Mar. 1922
KGG	Hallock & Watson Radio Service	Portland, Oregon	Apr. 1922
KGN	Northwestern Radio Manufacturing Co.	" "	Apr. 1922
KGO	Altadena Radio Laboratory	Altadena, Calif.	Apr. 1922
KGU	Marion A. Mulrony	Honolulu, Hawaii	Apr. 1922
KGW	Oregonian Publishing Co.	Portland, Oregon	Apr. 1922
KGY	St. Martin's College (Rev. S. Ruth)	Lacey, Wash.	Mar. 1922
KHD	C. F. Aldrich Marble & Granite Co.	Colorado Springs, Colo.	May 1922
KHJ	C. R. Kierulff & Co.	Los Angeles, Calif.	Apr. 1922
KHQ	Louis Wasmer	Seattle, Wash.	Mar. 1922
KJC	Standard Radio Co.	Los Angeles, Calif.	May 1922
KJJ	The Radio Shop	Sunnyvale, Calif.	Jan. 1922
KJQ	C. O. Gould	Stockton, Calif.	Jan. 1922
KJR	Vincent I. Kraft	Seattle, Wash.	Apr. 1922
KJS	Bible Institute of Los Angeles	Los Angeles, Calif.	Apr. 1922
KLB	J. J. Dunn & Co.	Pasadena, Calif.	Feb. 1922
KLN	Noggle Electric Works	Monterey, Calif.	Apr. 1922

Call Signal	Owner of Station	Location of Station	First Listed in Bulletin
KLP	Collin P. Kennedy Co.	Los Altos, Calif.	Feb. 1922
KLS	Warner Brothers	Oakland, Calif.	Apr. 1922
KLZ	Reynolds Radio Co.	Denver, Colo.	Apr. 1922
KMC	Lindsay-Weatherill & Co.	Reedley, Calif.	Apr. 1922
KMJ	San Joaquin Light & Power Corp.	Fresno, Calif.	Apr. 1922
KMO	Love Electric Co.	Tacoma, Wash.	Apr. 1922
KNI	T. W. Smith	Eureka, Calif.	May 1922
KNJ	Roswell Public Service Co.	Roswell, N. M.	May 1922
KNN	Bullock's	Los Angeles, Calif.	May 1922
KNR	Beacon Light Co.	" " "	May 1922
KNT	North Coast Products Co.	Aberdeen, Wash.	May 1922
KNV	Radio Supply Co.	Los Angeles, Calif.	May 1922
KOA	Young Men's Christian Association	Denver, Colo.	Apr. 1922
KOB	New Mexico College of Agriculture and Mechanic Arts	State College, N. M.	May 1922
KOE	Spokane Chronicle	Spokane, Wash.	May 1922
KOG	Western Radio Electric Co.	Los Angeles, Calif.	May 1922
KON	Holzwasser (Inc.)	San Diego, Calif.	May 1922
KOP	Detroit Police Department	Detroit, Mich.	Apr. 1922
KOQ	Modesto Evening News	Modesto, Calif.	May 1922
KPO	Hale Brothers	San Francisco, Calif.	May 1922
KQL	Arno A. Kluge	Los Angeles, Calif.	Nov. 1921
KQP	Blue Diamond Electric Co.	Hood River, Oregon	Mar. 1922
KQT	Electric Power & Appliance Co.	Yakima, Wash.	Apr. 1922
KQV	Doubleday-Hill Electric Co.	Pittsburgh, Pa.	Nov. 1921
KQW	Charles D. Herrold	San Jose, Calif.	Jan. 1922
KQY	Stubbs Electric Co.	Portland, Ore.	Apr. 1922
KRE	Maxwell Electric Co.	Berkeley, Calif.	Apr. 1922
KSC	O. A. Hale & Co.	San Jose, Calif.	May 1922
KSD	Post Dispatch	St. Louis, Mo.	Apr. 1922
KSL	The Emporium	San Francisco, Calif.	Apr. 1922
KSS	Prest & Dean Radio Research Laboratory	Long Beach, Calif.	May 1922
KTW	First Presbyterian Church	Seattle, Wash.	May 1922
KUO	Examiner Printing Co.	San Francisco, Calif.	May 1922
KUS	City Dye Works & Laundry Co.	Los Angeles, Calif.	May 1922
KUY	Coast Radio Co.	El Monte, Calif.	May 1922
KVQ	J. C. Hobrecht	Sacramento, Calif.	Jan. 1922
KWG	Portable Wireless Telephone Co.	Stockton, Calif.	Jan. 1922
KWH	Los Angeles Examiner	Los Angeles, Calif.	May 1922
KXD	Herald Publishing Co.	Modesto, Calif.	May 1922
KXS	Braun Corporation	Los Angeles, Calif.	May 1922
KYF	Thearle Music Co.	San Diego, Calif.	May 1922
KYG	Willard P. Hawley, Jr.	Portland, Oregon	Apr. 1922
KYJ	Leo J. Meyberg Co.	Los Angeles, Calif.	Jan. 1922
KYW	Westinghouse Electric & Manufacturing Co.	Chicago, Ill.	Dec. 1921
KYY	The Radio Telephone Shop	San Francisco, Calif.	Jan. 1922
KZC	Public Market & Stores Co.	Seattle, Wash.	Jan. 1922
KZI	Irving S. Cooper	Los Angeles, Calif.	May 1922
KZM	Preston D. Allen	Oakland, Calif.	Jan. 1922
KZN	The Desert News	Salt Lake City, Utah	May 1922
KZY	Atlantic-Pacific Radio Supplies Co.	Oakland, Calif.	Jan. 1922
WAAB	Times-Picayune	New Orleans, La.	May 1922
WAAC	Tulane University	" " "	May 1922
WAAE	St. Louis Chamber of Commerce	St. Louis, Mo.	May 1922
WAAF	Union Stock Yards & Transit Co.	Chicago, Ill.	May 1922
WAAG	Elliott Electric Co.	Shreveport, La.	May 1922

Call Signal	Owner of Station	Location of Station	First Listed in Bulletin
WAAH	Commonwealth Electric Co.	St. Paul, Minn.	May 1922
WAAJ	Eastern Radio Institute	Boston, Mass.	May 1922
WAAK	Gimbel Brothers	Milwaukee, Wis.	May 1922
WAAL	Minnesota Tribune Co. & Anderson- Beamish Co.	Minneapolis, Minn.	May 1922
WAAM	I. R. Nelson Co.	Newark, N. J.	May 1922
WAAN	University of Missouri	Columbia, Mo.	May 1922
WAAO	Radio Service Co.	Charleston, W. Va.	May 1922
WAAP	Otto W. Taylor	Wichita, Kan.	May 1922
WAAQ	New England Motor Sales Co.	Greenwich, Conn.	May 1922
WAAR	Groves-Thornton Hardware Co.	Huntington, W. Va.	May 1922
WAAS	Georgia Radio Co.	Decatur, Ga.	May 1922
WAAV	Athens Radio Co.	Athens, Ohio	May 1922
WAAW	Omaha Grain Exchange	Omaha, Neb.	May 1922
WAAX	Radio Service Corp.	Grafton, Pa.	May 1922
WAAY	Yahrling-Rayner Piano Co.	Youngstown, Ohio.	May 1922
WAAZ	Hollister-Miller Motor Co.	Emporia, Kan.	May 1922
WAH	Midland Refining Co.	El Dorado, Kan.	Apr. 1922
WBAA	Purdue University	West Lafayette, Ind.	May 1922
WBAB	Andrew J. Potter	Syracuse, N. Y.	May 1922
WBAD	Sterling Electric Co. and Journal Printing Co.	Minneapolis, Minn.	May 1922
WBAE	Bradley Polytechnic Institute	Peoria, Ill.	May 1922
WBAF	Fred M. Middleton	Moorestown, N. J.	May 1922
WBAG	Diamond State Fibre Co.	Bridgeport, Pa.	May 1922
WBAH	The Dayton Co.	Minneapolis, Minn.	May 1922
WBAJ	Marshall-Gerken Co.	Toledo, Ohio	May 1922
WBAM	I. B. Rennyson	New Orleans, La.	May 1922
WBAN	Wireless Phone Corp.	Paterson, N. J.	May 1922
WBAO	James Millikin University	Decatur, Ill.	May 1922
WBAP	Wortham-Carter Publishing Co.	Fort Worth, Tex.	May 1922
WBAQ	Myron L. Harmon	South Bend, Ind.	May 1922
WBAU	Republican Publishing Co.	Hamilton, Ohio	May 1922
WBAV	Erner & Hopkins Co.	Columbus, Ohio	May 1922
WBAW	Marietta College	Marietta, Ohio	May 1922
WBAX	John H. Stenger, Jr.	Wilkes-Barre, Pa.	May 1922
WBAY	American Telephone & Telegraph Co.	New York, N. Y.	May 1922
WBAZ	Times Dispatch Publishing Co.	Richmond, Va.	May 1922
WBL	T. & H. Radio Co.	Anthony, Kan.	May 1922
WBS	D. W. May (Inc.)	Newark, N. J.	Apr. 1922
WBT	Southern Radio Corp.	Charlotte, N. C.	Apr. 1922
WBU	City of Chicago	Chicago, Ill.	Mar. 1922
WBZ	Westinghouse Electric & Manufac- turing Co.	Springfield, Mass.	Oct. 1921
WCE	Findley Electric Co.	Minneapolis, Minn.	May 1922
WCJ	A. C. Gilbert Co.	New Haven, Conn.	Oct. 1921
WCK	Stix-Bear-Fuller	St. Louis, Mo.	May 1922
WCM	University of Texas	Austin, Tex.	Apr. 1922
WCN	Clark University	Worcester, Mass.	Apr. 1922
WDV	John O. Yeiser, Jr.	Omaha, Neb.	Apr. 1922
WDW	Radio Construction & Electric Co.	Washington, D. C.	Jan. 1922
WDY	Radio Corporation of America	Roselle Park, N. J.	Oct. 1921
WDZ	James L. Bush	Tuscola, Ill.	Apr. 1922
WEB	Benwood Co.	St. Louis, Mo.	May 1922
WEH	Midland Refining Co.	Tulsa, Okla.	Apr. 1922
WEV	Hurlburt-Still Electrical Co.	Houston, Tex.	Apr. 1922
WEW	St. Louis University	St. Louis, Mo.	Apr. 1922

Call Signal	Owner of Station	Location of Station	First Listed in Bulletin
WEY	Cosradio Co.	Wichita, Kan.	Apr. 1922
WFI	Strawbridge & Clothier	Philadelphia, Pa.	Apr. 1922
WFO	Rike Kumler Co.	Dayton, Ohio	Mar. 1922
WGF	The Register & Tribune	Des Moines, Iowa	Apr. 1922
WGH	Montgomery Light & Power Co.	Montgomery, Ala.	Mar. 1922
WGI	American Radio & Research Corp.	Medford Hillside, Mass.	Feb. 1922
WGL	Thomas F. J. Howlett	Philadelphia, Pa.	Mar. 1922
WGM	Georgia Railway & Power Co. (Atlanta Constitution)	Atlanta, Ga.	Apr. 1922
WGR	Federal Telephone & Telegraph Co.	Buffalo, N. Y.	Apr. 1922
WGU	The Fair	Chicago, Ill.	Apr. 1922
WGV	Interstate Electric Co.	New Orleans, La.	Apr. 1922
WGY	General Electric Co.	Schenectady, N. Y.	Mar. 1922
WHA	University of Wisconsin	Madison, Wis.	Feb. 1922
WHD	West Virginia University	Morgantown, W. Va.	Apr. 1922
WHK	Warren R. Cox	Cleveland, Ohio	Mar. 1922
WHN	Ridgewood Times Printing & Publishing Co.	Ridgewood, N. Y.	Apr. 1922
WHQ	Rochester Times Union	Rochester, N. Y.	Mar. 1922
WHU	William B. Duck Co.	Toledo, Ohio	Mar. 1922
WHW	Stuart W. Seeley	East Lansing, Mich.	Mar. 1922
WHX	Iowa Radio Corp.	Des Moines, Iowa	Apr. 1922
WIK	K & L Electric Co.	McKeesport, Pa.	Apr. 1922
WIL	Continental Electrical Supply Co.	Washington, D. C.	Apr. 1922
WIP	Gimbel Brothers	Philadelphia, Pa.	Apr. 1922
WIZ	Cino Radio Manufacturing Co.	Cincinnati, Ohio	May 1922
WJD	Richard H. Howe	Granville, Ohio	May 1922
WJH	White & Bower Co.	Washington, D. C.	Jan. 1922
WJK	Radio Service Equipment Co.	Toledo, Ohio	Mar. 1922
WJT	Electric Equipment Co.	Erie, Pa.	Apr. 1922
WJX	De Forest Radio Telephone & Telegraph Co.	New York, N. Y.	Nov. 1921
WJZ	Westinghouse Electric & Manufacturing Co.	Newark, N. J.	July 1921
WKC	Joseph M. Zamoiski Co.	Baltimore, Md.	Apr. 1922
WKN	Riechman-Crosby Co.	Memphis, Tenn.	Apr. 1922
WKY	Oklahoma Radio Shop	Oklahoma City, Okla.	Apr. 1922
WLB	University of Minnesota	Minneapolis, Minn.	Feb. 1922
WLK	Hamilton Manufacturing Co.	Indianapolis, Ind.	Feb. 1922
WLW	Crosley Manufacturing Co.	Cincinnati, Ohio	Apr. 1922
WMA	Arrow Radio Laboratories	Anderson, Ind.	May 1922
WMB	Auburn Electrical Co.	Auburn, Me.	Mar. 1922
WMC	Columbia Radio Co.	Youngstown, Ohio	Apr. 1922
WMH	Precision Equipment Co.	Cincinnati, Ohio	Jan. 1922
WMU	Doubleday-Hill Electric Co.	Washington, D. C.	Apr. 1922
WNJ	Shotton Radio Manufacturing Co.	Albany, N. Y.	Apr. 1922
WNO	Wireless Telephone Co. of Hudson County, N. J.	Jersey City, N. J.	Feb. 1922
WOC	Palmer School of Chiropractic	Davenport, Iowa	Mar. 1922
WOE	Buckeye Radio Service Co.	Akron, Ohio	May 1922
WOH	Hatfield Electric Co.	Indianapolis, Ind.	Apr. 1922
WOI	Iowa State College	Ames, Iowa	May 1922
WOK	Pine Bluff Co.	Pine Bluff, Ark.	Mar. 1922
WOO	John Wanamaker	Philadelphia, Pa.	Apr. 1922
WOQ	Western Radio Co.	Kansas City, Mo.	Mar. 1922
WOR	L. Bamberger & Co.	Newark, N. J.	Mar. 1922
WOS	Missouri State Marketing Bureau	Jefferson City, Mo.	Mar. 1922

Call Signal	Owner of Station	Location of Station	First Listed in Bulletin
WOU	Metropolitan Utilities District	Omaha, Neb.	Jan. 1922
WOZ	Palladium Printing Co.	Richmond, Ind.	Mar. 1922
WPA	Fort Worth Record	Fort Worth, Tex.	Apr. 1922
WPB	Newspaper Printing Co.	Pittsburgh, Pa.	Feb. 1922
WPE	Central Radio Co.	Kansas City, Mo.	May 1922
WPG	Nushawg Poultry Farm	New Lebanon, Ohio	Apr. 1922
WPI	Electric Supply Co.	Clearfield, Pa.	May 1922
WPJ	St. Joseph's College	Philadelphia, Pa.	May 1922
WPL	Fergus Electric Co.	Zanesville, Ohio	May 1922
WPM	Thomas J. Williams	Washington, D. C.	Apr. 1922
WPO	United Equipment Co.	Memphis, Tenn.	Apr. 1922
WRL	Union College	Schenectady, N. Y.	Apr. 1922
WRM	University of Illinois	Urbana, Ill.	Apr. 1922
WRP	Federal Institute of Radio Telegraphy	Camden, N. J.	Apr. 1922
WRR	City of Dallas (police and fire signal department)	Dallas, Tex.	Sept. 1921
WRW	Tarrytown Radio Research Laboratory	Tarrytown, N. Y.	Apr. 1922
WSB	Atlanta Journal	Atlanta, Ga.	Apr. 1922
WSL	J & M Electric Co.	Utica, N. Y.	Apr. 1922
WSN	Shipowners Radio Service	Norfolk, Va.	May 1922
WSV	L. M. Hunter & G. L. Carrington	Little Rock, Ark.	Apr. 1922
WSX	Erie Radio Co.	Erie, Pa.	Apr. 1922
WSY	Alabama Power Co.	Birmingham, Ala.	Apr. 1922
WTG	Kansas State Agricultural College	Manhattan, Kan.	May 1922
WTK	Paris Radio Electric Co.	Paris, Tex.	Apr. 1922
WTP	George M. McBride	Bay City, Mich.	Apr. 1922
WWB	Daily News Printing Co.	Canton, Ohio	Apr. 1922
WWI	Ford Motor Co.	Dearborn, Mich.	Apr. 1922
WWJ	Detroit News	Detroit, Mich.	June 1922
WWL	Loyola University	New Orleans, La.	Apr. 1922
WWT	McCarthy Bros. & Ford	Buffalo, N. Y.	Apr. 1922
WWZ	John Wanamaker	New York, N. Y.	Apr. 1922

"EXHIBIT H"

FIRST WEAF COMMERCIAL CONTINUITY

DAYTIME: 5:15–5:30

MONDAY, August 28, 1922

BROADCASTING PROGRAM HAWTHORNE COURT INTRODUCTION

This afternoon the radio audience is to be addressed by Mr. Blackwell of the Queensboro Corporation, who through arrangements made by the Griffin Radio Service, Inc., will say a few words concerning Nathaniel Hawthorne and the desirability of fostering the helpful community spirit and the healthful, unconfined home life that were Hawthorne ideals. Ladies and Gentlemen: Mr. Blackwell.

BROADCASTING PROGRAM HAWTHORNE COURT

It is fifty-eight years since Nathaniel Hawthorne, the greatest of American fictionists, passed away. To honor his memory the Queensboro Corporation, creator and operator of the tenant-owned system of apartment homes at Jackson Heights, New York City, has named its latest group of high-grade dwellings "Hawthorne Court."

I wish to thank those within sound of my voice for the broadcasting opportunity afforded me to urge this vast radio audience to seek the recreation and the daily comfort of the home removed from the congested part of the city, right at the boundaries of God's great outdoors, and within a few minutes by subway from the business section of Manhattan. This sort of residential environment strongly influenced Hawthorne, America's greatest writer of fiction. He analyzed with charming keenness the social spirit of those who had thus happily selected their homes, and he painted the people inhabiting those homes with good-natured relish.

There should be more Hawthorne sermons preached about the utter inadequacy and the general hopelessness of the congested city home. The cry of the heart is for more living room, more chance to unfold, more opportunity to get near to Mother Earth, to play, to romp, to plant and to dig.

Let me enjoin upon you as you value your health and your hopes and your home happiness, get away from the solid masses of brick, where the meagre opening admitting a slant of sunlight is mockingly called a light shaft, and where children grow up starved for a run over a patch of grass and the sight of a tree.

Apartments in congested parts of the city have proven failures. The word neighbor is an expression of peculiar irony—a daily joke.

Thousands of dwellers in the congested district apartments want to remove to healthier and happier sections but they don't know and they can't seem to get into the belief that their living situation and home environment can be improved. Many of them balk at buying a house in the country or the suburbs and becoming a commuter. They have visions of toiling down in a cellar with a sullen furnace, or shovelling snow, or of blistering palms pushing a clanking lawn mower. They can't seem to overcome the pessimistic inertia that keeps pounding into their brains that their crowded, unhealthy, unhappy living conditions cannot be improved.

The fact is, however, that apartment homes on the tenant-ownership plan can be secured by these city martyrs merely for the deciding to pick them—merely for the devoting of an hour or so to preliminary verification of the living advantages that are within their grasp. And this too within twenty minutes of New York's business center by subway transit.

Those who balk at building a house or buying one already built need not remain deprived of the blessings of the home within the ideal residential environment, or the home surrounded by social advantages and the community benefits where neighbor means more than a word of eight letters.

In these better days of more opportunities, it is possible under the tenant-ownership plan to possess an apartment-home that is equal in every way to the house-home and superior to it in numberless respects.

In these same better days, the purchaser of an apartment-home can enjoy all the latest conveniences and contrivances demanded by the housewife and yet have all of the outdoor life that the city dweller yearns for but has deludedly supposed could only be obtained through purchase of a house in the country.

Imagine a congested city apartment lifted bodily to the middle of a large garden within twenty minutes travel of the city's business center. Imagine the interior of a group of such apartments traversed by a garden court stretching a block, with beautiful flower beds and rich sward, so that the present jaded congested section dweller on looking out of his windows is not chilled with the brick and mortar vista, but gladdened and enthused by colors and scents that make life worth living once more. Imagine an apartment to live in at a place where you and your neighbor join the same community clubs, organizations and activities, where you golf with your neighbor, tennis with your neighbor, bowl with your neighbor and join him in a long list of outdoor and indoor pleasure-giving health-giving activities.

And finally imagine such a tenant-owned apartment, where you own a floor in a house the same as you can own an entire house with a proportionate ownership of the ground the same as the ground attached to an entire house but where you have great spaces for planting and growing the flowers you love, and raising the vegetables of which you are fond.

Right at your door is such an opportunity. It only requires the will to take advantage of it all. You owe it to yourself and you owe it to your family to leave the hemmed-in, sombre-hued, artificial apartment life of the congested city section and enjoy what nature intended you should enjoy.

Dr. Royal S. Copeland, Health Commissioner of New York, recently declared that any person who preached leaving the crowded city for the open country was a public-spirited citizen and a benefactor to the race. Shall we not follow this advice and become the benefactors he praises? Let us resolve to do so. Let me close by urging that you hurry to the apartment home near the green fields and the neighborly atmosphere right on the subway without the expense and the trouble of a commuter, where health and community happiness beckon—the community life and friendly environment that Hawthorne advocated.

INDEX

Abbott, Gordon, 180

Act of 1912, wireless, 106, 367, 370

Actors, "mike-fright," 243 f.; reaction to radio, 244, 262, 352

Addison, Joseph, *Spectator*, 7

Advertising, first sponsored programs, 199, 275, 287; outcry against, 285; early commercial advertisers, lists, 288, 289*n.*; RCA plans to give free time on air, 304; sponsors' problems, 320; income from: rates for broadcasting time, 360; movement toward sponsorship gains ground, 361; proposed bill to abolish, 363; music as lure, 368

Aeolian Company, 224

Aeolian Hall Building, station at, 301, 302, 303

Aerial, Marconi discovers principles of, 57

Agamemnon, laying of Atlantic Cable, 39

Akenside, Mark, quoted, 7

Alexander bill, 157, 158

Alexanderson, A. M., 83*n.*

Alexanderson-Beverage static eliminator, 146-48

Alexanderson, Ernst F. W., vi, 138; sketch of life, 83*n.*; quoted, 85; magnetic amplifier, 118-19; mercury vapor tube, 119; electronic amplifier, 119-20; multiple tuned antenna, 121; Marconi's visit to, 129; devices make New Brunswick station most powerful in world, 140; work in static control, 146; eliminator: Barrage receiver, 147; Wilson-Burleson wireless a testimonial to genius of, 152; Navy requests report by, 161; predicts crowded ether waves, 182; connection with RCA, 183; son kidnaped, 300; *see also* Alternator, Alexanderson's

Alexanderson, Verner, 301

Alternating current transmitter, 81

Alternator, Alexanderson's, 83, 85, 115-18, 124, 141, 144, 192; Marconi's interest in, 128 ff.; Marconi Company's efforts to buy, 130, 155, 159; perfected at last, 131; installed at New Brunswick, 138-40, 159; protection of American rights

in, 153 ff.; dependence of Marconi negotiations upon, 168; superseded by tube transmitter, 294

Alternator, Fessenden's, 83, 85, 86, 102, 115 ff., 192

Alternator, high frequency, 69

Amateurs, interest in wireless, 67, 91, 99, 100, 104; demand for equipment, 91; increase wireless confusion, 104-5, 182; Pittsburgh broadcast and listeners, 199 ff.; stations dismantled during war, 136, 137; Government radio instruction, 142 f.; inconvenienced by programs: feud with KDKA, 209

Amber, use of in electrical phenomena, 6, 8

American, New York, first news broadcast, 134

American Commission to Negotiate Peace, 151

American Committee for Devastated France, 215

American de Forest Wireless, 71

American Marconi, *see* Marconi Company, American

American Newspaper Publishers Association, 360

American Opera Ensemble, 355

American Radio and Research Company, 132

American Radio Relay League, 159

American Society of Composers, Authors and Publishers, 268; fights copyright infringement, 308 f., 313

American Telegraph Company, 35

American Telephone and Telegraph Company, vi; and de Forest, 106-9; purchases audion, 107; orders alternator, 116; achieves cross-continent and trans-oceanic transmission, 131; experiments with and use of, vacuum tubes, 131, 255, 263; buys full rights to audion, 135; patents, 169; alliance with RCA, 194-95; cross licensing agreements, 194-95, 256, 327; plans to open experimental station, 255; motives, 256-57; radio toll service: outline of plans, 257-58, 265; enters broadcasting field, 263; Sta-

ADDENDA

"HISTORY OF RADIO TO 1926"

By Gleason L. Archer, LL.D.

Since the publication of the "History of Radio" in the Autumn of 1938 the author has been able to gain access to records that throw additional light upon certain passages in the book that were written while such facts were unobtainable. In the interest of historical accuracy the following addenda is supplied to readers of "Big Business and Radio" in a belief that those of them who have read the earlier volume may be glad to correct any possible erroneous impressions created by the text.

Page 227—Sec. 126.

Article VII in the original RCA-British Marconi agreement (November 21, 1919), as disclosed by the Radio Corporation files demonstrates that the provisions for American participation in South American radio were much more favorable than the author had been led to believe by the scanty references which he had found. The actual language was as follows:

"The sole control and management of the South American Company shall be entrusted to officers appointed by the Radio Corporation, and the British Company agrees to vote for the confirmation of the said officers in the posts to which they are nominated by the Radio Corporation; and there shall be seven directors of the Company, of whom five shall be appointed by the Radio Corporation and two by the British Company."

Article VII contained various other provisions favorable to RCA—in fact more favorable to the corporation than were possible when the South American consortium was actually signed in October, 1921. The statement in the text that "This clause in the contract brought back by Nally and Davis had caused considerable embarrassment to Owen D. Young and his associates" is erroneous, since whatever "embarrassment" may have arisen touched Mr. Isaacs and his associates. It is obvious that because the provision was so strongly in favor of RCA was one of the chief reasons why the British Marconi Company later urged reconsideration of the provision. It is reported that the British government objected to this clause in the contract.

It appears that in July, 1920, President Edward J. Nally of RCA and Albert G. Davis met Godfrey Isaacs in Cobourg and took him to task for failing to act in the South American matter. Mr. Isaacs finally admitted that he had no intention of going forward with the plan, declaring that he was under great pressure from his government. After an earnest debate on the subject, Mr. Isaacs finally agreed to go through with the project provided the directors of RCA should insist upon it.

At a meeting of the RCA Board on September 15, 1920, it was voted to agree to an increased membership—four Britishers and five Americans. In November, 1920, Mr. Isaacs came to New York and urged that eight directors, evenly divided, be substituted. He agreed that one of the American directors should be chairman and should have two votes in case of a deadlock. This latter provision is what was referred to on page 228 as being contrary to the laws of Delaware, where no director may have two votes.

Pages 233-236—Sec. 129, 130.

Objection has been registered by M. Emile Girardeau, chief executive of the French Wireless Company—La Compagnie Générale de Télégraphie Sans Fil—that the author's version of the Paris conference does an injustice to himself and to his company. Dr. Carl Schapira of the Telefunken Company, as well as representatives of the British Marconi Company, likewise object to certain portions of the story. The author believes that he has unintentionally overstressed the part played by the American delegates due to the fact that his original information was the oral recollection of the chief actors from this side of the ocean. It is well known, however, that no two persons remember the same event in the same manner. Much time had elapsed—seventeen years—and the surprising fact is that original memoranda of

1

the conference, recently unearthed from files long inactive, confirm so much of oral recollections first given to the author by Owen D. Young about June, 1938. Turning now to detailed objections:

1. That Invitation to Germans to attend Conference was not done at Mr. Young's initiative.

The author relied upon Owen D. Young's radiogram ("History of Radio" p. 230) and Mr. Isaacs' radiogram (p. 231), in which occurred the expression "I will at once fix meeting at convenient place on continent with French and Germans as you propose" as authority for the allegation. In justice to French and British radio officials, however, it should be pointed out that they had already held conferences with the Germans on the South American situation in London (January, 1921) and in Berlin immediately thereafter—also in Cologne in February, 1921.

Edward J. Nally, then President of RCA, and one of the most potent figures in the communications field has recently given the author new light on why Paris was chosen. He states that the original plan had been to meet in London but while in mid-ocean the American delegates had decided that "the glamorous city" of Paris would be a pleasanter meeting place. Mr. Nally thereupon sent a radiogram to Godfrey Isaacs and the latter obligingly changed the plans accordingly.

2. That German delegates were not regarded with hostility in Paris in Summer of 1921.

The author confesses that he is puzzled over the clash of recollections on this point. Mr. Young stated in June, 1938, that he and Mr. Isaacs were obliged to intercede with the French government to permit Dr. Schapira and Mr. Ulpers to come to Paris. On August 3, 1939, John W. Elwood, who was Secretary of the American delegation, confirmed Mr. Young's recollection and declared that he well remembered the incident.[1]

We who recall the bitterness of feeling engendered against the Germans by the war, especially in devastated France, can easily believe that post-war animosities still rankled in Paris in September, 1921, and that Mr. Young may have recalled this phase of the German reception. It at least is certain that the Germans did not appear in Paris until Wednesday, September 7, 1921, although the conferences began at the Ritz on September first, on which date Charles Neave, Esq., who made copious notes of the conferences, wrote the following cryptic reference to the matter: "Telegram from Germans, coming here Monday."

On September second we find a further memorandum indicating that Dr. Schapira and Mr. Ulpers would represent the Telefunken Company and Mr. Diercks, the German Argentine Company.

On September third: "Isaacs said found Germans could not be here until Tuesday and probably Wednesday."

On September seventh is the following entry:

"Beginning of 4-party conferences
Wednesday 4:00 P.M.
Young, Nally, Elwood, Neave
Isaacs, Steadman, Burch
Schapira, Ulpers, Diercks
Garnier (Girardeau could not be found)
"In view of Girardeau's absence it was decided not this afternoon to enter upon any negotiations but merely to state to the Germans what the situation is, so as to bring them up to date."

Mr. Elwood's memoranda of the same session states that M. Girardeau arrived at the conference at 6:00 P.M.

---

[1] M. Girardeau's comment on the incident is as follows:
"A stiffly polite reception by the British and even less polite reception by the French never existed. The facts referred to above belie the possibility that a scene like the one described by the author of the book, could have existed. Dr. Schapira and the two French delegates have a good recollection of a reception that was equally polite on the part of the American delegates and the British and French as well.

"The strange attitude ascribed to the French is nothing but an invention of a person unfamiliar with both the truth as well as the French mentality."

Again Mr. Nally supplies interesting details in the following language:

"I give you this probable explanation of the delay of the Germans in reaching France. They had made their plans for England—a comparatively easy route for passport visés, whereas, in view of the results of the war, France had not yet opened its doors to them. Hence it must have taken several days for them to obtain the needed visés."

The author is again indebted to Mr. Nally for a bit of information that may indeed reconcile the conflict in recollection between some of the American delegates and M. Girardeau on the question of hostility to Germans in Paris at that time. Mr. Nally writes as follows:

"I learned that the French government had refused a visé for Baron Gebsottel, whom they wished to make a member of their international delegation. The reason for the refusal was that the Baron was an active member of the staff of the German Crown Prince, hence because of his activities during the War, was *persona non grata*."

In the American notes there is no evidence of hostility to the Germans, except the unexplained delay in their arrival in Paris. The very fact that French and Germans had met at previous conferences to discuss the same situation would seem to confirm M. Girardeau's denial of hostility. It is well known, however, that animosities engendered by the war persisted in allied countries for a long time after 1921. A general "frosty" attitude in Paris may have been meant, rather than personal hostility of French delegates. The author offers apology for having dramatized a situation without proof beyond oral recollection of certain American delegates.

In justice to himself, however, the author desires to state that after writing Chapter XIV he submitted it to the Secretary of the American delegation, John W. Elwood, for verification. Mr. Elwood stated that he had long ago parted with written memoranda of the conference but that the story as written was in accord with his memory of events.

3. *That Mr. Young's struggle with Mr. Isaacs has been overdramatized and inaccurately set forth.*

M. Girardeau's viewpoint is ably set forth in the following from his protest of December 12, 1938.

Pages 234-235-236-237-238-239:

The whole story of the negotiations is presented inaccurately, giving an impression of a peculiar struggle between Messrs. Young and Isaacs whom the author attempts to depict as the two respective protagonists of American and British imperialism. Actually the difficulty did not arise from any failure of the four delegations to accept the principle of equal sharing of future advantages since this was agreed already in January, 1921, but rather from arriving at a practical and equitable solution of a situation of fact which resulted from the initiatives already taken by the three European companies, and especially by Telefunken in Argentine, where the issuance of stock by a company associated with Telefunken as well as purchases of land and enormous quantity of material had to be reckoned with.

One of the chief tasks which we had to solve—in which solution Mr. Young displayed his outstanding qualities of a negotiator—consisted of the substitution of German interests on the same basis as those of the other companies and to transform the Argentine-German Company into an international combine.

It was not by reason of any hostile attitude of the French or British that the Germans had to interrupt their stay in Paris and spend two days in Berlin, but because they had to obtain the consent of their associated company to such vast change in the position acquired by the German company in Argentine.

This fact should be sufficient to explain the incident without injecting any thought of resentment between former enemies who all of them were intelligent enough to grasp the necessity of reestablishing cooperation in a field that was essentially international.

It is not possible to agree with the essence nor the form, nor even the conclusions arrived at in chapter fourteen, where the author finally presents the contract as an American victory and a British defeat. This is so much more inaccurate and unjust as the initiative aiming at the agreement of the four was actually taken by the British company in understanding with the French company. If men meet for the purpose of establishing cooperation for a vast international undertaking beneficial to humanity, and if they succeed, they are victors, all of them.

To this the author makes reply that the original minutes of these conferences, rediscovered in August, 1939, appear to justify all that he has written concerning the Young-Isaacs duel. In justice to Mr. Girardeau it should be noted that some of the serious clashes between Young and Isaacs occurred when he was not present. On September third, for instance, when British and American delegations were endeavoring to arrive at a preliminary understanding (the RCA-Marconi agreement of 1919 still in force) they reached an impasse over the question of "Monroe Doctrine" in setting up the South American Company, even though it had been recognized in the RCA-Marconi agreement of 1919. Mr. Young accused Mr. Isaacs of attempting to change the basis of negotiations and threatened to break off the conferences before either French or Germans came in. Mr. Isaacs was apparently unwilling to bring the RCA-Marconi agreement into the conference at all. The existence of a powerful German wireless company in the Argentine (Transradio Company) proved a complicating factor, especially since Transradio had already made traffic agreements with the Mackay (Postal Telegraph) interests.

Days of the four-party conference were consumed in wrangles which, on September tenth, Mr. Young is reported by Charles Neave, Esq., to have characterized as "child's play." This was the very day when the Germans walked out of the conference. Mr. Elwood summarized Mr. Young's statement in the following manner:

"Mr. Young's Position
(1) Came here to discuss coöperative program in South (America) and prepared to discuss it for world.
(2) Been unable to get any consideration of that subject.
(3) Deteriorated into bargaining for small amounts of shares.
(4) Go in on basis of what all parties had expected.
(5) Asked Germans what their expenditures (in South America).
(6) No reply as to that question.
(7) Only statement, they must have par value—or leave meeting and say goodbye.
(8) If progress for world communication can only begin and end that way then certainly my trips over for discussion of world program is most unsatisfactory."

On September thirteenth the Germans were present in conference but on this day they left for Berlin. The author has stated (on page 236) that Mr. Young accompanied them yet Mr. Neave's minutes demonstrate that this was not the fact. Mr. Neave made the following entry:

"Young to call on Isaacs at 2:30 tomorrow afternoon, at Isaacs' suggestion."
It was evidently at this conference with Mr. Isaacs on September fourteenth that Mr. Young agreed, as stated by the author, not to make a separate pact with the Germans.

Mr. Elwood's notes establish the fact that from September nineteenth to the twenty-first the American negotiators were in Berlin holding conferences at the office of the Telefunken Company. On the day last named an interesting debate occurred between Mr. Young and Dr. Schapira over the "Monroe Doctrine" contention but no definite decision was reached, Schapira stoutly insisting that if the German Company were to waive its very tangible rights in the Argentine Company, RCA should abandon its effort for American control of South American wireless communications. Mr. Young was adamant, however, endeavoring to persuade Dr. Schapira that German interests could thus be safeguarded.

In conclusion we know that Mr. Young won his contention. It is written into the South American Consortium itself. The newly discovered minutes of the conferences seem to the author to justify in full measure the praise that he has accorded to Owen D. Young for a great American victory in the Paris four-party conferences in September and October, 1921. While it is a matter of regret that the author's expressions should have caused distress to European participants or their friends, yet honest differences of opinion on the significance of any great historical occurrence not infrequently arise. The author yields to no man in his admiration for the gallantry and devotion of the notable men, each for his own country, who participated in the Paris conferences; but he believes that the text of the Consortium is the evidence upon which the issue should be decided. The American Company was therein given not only an equal number of delegates with British, French and German companies but the right to name the all powerful neutral chairman—an American. These were the fruits of Mr. Young's labors.

HISTORY OF BROADCASTING:
Radio To Television
An Arno Press/New York Times Collection

Archer, Gleason L.
Big Business and Radio. 1939.

Archer, Gleason L.
History of Radio to 1926. 1938.

Arnheim, Rudolf.
Radio. 1936.

Blacklisting: Two Key Documents. 1952–1956.

Cantril, Hadley and Gordon W. Allport.
The Psychology of Radio. 1935.

Codel, Martin, editor.
Radio and Its Future. 1930.

Cooper, Isabella M.
Bibliography on Educational Broadcasting. 1942.

Dinsdale, Alfred.
First Principles of Television. 1932.

Dunlap, Orrin E., Jr.
Marconi: The Man and His Wireless. 1938.

Dunlap, Orrin E., Jr.
The Outlook for Television. 1932.

Fahie, J. J.
A History of Wireless Telegraphy. 1901.

Federal Communications Commission.
Annual Reports of the Federal Communications Commission.
1934/1935–1955.

Federal Radio Commission.
Annual Reports of the Federal Radio Commission. 1927–1933.

Frost, S. E., Jr.
Education's Own Stations. 1937.

Grandin, Thomas.
The Political Use of the Radio. 1939.

Harlow, Alvin.
Old Wires and New Waves. 1936.

Hettinger, Herman S.
A Decade of Radio Advertising. 1933.

Huth, Arno.
Radio Today: The Present State of Broadcasting. 1942.

Jome, Hiram L.
Economics of the Radio Industry. 1925.

Lazarsfeld, Paul F.
Radio and the Printed Page. 1940.

Lumley, Frederick H.
Measurement in Radio. 1934.

Maclaurin, W. Rupert.
Invention and Innovation in the Radio Industry. 1949.

Radio: Selected A.A.P.S.S. Surveys. 1929–1941.

Rose, Cornelia B., Jr.
National Policy for Radio Broadcasting. 1940.

Rothafel, Samuel L. and Raymond Francis Yates.
Broadcasting: Its New Day. 1925.

Schubert, Paul.
The Electric Word: The Rise of Radio. 1928.

Studies in the Control of Radio: Nos. 1–6. 1940–1948.

Summers, Harrison B., editor.
Radio Censorship. 1939.

Summers, Harrison B., editor.
**A Thirty-Year History of Programs Carried on
National Radio Networks in the United States, 1926–1956.** 1958.

Waldrop, Frank C. and Joseph Borkin.
Television: A Struggle for Power. 1938.

White, Llewellyn.
The American Radio. 1947.

World Broadcast Advertising: Four Reports. 1930–1932.